CONTRACT, CULTURE, AND CITIZENSHIP

CONTRACT, CULTURE, AND CITIZENSHIP

TRANSFORMATIVE LIBERALISM FROM HOBBES TO RAWLS

Mark E. Button

THE PENNSYLVANIA STATE UNIVERSITY PRESS
UNIVERSITY PARK, PENNSYLVANIA

Library of Congress Cataloging-in-Publication Data

Button, Mark E.
Contract, culture, and citizenship : transformative liberalism
from Hobbes to Rawls / Mark E. Button.
p.   cm.
Summary: "Explores the concept of the social contract and how it shapes citizenship.
Argues that the modern social contract is an account of the ethical and cultural conditions
upon which modern citizenship depends"—Provided by publisher.
Includes bibliographical references and index.
ISBN 978-0-271-03382-2 (pbk : alk. paper)
1. Social contract.
2. Political science—Philosophy—History.
I. Title.

JC336.B88 2008
320.1'1—dc22
2008005904

The Pennsylvania State University Press is a member
of the Association of American University Presses.

It is the policy of The Pennsylvania State University
Press to use acid-free paper. This book is printed on
uncoated stock that
meets the minimum requirements of American
National Standard for Information Sciences—
Permanence of Paper for Printed Library Material,
ANSI Z39.48–1992.

For Sarah,
WITH LOVE AND GRATITUDE

CONTENTS

ACKNOWLEDGMENTS

As my friends and family will ruefully attest, this book has been a long time in the making. That it has finally arrived is owed in no small part to many kind people it is my pleasure to thank here. This project was first inspired by the confluence of a remarkable group of scholars I had the great fortune to study with as a graduate student in political theory at Rutgers University. For all of the changes that this work (and its author) have undergone over the years, many of its central concerns can be traced back to my formative days on the banks of the Raritan. My greatest intellectual (and personal) debt is to Benjamin Barber, who not only guided this project in its infancy but also shepherded my journey into the study of political theory—and for both I will always be immensely grateful. Linda Zerilli, Drucilla Cornell, Gordon Schochet, and the late Carey McWilliams all played (and continue to play) an important role in my thinking, and I count myself incredibly lucky to have had the chance to study with all of them. "You could not step twice into the same river," according to Heraclitus, but the memory of so important a sojourn can buoy our spirits amid the flux of things.

I have been blessed with many wise friends and colleagues who cannot agree with me; may it ever be so. Central among these beneficent agonistes is Chandran Kukathas, who graciously read numerous versions of most of this manuscript. To Chandran I owe a great deal, not only for his critical eye but for the example of a fiercely independent mind wedded to so generous a spirit. For their many comments and helpful guidance on various portions of this evolving manuscript over the years I would also like to thank (without implying any responsibility for its contents) Stephen Holmes, Kevin Mattson, Richard Boyd, Andrew Murphy, David Gutterman, Lisa Disch, Dan Levin, Brenda Lyshaug, Casiano Hacker-Cordón, Richard Dagger, and Stephen White.

Sandy Thatcher at Penn State University Press has proved to be an ideal editor—probing, thoughtful, and sagacious. I thank Sandy for supporting this project, and then pushing me to make it better. I also owe a great debt of gratitude to Stephen Macedo, who kindly agreed to read the manuscript for Penn State and offered numerous helpful suggestions that have improved this book. I would also like to acknowledge the patient assistance of an anonymous reviewer for Penn State Press whose critical reading helped spur some important additions to the manuscript. Suzanne Wolk provided expert editorial guidance on this project—my sincere thanks to her. My thanks, as well, to Jessica Taverna, for preparing the index.

Early funding in support of my research for this book was provided by the Center for the Critical Analysis of Contemporary Culture. I thank Michael Warner and the Center fellows for their helpful advice on this project. A research fellowship with the Tanner Humanities Center at the University of Utah enabled me to complete this manuscript within a collegial, interdisciplinary environment. For that I would like to thank Michael Cheng and the rest of the "democracy and diversity" fellows at the Tanner Humanities Center.

I would also like to thank Sage Press for permission to draw from my originally published article "'A Monkish Kind of Virtue'? For and Against Humility," *Political Theory* 33, no. 6 (December 2005): 840–68. A slightly modified portion of this article appears in Chapter 5 of this book. A further portion of Chapter 5 first appeared in "Arendt, Rawls, and Public Reason," *Social Theory and Practice* 31, no. 2 (April 2005): 257–80. My thanks to *Social Theory and Practice* for allowing me to reprint a section of that essay here.

Finally, I thank my parents, Gene and Linda Button, for their constant encouragement over these many years. Together with my parents, the gracious support of Randi Robinson and Jim Robinson won't soon be forgotten.

I dedicate this book to my wife, Sarah, who is owed more than words can ever recount or adequately repay. To her, and to our daughters Kate and Leah, I offer my deep thanks for their patience, when mine had all but run out, and for their confidence, when mine was nearly depleted.

INTRODUCTION

> All political business is, and always has been, transacted within an elaborate
> framework of ties and bonds for the future—such as laws and constitutions,
> treaties and alliances—all of which derive in the last instance from
> the faculty to promise and to keep promises in the face of the
> essential uncertainties of the future.
> —Hannah Arendt, *Between Past and Future*

Theories of the social contract are stories about the origins of life in political society. They are stories that recount how and for what purposes diverse peoples might have come to live together, and remain living together, in those uniquely unnatural arrangements we call states. Like any good story, these are works of creative license, full of imagination, phantasmagoria, light and darkness, specters to move the heart, shape the mind, and form the will. As a moral and political narrative, the social contract provides its readers a framework with which to understand the world around them and their place within it—of whence they have come and whither they are going. Like any story that is told and retold by a host of different authors, writing within a wide range of different historical circumstances and for diverse audiences, the very prominence of the story amid the diversity of its retelling is an index to a broad set of social, political, and cultural developments to which the story is both testimony and agent. Some of the important developments that the modern contract story both announces and helps accelerate include widespread beliefs in the natural liberty and equality of persons, and the corresponding understanding of political societies as artificial and contingent; the inviolability and moral significance of private conscience and natural rights, and the corresponding denaturalization and gradual de-centering of singular, authoritative ways of being; the moral legitimacy of those political orders secured by the consent of the governed, and the corresponding right and duty of a people to "throw off governments" destructive of these commitments.[1] This partial list helps to reveal that even as past and present critics have questioned the credibility and usefulness of this tale, the landscape the social contract story imaginatively invokes and constitutes is the moral and political terrain of both the present and the foreseeable (desirable) future.

Thus, to offer a new interpretation of this archetypal story, as I aim to do in this book, is in part a hermeneutical task that ineluctably confronts some of the most fundamental features of Western moral and political life. Since so much of our present moral and political self-understanding is drawn from the modern social contract tradition, the historical dimensions of this book also provide an account of the political, cultural, and ethical lineages of contemporary citizenship and government. And if my reading of the historical significance of narrative retelling is correct, then offering new ways of reconsidering this story may also provide new ways of thinking and acting in accordance with the moral and political frame that the social contract story continues to shape and inform. Every contract story is both interpretive and normative in nature, offering a language and a framework of moral and civic self-understanding alongside a vision of the just and proper ends that political societies ought to pursue. This book operates on both of these registers (the interpretive and the normative) as well. I write in the conviction that two of the most important tasks for political theory today are to sustain critical attention toward the streams of thought that have shaped our political culture in fundamental ways, and, by sifting through the rich and strange deposits carried along by these currents, to continuously work out normative possibilities and practical strategies for moral and political life for both present and future generations.[2]

---

1. To invoke the words of the American Declaration of Independence, a document that still provides the best evidence of the immense influence that social contract theory has had on political practice, and one that supplies the clearest testimony to the immense power that the social contract story will always have on the self-understanding of American citizens—at least so long as the American republic endures.

2. For similar thoughts along these lines, see Quentin Skinner, *Liberty Before Liberalism* (Cambridge: Cambridge University Press, 1998), 112. See also Hannah Arendt, "Walter Benjamin," in *Men in Dark Times* (San Diego: Harcourt Brace Jovanovich, 1968), 205–6.

Contracts, Promises, and Civic Fidelity

The central thesis of this book is that *contract makes citizens,* never simply the other way around. To say that contract makes citizens is to say, first, that the familiar social contract story that recounts how individuals secure the benefits of political order and the rule of law by forming a social compact for their mutual well-being is a story that does not end with the escape from (or the loss of) the "state of nature." There are several important ways in which the social contract story has really only just begun once individuals have pledged themselves to a common political association, but the most fundamental of these can be seen by reflecting upon the all-important difference between the act of making a contract or promise, and the forms and qualities of being that are necessary for keeping a promise, once made. One of the central insights of the social contract tradition, as I read it, is the recognition that the making of a compact or promise is one (fairly easy) thing, keeping a promise—in the face of the vagaries and uncertainties of time, the opacity of human motives, and the perpetually unfinished character of human becoming and identity—is quite another. As Benedict Spinoza declared, "the preservation of the state chiefly depends on the subjects' fidelity and constancy," yet he admitted that "how subjects ought to be guided so as best to preserve their fidelity and virtue is not so obvious."[3] The social contract theorists, from Hobbes to Rawls, endeavor to fashion citizens and "guide" the formation of civic identities and virtues because promising, fidelity, and stability are so fundamental to moral and political life and so fraught with difficulty.

Promises are one of the more direct ways that individuals mutually coordinate reciprocal plans, commitments, and actions for the future. Promising is a mode of self-binding that, while circumscribing some dimension of our autonomy and freedom, also enables us to pursue choices and ways of being that would not be possible (or as reliable) without this moral practice. Put in these terms, promises stand to individuals as constitutions do to states: they are forms of precommitment that restrain and free us at once.[4] Yet noting this structural parallel introduces a troubling

---

3. Spinoza, *A Theologico-Political Treatise,* trans. R. H. M. Elwes (New York: Dover, 1951), chapter 17, p. 216.

4. I have been influenced here by the work of Stephen Holmes, *Passions and Constraint: On the Theory of Liberal Democracy* (Chicago: University of Chicago Press, 1995), esp. chapter5. See also Jon Elster, *Ulysses Unbound: Studies in Rationality, Precommitment, and Constraints*

range of moral and political questions that are as significant today as they were for the social contract theorists who drew so prodigiously upon the language of promising to conceive the nature of the political relationship as such.[5] For how are promises even possible for beings who are always in a process of becoming who they are? How can a once pledged word, like a constitution signed by an earlier generation, continue to possess living meaning in the present, and endure as a legitimate organizing structure for the future? Under what conditions are promises normatively binding, and under what conditions, and for what purposes, may these willful constraints legitimately be broken? Perhaps most important, is it possible for compacts and promises to serve as "islands of predictability"[6] for human life without becoming petrified barriers to individual and collective development?

(New York: Cambridge University Press, 2000); Benjamin Barber, "Foundationalism and Democracy," in Barber, *A Passion for Democracy* (Princeton: Princeton University Press, 1998); and Bruce Ackerman, *We the People: Foundations* (Cambridge: Belknap Press of Harvard University Press, 1991). Sheldon Wolin has also written a provocative set of essays on these themes; see in particular "Tending and Intending a Constitution: Bicentennial Misgivings," in *Presence of the Past: Essays on the State and the Constitution* (Baltimore: Johns Hopkins University Press, 1989); "Norm and Form: The Constitutionalizing of Democracy," in *Athenian Political Thought and the Reconstruction of American Democracy*, ed. J. Peter Euben, John R. Wallach, and Josiah Ober (Ithaca: Cornell University Press, 1994); and "Fugitive Democracy," in *Democracy and Difference: Contesting the Boundaries of the Political*, ed. Seyla Benhabib (Princeton: Princeton University Press, 1996). See also Jürgen Habermas, "Constitutional Democracy: A Paradoxical Union of Contradictory Principles?" *Political Theory* 29, no. 6 (2001): 766–81; and, in the same issue, Bonnie Honig, "Dead Rights, Live Futures: A Reply to Habermas's 'Constitutional Democracy,'" 792–805.

5. I am hardly the first to recognize that modern social contract theorists use the language of promising to express ideas about the legitimate sources of civil society, the boundaries of just authority, and the conditions for and meaning of political obligation. As John Dunn has argued, "The master conception of classical contractarianism was the capacity of individual human beings to bind their own future actions by making a promise." See his "Contractualism," in Dunn, *The History of Political Theory and Other Essays* (Cambridge: Cambridge University Press, 1996), 61. Other interpreters who have given attention to the manner in which promising is at least an expression of the type of obligations that different contract theorists present include Hannah Pitkin, "Obligation and Consent," *American Political Science Review* 59, no. 4 (1965) (part I), and 60, no. 1 (1966) (part II); Carole Pateman, *The Problem of Political Obligation: A Critique of Liberal Theory* (Berkeley and Los Angeles: University of California Press, 1979); and A. John Simmons, *Moral Principles and Political Obligations* (Princeton: Princeton University Press, 1979). See also Victoria Kahn's insightful historical study, *Wayward Contracts: The Crisis of Political Obligation in England, 1640–1674* (Princeton: Princeton University Press, 2004).

6. I am borrowing here from Hannah Arendt, *The Human Condition* (Chicago: University of Chicago Press, 1958), 244. For a useful discussion, see Alan Keenan, *Democracy in Question: Democratic Openness in a Time of Political Closure* (Stanford: Stanford University Press, 2003), chapter 2. There is now an extensive literature on the normative status of promissory obligations. I have been influenced in particular by H. A. Prichard, *Moral Obligation* (Oxford: Clarendon Press, 1949); John Rawls, "Two Concepts of Rules," *Philosophical Review* 64, no. 1

If, then, one of the "real problems regarding man," in Nietzsche's famous words, is "to breed an animal with the right to make promises,"[7] I believe that the modern social contract theorists offer us a compelling set of answers to this dilemma, a dilemma that can be understood as the challenge of balancing liberty and the full conditions for self-flourishing with the need for political stability and order. Yet, to appreciate the full response that these thinkers provide to squaring freedom with order and moral pluralism with civic fidelity, we must attend to the ways in which social contract theory works as an account of the enduring sources of civic commitment and political stability, and not only as an account of political obligation and the rule of law. The modern social contract theorists, in particular Thomas Hobbes, John Locke, Jean-Jacques Rousseau, and the contemporary philosopher John Rawls, not only confront the challenges of political and legal justification for free and equal persons, but address the even more vexing problem of sustaining ethical attachments to artificial bonds over time. In this book I challenge the long-standing notion that the social contract is a strictly backward-looking idea answering to questions of justification, legitimacy, and obligation and show how these important concerns give rise to a substantial formative project concerned with civic fidelity, allegiance, and political (moral) virtue.

The project of securing fidelity to promises and allegiance to political institutions over generations motivates a significant *transformative ethos* within the heart of modern liberalism that is often overlooked by critics and defenders alike.[8] By transformative ethos I mean a shared

---

(1955); H. L. A. Hart, "Legal and Moral Obligation," in *Essays in Moral Philosophy*, ed. A. I. Melden (Seattle: University of Washington Press, 1958); Henry Sidgwick, *The Methods of Ethics* (New York: Dover, 1966); John R. Searle, *Speech Acts* (Cambridge: Cambridge University Press, 1969); R. M. Hare, "The Promising Game," in *The Is-Ought Question*, ed. W. D. Hudson (New York: St. Martin's Press, 1969); Charles Fried, *Contract as Promise* (Cambridge: Harvard University Press, 1981); P. S. Atiyah, *Essays on Contract* (Oxford: Clarendon Press, 1986); and Thomas Scanlon, "Promises and Practices," *Philosophy and Public Affairs* 19, no. 3 (1990). Mark Tunick provides a very helpful discussion of this literature through the frame of Kant and Hegel, that is, between those who defend the obligations of promises according to moral principles (via Kant) and those who defend such obligations through the standards of cultural or linguistic practices (via Hegel). Tunick, *Practices and Principles: Approaches to Ethical and Legal Judgment* (Princeton: Princeton University Press, 1998).

7. Friedrich Nietzsche, *The Genealogy of Morals*, trans. Walter Kaufmann and R. J. Hollingdale (New York: Vintage Books, 1967), second essay, 1.

8. The work of Stephen Macedo is an important exception to this. See his *Liberal Virtues* (Oxford: Clarendon Press, 1990); "Transformative Constitutionalism and the Case of Religion: Defending the Moderate Hegemony of Liberalism," *Political Theory* 26, no. 1 (1998): 56–80; and, more recently, *Diversity and Distrust: Civic Education in a Multicultural Democracy* (Cambridge: Harvard University Press, 2000). See also Duncan Ivison, *The Self at Liberty:*

commitment to the formation of civic character and the cultivation of forms of political self-understanding and ethical sensibility upon which a liberal political order depends. In referring to this as a transformative ethos I mean to convey two important sets of ideas: the first is that the manner in which persons enter the social contract is a very poor predictor for characterizing who or what they will become by remaining within the terms of that compact. The second is that this transformative process is not the exclusive purview of government or political power but is best conceived as operating through the interplay of institutions, culture, and identity. As we will see, the transformative ethos working throughout the social contract tradition is manifested in widespread concerns about the virtues, habits, and opinions of citizens that are deemed foundational to the long-term sustainability of a just political society. This transformative ethos is given diverse normative expression through ideas about education, law, religion, and public reason. At the same time, this transformative impulse often appears to stand in tension with such other important commitments within this broad tradition as individual freedom, self-direction, and moral pluralism. This tension comes about because, as Harvey C. Mansfield has put it, "liberty appears to mean living as you please and virtue appears to mean living not as you please but as you ought."[9]

Of course, appearances are often deceiving. Virtue and liberty are not so much at odds in this tradition as they are bound up in a historic relationship of agonistic interdependence that derives from a basic tension between commitments to moral justification on the one hand, and commitments to ethical-political transformation on the other. For how can political justification—a process addressed to and by diverse persons who disagree about fundamental conceptions of the good—meaningfully coincide with a commitment to the formation of civic identity? That is, how

---

Political Argument and the Arts of Government (Ithaca: Cornell University Press, 1997). Scholars who have provided insightful studies of certain transformative ideals specific to individual thinkers within the social contract tradition include James Tully, *An Approach to Political Philosophy: Locke in Contexts* (Cambridge: Cambridge University Press, 1993); Peter Josephson, *The Great Art of Government: Locke's Use of Consent* (Lawrence: University Press of Kansas, 2002); David Johnston, *The Rhetoric of Leviathan: Thomas Hobbes and the Politics of Cultural Transformation* (Princeton: Princeton University Press, 1986); Zev M. Trachtenberg, *Making Citizens: Rousseau's Political Theory of Culture* (London: Routledge, 1993); and Joseph R. Reisert, *Jean-Jacques Rousseau: A Friend of Virtue* (Ithaca: Cornell University Press, 2003).

9. Harvey C. Mansfield, "Liberty and Virtue in the American Founding," in *Never a Matter of Indifference: Sustaining Virtue in a Free Republic*, ed. Peter Berkowitz (Stanford: Hoover Institution Press, 2003), 3.

might political justification and civic formation fit together without, on the one hand, jeopardizing the freedom, equality, and rights of persons by pushing a transformative ethic too far, or, on the other hand, leaving the reasoned justification of political principles without motivational support or affective attachment by forswearing or ignoring the transformative role of political institutions? By critically attending to the political and ethical tensions that inhere in the transformative aims of social contract theory, I hope to deepen our understanding of this influential tradition and spur a critical reevaluation of it.[10] I also write with the intention of drawing on these thinkers in a manner that might make them relevant to us in new and surprising ways—specifically, as critical aids to a historically minded reconsideration of the ethical, cultural, and political preconditions for sustaining liberty and stability amid pluralism today.

In claiming that contract makes citizens I mean to stress the idea that the central modern problem of political justification—how to justify political order and coercive laws to persons conceived as free and equal citizens—entails and calls upon a range of transformative ethical-cultural practices in order to cultivate and solidify the qualities of self and citizenship required by the ideal of a political society rooted in a social compact,

---

10. The critical literature dealing with social contract theory is voluminous. The classic studies that I have consulted include Otto von Gierke, *The Development of Political Theory,* trans. Bernard Freyd (New York: W. W. Norton, 1939), and Gierke, *Natural Law and the Theory of Society, 1500 to 1800,* trans. Ernest Barker (London: Cambridge University Press, 1958); D. G. Ritchie, "Contributions to the History of the Social Contract Theory," in *Darwin and Hegel* (London: Swan Sonnenschein and Co., 1893); J. W. Gough, *The Social Contract: A Critical Study of Its Development,* 2d ed. (Oxford: Clarendon Press, 1957); and Ernest Barker, "Introduction," in *Social Contract: Essays by Locke, Hume, and Rousseau* (New York: Oxford University Press, 1962). Among the more recent treatments of social contract theory, perhaps the single best study is Patrick Riley's *Will and Political Legitimacy* (Cambridge: Harvard University Press, 1982). See also Michael Lessnoff, *Social Contract* (Atlantic Highlands, N.J.: Humanities Press International, 1986); Jean Hampton, *Hobbes and the Social Contract Tradition* (Cambridge: Cambridge University Press, 1986); Peter J. McCormick, *Social Contract and Political Obligation: A Critique and Reappraisal* (New York: Garland, 1987); Martyn P. Thompson, *Ideas of Contract in English Political Thought in the Age of Locke* (New York: Garland, 1987); Harro Höpfl and Martyn P. Thompson, "The History of Contract as a Motif in Political Thought," *American Historical Review* 84, no. 4 (1979); Andrzej Rapaczynski, *Nature and Politics: Liberalism in the Philosophies of Hobbes, Locke, and Rousseau* (Ithaca: Cornell University Press, 1987); Carole Pateman, *The Sexual Contract* (Stanford: Stanford University Press, 1988); Ron Replogle, *Recovering the Social Contract* (Totowa, N.J.: Rowman and Littlefield, 1989); Vincente Medina, *Social Contract Theories: Political Obligation or Anarchy?* (Savage, Md.: Rowman and Littlefield, 1990); James Gordly, *The Philosophical Origins of Modern Contract Doctrine* (Oxford: Clarendon Press, 1991); and Charles W. Mills, *The Racial Contract* (Ithaca: Cornell University Press, 1997). A useful set of critical essays are collected in David Boucher and Paul Kelly, eds., *The Social Contract from Hobbes to Rawls* (New York: Routledge, 1994).

mutual covenant, or reasonable agreement. Compacting, covenanting, and promising presuppose a certain kind of ethical subject (at least *in potentia*), that is, a subject of veracity, fidelity, and foresight. The social compact and the institutional and cultural forms invoked by it must sponsor and cultivate the very beings who have "authored" or "consented" to the *pactio inter cives*.[11] This is not as illogical as it may sound. For something like this occurs whenever we make a promise or self-consciously commit ourselves to something or someone, and then discover that we have to call forth new or previously untapped dimensions of our own nascent reservoir of character traits, dispositions, and skills to make good on our pledge. In cases like this, ethical arts of self-cultivation coincide with the projection of a self that one is not yet but, by virtue of a mix of foresight, hope, and fear, strives to become.[12] This is part of what it means to talk of promising or covenanting as a mode of sponsoring a specific kind of ethical being and of shaping unique forms of self- and collective understanding. To cultivate a self with the capacity and disposition to sustain promises and agreements over time requires first that one is practiced in the art of making them, and then practiced in striving to live within the changed circumstances, internally and externally, that these commitments bring about.

For individuals and states alike, then, some promises are more than mutual transfers of rights over some definite period of time. Some promises are based on who or what we would like to become. With this forward-looking, developmental logic in mind—one that neither follows a strictly deonotological account, as per (one side of) Kant, nor assumes already settled cultural or linguistic practices, as per Hegel—I treat the social contract theorists of the modern period as thinkers who were as concerned with securing the practical conditions—moral, political, and cultural—for

11. This is how the Renaissance jurist Salamonio (1450–1532) conceived the origins of political society (*civilis societas*). For a useful discussion of Salamonio and contract theory's debts to Roman law conceptions of civil society, see Antony Black, "The Juristic Origins of Social Contract," *History of Political Thought* 14, no. 1 (1993): 69–70. See also Richard Tuck, *Natural Rights Theories: Their Origin and Development* (Cambridge: Cambridge University Press, 1979), chapter 2; Lessnoff, *Social Contract*, 25–27; and Quentin Skinner, *The Foundations of Modern Political Thought*, vol. 1, *The Renaissance* (Cambridge: Cambridge University Press, 1978), 148–52.

12. Hubris and pride might also need to be added to this list, at least if we have the contract theory of Thomas Hobbes in mind. For, as Hobbes conceived it, "the pacts and covenants, by which the parts of this body politic were at first made, set together, and united, resemble that fiat, or let us make man, pronounced by God in the creation." Michael Oakeshott, introduction to *Leviathan*, ed. Michael Oakeshott (New York: Collier Books, 1962), 19. All citations of the *Leviathan* are to this edition.

the long-term fulfillment of contracts and promises as they were with providing formal, foundational accounts of political legitimacy and political obligation. Indeed, one of the primary goals of this book is to show what the latter owes to the former, that is, to reveal the extent to which political justification depends upon an ethics of character formation. The social contract is no mere exchange of unstable liberty for the rule of law, nor of course is it a discrete moment in time that can be readily modeled after a transaction in the marketplace.[13] Rather, the social compact is a promise whose terms and requirements form the cultural-political conditions (variable to be sure) in relation to which citizens appear and take shape within a social world that is always in flux. By encouraging individuals to live up to the imaginary self/society relationship forged by the ideal of an originating mutual social compact, the hope expressed throughout this tradition is that this unique form of political and ethical being would become habitual over time, influencing the opinions, manners, judgments, and *mores* of citizens. Because they all want stability for the "right reasons," Hobbes, Locke, Rousseau, and Rawls are perhaps best viewed as theorists of the ethical and cultural labor involved in cultivating beings of civic fidelity.[14] This means that the modern social contract is not simply a story about the origins and justification of political power. Nor is the social contract best understood as a pure idea of reason in accordance with which we can judge the conduct of states and/or the "rightfulness" of laws (Kant). Rather, the social contract is, even more significantly, an account of the ethical and cultural conditions upon which contemporary citizenship continues to depend.

In light of what has been claimed so far, Kant's moral and political thought will serve as an important point of contrast to the main themes

13. For an influential reading of the contract tradition along these lines, see C. B. Macpherson, *The Political Theory of Possessive Individualism: Hobbes to Locke* (Oxford: Oxford University Press, 1988).

14. It is worth pointing out that there is an interesting etymological association at work here as well. Promise, from the Latin *foedus* (which can also mean covenant) requires and elicits *fides*, or faith. Cicero discusses this linguistic-conceptual relationship in his highly influential *De officiis*. In doing so, Cicero defines the foundation of justice as "good faith—that is, truth and fidelity to promises and agreements." Cicero goes on to note, following earlier Stoic arguments on this point, that "good faith" is so called because a promise is fulfilled or "made good." Cicero, *De officiis*, trans. Walter Miller (Cambridge: Harvard University Press, 1921), 1.7.23, 2.7. Cicero's importance to modern social contract theory can be gauged by the fact that the only book that receives Locke's endorsement for instruction in morals, besides the Bible, is Cicero's *De officiis*. See Locke's *Some Thoughts Concerning Education*, as well as "Some Thoughts Concerning Reading and Study for a Gentleman," both in *The Educational Writings of John Locke*, ed. James L. Axtell (Cambridge: Cambridge University Press, 1968), 294, 400.

and thinkers in this argument. In this study I consider how the interplay of contract, culture, and citizenship might help reorient contemporary understandings of how citizens within liberal regimes relate to political society, authority, and their fellow *cives*. With this aim in mind, Kant's distinctive treatment of the social contract stands a rather significant distance removed from those figures within the contract tradition who preceded him (including Rousseau, who had such a significant impact on Kant), and those who came after him (including Rawls, who was of course deeply influenced by Kant).[15] This is a complicated matter that I will return to throughout my discussions in each chapter, but the basic difference between Kant and the rest of the contract tradition might be understood along the following lines. In accordance with Kant's ideas of the person as rational and reasonable as such, of the will (practical reason) as a source of moral causality that gives universal laws, and of the social contract as purely an idea of reason, Kant offers a hypothetical account of contract and commonwealth as a regulative and "eternal norm" that need not have any resonance or purchase with actual citizens.[16] Indeed, part of the purpose of Kantian contractarianism (and part of its unique value, by some lights) is precisely that "Kant does not have to struggle, like Rousseau, to get the particular will to generalize itself, to think as a

15. As I discuss at greater length in Chapter 5, Rawls's movement away from Kantianism and Kantian conceptions of autonomy (after the Dewey Lectures of 1980) brings him closer to the pre-Kantian social contract tradition, which gave an important role (in my reading) to the formation of civic identities. For a useful discussion of Rawls's gradual separation from Kantianism, see Samuel Freeman, "Congruence and the Good of Justice," in *The Cambridge Companion to Rawls*, ed. Samuel Freeman (Cambridge: Cambridge University Press, 2003), chapter 7, esp. 303–8. See also Freeman, "Political Liberalism and the Possibility of a Just Democratic Constitution," *Chicago-Kent Law Review* 69, no. 3 (1994): 619–68. In this respect I think that Onora O'Neill is right to claim that Rawlsian justification is more Rousseauian than Kantian. I read this, however, as a gain for Rawls and the contract tradition of which he is a part, rather than a loss for Kantian constructivism. See O'Neill, "Constructivism in Rawls and Kant," in Freeman, *Cambridge Companion to Rawls*, 353. See also O'Neill, "Political Liberalism and Public Reason: A Critical Notice of John Rawls, *Political Liberalism*," *Philosophical Review* 106, no. 3 (1997): 411–28. J. Donald Moon also finds non-Kantian roots in Rawls's political theory, referring to these as a Humean (or neo-Humean) concern with the "circumstances of justice." Moon, "Rawls and Habermas on Public Reason: Human Rights and Global Justice," *Annual Review of Political Science* 6 (2003): 257–74. It is also worth noting that Habermas, in recent years, has also moved away from Kantian conceptions of autonomy. See, for just one example of this, *Between Facts and Norms: Contributions to a Discourse Theory of Law and Democracy*, trans. William Rehg (Cambridge: MIT Press, 1998), 120–22. Cf. Habermas, *The Structural Transformation of the Public Sphere*, trans. Thomas Burger (Cambridge: MIT Press, 1992), 102–17.

16. Kant, "On the Common Saying: 'This May Be True in Theory, but It Does Not Apply in Practice,'" in *Political Writings*, ed. Hans Reiss, trans. H. B. Nisbet (New York: Cambridge University Press, 1991), 79–81; see also *The Contest of Faculties*, ibid., 187.

citizen and not as a man, because consent can be treated as a standard."[17] When contract and consent are treated as an *a priori* standard of right, such an approach—albeit in other respects useful for public authorities who make laws—largely does away with the concern to ensure that *citizens* will possess the capacities and motivations to sustain a political society over time. In contrast to Kant and Kantian-inspired accounts of moral autonomy, none of the social contract thinkers that are the focus of this book presuppose a conception of practical reason or human will that allows for the articulation of a categorical, apodictic morality, and given this, that is, owing to fewer and more minimal assumptions about human rationality and the nature of moral motivation, Hobbes, Locke, and Rousseau (and later, Rawls) give more attention than does Kant to the ways in which social and political institutions give shape to the culture and character of citizenship. This is not to deny that Kant, in his own way, was concerned with the education and cultivation of persons, or that he was insensitive to the empirical, historical, and "anthropological" constraints on individual agency and moral development; but it is to say that Kant's commitment to a progressive, universal *Aufklärung* is distinct from the rest of the contract tradition's concern with political education and the cultivation of civic attachments.[18] More generally, a practical concern for the conditions under which a "social contract" is at all possible for citizens over generations entails a measure of cultural and ethical work, on and by political subjects, that is largely remote from and in tension with Kantian ideals of rationality, moral autonomy, and virtue.[19]

17. Riley, *Will and Political Legitimacy*, 127. Riley is surely also correct to claim that part of Kant's motivation here was to avoid the historicist challenge to (Lockean) contract theory provided by Hume in his essay "Of the Original Contract." I address, and seek to rebut, Hume's challenge to Locke in Chapter 3.

18. As Mika LaVaque-Manty notes, Kant's pedagogical focus is more *Erziehung* (upbringing) than *Bildung* (education or formation). See LaVaque-Manty, "Kant's Children," *Social Theory and Practice* 32, no. 3 (2006): 365–88. Barbara Herman also provides a very helpful discussion of Kant's treatment of moral education, stressing its significant social dimensions, in "Training to Autonomy: Kant and the Question of Moral Education," in *Philosophers on Education: Historical Perspectives*, ed. Amélie Oksenberg Rorty (London: Routledge, 1998), chapter 19.

19. Still, it must be acknowledged that over the past several decades Kant scholars have provided an increasingly capacious view of Kantian ethics and politics that has begun to chip away at the image of Kant's philosophy as excessively formal, cerebral, and individualistic. In the process, we are given an intriguing view of Kantian ethics that is more attuned to its social and communicative conditions, and a view of Kantian politics that is more provisional and historicist. In large part these developments arise from a welcome (and belated) effort to read Kant's expansive and complex corpus as a whole, taking the critical, the *a priori*, and the anthropological Kant together. While I continue to see him as largely outside the main tradition of social

What is at stake in this interpretation of the social contract tradition, and why should we attend to it now? A brief answer is that there is simply no getting around the (trans)formative experiences and demands that life in political society has for those who would be members of these associations. This remains true even when these political arrangements are self-consciously understood as a form of *societas,* not of *universitas,* that is, a civic association composed of a plurality of self-enacting individuals and groups who do not share a common substantive purpose or aim.[20] Despite the absence of a shared *summum bonum* among diversely appetitive beings, Thomas Hobbes argued that "civil societies are not mere meetings, but bonds, to the making whereof faith and compacts are necessary." Yet Hobbes was quick to point out that many, "perhaps most men," are ignorant of the virtues of political society and thus remain "unapt" to properly understand or care for such a society. "Wherefore," Hobbes reasoned, "man is made fit for society not by nature, but by education."[21] I will have a great deal more to say about Hobbes's education for political membership in Chapter 1, as I will of the education for civic

---

contract theory, my appreciation for Kant has been significantly enriched by these works. See Henry E. Allison, *Kant's Theory of Freedom* (Cambridge: Cambridge University Press, 1990); Thomas E. Hill Jr., *Dignity and Practical Reason in Kant's Moral Theory* (Ithaca: Cornell University Press, 1992); Elizabeth Ellis, *Kant's Politics: Provisional Theory for an Uncertain World* (New Haven: Yale University Press, 2005); Barbara Herman, "A Cosmopolitan Kingdom of Ends," in *Reclaiming the History of Ethics: Essays for John Rawls,* ed. Andrews Reath, Barbara Herman, and Christine M. Korsgaard (Cambridge: Cambridge University Press, 1997); Christine M. Korsgaard, *The Sources of Normativity* (Cambridge: Cambridge University Press, 1996); Mika LaVaque-Manty, *Arguments and Fists: Political Agency and Justification in Liberal Theory* (New York: Routledge, 2002); Onora O'Neill, *Constructions of Reason* (Cambridge: Cambridge University Press, 1989); Andrews Reath, "Legislating for a Realm of Ends: The Social Dimension of Autonomy," in *Reclaiming the History of Ethics;* and Nancy Sherman, *Making a Necessity of Virtue: Aristotle and Kant on Virtue* (Cambridge: Cambridge University Press, 1997).

20. I am drawing here on Michael Oakeshott's famous discussion of the old distinction between *societas* and *universitas,* in *On Human Conduct* (Oxford: Clarendon Press, 1975). Further useful discussion of this can be found in Richard Flathman, *Pluralism and Liberal Democracy* (Baltimore: Johns Hopkins University Press, 2005), chapter 5.

21. Thomas Hobbes, *De cive,* 1.2n*. In this passage Hobbes is challenging the Greek (Aristotlean) notion of man as ζωον πολιτκον. In doing so, Hobbes exaggerates (as was his custom) the differences between Aristotle's appreciation of the importance of education relative to a regime's laws and pattern of life and Hobbes's own understanding of the need to fashion dispositions, manners, and opinions in accordance with the requirements (as he conceived them) of sustaining political order. *Man and Citizen: Thomas Hobbes's De homine and De cive* (also known as *Philosophical Rudiments Concerning Government and Society*), ed. Bernard Gert (Garden City, N.Y.: Anchor Books, 1972). For an extensive discussion of the complex philosophical relationship between Hobbes and Aristotle, see Thomas A. Spragens Jr., *The Politics of Motion: The World of Thomas Hobbes* (London: Croom Helm, 1973).

identity throughout the entire contract tradition, culminating in John Rawls's effort to cultivate citizens who will become "wholehearted members of a democratic society."[22] Here I simply want to introduce the idea that if there is no way to cancel or deny the transformative expectations that are present from the start of what we have come to identify (retrospectively) as a central expression of the modern liberal tradition of political thought, there is nonetheless important space within this tradition to challenge and rework the manner, scope, and aims of this transformative ethos. Indeed, I argue that this is work that must be done if we have hopes of sustaining liberty and stability within an increasingly complex and diverse social world.

Yet to undertake this normative project in a manner that is responsive to the norms and constraints that have been fashioned over the course of the last several hundred years of moral and political development, we must first critically attend to the full ethical weight of the pattern of ideas that have done so much to shape who we (citizens of liberal democratic regimes) have become. Such an examination requires that we replace an exclusively backward-looking orientation to our understanding of social contract theory, one that asks "why political legitimacy and political obligation should be viewed as the voluntary creation of equal moral agents,"[23] with one that is able to appreciate its forward-looking, transformative aims and ends, by asking instead: how is it possible for these artificial relations and obligations to endure and hold meaning over time? When we have taken the full measure of the complex interrelationships between contract, culture, and citizenship—when we are critically attuned to the intimate relationship between strategies of public justification and ethical-civic transformation—several new avenues of political inquiry and moral reflection may come to the fore.[24] In what immediately follows I want to introduce a few of the critical paths that I explore in the chapters that follow.

22. John Rawls, "The Idea of Public Reason Revisited," in Rawls, *The Law of Peoples* (Cambridge: Harvard University Press, 1999), 149–50.

23. Riley, *Will and Political Legitimacy*, x.

24. I have been influenced by Foucault here. "The function of any diagnosis concerning what today is . . . does not consist in a simple characterization of what we are but, instead—by following lines of fragility in the present—in managing to grasp why and how that which is might no longer be that which is. In this sense, any description must always be made in accordance with these kinds of virtual fracture which open up the space of freedom understood as a space of concrete freedom, that is, of possible transformation." Foucault, "Structuralism and Post-Structuralism," in *The Essential Foucault*, ed. Paul Rabinow and Nikolas Rose (New York: New Press, 2003), 94.

Public Reason and the Challenges of Transformative Liberalism

The transformative practices and institutions within the modern contract tradition that speak to the challenge of "sustaining affirmation" to political conventions and civic bonds differ in important ways from one thinker to the next.[25] Yet, notwithstanding this diversity in design and purpose, the law (both natural and civil), education (both private and public), religious belief and practice, and public reason all play significant roles here. As I explain further below, the idea of public reason, operating in various ways throughout the social contract tradition, is both a crucial expression of a modern (increasingly liberal) transformative ethos and an effort (albeit an uneven one) to confront the internal dilemmas posed by the recognition that contract must make citizens. In the case of John Locke, for example, I show how his overall moral, political, and educational writings seek to shape and govern individual judgment from the inside out in accordance with the guidelines of the natural law. In doing so, political self-rule, understood as a civic virtue, is intimately connected to, in fact presupposes, the rule of self as a moral virtue (see Chapter 3). To emphasize these important features of modern contract thought is not to deny the deeply voluntarist commitments inherent in social contractarianism, nor is it to deny the significant ways in which contract theory (and liberal-democratic constitutions inspired by these accounts) view the presence and structure of political institutions as the common creation of the words and deeds of citizens. Nonetheless, alongside these important commitments resides a critical recognition that the moral and civic qualities that are needed in a society conceived as the product of willed free consent, qualities like trust, reciprocity, fidelity, and allegiance (among others), are features that arise neither naturally nor easily. Indeed, this kind of moral and ethical reliance is a basic condition for every joint undertaking or association that is meant to endure for any significant length of time, whether small or large, whether essentially private or public.

Yet a liberal political society, rooted in a moral commitment to the equal freedom of persons, stands in particularly acute need of mutual trust.[26]

---

25. I have borrowed the felicitous phrase "sustaining affirmation" from Stephen K. White, *Sustaining Affirmation: The Strengths of Weak Ontology in Political Theory* (Princeton: Princeton University Press, 2000).

26. See Mark E. Warren, ed., *Democracy and Trust* (Cambridge: Cambridge University Press, 1999).

A free society requires frequent and meaningful signals of veracity, reciprocity, and good faith from its members to offset persistent and rational fears that others are not abiding by the rules of the regime, not sharing in collective burdens, or abusing positions of relative social or economic power.[27] In an increasingly interdependent and global world, this type of ethical reliance shapes (and distorts) the very possibility of reciprocal relations between states, as much as it does the nature and status of civic associations within states.[28] Contracts, promises, and agreements are devices of mutual coordination that address this condition of moral and political uncertainty. As Hugo Grotius put it, "since man's will is from its nature changeable, means had to be found to fix that will for time to come, and such means are called 'promise.'"[29] Of course, contracts and promises can also reinforce and heighten basic anxieties about the veracity and reliability of others, and ourselves, especially under material circumstances that are less than ideal (that is to say, always). Thus, as Hobbes famously claimed, "Covenants, without the sword, are but words, and of no strength to secure a man at all."[30] One of the central political questions to which all of this gives rise is the following: how can liberal societies acknowledge this moral and ethical dependence on the character and dispositions

27. In light of the work of Michael Suk-Young Chwe, we might also think of public reason as both a ritual and a form of "common knowledge," that is, a way of creating the conditions in which a people come to believe or hold certain determinate things in common (knowledge, identity, and values) and also know that others know and share in these elements as well. Common knowledge is not only essential for solving coordination problems, but the very publicity inherent in modes and rituals of common knowledge shapes political self-understanding as well—indeed, it shapes a metalevel form of political self-understanding insofar as all citizens come to know that others know and share in this knowledge, and know that others know that as well. See Chwe, *Rational Ritual: Culture, Coordination, and Common Knowledge* (Princeton: Princeton University Press, 2001). My thanks to Stephen Macedo for suggesting this work to me.

28. For a timely and acute analysis of this condition and the multiple perils of ignoring global conditions of mutual interdependence, see Benjamin Barber, *Fear's Empire: War, Terrorism, and Democracy* (London: W. W. Norton, 2003).

29. Grotius, *The Jurisprudence of Holland*, quoted in Tuck, *Natural Rights Theories*, 69–70. In his "Preliminary Discourse" to *The Rights of War and Peace*, Grotius argues as follows: "Since the fulfilling of Covenants belongs to the Law of Nature (for it was necessary there should be some Means of obliging Men among themselves, and we cannot conceive any other more conformable to Nature) from this very Foundation Civil Laws were derived." *The Rights of War and Peace*, ed. Richard Tuck (Indianapolis: Liberty Fund, 2005), 93; see also book 2, chapter 16, 848–49. Even earlier, Althusius claimed that "the subject matter of politics is therefore association (*consociatio*), in which the symbiotes pledge themselves each to the other, by explicit or tacit agreement, to mutual communication of whatever is useful and necessary for the harmonious exercise of social life." *Politica*, ed. and trans. Fredrick S. Carney (Indianapolis: Liberty Fund, 1995), 1, §2.

30. Hobbes, *Leviathan*, chapter 17, p. 129. See also Hobbes's discussion of the fallible conditions for covenants of mutual trust in chapter 14.

of its citizens and leaders and seek to fulfill this need in meaningful ways, while honoring commitments to individual liberty, self-direction, freedom of association, and moral pluralism?

To be sure, the question of how far (if at all) a liberal society may legitimately seek to influence the character, dispositions, and skills of its members has become one of the most controversial fault lines within contemporary liberal thinking over the past several decades.[31] While liberal societies presuppose and rely on a range of important moral qualities and virtues for their very identity and stability (toleration, mutual respect, civility, reciprocity, to name a few), liberal political regimes have a difficult time conceiving how these qualities could legitimately be the object of cultivation, given fundamental commitments to natural freedom and equality and an overriding concern to limit the coercive powers of government.[32] I will refer to this as the paradox of civic virtue for liberal

31. The literature here is vast and growing. In many ways the following sources are a response to the powerful challenge presented by Alasdair MacIntyre in *After Virtue* (Notre Dame: University of Notre Dame Press, 1984), as well as Michael Sandel, *Liberalism and the Limits of Justice* (Cambridge: Cambridge University Press, 1982), and Charles Taylor, *Sources of the Self* (Cambridge: Harvard University Press, 1989). Those who have defended an important role for virtue within liberal political theory include Ronald Beiner, *What's the Matter with Liberalism?* (Berkeley and Los Angeles: University of California Press, 1992); Peter Berkowitz, *Virtue and the Making of Modern Liberalism* (Princeton: Princeton University Press, 1999); Eamonn Callan, *Creating Citizens: Political Education and Liberal Democracy* (Oxford: Clarendon Press, 1997); George Crowder, *Liberalism and Value Pluralism* (London: Continuum, 2002); Richard Dagger, *Civic Virtues* (New York: Oxford University Press, 1997); William Galston, *Liberal Purposes: Goods, Virtues, and Diversity in the Liberal State* (Cambridge: Cambridge University Press, 1991); Amy Gutmann and Dennis Thompson, *Democracy and Disagreement* (Cambridge: Belknap Press of Harvard University Press, 1996); Mark Kingwell, *A Civil Tongue: Justice, Dialogue, and the Politics of Pluralism* (University Park: Pennsylvania State University Press, 1995); Macedo, *Liberal Virtues;* and Thomas A. Spragens Jr., *Civic Liberalism* (Lanham, Md.: Rowman and Littlefield, 1999). Of course we should not overlook in this respect the ways in which John Rawls was also acutely aware of the importance of moral and political virtues for sustaining liberal institutions. See especially part 3 of *A Theory of Justice* (Cambridge: Harvard University Press, 1971). See also Judith Shklar, *Ordinary Vices* (Cambridge: Belknap Press of Harvard University Press, 1984), 5. The work of "liberal perfectionists" is also relevant here. See Joseph Raz, *The Morality of Freedom* (Oxford: Clarendon Press, 1986); Thomas Hurka, *Perfectionism* (New York: Oxford University Press, 1993); and Steven Wall, *Liberalism, Perfectionism, and Restraint* (New York: Cambridge University Press, 1998). For diverse expressions of liberal political theory that vigorously resist this "return" to the virtues, see John Gray, *Two Faces of Liberalism* (New York: New Press, 2000); Richard Flathman, *Reflections of a Would Be Anarchist: Ideals and Institutions of Liberalism* (Minneapolis: University of Minnesota Press, 1998); Chandran Kukathas, *The Liberal Archipelago: A Theory of Diversity and Freedom* (Oxford: Oxford University Press, 2003); and Douglas B. Rasmussen and Douglas J. Den Uyl, *Norms of Liberty: A Perfectionist Basis for Non-Perfectionist Politics* (University Park: Pennsylvania State University Press, 2005).

32. See Skinner on this point, *Liberty Before Liberalism;* see also Berkowitz, *Virtue and the Making of Modern Liberalism.*

political societies. I say paradox here advisedly, because this tension need not be seen as a contradiction; it is possible to hold that there is a distinct scheme of liberal virtues/characterological requirements, and to maintain without fear of logical contradiction that the state and its institutions should not be charged with the duty of their promotion.[33] In all of this, liberal societies at least seem to give the lie to the ancient faith in the unity of the virtues and the moral values they express, for in our case, freedom, autonomy, individuality, and rights (and modern deontological ethics) create formidable restraints on virtue talk (and broadly teleological ethical outlooks).

By posing the challenge of the ethical preconditions for the endurance of liberal citizenship in relation to the contract theorists of the modern period, I mean to stress that the (trans)formative dimensions of social contract theory are, on the one hand, important steps toward an answer to widespread and still lively concerns about the sustainability of liberal political societies. On the other hand, these same transformative features are a source of internal trouble and anxiety for this tradition, and by extension, for liberal citizens and liberal regimes today. It is precisely here, in this dual reliance upon and anxiety about the moral and ethical qualities necessary for modern citizenship, that the social contract thinkers hold immense value and relevance for our own time. If there is any hope for an ideal of ethical-civic transformation as a hospitable, indeed crucial, dimension within the Western liberal tradition of freedom and equality, it will be found within the modern (broadly nonperfectionist) social contract tradition, or it will probably always remain a fugitive element in liberal political societies. I believe that there are important commitments to ethical cultivation within a liberal frame that can be defended both historically and politically. But I also argue (especially in Chapter 5) that these commitments need to be critically refashioned and pluralized in order to better accord with other equally important features of contemporary moral and political life.

The significance of this analysis for us today is to urge a different way of conceiving (interpretively) and approaching (normatively) the complex interrelationships between contract, culture, and citizenship. The central question to which this analysis gives rise is not whether liberal political societies rightfully undertake morally and politically significant forms of transformative influence on their members for the sake of meeting certain

33. See Shklar, *Ordinary Vices*, chapter 6.

perceived needs for social stability. For, as we will see, in no case was this idea seriously doubted. Indeed, I will show that the modern social contract was always less atomistic, disengaged, and deontological (or relentlessly anti-Aristotelean) than we have long supposed.[34] Likewise, for all the thinkers considered here, the liberal subject is never a simple, originating source of morals or politics but always a highly uncertain, incomplete, and fragile achievement. Accordingly, the critical question we need to pursue in relation to this influential tradition is not simply whether social contract theory is invested in the development of particular forms of ethical being or committed to specific modes of self- and collective understanding, but how well these necessary configurations and strategies of cultivation honor other commitments that are no less fundamental for liberal democratic citizens today, commitments to individual freedom and moral pluralism foremost among them. As I demonstrate throughout the chapters of this book, the social contract tradition—if read as a broad normative account of both political legitimation *and* ethical cultivation—holds significant insights for diverse liberal regimes that must still confront this question today. At the same time, this is a tradition that continues to form a powerful internal challenge for pluralistic liberal democracies, creating significant political and moral constraints on the prospects for normative political theory that need to be critically reappraised by each new generation of citizens.

Along these lines, previous scholarship by Carole Pateman and Charles W. Mills has shown how the abstract, liberal language of the modern social contract reproduces and solidifies sexual and racial privilege in ways that both belie ideals of liberty and equality and shield underlying dynamics of exclusion and domination.[35] Like Pateman and Mills, I believe that

---

34. For critiques of contract theory along these lines, see Hegel, *Philosophy of Right*, trans. T. M. Knox (New York: Oxford University Press, 1967), §§75, 258, and "Additions," §47. Also see the discussion of social contract theory and modern natural law in Alexander Passerin d'Entrèves, *Natural Law: An Introduction to Legal Philosophy* (New Brunswick, N.J.: Transaction Publishers, 1994), chapter 4. J. G. A. Pocock's extensive historical work into the republican tradition is also relevant here. See *The Machiavellian Moment: Florentine Political Thought and the Atlantic Republic Tradition* (Princeton: Princeton University Press, 1975); *Virtue, Commerce, and History* (Cambridge: Cambridge University Press, 1985); and Pocock's very helpful essay, "Cambridge Paradigms and Scotch Philosophers: A Study of the Relations Between the Civic Humanist and the Civil Jurisprudential Interpretation of Eighteenth-Century Social Thought," in *Wealth and Virtue: The Shaping of Political Economy in the Scottish Enlightenment*, ed. Istvan Hont and Michael Ignatieff (Cambridge: Cambridge University Press, 1983).

35. See Pateman, *Sexual Contract*, and Mills, *Racial Contract*. For similar critiques of the ways in which liberal procedural conceptions of justice proffer a false universalism that perpetuates antecedent structural inequalities, see Susan Moller Okin, *Justice, Gender, and the Family*

the nature of modern freedom and authority cannot be adequately understood without attending to the full story of the social contract, and that
a more just and inclusive democratic future resides, at least in part, in a
normative reworking of this tradition. With this in mind I consider how
the transformative institutions within social contract theory—like public reason—might be rendered more responsive to the diverse moral
agents these institutions seek to govern and shape. As I argue at greater
length in Chapter 5, we are in particularly acute need today of ethical
qualities (like democratic humility) that can forestall the drive to define
liberalism and public reasoning along a narrow range of value and encourage a more self-reflexive orientation toward its own transformative
ambitions.

Before I introduce this latter project, I need to say a little more about
the promise and the challenge presented by the idea of public reason
within the social contract tradition. Public reason can be defined, briefly,
as a commitment to public reasonableness as a necessary standard for
the morally legitimate exercise of political power. At a more general level,
when public reason is introduced as a moral and political duty, this is a
concept whose aim is to articulate the substance and form of sharing citizenship with diverse others. If contract makes citizens, never simply the
other way around, public reason is one of the central means by which
this moral and civic development is imagined to take place. The transformative role played by the idea of public reason in social contract theory is one that seeks to ameliorate, if never entirely resolve, the tension
presented by free and equal persons living within institutional forms that
possess their own ethical preconditions. The idea of public reason enters
this story (and well before Kant made the idea famous) as a means of
sustaining the social compact, or, in the case of John Rawls and contemporary political liberalism, of affirming a society conceived as a fair system of cooperation over time.[36] Public reason serves to facilitate and guide

(New York: Basic Books, 1989); Will Kymlicka, *Liberalism, Community, and Culture* (Oxford:
Oxford University Press, 1989); and Iris Marion Young, "Polity and Group Difference: A Critique
of the Ideal of Universal Citizenship," *Ethics* 99, no. 2 (1989): 250–74. A very useful discussion
and critical engagement with this literature is provided by Melissa S. Williams in "Justice Toward
Groups: Political Not Juridical," *Political Theory* 23, no. 1 (1995): 67–91.

36. Here, then, is another important difference between Kant and the social contract thinkers
explored in this book. Hobbes, Locke, and Rousseau (and later Rawls) offer an account of public reason that works on the boundary conditions of law (public right) and ethics (virtue) in a
manner that seems to be foreclosed in Kant's thought, especially if we have in mind the strict
separation that Kant makes between right (*Recht*) and virtue (*Tugend*). See his *Metaphysics of*

this task of political and ethical cultivation in blunt and forceful ways, through law and punishment (Hobbes), and in more subtle, indirect ways through a variety of different social and cultural institutions (Locke and Rousseau).

Thus, in the chapters that follow I treat public reason rather broadly as part of a theory of public political culture and as an ideal of citizenship within the institutions and culture of which public reason is an integral part. The overlapping commitment within the social contract tradition to something like public reason—of having and sharing reasons as citizens of a specific political culture, of possessing and being attached to specific forms of self- and collective understanding—helps reveal the extent to which contract constitutes certain distinctive forms of civic identity and moral conduct. It is critical for us to attend to this because political justification and public reason are two of the most significant and controversial domains of moral and political reflection at present.[37] This ongoing

---

Morals, ed. and trans. Mary Gregor (Cambridge: Cambridge University Press, 1996), 20–21 (6:219–20). To put this point slightly differently, the function of publicity and public reasoning in the main contract tradition is to help meet the motivational challenges of a society patterned after the idea of a social compact or agreement. In this sense public reasoning is always a civic formative project that entails the cultivation of shared principles, opinions, manners, and virtues that were assumed (but not provided for) by the ideal of a social compact. For these thinkers, the idea of public right, as something publicly shared by all citizens, is an idea whose intelligibility and long-term stability depend on mechanisms of cultural, and quite explicitly civic, formation. By contrast, publicity and the public use of reason in Kant serve to secure the free conditions necessary for the realization of the universal moral law (as a principle of practical reason) and for a cosmopolitan conception of justice. There are great merits in this last view, as developed, for example, by O'Neill, *Constructions of Reason;* see esp. chapter 2. My point here is simply to note how public reason in Kant differs from that found in the earlier contract tradition.

37. Gerald Gaus has produced a very useful text dedicated to a critical discussion of alternate conceptions of public reason within contemporary normative theory. See Gaus, *Contemporary Theories of Liberalism: Public Reason as a Post-Enlightenment Project* (Thousand Oaks, Calif.: Sage, 2003). Some of the most important recent articulations of public reason can be found in John Rawls, *Political Liberalism* (New York: Columbia University Press, 1996); and Rawls, "Idea of Public Reason Revisited." See also Kent Greenawalt, *Private Consciences and Public Reasons* (New York: Oxford University Press, 1995); Charles Larmore, *The Morals of Modernity* (New York: Cambridge University Press, 1996), chapters 6 and 7; Robert Audi, *Religious Commitment and Secular Reason* (New York: Cambridge University Press, 2000); and Fred Frohock, *Public Reason: Mediated Authority in the Liberal State* (Ithaca: Cornell University Press, 1999). For more critical treatments of public reason, see James Bohman, "Public Reason and Cultural Pluralism: Political Liberalism and the Problem of Moral Conflict," *Political Theory* 23 (1995): 253–79; Veit Bader, "Religious Pluralism: Secularism or Priority of Democracy?" *Political Theory* 27 (1999): 597–633; Paul J. Weithman, *Religion and the Obligations of Citizenship* (Cambridge: Cambridge University Press, 2002), chapter 7; John Horton, "Rawls, Public Reason, and the Limits of Liberal Justification," *Contemporary Political Theory* 2 (2003): 5–23; and Jeffrey C. Isaac, Matthew F. Filner, and Jason C. Bivins, "American Democracy and the New Christian Right: A Critique of Apolitical Liberalism," in *Democracy's Edges,* ed. Ian Shapiro and Casiano Hacker-Cordón (Cambridge: Cambridge University Press, 1999), 222–64.

attention to the question of public justification is motivated by the concern that the basis and exercise of political authority should be capable of justification to all those who will be subject to it. Put in these terms, it is fairly easy to see that a concern for political justification—witnessed in the contemporary period in the philosophical work of John Rawls, T. M. Scanlon, and Jürgen Habermas, as well as in the drafting of new constitutional regimes throughout the world—originates largely with the modern social contract tradition and its preoccupation with addressing the problem of political legitimacy in the context of religious civil wars. The idea of a social contract is itself a mechanism of public justification, a normative model by which to imagine the principles (or the procedures) that could govern otherwise free and equal individuals.[38] Closely related to this, the contemporary focus on public reason—of having and providing reasons for the direction and use of political power that all can reasonably accept—is likewise ushered into modernity with the moral centrality given to the idea of consent, buttressed by the commitment to the natural freedom and equality of persons in the contract tradition.

It may be that as liberal societies continue to experience the moral responsibilities and political burdens of public justification—shaped by the inheritance of this tradition and its moral categories and yet confronted by an increasingly diverse, complex, and global social universe in which these categories seem ill suited—a stronger sense of exigency will attend the critical reappraisal of their own political-historical formation. We may fervently hope that our times will spur this kind of cultural/intellectual introspection, for as this book aims to show, this tradition holds underexplored lessons and possibilities for the present.

To begin to appreciate this, we must first see that public justification in the social contract tradition stands alongside cultural-civic transformation in importance for making good on the promise of securing liberty with stability and individual autonomy with legal order. More to the point, public justification (signaled by the language of consent and legitimacy) was never imagined to be sufficient, or fully realizable, without significant ethical and cultural work on and by citizens. When we turn to more contemporary expressions of this mutually constitutive relationship between justification and civic transformation (in the work of John Rawls and, even more tellingly, in Stephen Macedo), we will see

---

38 See here Jeremy Waldron, "Theoretical Foundations of Liberalism," in his *Liberal Rights: Collected Papers, 1981–1991* (Cambridge: Cambridge University Press, 1993), 43–50.

that public reason is never neutral in aim or effect. This is something that should be neither lamented nor uncritically embraced. Rather, we need to ask a distinctly more relevant and potentially fruitful question for our times: the question is not whether but how a liberal society should best understand and undertake its transformative influences on the character and self-understanding of its citizens and the culture that sustains them? With this as our motivating line of inquiry, each chapter of this book examines the different strategies by which Hobbes, Locke, Rousseau, and Rawls confronted this challenge.

With this latter, more normative set of purposes in mind, I mean to challenge and modestly refashion the liberal tradition of public reason that I discuss here. From Hobbes to Rawls, the social contract tradition has shown a robust commitment to the idea of public reason as a uniquely valuable way of understanding the proper (ethical) relationship among and between citizens and leaders who share a political society. I attend critically to the idea and use of public reason in social contract thought because it provides a conceptual point at which these thinkers reveal an appreciation for the necessary interdependencies of contract, culture, and citizenship. If the contract story does not really end with the making of a collective political promise or covenant, but instead creates a framework within which it becomes meaningful to say that the contract shapes and constitutes citizens, then the development and diverse use of public reason—and related concepts like public conscience and civic manners and mores—are some of the most important places for analyzing where and how this project of moral and civic formation is undertaken.

With this in mind I go on to argue that what is increasingly needed today is a greater measure of critical self-consciousness about the nature and direction of liberalism's transformative ethos. More specifically, we need a greater appreciation for the *mutually transformative possibilities* that can arise in any public encounter between citizens in a pluralistic democratic society. To this end I make a case in Chapter 5 for an ethos of democratic humility as a critical supplement to public reason. I define *democratic* humility as a cultivated sensitivity to the limitations, incompleteness, and contingency of both one's personal moral powers and commitments and the particular forms, laws, and institutions that structure one's political and social life with others. Contemporary conditions for political judgment and action should spur us to cultivate forms of civic attentiveness that can help maximize the possibilities for reciprocal learning and moral growth from our mutual interactions with others, even when (or especially when) our democratic entanglements are themselves the outgrowth of deeper moral or religious disagreements. To the extent that an ethos of democratic humility can be effectively cultivated among a diverse array of citizens and leaders, we might find that our civic lives and what we are willing to label just and reasonable will be complicated and expanded not by prior orchestrations of public reason but by forms of political expression and action moderated by and received in humility.

To more clearly distinguish the significance of this analysis of social contract theory and to highlight the interpretive and normative gains that follow from the arguments of this book, I want to contrast (briefly) the approach I take to these venerable figures in the history of Western moral and political thought with some of the dominant ways in which they have been traditionally understood.

The Social Contract Story Retold

It has become a respectable commonplace to think of social contract theory, in spite of its many variations and internal differences, as an account of social institutions conceived as the outcome of a rational bargain between free and equal persons concerned to advance their own self-regarding good. Habermas, for example, claims that "social contract theories have constructed the autonomy of citizens in the categories of bourgeois contract law, that is, as the private choice of parties who conclude a contract."[39] To be sure, the social institutions that are taken as the proper object of contractarian thought differ from one account to the next. In the case of modern theories of contract, the object under consideration was political society itself. In more recent articulations, the objects of agreement are things like principles of justice by which to regulate the basic institutions and laws of society (Rawls) or morality itself

---

39. Habermas, *Between Facts and Norms*, 449. In these terms, Habermas claims, "the Hobbesian problem of founding a social order could not be satisfactorily resolved in terms of the fortuitous confluence of rational choices made by independent actors." Yet there is in fact nothing fortuitous at work in the Hobbesian founding of social and political order, as can be witnessed by both the dearth of rational resources with which to fashion a stable commonwealth (there are very few rational actors walking about in the "state of nature"), and Hobbes's unwillingness (as per Kant) to "equip the parties in the state of nature with genuinely moral capacities" (read: moral autonomy). So Habermas is correct to point to this problem in Hobbes, but wrong, in my view, to suppose that Hobbes offered no other means of addressing the challenge of political order. See Chapter 1.

(Gauthier).[40] Still, while the focus of the contractarian enterprise may shift, the idea that contract itself is properly understood as a procedure of rational choice or reasonable agreement (under certain specified conditions) remains. The promise and appeal of this traditional understanding of contract, taken both philosophically and practically, is that if it is possible to show what rational individuals seeking their own various ideas of the good would (or could) agree to as reasonable rules for their common association, then we would have a coherent and persuasive way of thinking about the proper ends and limits of political society, justice, and morality. We would possess standards of justice and an understanding of political morality that could be applied to all kinds of contemporary practices as a test of their legitimacy.[41]

Part of my purpose in this book is to show that this widespread understanding of contract theory is not so much wrong as woefully incomplete. This incompleteness is a problem not simply because we (students of political ideas and citizens of pluralistic liberal regimes) desire theoretical completeness for its own sake, but more fundamentally because it shields from view both important challenges for this tradition of political thought and intriguing latent possibilities that we would do well to reconsider. By claiming that contract makes citizens, and never simply the other way around (as the contract as bargain model assumes), I mean to emphasize the ways in which justice, morality, and public political culture operate as mechanisms of transformative influence within this tradition. What I will show, in reference to all of the thinkers discussed here, is that contract is always an ethical, formative enterprise, never purely reductionist (reducing morality/duty to interest and prudence, as is said of Hobbes), or strictly foundationalist (as is said of Locke and the liberalism he helped to inspire), or solely or exclusively political (as Rawls endeavored to show). Political justification and ethical transformation are two constitutive dimensions of social contract theory, past and present, that cannot be separated without great loss both to a full understanding of these central figures in Western political theory and to the ongoing need to face this inheritance self-critically.

40. See David Gauthier, *Morals by Agreement* (Oxford: Clarendon Press, 1986). In the same vein, see John C. Harsanyi, "Morality and the Theory of Rational Behaviour," in *Utilitarianism and Beyond*, ed. Amartya Sen and Bernard Williams (Cambridge: Cambridge University Press, 1982).

41. See Samuel Freeman's very helpful essay, "Reason and Agreement in Social Contract Views," *Philosophy and Public Affairs* 19, no. 2 (1990): 122–57; see also Ian Shapiro, *The Moral Foundations of Politics* (New Haven: Yale University Press, 2003), chapter 5.

Thus the project of outlining the social institutions and moral principles that plural and at least quasi-rational agents would or could agree
to under certain specified conditions is only one (deeply Kantian) side of
social contract theory. The other side, more implicit but of equal importance, is a concern for the qualities, dispositions, beliefs, and virtues citizens must possess in order to make and, most important, to abide by
their mutual agreements and promises. In the chapters that follow I show
how the social contract theorists addressed both sides of this general problem: articulating moral norms and political principles that are to govern
people's relationships with one another, and confronting the question of
the motivating moral sources for abiding by and sustaining those principles over time. If I am right about the nature and the importance of
these transformative commitments for modern social contractarianism,
then Hume was surely correct to claim that the ongoing legitimacy of
regimes has little to do with their origins (let alone counterfactual beginnings), but wrong to think that social contract thinkers were insensitive
to the problems of civic identity and allegiance that thereby follow for
future generations. Likewise, Hegel was right to worry about the inad-
equacies of a theory of the state that is rooted in the subjective needs and
choices of individuals in a presocial condition, but wrong to suppose that
contractarian accounts do not seek to cultivate habitual practices of ethical and political belonging that Hegel understood to be central to the very
idea of moral and political order.[42] And, more recently, Michael Sandel
may be right to worry about the rise of a purely procedural republic, but
wrong to place the responsibility for this aberration (assuming it exists)
at the feet of the liberal contract tradition and to overlook the resources
internal to this tradition for sustaining free self-government over time.[43]

Part of what continues to make the modern contract theorists so fascinating and still so timely is that, *qua* theorists of liberty, consent, and
legitimacy, they attended to the formation of civic-ethical character and
the cultivation of a supporting civic culture to facilitate uniquely modern
and (over time) increasingly liberal forms of being and self-understanding.
None of the thinkers explored here believed that the problem of establishing or securing a political order could be completed without considering
the mutually interdependent relationships between contract, culture, and
citizenship. In large part this is because there is no reason to assume that

42. See Hegel, *Philosophy of Right*, §§150–53.
43. See Michael Sandel, *Democracy's Discontent: America in Search of a Public Philosophy*
(Cambridge: Harvard University Press, 1996), chapter 1.

the particular institutions and predominant elements within a political culture will necessarily support the type of citizens (and the corresponding dispositions, virtues, and forms of self-understanding) needed to sustain a particular regime or to help it flourish. Indeed, to assume that there is any kind of natural or necessary relationship here (as Aristotle and Montesquieu also warned) is to take far too much for granted—both historically and morally.[44] There are numerous signs across many different regimes around the globe that the question of consolidating new or sustaining older liberal democratic societies is now one of the leading challenges for our time.[45] All of the thinkers explored here recognized an early version of this problem, owing to their own experiences with significant political change, and saw it as a dilemma to which their own brand of normative moral and political thought could contribute, however haltingly or incompletely. To be sure, there are significant differences between the type of citizens that Hobbes's political thought is dedicated to producing and the character of the citizen in Locke, or again, more recently, in the thought of John Rawls. Yet by foregrounding the significant interrelationships between contract, culture, and citizenship—and the crucial connecting role that public reason plays in this—we may be able to draw upon some valuable intellectual resources with which to confront, more self-consciously and self-critically, ongoing challenges within liberal citizenship today.

Contract, Culture, and Citizenship: Past and Present

Still, the question will naturally and forcefully obtrude: why should we attend to the social contract theorists of the seventeenth and eighteenth centuries, given that so much has changed (politically, technologically, and economically) over the course of the intervening centuries? What I hope to show throughout this book is that Thomas Hobbes, John Locke, Jean-Jacques Rousseau, and the social contract "tradition" more broadly, can

44. See Stephen Macedo's *Diversity and Distrust* for a recent provocative argument along these same lines. See also Quentin Skinner, "Paradoxes of Political Liberty," in *The Tanner Lectures on Human Values,* vol. 7, ed. Sterling M. McMurrin (Salt Lake City: University of Utah Press, 1986), 225–50.

45. See, for example, Robert Putnam, *Making Democracy Work: Civic Traditions in Modern Italy* (Princeton: Princeton University Press, 1993), and Larry Diamond and Marc F. Plattner, eds., *The Global Divergence of Democracies* (Baltimore: Johns Hopkins University Press, 2001).

help us reconsider the ethical and institutional conditions necessary for sustaining meaningful commitments to the idea of freedom within diversity, and for sustaining practices of liberty within the necessary constraints of political order. I believe that the contract story needs to be retold in light of recent developments in the critical reinterpretation of modern liberalism, and in light of ongoing moral and political challenges for securing freedom and stability under conditions of growing social diversity and global complexity. The modern theorists of social contract are typically read for the contributions they have made to our thinking about the general problems of political legitimacy and obligation during the rise and consolidation of the modern state. And of course these remain lively issues for the present, notwithstanding the many premature dirges and celebrations we hear today about the end of the nation-state. Yet the thinkers discussed in this book not only addressed themselves to questions about how to justify rule over others, for alongside these traditional concerns resides another range of problems that are no less constitutive of modernity and that continue to confound diverse liberal societies. The most general way to articulate this problem is as follows: how should pluralistic societies go about cultivating forms of ethical attachment to political artifice? Or, as John Rawls asked in *Political Liberalism*, "How is it possible that there may exist over time a stable and just society of free and equal citizens profoundly divided by reasonable though incompatible religious, philosophical, and moral doctrine?"[46]

From this general question three distinct yet interconnected lines of inquiry are at the center of social contract thinking, and each of them serves as the analytic framework for my discussion throughout the chapters that follow. We might express them thus: (1) How to shape political *institutions* that are legitimate, stable, and capable of eliciting the voluntary and affectional attachments of their diverse members? This is the question of *compact* or *contract*, and it identifies the basic problem of political justification that unites thinkers as diverse as Hobbes, Locke, Rousseau, and Rawls. (2) What disciplines of *cultural and self-fashioning* are requisite to sustaining political order and equal freedom amid pluralism? Specifically, what forms of reasoning, self-understanding, and collective identity are needed to sustain diverse liberal societies over time? This is the *ethical-cultural* question incumbent upon the first question. (3) How to undertake projects of *civic cultivation* while sustaining commitments

46. Rawls, *Political Liberalism*, xviii; see also 160–61.

to autonomy, freedom, and diversity? This is the question of liberal *civic membership* incumbent upon answering the second.

In my view there are better and worse ways of answering each one of these questions. Or, rather, each answer is itself a contestable response that flows from a more general range of moral and political assumptions about things like the human self, the nature of power, the sources of moral belief, the motivations for ethical action, the possibilities for moral agreement, and much else besides. Thus every response to the questions posed above, answering to the complex interrelationships between *contract, culture, and citizenship* stands in need of critical scrutiny. This book provides such an analysis not only with the goal of shedding new light on a tradition whose influence is still in need of interrogation, but in order to assemble a general political-ethical framework—with its own political alignments and philosophical commitments, to be sure—that could help us think anew about citizenship within diversity today.[47]

The above questions also speak to an interpretive-historical point that I defend throughout this book. For embedded in all of these questions is a concern to make a distinction between the deductions of sovereignty, on the one hand, and what John Locke referred to as the "art of conducting men right in society," on the other.[48] At the heart of this distinction is the concern to distinguish the formal establishment of sovereignty, legitimate authority, and rights from the more general moral and cultural work that must be undertaken once the institutions of public authority and law have been generated.[49] One reason why this distinction has not been prevalent in either the study of political ideas or our inherited understandings of the moral and political contours of liberal societies surely has to do with a basic conceit of modern liberalism: that liberal societies need not concern themselves with the character, dispositions, or moral qualities of those governed by a liberal state. This was perhaps made most famous by Kant's assertion that "the problem of setting up a state can be solved even by a nation of devils (so long as they possess

---

47. I have been inspired here by the work of William Connolly. See, in particular, *The Ethos of Pluralization* (Minneapolis: University of Minnesota Press, 1995), and *Why I Am Not a Secularist* (Minneapolis: University of Minnesota Press, 1999).

48. Locke, "Draft Letter to the Countess of Peterborough," MS Locke c. 24, fols. 196–97, in *Educational Writings of Locke*, 395–96.

49. In many ways this is a distinction that is owed, in the modern context, to Locke. But see also Foucault, "The Subject and Power," and "Governmentality," in *Essential Foucault*, 126–44, 229–45; Ivison, *Self at Liberty*, esp. chapters 5 and 6; and Tully, *Approach to Political Philosophy*.

understanding)."[50] This was a sentiment that seemed to take practical, institutional form in the American setting with the framing of the U.S. Constitution. While men may not be rational devils, James Madison rue-fully conceded that they are certainly not angels, and should be governed accordingly.[51] In this respect Madison was closer to Hume's recommended *political* maxim "that, in contriving any system of government, and fix-ing the several checks and controls of the constitution, every man must be supposed a knave."[52]

There are strong principled and prudential reasons to support this broad antipathy to the talk of virtue or ethical (trans)formation, given justifi-able fears about state paternalism, "soul craft," and the stultifying effects of social straitjackets. Yet, as this book aims to show, liberal societies have always been essentially dependent upon the (trans)formative dimen-sions of their institutions and culture: political justification elicits ethical-cultural formation, and deontological categories of right and obligation depend for their reliable performance upon the character and dispositions of human agents. I give shorthand expression to this idea by arguing that for all of thinkers examined here, *contract makes citizens*, never sim-ply the other way around. This, however, is not to say that the cultiva-tional strategies adopted always work, or work in the ways that these authors had hoped. Indeed, since human beings are neither plastic crea-tures nor readily shaped by the writings of political philosophers, the social contract theorists face a variety of challenges with respect to their own moral and political ambitions.[53] As we will see, this is especially true

50. Kant, "Perpetual Peace," in *Political Writings*, 112. Such a view is also well captured by another justly famous Kantian line: "Nothing straight can be constructed from such warped wood as that which man is made of." "Idea for a Universal History with a Cosmopolitan Pur-pose," ibid., 46.

51. James Madison, Federalist no. 51, in *The Federalist*, ed. Clinton Rossiter (New York: Mentor Books, 1961), 322.

52. David Hume, "Of the Independency of Parliament," in Hume, *Essays: Moral, Political and Literary*, ed. Eugene F. Miller (Indianapolis: Liberty Fund, 1985), 42–43. It should, of course, be noted that such a view, while generative for political institutions and law, did not exhaust Madison's (or Hume's) understanding of the preconditions for the sustainability of a republic, especially as regards the all-important branch of Congress. Thus, for example, Madison argued as follows in his speech at the Virginia Ratifying Convention, June 20, 1788: "I go on this great republican principle, that the people will have virtue and intelligence to select men of virtue and wisdom. Is there no virtue among us? If there be not, we are in a wretched situation. No theoretical checks—no form of government can render us secure. To suppose that any form of government will secure liberty or happiness without any virtue in the people, is a chimerical idea." James Madison, *Writings*, ed. Jack N. Rakove (New York: Library of America, 1999), 398.

53. For a critical treatment of the transformative ambitions within modern democratic the-ory as an undiagnosed impulse to "perfectibility," see Patrick J. Deneen, *Democratic Faith* (Princeton: Princeton University Press, 2005).

in the case of John Locke. Yet, I insist, they all confronted the dilemmas of uniting contract, culture, and citizenship quite self-consciously. In doing so, they continue to provide important moral and intellectual resources for normative thought today. The point, then, of taking seriously the idea that contract makes citizens is not to simply endorse this conception but to critically reconsider the relationship between contract, culture, and citizenship, and to imagine how these constitutive but often submerged features of modernity might be better adapted to the complex moral and political conditions of our own time.

The Road Ahead

I begin this reexamination of the modern social contract tradition with Thomas Hobbes's important contributions to the ideas of public reason and civic-ethical formation. For all of Hobbes's notoriety as a theorist of political absolutism, he was also a thinker fundamentally concerned with "those qualities of mankind, that concern their living together in peace, and unity."[54] "Those qualities" to which Hobbes refers his readers are moral virtues, virtues that he believes are necessary for a peaceful, stable, and flourishing political society. The virtues include such things as justice, fidelity, and equity, as well as modesty, gratitude, and charity, among others. To emphasize these points is not to deny the significance of state-enforced fear as a means of maintaining obedience to the laws of a regime. Yet alongside the implements of fear over the body of the subject is an account of the virtues directed at the interior of the citizen. Naturally this has led scholars to a puzzle: what is the status and import of the moral virtues in Hobbes's thought, given the centrality of fear in his account? This question is typically posed in relation to Hobbes's distinctive form of natural law theorizing: do these "natural laws" stand as moral obligations, prudential rules, traditional window dressing, or what?[55]

---

54. Hobbes, *Leviathan*, chapter 11.

55. I refer here, of course, to the so-called Taylor-Warrender thesis, and to the alternative reading of Leo Strauss. See A. E. Taylor, "The Ethical Doctrine of Hobbes," *Philosophy* 13, no. 52 (1938), and Howard Warrender, *The Political Philosophy of Hobbes* (Oxford: Clarendon Press, 1957). See also Bernard Gert, "Introduction," in Hobbes, *Man and Citizen*. For a more recent treatment of Hobbes as a divine-command theorist, see A. P. Martinich, *The Two Gods of Leviathan: Thomas Hobbes on Religion and Politics* (Cambridge: Cambridge University Press, 1992). For Strauss, see *The Political Philosophy of Hobbes: Its Basis and Its Genesis* (Chicago: University of Chicago Press, 1963). For a more recent defense of the Straussian approach, see

I pursue a different line of inquiry—one that I believe can help us think anew not only about Hobbes but about the ethical conditions upon which diverse liberal societies depend today.

The central question here, as throughout this study of the social contract tradition, is how to live together as citizens under conditions of diffuse moral pluralism. In other words, what are the political-institutional and cultural-ethical conditions necessary for balancing freedom and common citizenship under pluralism? What I want to emphasize is that this is not a new, late modern dilemma brought on by the forces of globalization, transnational migrations, or technological advancements. While these and other developments have surely made the problems of liberty and citizenship within diversity more acute and widespread, this general problem is at the heart of Hobbes's thinking, and his response to the challenges of citizenship and pluralism is both more complex and more instructive than is often realized. To see this, and to see the specific ways in which Hobbes's intervention on these questions still resonates today, we must examine the relationship between private and public conscience in his theory of public reason. In doing so I present a new account of Hobbesian public reason as one that is as concerned with the internal sources of a people's ethical and political commitments as it is with providing external constraints on human conduct. In contrast to more familiar interpretations, I argue that public reason in Hobbes does not merely seek to supplant private reason and independent judgment, but rather seeks to educate and frame those judgments in accordance with the virtues of justice. The first extensive account of contract and public reason in the modern period is found not in Kant but in Hobbes. When this comes more fully into view, we will also see that social contract theory and public reason are tied to a transformative ethic that changes over time, but whose significance for conceiving a lasting normative relationship between citizenship and diversity lives on into the present.

I dedicate two chapters to John Locke because his moral and political theory represents an important shift away from the strategy of public reason/public conscience in Hobbes, yet the constitutive link between public justification and ethical cultivation remains a powerful, anxious, and underexplored dimension of his thinking. Since those who hold political

---

Paul D. Cooke, *Hobbes and Christianity: Reassessing the Bible in Leviathan* (Lanham, Md.: Rowman and Littlefield, 1996); see also Greg Forster, "Divine Law and Human Law in Hobbes's *Leviathan*," *History of Political Thought* 24, no. 2 (2003): 189–218.

power are distinguished above all by the fact that they possess the authority to use coercive sanctions against the members of a political society, the grounds for the employment of this power should be capable of being justified to everyone. In short, the use of political power should be reasonable. This is an all-important piece of political morality that we have inherited from Locke. But what this commitment primarily meant for Locke is that citizens must be shaped to think, judge, and act with this moral commitment in mind. And as Locke fully appreciated, this is a more complex and demanding project than many are willing to admit. In this Locke recognized something that is as important today as it was during the political crises of his own time: the endurance of a free society requires civic vigilance, critical attentiveness, and a prudent dose of active suspicion wedded to capacities and dispositions for concerted political action. All of this in turn depends upon certain traits, habits, and skills (of observation, understanding, deliberation, and judgment) that are always untimely, uncertain, and frequently undeveloped. Yet, as Locke can still point out to us today, a demobilized, disinterested, and distrustful polity is not born, but made and sustained by a variety of different social, political, and cultural forces against which citizens should be on guard.

Lockean public reason represents a strategy of transformative political and ethical cultivation that aims to disrupt persistent forces of naturalization that would situate political institutions beyond the purview and agency of citizens, while simultaneously striving to place the conditions for social stability on more solid ground. In this way Locke must confront the pulls of time, custom, and convention, and the corresponding power of human passions and the limits of reason. If we consider Locke's political theory alongside his epistemological, educational, and religious writings, we will see that he provides a coherent account of the ethical and political conditions necessary for securing liberty and stability amid moral pluralism, but it is an account that provides a critical foil for contemporary accounts of public reason, not one that is an already liberal antecedent to it. The internal dilemmas of Lockean public reason should serve as a forceful reminder today about the limits of human reason and the essential tensions between liberty and virtue.

Despite the enduring fame of Rousseau's great work, *The Social Contract*, Rousseau's place within the social contract tradition proper, as with his relationship to natural jurisprudence more generally, has long been plagued by interpretive and philosophical difficulties. It has been far more customary to see Rousseau as a thinker deeply committed to a transformative project of moral and political cultivation—his great educational work, *Emile*, reveals this on nearly every page. Indeed, the seeming centrality of civic formation in Rousseau's thought has given rise to the suspicion that Rousseau may not be a contract theorist at all (especially if we have Kant's influential adaptations in mind). In Chapter 4 I provide a reading of Rousseau that seeks to take seriously and unite both his contractarianism and his substantive (republican) conception of politics and ethics. I argue that the means of connecting these otherwise discontinuous features of his (and therewith modern) political thought is provided by the ways in which Rousseau speaks to the motivational bases of a public-spirited society within the limits created by man's private passions, self-interest, and *amour propre*. By highlighting the underlying connections between contract and culture, personal will and social *moeurs*, I show how Rousseau offers a practical way of reappraising the relationship between private vices and public virtues. The aim of this chapter is to bring Rousseau's political theory into the modern conversation about the preconditions for sustaining liberty and order in general, and into debates about the nature and scope of public reason in particular. I argue that Rousseau's idea of the general will is a model of public reasoning that holds surprising insights and value for us today. Indeed, I show that any conception of public reason that aims to respect liberty and diversity while cultivating the civic qualities and virtues necessary to sustain a regime over time will have to attend to some of the unique institutional mechanisms and cultural forms that Rousseau articulated. Crucial among these is what I refer to as an ethos of political revisability—an ethos that makes Rousseau highly relevant for large, complex, and increasingly interdependent political regimes.

Chapter 5 brings the discussion of the formative interrelationship between contract, culture, and citizenship up to date by turning to the work of John Rawls and contemporary liberalism. In the first part of this chapter I provide a critical interpretation of liberal public reason and discuss some of the problems inherent in this model of political and moral transformation. I show how public reason's educative, disciplinary features are a one-way street of civic formation in contemporary liberalism. As such, public reason and the transformative ethos it represents cannot serve as a fully adequate source for securing reciprocity and mutual respect within diverse regimes today. Thus, in the second part of this chapter I offer an account of democratic humility as a critical supplement to public reason and liberal political cultures in general. The ultimate aim in this final chapter is to offer some ideas for a positive reconstruction of the ways in which we understand and approach the relationship between moral pluralism and democratic citizenship today.

ONE

"WHERE JUSTICE IS CALLED A VIRTUE":
PUBLIC REASON AND CIVIC FORMATION IN THOMAS HOBBES

The just shall live by faith.
—Romans 1:17

At the end of his remarkable study of "the matter, form, and power" of political societies, Thomas Hobbes claims, in a disarming parenthetical aside, "there is scarce a commonwealth in the world whose beginnings can in conscience be justified."[1] If this piece of chastened politico-historical wisdom holds true for Hobbes, what does this mean for the whole of his moral and political theory, a theory that sought, among other things, to justify social and political institutions by rooting their origins and a subject's obligations to political society in the will and consent of each person? If it is the case that, upon completion of the most comprehensive

---

1. Hobbes, "A Review, and Conclusion," in *Leviathan*, ed. Michael Oakeshott (New York: Collier Books, 1962), p. 506. All references to Hobbes are to the following texts: *The Elements of Law Natural and Politic: Human Nature and De corpore politico*, ed. J. C. A Gaskin (New York: Oxford University Press, 1994) (hereafter *EL*); *Man and Citizen: Thomas Hobbes's De homine and De cive* (also known as *Philosophical Rudiments Concerning Government and Society*), ed. Bernard Gert (Garden City, N.Y.: Anchor Books, 1972); *Behemoth, or The Long Parliament*, ed. Ferdinand Tönnies (Chicago: University of Chicago Press, 1990); and *The English Works of Thomas Hobbes*, ed. Sir William Molesworth, 12 vols. (London: John Bohn, 1839–45). A brief note concerning my use of Hobbes's works is in order here. Since I do not find any significant (philosophical or political) differences in the way that Hobbes treats the need for or the nature and limits of moral and political education in his various writings, I will draw freely on all of these works in the discussion that follows. I do so knowing that both a significant span of time exists between works such as *The Elements of Law* (first circulated in 1640), the original English version of *Leviathan* (1651), and *Behemoth* (completed in 1668), and that noted Hobbes scholar Quentin Skinner has argued that Hobbes's ideas about liberty and his approach to "civil philosophy" underwent important changes between *The Elements of the Law*, *De cive* (1642 Latin edition), and *Leviathan*. See Skinner, *Visions of Politics*, vol. 3, *Hobbes and Civil Science* (Cambridge: Cambridge University Press, 2002), chapters 3 and 7. There are, of course, differences between these texts, but none that in my view touches significantly on the central issues of this chapter.

account of modern contractarian philosophy, Hobbes acknowledges that life in civil society nonetheless entails a crisis of conscience that can be neither avoided nor subverted, what does this confrontation with (or confession of) moral conflict tell us about the nature and meaning of Hobbes's project? What lessons does this hold for thinking about the relationship between political justification and private conscience today?

There are, of course, numerous ways in which we could approach Hobbes's political thought with these questions in mind. First, the tension between conscience and commonwealth might be taken as Hobbes's acknowledgment of the limitations and challenges that will constrain any attempt to establish a commonwealth by "institution," that is, by the will, choice, and consent of diverse individuals. More broadly put, we might identify this sense of irreconcilability as recognition of the limits and insufficiencies of normative political philosophy as such, a recognition that isn't often attributed to this seemingly self-confident author.[2] Alternatively, we could read this expression as entirely consistent with a historical understanding of Hobbes as a de facto theorist of obligation in the context of the English engagement controversy, a thinker who wanted to "set before men's eyes the mutual relation between protection and obedience."[3] In either case, Hobbes might be taken as reflecting upon an irresolvable gap between acts of consent and the conditions necessary for the full moral approbation of that to which one consents, whether under conditions of conquest/acquisition or of choice.[4] Alongside these sensible readings there may also be a melancholy, personal dimension flowing through these last concluding lines of the *Leviathan*, with Hobbes trying to make some kind of public display of peace with Cromwell and the Puritans of the interregnum years (1646–60). If we were to probe this last suggestion more deeply, we might find room for a proto-Nietzschean

2. See in this respect *Leviathan*, chapter 31: "And now, considering how different this doctrine is, from the practice of the greatest part of the world, especially of these western parts, that have received their moral learning from Rome and Athens; and how much depth of moral philosophy is required, in them that have the administration of sovereign power; I am at the point of believing this my labour, as useless, as the commonwealth of Plato" (p. 270).

3. See ibid., "Review, and Conclusion," p. 511. See also the influential essays of Quentin Skinner, placing Hobbes's writings in the context of other de facto theorists such as Anthony Ascham and Marchamont Nedham. Skinner, "The Context of Hobbes's Theory of Political Obligation," in *Hobbes and Rousseau: A Collection of Critical Essays*, ed. Maurice Cranston and Richard S. Peters (New York: Anchor Books, 1972); see also Skinner, "Conquest and Consent: Thomas Hobbes and the Engagement Controversy," in *The Interregnum: The Quest for Settlement, 1646–1660*, ed. G. E. Aylmer (London: Macmillan, 1974).

4. For the distinction between regimes established by acquisition and those established by institution, see *Leviathan*, chapter 20, as well as Hobbes's "Review, and Conclusion."

"pathos of distance" in Hobbes,[5] or (less anachronistically) a skeptical, neo-Stoic separation from and devaluation of the political realm as such.[6]

I want to develop an alternative account of Hobbes's moral and political thought, one that is at once more hopeful, challenging, and relevant for the present, by emphasizing the role of public reason and the cultivation of virtue as the means toward the resolution, or at least amelioration, of the tension between conscience and commonwealth. Can a commonwealth, and the laws and moral principles that it instantiates, ever be justified to the diverse consciences of individual citizens? Can common political artifice (civil society) coexist in a meaningful and stable way with ethical and religious particularity? As we have already seen, Hobbes holds some significant reservations about whether this question is capable of anything like a fully satisfactory resolution. Noting this at the outset is important not only for a proper understanding of Hobbes, but also for a historically minded reconsideration of contemporary liberal thought. Today liberal political theory is increasingly dominated by the question of justification.[7] Faced with a social world that confronts us with "choices between ends equally ultimate, and claims equally absolute,"[8] the essential liberal strategy—in politics, morals, and law—is to construct fair procedures by which diverse citizens may converge on reasonable and mutually acceptable principles for the regulation of their society. Political liberalism and deliberative democracy are two of the most well known of such strategies on offer today. Taken historically, they both represent the continuation of a moral-theoretical impulse that has both informed and been inspired by revolutionary political practices in Europe and America.[9]

5. See Richard Flathman, *Thomas Hobbes: Skepticism, Individuality, and Chastened Politics* (Newbury Park, Calif.: Sage, 1993).

6. See three works by Richard Tuck: *Hobbes* (Oxford: Oxford University Press, 1989); *Philosophy and Government: 1572–1651* (Cambridge: Cambridge University Press, 1993), chapter 7; and "Hobbes's Moral Philosophy," in *The Cambridge Companion to Hobbes*, ed. Tom Sorell (Cambridge: Cambridge University Press, 1996).

7. See T. M. Scanlon, "Contractualism and Utilitarianism," in *Utilitarianism and Beyond*, ed. Amartya Sen and Bernard Williams (Cambridge: Cambridge University Press, 1982); Thomas Nagel, "Moral Conflict and Political Legitimacy," *Philosophy and Public Affairs* 16, no. 3 (1987): 215–40; Jeremy Waldron, "Theoretical Foundations of Liberalism," in his *Liberal Rights: Collected Papers, 1981–1991* (Cambridge: Cambridge University Press, 1993); and John Rawls, *Political Liberalism* (New York: Columbia University Press, 1996).

8. Isaiah Berlin, "Two Concepts of Liberty," in his *Four Essays on Liberty* (Oxford: Oxford University Press, 1969), 168.

9. One of the greatest justificatory expressions of the modern period, the American Declaration of Independence, testifies to this fertile relationship between social contract theory and political action.

Hobbes is still deeply relevant for considering the contemporary challenges of moral and political justification because, while he clearly recognizes the multiple levels of dissonance that will inevitably arise between the life of conscience and the formation and endurance of common political bonds, and further appreciates the potentially wide distances (both cognitive and affective) between acts of consent and the moral approbation of and allegiance to that to which one has consented, he nonetheless understands the problem of justification as one to which moral and political thought can meaningfully contribute. Yet some of the most widely accepted understandings of Hobbes's response to the challenges for political stability have either overlooked or have not adequately explored the significance of his theory's transformative cultural-ethical aims.[10] In this chapter I will show that public reason in Hobbes (which includes the civil law as well as "public instruction, both of doctrine, and example") is not only directed at securing obedience and lawful external behavior following a procedural logic of authorization and subordination, but is also oriented toward the gradual ethical-political cultivation of individuals in accordance with a deeper understanding of justice beyond the observance of covenants, and deeper sources of stability and allegiance beyond coercion and fear. Hobbes is seeking to provide political stability for the "right reasons" (as Rawls puts it), that is, "not by the terror of penalties, but by the perspicuity of reasons."[11] In doing so, Hobbes shows how the political legitimating function of public reason depends for its long-term success on its transformative ethical potential, the possibilities for which are addressed in Hobbes's treatment of moral and political education.

Long before justification came to possess the strictly rational, legal, and procedural understanding it has come to acquire today, "justification," drawn in distinction to "sanctification," held deep religious meaning. To talk of justification in the sixteenth and seventeenth centuries was, more often than not, to participate in an expression of deep wonder about how

---

10. There are some important exceptions here. See, for example, David Johnston, *The Rhetoric of Leviathan: Thomas Hobbes and the Politics of Cultural Transformation* (Princeton: Princeton University Press, 1986); S. A. Lloyd, *Ideals as Interests in Hobbes's Leviathan: The Power of Mind over Matter* (Cambridge: Cambridge University Press, 1992); Lloyd, "Coercion, Ideology, and Education in *Leviathan*," in *Reclaiming the History of Ethics: Essays for John Rawls*, ed. Andrews Reath, Barbara Herman, and Christine M. Korsgaard (Cambridge: Cambridge University Press, 1997), 36–65; and Geoffrey M. Vaughan, *Behemoth Teaches Leviathan: Thomas Hobbes on Political Education* (Lanham, Md.: Lexington Books, 2002).

11. *De cive*, 13.9.

the individual might come to stand in a proper, redemptive relationship to a salvific God. Both of these senses of justification, the political-legal and the internal religious, play an important and I think mutually constitutive role in Hobbes's moral and political thought. We can begin to see the importance of this relationship if we attend critically to Hobbes's abiding concern not only with right, law, and obedience ("works"), but with the internal disposition and "endeavor" of persons toward both the natural and the civil law ("faith"). To put it slightly differently, right and virtue, or the delineation of lawful actions on the one hand and the cultivation of virtuous character on the other, are the core dimensions of Hobbes's normative theory that meet in the idea of public reason and serve as an answer to the question of how to provide a stable and well-ordered relationship between conscience and commonwealth.

In accordance with a renewed appreciation for the transformative role and ethical depths of Hobbesian public reason, we will see that moral and political justification in Hobbes is best understood as a long-range, culture-wide task whose proper aim and end is to unite the interior sources of character, belief, and identity with the necessary demands of life in a *civitas*. This is an undertaking that is not satisfied, or capable of being satisfied, by the willful formation of contractual arrangements and the provision of security and safety by a coercive state—the traditional reading of social contract as a rational exchange of unstable liberty for ordered freedom through law. Nor can the Hobbesian state be properly characterized as extending to "private belief the radical tolerance of indifference."[12] Rather, the justification, stability, and endurance of a state require a significant measure of political and ethical cultivation undertaken by a range of different social and political institutions. In other words, if "there is scarce a commonwealth in the world whose beginnings can in conscience be justified," then the transformative aims of Hobbes's moral and political thought are best seen as working on and trying to shape conscience, belief, and opinion in an effort to remove, or least diminish and soften, the inevitable antinomies that arise between conscience and commonwealth, private judgment and public reason. As we will see, this is a central part of what Hobbes means when he speaks of "framing" the will by justice, and it informs a crucial part of what Hobbes is up to when he turns to the moral and political arts necessary for the "well-governing of opinions."[13]

---

12. See John Gray, *Two Faces of Liberalism* (New York: New Press, 2000), 25; see also Gray, *Post-Liberalism: Studies in Political Thought* (New York: Routledge, 1993), 9–10.

13. See chapters 15 and 18 of *Leviathan*.

Yet it must be noted immediately that the multiple efforts by which Hobbes seeks to ameliorate the tensions between conscience and commonwealth place him in a paradoxical position that is as deeply instructive as anything else one will find in his corpus. Indeed, in this paradox we can locate a central challenge for modern political thought with which we are still grappling today. To put it briefly, and in the terms of Hobbes's theory, the law and public reason of a state can only legitimately direct the actions and behavior of subjects; individual conscience, judgment, and opinion are always ultimately and rightly free from the powers of coercion and command.[14] A contemporary version of this understanding of the boundary conditions of politics and ethics is contained in the idea that public reason and liberal principles of justice are defined so as to apply only to the public political domain; they are not meant to be written on the hearts of citizens.[15] While this commitment is certainly more robust today than it was in the seventeenth century, Hobbes articulates an important version of this view in claiming that "no human law is intended to oblige the conscience of a man, but the actions only."[16] Yet, as I will show, the full ethical and political design of Hobbes's theory is to work on the interior sources of character, belief, and action, uniting

14. This is a position that Hobbes articulates consistently throughout his life, from his earliest political writings in the *Elements of Law* to his later works, and it is a position that he defends with particular force in parts 3 and 4 of the *Leviathan*. See *EL*, 2.28.8. From *Leviathan*, see chapter 37, p. 324; chapter 42, pp. 362–64, 380; and chapter 46, p. 491. It should also be noted here that while Hobbes initially establishes a set of distinct meanings for conscience, judgment, and opinion (*Leviathan*, chapter 7), his more common tendency is to use these terms interchangeably. Thus Hobbes argues, "For a man's conscience, and his judgment is the same thing, and as the judgment, so also the conscience may be erroneous" (chapter 29, p. 239). Further on in this paragraph Hobbes also equates private conscience with private opinion. This represents an obviously contestable reduction, given the various ways in which conscience has been imagined in Western moral and religious thought. Nonetheless, I will follow Hobbes in this usage, since the interchangeability of conscience, judgment, and opinion is consistently held throughout his writings and quite important to his normative project. For an excellent discussion of the meaning and politics of conscience in early modern England and America, see Andrew R. Murphy, *Conscience and Community* (University Park: Pennsylvania State University Press, 2001). For a more general discussion of the history of conscience, see Douglas C. Langston, *Conscience and Other Virtues* (University Park: Pennsylvania State Press University Press, 2001).
15. See here Rawls, *Political Liberalism*; and Rawls, "The Idea of Public Reason Revisited," in *The Law of Peoples* (Cambridge: Harvard University Press, 1999); see also Charles Larmore, *The Morals of Modernity* (New York: Cambridge University Press, 1996), chapters 6–7; Larmore, "Public Reason," in *The Cambridge Companion to Rawls*, ed. Samuel Freeman (Cambridge: Cambridge University Press, 2003); and Stephen Macedo, *Diversity and Distrust: Civic Education in a Multicultural Democracy* (Cambridge: Harvard University Press, 2000), chapters 7–9. I provide a critical discussion of contemporary theories of liberal public reason in Chapter 5.
16. *EL*, 2.25.3; see also *De cive*, 4.24; and *Leviathan*, chapter 26, p. 213.

the "internal court" and the external life of citizens for the purposes of securing the stability of the state and the felicity of its members.[17] The importance of such a project arises for Hobbes from the recognition that "the actions of men proceed from their opinions, and in the well governing of opinions, consisteth the well-governing of men's actions, in order to their peace, and concord."[18] How can individual opinion and conscience be simultaneously free and well governed by sovereign authority? How does Hobbes propose to deal with this tension between free conscience and public reason? What challenges or limitations are identified here, and how are they confronted? These are the central questions of this chapter. By addressing them we will see how "contract makes citizens" in Hobbes's thought, or how mutual covenant sponsors the development of a particular kind of subject-citizen. In addition, we will have a better understanding of one of the modes by which contract, culture, and citizenship have been intertwined in this tradition, enabling us to make some new and illuminating comparisons with later thinkers like Locke, Rousseau, Kant, and Rawls, explored in the chapters that follow. As these later chapters will show, the transformative aims of social contract theory change over time, but the challenges for this ethical-political commitment endure.

The Conditions and Sources of Public Reason

At the center of Hobbes's political thought is a concern with the nature of public opinion—its sources, constitution, influences, and governance. In the most fundamental sense, the unsustainable state of uncertainty, controversy, and war that Hobbes imagines outside life in civil society is not the result of a mere clash of interests and private vanities but is rather a condition of strife owing to the irreducible diversity of beliefs and private judgments about what conduces to an individual's or group's

17. Thus, while I agree with those scholars who observe the ways in which Hobbes, following traditional Protestant understandings, sought to distinguish between inner faith and outward conduct, my reading of Hobbes stresses the ways that he seeks to reconnect these dimensions of human life through public reason, or what he also refers to as the "public conscience." See, for example, Eldon J. Eisenach, *Two Worlds of Liberalism* (Chicago: University of Chicago Press, 1981), chapters 4–5; and Eisenach, *Narrative Power and Liberal Truth* (Lanham, Md.: Rowman and Littlefield, 2002), chapter 2. See also Joshua Mitchell, *Not by Reason Alone: Religion, History, and Identity in Early Modern Political Thought* (Chicago: University of Chicago Press, 1993), chapter 2.
18. *Leviathan*, chapter 18, p. 137.

preservation and happiness. To cite just one example of this understanding, consider the following passage from *The Elements of Law:*

> In the state of nature, where every man is his own judge, and differeth from other concerning the names and appellations of things, and from those differences arise quarrels, and breach of peace; it was necessary there should be a common measure of all things that might fall in controversy; as for example: of what is to be called right, what good, what virtue, what much, what little, what *meum* and *tuum*, what a pound, what a quart, etc. For in these things private judgment may differ, and beget controversy.[19]

From moral evaluations to calculations of weights and measurements, the diversity of judgments and the partiality of evaluations are the epistemological and moral fundaments of a life outside civil society, a life devoid of a reliable "common measurement" provided by public law. The sources of these differences in judgment, and with them the diversity in the modes of human life, are multiple, and they include considerations such as human fallibility, human contingency/temporality, self-love (partiality and pride), and the very weakness of human reason in comparison to the powerful sway of human passions, appetites, and aversions. Added to this, the general condition in which these beings think, judge, and act lacks an objective standard of morality, "for want of a right reason constituted by nature."[20] Thus an individual's or group's claim to possess "right reason" under these conditions is more likely than not to be an arrogant and erring (epistemically unwarrantable) grab for power shaped by self-interested passions. Until a legitimate public power has been instituted by the consent of each person, the effort to install one's standard of reasoning for the authoritative rule and governance of others is the very kind of action that will perpetuate an "intolerable" condition of resentment, revenge, and conflict. Indeed, this continues to be a problem even within political society, for "men seek not only liberty of conscience, but of their actions; not that only, but a farther liberty of persuading others to their opinions; not that only for every man desireth, that the sovereign authority should admit no other opinions to be maintained but such as he himself holdeth."[21]

19. *EL,* 2.29.8. See also *Leviathan,* chapter 5, p. 42, and chapters 15, 26, and 28.
20. *Leviathan,* chapter 5, and chapter 6, 48–49.
21. *EL,* 2.25.13. As Rawls would put it, persons fitting this description are "unreasonable" because they have failed to see how the "burdens of judgment" set limits on what can be justified

Hobbes's description of the sources of diversity and the politics of disagreement still resonate deeply today. While the specific reasons that
Hobbes adduces for ethical diversity and moral conflict undergo important changes in the work of more contemporary figures like Berlin, Larmore, Nagel, Rawls, and Connolly (as do the normative evaluations of
this diversity and the politics it generates), the fact that Hobbes placed
such disagreements at the center of his thought is a testament to his
modernity and one of the important sources for students' continuing
fascination with his writings.[22] In contrast, for example, to both Kant and
Leibniz, the free exercise of individual reason does not generate agreement or convergence on truths of any kind. Further, Hobbes saw the immense trouble that comes from the passionate urge to install one's own
partial and contestable conception of the moral truth at the center of
political life, even as he understood the insatiable and restless pull of such
claims.[23] Hence, one of the central normative questions motivating this
book—how to live together as citizens under diffuse moral pluralism—
is not a new, late modern dilemma ushered in by globalization, transnational migration, and technological advancement. While these and other
developments have surely made the challenges of sustaining liberty and
citizenship within diversity more acute and widespread, this general problem is at the heart of Hobbes's moral and political thought, as it is in a
host of post-Reformation thinkers. But what shall we make of his strategies for responding to this, our political-ethical condition?

The famous Hobbesian solution is to authorize a public arbitrator with
(mostly) unconstrained powers to establish the standards, through law,
for the regulation and settlement of public controversies.[24] Thus, for beings

---

to diverse others. The difference between Hobbes and Rawls on this point is that for Hobbes
the "burdens of judgment" run deeper than they do for Rawls; that is, Rawls avoids ascribing
any metaphysical or epistemological meaning to the burdens of judgment for human reason,
whereas Hobbes is far less reticent about doing so. Hobbes's pluralism, in other words, goes all
the way down. Richard E. Flathman has come to a similar conclusion in his considerations of
Hobbes. See Flathman, *Willful Liberalism: Voluntarism and Individuality in Political Theory and
Practice* (Ithaca: Cornell University Press, 1992), chapter 1; see also Flathman, *Thomas Hobbes*.

22. See, for example, Richard Boyd's illuminating discussion of Hobbes and the challenge
that Hobbes's thought poses for the contemporary revival in civil society, in *Uncivil Society:
The Perils of Pluralism and the Making of Modern Liberalism* (Lanham, Md.: Lexington Books,
2004), chapter 1.

23. See *Leviathan*, chapter 11, p. 80, and chapter 17, where Hobbes argues: "amongst men,
there are very many, that think themselves wiser, and abler to govern the public, better than
the rest; and these strive to reform and innovate, one this way, another that way; and thereby
bring it into distraction and civil war" (p. 131).

24. I say "mostly unconstrained" because in chapter 21 of the *Leviathan* Hobbes's discussion
of the liberty of subjects suggests that there are constraints on the extent to which individuals

who discover that "no one's reason, nor the reason of any one number of men" confers any certainty on the possibility of resolving conflicts in their mutual dealings with one another,[25] beings who realize that, even while striving to be as reasonable as you please, "on matters of supreme importance, the more we talk with one another, the more we disagree,"[26] the only way forward, according to Hobbes, is

> to confer all their power and strength upon one man, or upon one assembly of men, that may reduce all their wills, by plurality of voices, unto one will: which is as much to say, to appoint one man, or assembly of men, to bear their person; and every one to own, and acknowledge himself to be author of whatsoever he that beareth their person, shall act, or cause to be acted, in those things which concern the common peace and safety; and therein to submit their wills, every one to his will, and their judgments, to his judgments.[27]

Public reason for Hobbes is the civil law that is made possible by this act of covenant *cum* authorization. As such, public reason represents the unifying legal and moral force to which all will stand concerning those matters that directly pertain to the ends for which a commonwealth is instituted, that is, peace and security. Under the rule of public reason, the civil law stands in for that measure of "right reason" that nature otherwise does not objectively or transparently reveal to individuals.[28] This represents a morally significant development, as propitious and foreboding as anything else in the contract tradition.[29] Passing through a kind

---

must conform to sovereign power, and thus there are limits on the scope of public reason. This has led to numerous discussions, from Bishop Bramhall to the present, about internal challenges for Hobbes's account. See Bramhall, *The Catching of Leviathan, or the Great Whale*, in *Leviathan: Contemporary Responses to the Political Theory of Thomas Hobbes*, ed. G. A. J. Rogers (Bristol: Thoemmes Press, 1995); see also Jean Hampton, *Hobbes and the Social Contract Tradition* (Cambridge: Cambridge University Press, 1986), chapter 7.

25. *Leviathan*, chapter 5, p. 42.

26. Larmore, *Morals of Modernity*, 122.

27. *Leviathan*, chapter 17, p. 132.

28. As Hobbes argues in his exchange with Bishop Bramhall: "The law is all the right reason we have." *English Works of Hobbes*, 5:194. But see the following passage in *De cive*, where Hobbes seems to allow for a more direct relationship to a traditional (scholastic) conception of "right reason": "For although they who among men obtain the chiefest dominion, cannot by subject to laws properly so called . . . yet is it their duty in all things, as much as possibly they can, to yield obedience unto right reason, which is the natural, moral, and divine law" (13.2).

29. See Rousseau's classic description of just this moment in his own conceptualization of political society, *The Social Contract*, 1.8, pp. 55–56. All citations of *The Social Contract* are to Roger D. Masters's edition (New York: St. Martin's Press, 1978).

of moral threshold opened by a mutual covenant of their own making, formerly independent beings who were the private judges of good and evil are now, by virtue of their joint undertaking, both the authors and the subjects of the moral judgments of an absolute sovereign. A political society is, succinctly put, a form of life in which one is no longer guided by one's own individual lights alone. For now "civil law, is to every subject, those rules, which the commonwealth hath commanded him, by word, writing, or other sufficient sign of the will, to make use of, for the distinction of right, and wrong."[30] Hobbes always wears his conventionalism on his sleeve; that is, there is no pretension here that what the sovereign declares is truth with a capital "T," for, again, there is no right reason constituted by nature. Yet without a standard of artificial "right" reason, according to Hobbes, there is only a multitude, not a people, or a *civitas;* and without a commonwealth, there is no peace, security, or hope for contentment in this life. As we will see further below, this conception of reason is (politically speaking) an absolutist one, but it is not (by Hobbes's lights) an arbitrary one, even though it is always self-consciously understood as an "artificial chain."

While the civil condition is not without its own "inconveniences" and costs, especially in relation to the liberty of acting in accordance with conscience and the formerly independent right of moral judgment, Hobbes makes it plain that "if every man were allowed the liberty of following his conscience, in such differences of consciences, they would not live together in peace an hour."[31] In sum, the public reason of an entrusted sovereign authority represents the institutional means by which independent beings of natural right and private reason are formed into subject-citizens—that is, beings who not only possess a private conscience but are now also participants in a "public conscience."[32] The distance between one's conscience and the absolute liberty to act in accordance with the voice of one's conscience is the wages of a secure life in civil society.

30. *Leviathan,* chapter 26, p. 198; see also chapter 29, p. 238.
31. *EL,* 2.24.2; see also *Leviathan,* chapter 17.
32. I use the term *subject-citizen* to stress the idea that individuals fashion this public reason via an act of authorizing consent that gives substance to an active notion of citizenship, and to register the fact that they are also substantially governed and shaped by it in a way that does not entail (indeed largely prohibits) their ongoing authorship, rendering them the subjects of their public reason. Hobbes conveys this idea in the following passage from *Leviathan:* "Though he that is subject to no civil law, sinneth in all he does against his conscience, because he has no other rule to follow but his own reason; yet it is not so with him that lives in a commonwealth; because the law is the public conscience, by which he hath already undertaken to be guided" (chapter 29, p. 239).

Does all of this come at too high of a price? To address this question adequately we must first ask how the formation of subject-citizens is supposed to take place. How does Hobbes conceive individuals relating to this "public reason"? What is the content and scope of this reason? Indeed, *how is it possible to have a "public reason" at all?* Not only are these questions important for a critical understanding of Hobbes, but given that the very idea of public reason continues to hold out the promise of what diverse citizens of a liberal society might come to share as a basis for their common political association/civic identity, they are questions that go to the heart of a great deal of ongoing moral and political reflection today.

The Purpose and Scope of Public Reason

No one has done more in recent years to highlight the importance of public reason in Hobbes's political theory than David Gauthier. According to Gauthier, in the Hobbesian account of public reason "the individual mode of deliberation, in which each person judges for herself what she has reason to do, is to be *supplanted* by a collective mode, in which one person judges what all have reason to do."[33] The central idea here is that private reasoning and individual judgment are subordinated to or supplanted by the public reason of the sovereign, primarily through civil law and the punishments attached to the violation of those laws, in relation to those matters that affect the public good. While Gauthier recognizes certain internal difficulties and implicit dangers with respect to the scope of Hobbesian public reason ("to take the reason of one individual or assembly as if it were right reason is to risk creating a monster"),[34] he nonetheless finds in Hobbes a useful normative model for the construction of public reason. As Gauthier claims, "Public reason must be justified as *supplanting*—within limits—the individual reason of each citizen."[35]

33. David Gauthier, "Public Reason," *Social Philosophy and Policy* 12, no. 1 (1995): 31.
34. Ibid., 37. Of course, Hobbes is careful to say that it is not "right reason," as I have already stressed. The reason for this is that such a category of moral knowledge simply does not exist, in Hobbes's view. What is more, Hobbes never pursues the possibility that the sovereign might gain political leverage by either pretending or allowing the illusion to arise that the sovereign's reason is right reason as such (as perhaps a more Machiavellian ruler might). Jeremy Waldron is very good on this point. See his "Hobbes and the Principle of Publicity," *Pacific Philosophical Quarterly* 82, nos. 3–4 (2001): 447–74. S. A. Lloyd also notes a difference between Hobbes and Machiavelli on this question. See Lloyd, "Coercion, Ideology, and Education."
35. Lloyd, "Coercion, Ideology, and Education," 38.

The renewed attention to the role of public reason in Hobbes has helped reveal the extent to which Hobbes's political theory pursues something far more substantial, morally and politically speaking, than a *modus vivendi*.[36] This has been a valuable gain, and one that helps connect Hobbes to his more recent and more liberal counterparts in the social contract tradition. Yet the contemporary appreciation for and reconstruction of Hobbesian public reason has not gone far enough. By identifying public reason exclusively with the subordination of private reason, the full transformative aims of Hobbesian public reason—and the additional, intriguing challenges for this view—have not been adequately explored.

The problem into which contemporary readings of Hobbes fall is in thinking that public reason is derived (or derivable) from the natural private reason of individuals.[37] Now, in a certain restricted sense this is right: individuals come to acknowledge the intolerable condition of a pre- or postpolitical state, and reason (fallible, shifting, weak, and short-sighted as it is) suggests to them a way out. But public reason in Hobbes represents more than the coercive power of public law authorized by the people—it represents the beliefs, norms, and virtues that will, over time, form the very meaning of citizenship in a commonwealth. In other words, public reason represents a cultural-civic ideal directed at sustaining political bonds over generations.[38] Part of the evidence in support of such a view is provided by the fact that, according to Hobbes, public reason (embodied by the civil law) is to become the "public conscience" of civil society, and the pursuit of this kind of "shared knowledge" (*conscientia*) must be understood as a very distinct kind of aim.[39] That is, the goal in Hobbesian

36. For a very useful discussion, see Gerald F. Gaus, *Contemporary Theories of Liberalism: Public Reason as a Post-Enlightenment Project* (Thousand Oaks, Calif.: Sage, 2003), chapter 3. Also important here are R. E. Ewin, *Virtues and Rights: The Moral Philosophy of Thomas Hobbes* (Boulder: Westview Press, 1991); Lloyd, *Ideals as Interests in Leviathan;* George Shelton, *Morality and Sovereignty in the Philosophy of Hobbes* (New York: St. Martin's Press, 1992); and David Boonin-Vail, *Thomas Hobbes and the Science of Moral Virtue* (New York: Cambridge University Press, 1994).

37. See Michael Ridge's essay, "Hobbesian Public Reason," *Ethics* 108 (April 1998): 538–68.

38. See *De cive*, 1.2n*: "civil societies are not mere meetings, but bonds, to the making whereof faith and compacts are necessary."

39. *Leviathan*, chapter 29. Thus I mean to claim that more or, rather, something deeper is at work in Hobbes than his notorious Erastianism. That Hobbes subordinated the church to state policy was one of the most controversial features of his theory, at least as it appeared in *De cive* and *Leviathan*. For some excellent discussions of this, see Mark Goldie, "The Reception of Hobbes," in *The Cambridge History of Political Thought: 1450–1700*, ed. J. H. Burns (Cambridge: Cambridge University Press, 1991), 610–13; A. P. Martinich, *The Two Gods of Leviathan: Thomas Hobbes on Religion and Politics* (Cambridge: Cambridge University Press, 1992); and Partricia Springborg, "Leviathan and the Problem of Ecclesiastical Authority," *Political Theory* 3, no. 3

public reason is to give shape and content to a system-wide form of norm building that will regulate interpersonal relationships (justice) and relationships to political authority (allegiance). As Hobbes asks in *Behemoth*, "Why may not men be taught their duty, that is, the science of *just* and *unjust*, as divers other sciences have been taught, from true principles and evident demonstration?"[40]

Thus the question for Hobbes is not simply between retaining some measure of autonomous rational judgment and surrendering absolutely to the sovereign's judgment, for it is indeed true to say that, paradoxically, both of these things take place. Given Hobbes's appreciation of the irresolvable tensions between the free, internal life of conscience, judgment, and opinion, on the one hand, and one's adopted civic obligations, on the other, this should come as little surprise. Instead, the central question for Hobbes, and one that remains deeply relevant for the present age, is how to cultivate an acceptance and an appreciation of public reason and the virtues it represents in those domains over which it should properly influence the actions and dispositions of the diverse members of civil society. The issue is not that private reason will continue to hold influence in political society—how could it not, since as Hobbes emphasizes, "thought is free"?[41] Rather, the central challenge is how to shape and influence private judgments such that, over time, those judgments will be "framed" by virtues like justice, equity, gratitude, and mercy. This means coming to see oneself, and being recognized by others, as a particular kind of subject-citizen. In these terms the aim of public reason is not just to constrain external actions but to govern the conduct of citizens by shaping judgment, opinion, and belief in accordance with Hobbes's civic and moral pedagogy ("the science of just and unjust"). Hobbesian public reason is best viewed as a transformative project that seeks to embed free and equal individuals in a social and political framework with significant ethical content.

(1975): 289–303. One of the more interesting (if not fully persuasive) suggestions to come out of this historical research is the idea that beneath Hobbes's Erastianism is a policy of "tolerant indifference" toward religious difference. See in this respect Goldie's essay, but also see Alan Ryan, "Hobbes, Toleration, and the Inner Life," in *The Nature of Political Theory*, ed. David Miller and Larry Siedentop (New York: Oxford University Press, 1983); Ryan, "Hobbes and Individualism," in *Perspectives on Thomas Hobbes*, ed. G. A. J. Rogers and Alan Ryan (New York: Oxford University Press, 1988); and Richard Tuck, "Hobbes and Locke on Toleration," in *Thomas Hobbes and Political Theory*, ed. Mary G. Dietz (Lawrence: University Press of Kansas, 1990), 153–71.

40. *Behemoth*, Dialogue 1, p. 39.

41. *Leviathan*, chapter 37, p. 324.

As it will also become in the work of John Rawls, public reason in Hobbes is a way of articulating an ideal of citizenship that public reason both illuminates and helps to shape. To be sure, the Hobbesian ideal of citizenship is neither republican nor fully liberal—but it is an ideal that requires a significant measure of ethical work to bring about. Yet this ethical work, entailing both general, public cultivation and individual self-fashioning, cannot be recognized or critically appraised by identifying Hobbesian public reason with the subordination of private reason alone, or seeing in that subordination the full terminus of the "moral" transformation necessary for the endurance of a society.[42] The contract story does not end with the covenant and the authorization of public power. If "the *pacts* and *covenants* by which the parts of this body politic were at first made, set together, and united, resemble that *fiat*, or *let us make man*, pronounced by God in the creation," then the next question, in point of both divine creation and in the human imitation of that creation, concerns "what it is that preserveth and dissolveth it."[43] This is the appropriate context in which we should search for a full understanding of the nature, purpose, and ultimate aims of Hobbesian public reason. For public reason does not merely seek to address a rational coordination problem for the *origins* of political authority but answers to the question of what will serve to sustain citizens in their covenanted commitments over time. As I argued in the Introduction, making a promise is one thing; keeping it is quite another. The difficulty of this latter problem is one that Hobbes never underestimated, the blustery language of coercion and "swords" notwithstanding.

In contrast to widely accepted representations of Hobbesian public reason as something that *supplants* or subordinates the individual reason of each citizen, the alternative account of public reason that I develop in what follows shows the ways in which public reason and law seek to *cultivate* the moral and political character of citizens. There are limits to how far this cultivationist project may hope to succeed, given the

---

42. See David Gauthier, "Between Hobbes and Rawls," in *Rationality, Justice, and the Social Contract: Themes from Morals by Agreement*, ed. David Gauthier and Robert Sugden (Ann Arbor: University of Michigan Press, 1993), 34. See also Jean Hampton's identification of authorization with "conversion" in *Hobbes and the Social Contract Tradition*, 208–20. An alternative reading, provided by David Johnston in *Rhetoric of Leviathan*, stresses the idea that Hobbesian cultural transformation is aimed at fashioning "enlightened" reasoners and a rational polity. Thus, while I agree with Johnston about the importance of a cultural transformative aim in Hobbes, we disagree about the nature of this cultivationist ethic.

43. *Leviathan*, author's introduction, 19.

irreducible diversity and freedom of individual judgment/conscience, and given that no earthly power (civil or ecclesiastical) holds dominion over men's hearts. As a result of these important (if not yet fully liberal) set of constraints, the citizen-subject is neither a simple cause nor a mere effect of public reason. This is important to recognize, if only to offset the cynical notion that Hobbes is only offering us a picture of ideological indoctrination or brainwashing. Thus, for example, in relation to the important question of whether citizens should accept or suspect reports of miracles (or more directly, whether citizens should acknowledge or doubt the veracity of those who claim religious and/or political authority on the basis of miracles), Hobbes argues that

> we are not every one, to make our own private reason, or conscience, but the public reason, that is, the reason of God's lieutenant, judge; and indeed we have made him judge already, if we have given him a sovereign power, to do all that is necessary for our peace and defence. A private man has always the liberty, because thought is free, to believe or not to believe in his heart those acts that have been given out for miracles. . . . But when it come to confession of that faith, the private reason must submit to the public; that is to say, to God's lieutenant.[44]

To appraise both the possibilities and the challenges of Hobbesian public reason we must attend critically to Hobbes's ideas about virtue, education, and religion, all of which are explored in the following sections of this chapter. I hasten to acknowledge that most of Hobbes's interpreters who emphasize the role of supplanting with respect to the relationship between private and public reason are entirely in keeping with certain features of Hobbes's theory, as we have already seen. The problem as I see it is not with a misconstrued understanding of Hobbes's ideas, but rather with an incomplete accounting of them that leaves unexamined additional features and dilemmas for his theory. Crucially, what is left unexplored is the degree to which contract must make citizens, and public reason in Hobbes, as for the rest of the contract tradition, plays a central role in this setting. I turn now to a more complete discussion of the textual evidence for this alternative account of Hobbesian public reason.

44. Ibid., chapter 37, p. 324. My thanks to Andrew Murphy for correspondence on this passage in Hobbes.

Hobbes's Inward Turn

> For the power of the mighty hath no foundation but in the
> opinion and belief of the people.
> —Hobbes, *Behemoth*

As I have suggested, Hobbesian public reason is best understood as the institutional and cultural means by which individuals are to be cultivated as a particular kind of subject-citizen. This is a citizen who will, among other things, abide by his promises and covenants, be accommodating to others, forgive other's offenses, and be willing to stand by the judgments of the public arbitrator when the mutual respect for human equality and equal rights inevitably breaks down. But how is all of this to be done? What are the "moral sources" for this kind of political-ethical life?[45] To address these important questions we must turn to Hobbes's concern with the internal life of human beings, that is, to opinion and individual conscience. "For the actions of men proceed from their opinions, and in the well governing of opinions, consisteth the well-governing of men's actions, in order to their peace, and concord."[46]

Hobbes consistently held that the observation of the natural law in a precivil condition should never be taken so far as to make us "prey" to others who would not observe its dictates in turn. This is, of course, a significant limiting condition on the viability of the moral virtues such as justice, equity, and mercy, contained in the natural laws Hobbes otherwise sought to champion. To observe such virtues as these among people who would not keep peace or trust in return would be a violation, in its own way, of the fundamental law of nature to seek peace where it may be found, and where not, to avail oneself of the instruments of war.[47] In a certain way, holding such a position is to Hobbes's credit in that he will not countenance a moral theory of obligation that does not at the same time speak to the necessary and fallible conditions of human motivation.

While it may not always be safe or reasonable to *act* in conformity with natural law, Hobbes also argued that the natural law always binds and is obligatory over the subject's conscience, will, and mind.[48] Thus, crucially for Hobbes, there is still a way in which the laws of nature can

---

45. I am drawing on the idea of moral sources from Charles Taylor, *Sources of the Self* (Cambridge: Harvard University Press, 1989).

46. *Leviathan*, chapter 18, p. 137.

47. Ibid., chapter 14; *De cive*, 2.2. Hobbes also suggests that such a breach of the natural law, because it opens us to the assaults of others, would be "an injury against God." *De cive*, 3.27n.

48. See *EL*, 1.17.10, 13, 14; *De cive*, 3.27–32; *Leviathan*, chapter 15.

be observed in a meaningful way even while individuals inhabit a condition where the "primitive right of self-defense" reigns.[49] They can be so observed through a preparation of the mind for the time when the enactment of these virtues shall be secured for all—when, that is, acting in accordance with such laws will not make one a dupe or a victim. According to Hobbes, under such conditions the preparation or "endeavor" to observe these virtues is sufficient for, or in a sense is an equivalent sign of, the actual fulfillment of these laws. The laws of nature, which, Hobbes tells us, are in fact moral virtues or dispositions, always concern the internal life of persons and their character, and apply to their immediate outward actions only under certain appropriate (secure) conditions. As he argues in *De cive*: "*The laws of nature are immutable and eternal:* what they forbid, can never be lawful; what they command, can never be unlawful. For *pride, ingratitude, breach of contracts* (or *injury*), *inhumanity, contumely,* will never be lawful, nor the contrary virtue to these ever unlawful, as we take them for dispositions of the mind, that is, as they are considered in the court of conscience, where only they oblige and are laws."[50]

Here we have struck upon Hobbes's distinction between those things that oblige *in foro interno* and those that oblige *in foro externo*. As we have seen, this distinction turns on the question of what it is safe for the subject to do or cause to be done in relation to others who may just as easily be carried away by their self-love and partiality as observe equity and justice. Yet we have to ask what kind of an obligation is an *in foro interno* obligation? Are such duties expressive or consistent with a meaningful moral outlook? I believe that the answer to this question is yes.

In foro interno obligations, which are obligations on an individual's conscience or will, give the subjects in a "state of nature" a certain moral depth, a nascent but aggravated moral personality. This is not something equivalent to later Kantian or neo-Kantian ideas about highest-order moral powers—but this sense of obligation is a kind of interior, nagging dilemma for beings outside civil society. *In foro interno* obligations represent the type of ethical being that subjects would like to be or become, but for a variety of reasons—their own safety being the most fundamental—cannot.[51] What Hobbes presents us with is an internal moral dilemma

---

49. *De cive*, 5.1.

50. Ibid., 3.29; see also *EL*, 1.17.10.

51. John Rawls alludes to a similar idea in *Political Liberalism*, claiming that "without an established public world, the reasonable may be suspended and we may be left largely with the rational, although the reasonable always binds *in foro interno*, to use Hobbes's phrase" (54).

as much as an external conflict of bodies and resources in the pre- or postcivil state. In this conflict, within the soul and conscience of persons, what matters is endeavor—the will and desire to act in accordance with moral constraints and moral virtues (the natural law), not performance itself, since such moral performance is not always safe and hence not always possible. For Hobbes, the laws of nature (the moral virtues) require what he variously calls an "unfeigned and constant" or "true" endeavor that they be observed.[52] This means that while the actions of obedience may not be safe or consistent with one's own self-preservation, the subject is called upon nonetheless to a "readiness of mind" to perform these virtues. Hobbes understands this type of obligation as one that binds the subject to a constant internal ordering, or cultivation, in conformity with the moral qualities of justice, equity, modesty, and the like. All of this is important to establish, because when it comes to imagining the role of virtue and justice within civil society, Hobbes sustains this focus on endeavor, will, and the interior sources of moral virtue.

The concept of endeavor in Hobbes's political theory expresses the idea that not only do intentions matter, but the interior, dispositional moral life of human beings matters.[53] To endeavor is to self-consciously mean something by one's actions or pursuits. Endeavor is internal deliberation with a morally purposive content, a deliberation that is more than the reactive operations of appetite and aversion. Hobbes's use of endeavor as a normative principle bears a striking resemblance to Aristotle's distinction between voluntary acts done by choice and voluntary acts done without choice.[54] Aristotle's use of these categories allows him to make additional, more salient distinctions, including one between just men and just actions (something that I will discuss further in relation to Hobbes below). But the relevant parallel here is that for Aristotle voluntary acts that are committed by choice involve deliberation and as such disclose the self as virtuous or vicious, and not merely as one who acts appropriately or in ways that are not blamable. Endeavor for Hobbes likewise discloses the subject as just or unjust, not simply as one who is or is not in conformity with the laws. The object of moral endeavor is not peace or safety but a form of human character defined or framed by justice.

---

52. *De cive*, 3.30; *Leviathan*, chapter 15, p. 123.

53. For a slightly different account of the concept of "endeavor" in Hobbes, see Michael Oakeshott, "The Moral Life in the Writings of Thomas Hobbes," in *Rationalism in Politics and Other Essays* (Indianapolis: Liberty Fund, 1991), 310–12.

54. Aristotle, *The Nicomachean Ethics*, trans. David Ross (New York: Oxford University Press, 1980), 5.8.1135a25–b15.

Hobbes gives us good cause to think that it is an individual's true and just endeavor, and not simply performance or obedience, that matters most in the moral life of persons. The first reason for this is that Hobbes argues that even in cases where a subject acts in conformity with the natural law, if her purpose or endeavor was against it, then it is still a breach of the natural law. As we have seen, the laws of nature concern conscience or the "internal court," and in such a case, "though the act itself be answerable to [or in agreement with] the laws, yet his conscience is against them."[55] Hobbes is seeking more than mere conformity with external laws, or at least he is willing to make a clear distinction between such conformity and the deeper interior dispositions of persons.

All of this is worth attending to because it closely parallels Hobbes's theological discussion concerning those things required for human salvation. The question of human justification before God is extremely important for Hobbes, and not only because it turns on the prospects of eternal life. Rather, Hobbes clearly believes that if he can convince his readers of what is and what is not necessary for human salvation, then "the most frequent pretext of sedition, and civil war" will be removed,[56] that "pretext" being the idea that the commands of God and the commands of the commonwealth may differ and that in their controversy the conscientious Christian should prioritize the former. For Hobbes, the question of salvation can be reduced to two virtues: obedience to laws and faith in Christ. But in discussing the obedience required of human beings, Hobbes is careful to argue that it is "not *the fact*, but the *will* and *desire* wherewith we purpose, and endeavour as much as we can, to obey for the future."[57] God accepts from the faithful the will and endeavor to be obedient, as long as this is a "serious endeavour to obey him." Such forms of endeavor also go by the names of charity and love "because they imply a will to obey."[58]

Now, when Hobbes turns to those things that must be taught through the public reason of the sovereign for the purposes of securing a stable political life, he argues in much the same way concerning the importance of a subject's intentions and endeavors as we have seen him doing in relation to the natural law and human salvation. Crucially, subjects "are to be taught that not only the unjust facts, but the designs and intentions to do them, though by accident hindered, are injustice; which consisteth

55. *De cive*, 3.28.
56. *Leviathan*, chapter 43, p. 424.
57. *De cive*, 18.3; see the related discussion in *Leviathan*, chapter 43, pp. 425–28.
58. *Leviathan*, chapter 43, p. 425.

in the pravity of the will, as well as in the irregularity of the act."[59] While the sovereign "mortal God" may not have the same insight into the hearts and designs of men, and would be foolhardy to try, Hobbes is hopeful nonetheless that the right kind of moral instruction and the right kind of social institutions will prepare individuals not only to follow the laws but to do so "sincerely from the heart."[60] Indeed, public reason represents that measure of limited unification and shared attachment that is necessary within a Protestant Reformation setting in which each person "is allowed to take for the sense of the Scripture that which they make thereof, either by their own private interpretation, or by the interpretation of such as are not called thereunto by public authority: they that follow their own interpretation, continually demanding liberty of conscience."[61] As I will argue further below, the laws may have no direct influence over men's conscience, but Hobbes, as a theorist of public reason and moral virtue, writes with the purpose of shaping hearts and minds, seeking always to unite the internal and the external court, conscience and commonwealth.

Natural Laws/Moral Virtues

Part of what makes Hobbes so intriguing as a theorist of public reason is that while the laws and civic-pedagogical aims of sovereign authority are to be directed toward the cultivation of subject-citizens, Hobbes clearly appreciates the significant epistemological and social-psychological limits on the power of the state to transform individuals after its own image. "All men are by nature provided of notable multiplying glasses, that is their passions and self-love, through which, every little payment appeareth a great grievance; but are destitute of those prospective glasses, namely moral and civil science, to see afar off the miseries that hang over them, and cannot without such payments be avoided."[62] Some scholars are quick to identify statements like this with Hobbes's psychological realism; others call it historical pessimism; for still others it represents a nascent protoliberalism.[63] In my view what is most telling here is that

59. Ibid., chapter 30, p. 252.
60. Ibid.
61. *EL*, 2.25.2.
62. *Leviathan*, chapter 18, p. 141.
63. For valuable discussion, see Ewin, *Virtues and Rights*, chapter 2; and Lloyd, *Ideals as Interests in Leviathan*, chapter 1.

the subjectivist theory of value and the egoistic psychology that are clearly a part of Hobbes's initial picture of morality do not foreclose the fact that Hobbes thinks it possible, indeed necessary, to articulate a set of common moral standards and virtues that will regulate and help solidify a political commonwealth, a society, as we would say today, that is riven by reasonable but incommensurable conceptions of the good. What is more, Hobbes intends these moral virtues, habits, and dispositions to become elements of a common public life that will not only contend with a subjectivist conception of the good but also fashion the mutual relations between citizen and sovereign as deep allegiance, affection, and love. Hobbes never doubted either the difficulties or the importance of this transformative work:

> And to consider the contrariety of man's opinions, and manners, in general, it is, they say, impossible to entertain a constant civil amity with all those, with whom the business of the world constrains us to converse: which business consisteth almost in nothing else but a perpetual contention for honor, riches and authority. To which I answer, that these are indeed great difficulties, but not impossibilities: for by education, and discipline, they may be, and are sometimes reconciled.[64]

The particular problem, from Hobbes's perspective, is that "all writers do agree, that the natural law is the same with the moral"; yet the terms *good* and *evil* are used to signify diverse attributes, owing to man's diverse inclinations and aversions, customs and opinions.[65] This is even more the case where moral judgments touch on "the common actions of life, where what this man commends, that is to say, calls good, the other undervalues, as being evil. Nay, very often the same man at diverse times praises and dispraises the same thing."[66] Here, as in other, similar passages, we can see that it is incorrect to label Hobbes a moral relativist, if by that we mean someone who does not believe in the validity of moral categories or judgments. Rather, these moral judgments exist and refer to human appetites and desires, but they do not for Hobbes inhere in the objects of those inclinations or aversions themselves.[67] Hence the

---

64. *Leviathan*, "Review, and Conclusion," p. 503.
65. *De cive*, 3.31.
66. Ibid.
67. Here I have been helped by Ewin, *Virtues and Rights*, chapter 2.

problem this creates is not one where human beings face a disenchanted universe in which no standards of just and unjust, good and evil apply. Instead, it is a context marked by a veritable babble of moral significations and evaluations, shifting from person to person, and over time, within each subject. The uncertainty of this condition is exacerbated by the fact that even when persons within such a state find that they can agree on certain moral virtues as being good, "yet they disagree still concerning their nature, to wit, in what each of them doth consist."[68]

This is a problem that concerns human beings in general, but it also highlights for Hobbes the failings of moral philosophers who might otherwise have provided a remedy to this situation. It is important to see in Hobbes's repeated railings against the "schools" and certain ancient authors and texts, both for what they teach and for what they fail to teach, that Hobbes takes for granted that the philosopher has a crucial role to play in public political life. Hobbes places a sizable portion of the blame for what he takes as philosophy's failed public role on Aristotle and the popularity of Aristotle in the "schools."[69] Despite understanding morality as something that concerns human character and virtue, and despite fixing upon some of the same virtues that Hobbes also celebrated (in this context, fortitude and liberality), Aristotle and his followers situated these virtues as the mean (Hobbes labels it the mediocrity) between the passions, rather than the specific qualities necessary for the attainment of "peaceable, sociable, and comfortable living."[70] In his epistle dedicatory to *De cive* Hobbes levels this charge with characteristic verve: "If the moral philosophers had as happily discharged their duty [as the geometricians had with respect to natural bodies], I know not what could have been added by human industry to the completion of that happiness, which is consistent with human life." He claims further that "what hath hitherto been written by moral philosophers, hath not made any progress in the knowledge of truth."[71] In misconstruing the ends of moral philosophy, in failing to see in what the value or goodness of the virtues consists, the ancients (and Aristotle in particular) have left the modern world in a condition where subjects do not know the "moral law" and

---

68. *De cive*, 3.32.

69. See, for example, *Behemoth*, Dialogue 1, pp. 40–45.

70. *Leviathan*, chapter 15; see also *De cive*, 3.32; *EL*, 1.17.14. This is not to say that Hobbes got Aristotle right. Indeed, there is sufficient room to think that Hobbes's disagreement with Aristotle is overstated (for obvious polemical purposes) and tends to distort those features of their theories that they held in common.

71. *De cive*, epistle dedicatory.

cannot appreciate the contributions it can make to peace and the pre-vention of discord.

Hobbes means to correct this situation by providing a "science of vir-tue and vice." This labeling can be a bit deceptive if we are not sensitive to the fact that for Hobbes and his contemporaries in the seventeenth century, science and philosophy were not easily distinguishable. Science, as Hobbes understands it, is not the knowledge of facts derived from observations. Such knowledge for him is "absolute knowledge," involv-ing sense and the memories of sensed experiences. Science, by contrast, is a far more limited and conditional form of knowledge that comes from reasoning through (or "reckoning" upon) the consequences of words and definitions.[72] Philosophy, or science, is the activity of reasoning about causes and effects. The key distinction that we must note here is that philosophy and that branch of science that Hobbes is most concerned with are ineluctably bound up with language, not with sense or experience like natural philosophy (or what we would call the natural sciences) or physics. Hence, whatever degree of understanding or knowledge we may hope to achieve through reason is entirely dependent on language and the "right ordering of names in our affirmations."[73] Reason is abandoned, science is forsaken, and any benefits that might redound to humankind are lost unless we adopt the method of making exact and consistent use of words and definitions in our ratiocinations.[74] All of this is of crucial importance for understanding what Hobbes means by the claim to have provided the true and only moral science. As a science, it does not (it cannot) aspire to a truth claim. Hobbes's moral philosophy does not involve facts but the ratiocination of consequences from clearly stated significations and definitions concerning human dispositions and passions.[75]

Hobbes's deduction, then, is that so long as human beings continue with their right to all things, and so long as private and immediate appetite is the measure of good and evil, subjects will remain in the condition of a war of each against all. But to continue in such a state, Hobbes tells us, is a self-contradiction, something that no one could in fact will. "For

73. Hobbes makes this distinction most clearly in *De homine:* "Indeed, when one is deal-ing with the truth of fact, it is not properly called *science,* but simply *knowledge.* Therefore it is science when we know a certain proposed theorem to be true, either by knowledge derived from the causes, or from the generation of the subject by right reasoning" (10.4).

73. *Leviathan,* chapter 4, p. 36.

74. See ibid., chapter 5.

75. See here the very useful discussion by Quentin Skinner in *Reason and Rhetoric in the Philosophy of Hobbes* (Cambridge: Cambridge University Press, 1996), chapter 8.

man by natural necessity desires that which is good for him; nor is there any that esteems a war of all against all, which necessarily adheres to such a state, to be good for him."[76] While the passions separate and divide us, reason instructs us toward the means by which to secure ourselves and our future. The most succinct expression of the relationship Hobbes propounds between reason, peace, and the moral virtues is in *De cive:* "Reason declaring peace to be good, it follows by the same reason, that all the necessary means to peace be good also; and therefore that modesty, equity, trust, humanity, mercy (which we have demonstrated to be necessary to peace), are good manners or habits, that is, virtues. The law therefore, in the means to peace, commands also good manners, or the practice of virtue; and therefore it is called *moral.*"[77]

As we have seen, Hobbes is concerned with enumerating several distinct moral virtues: those that "appertain to the preservation of ourselves against those dangers which arise from discord."[78] Hence he is less concerned with virtues such as temperance or prudence, which speak to individuals as individuals, than he is with those that relate to persons in their role as interdependent citizens. The moral virtues that are politically relevant and conducive to peace include justice, trust, equity, modesty, charity, gratitude, and sociability, but the natural laws also include injunctions against the vices of pride, contumely, and revenge. There are, all told, twenty natural laws (which include the law Hobbes adds in his "Review, and Conclusion" to *Leviathan*). As we have noted, Hobbes acknowledges that these are in fact not laws but qualities or dispositions that direct men to peace and concord in political society.[79] The virtue of gratitude, for example, requires subjects to endeavor not to let others suffer from or regret gestures of good will. Without such gratitude, "all beneficence and trust, together with all kind of benevolence, would be taken from among men." Although a failure in this respect is not technically an injury

76. *De cive*, 1.13. Similar language is used in *EL*, 1.14.12. It is common to view Hobbes's argument from general equality and the absolute right, or liberty, of nature as leading to unnecessarily pessimistic assumptions concerning human diffidence, competition, and war. Yet to the extent that the right of nature leads to or involves a self-contradiction, there is in fact no real or substantive right to speak of. Hence to assert that subjective right is the foundation of Hobbes's theory of the state—as commentators such as Strauss have done—is to rest Hobbes's deductions on something he seems to have considered a necessary but empty category. See Strauss, *The Political Philosophy of Hobbes: Its Basis and Its Genesis* (Chicago: University of Chicago Press, 1963).

77. *De cive*, 3.31.

78. Ibid, 3.32.

79. See, among other places, *Leviathan*, chapter 15, p. 124; chapter 26, p. 200.

in Hobbes's language (because there is no contract or stipulation of trust), it is nonetheless a breakdown in standards of reciprocity and mutuality and can just as easily (re)create a state of war.[80] Likewise, complaisance and sociability are necessary to comport men to political life, and violations of equity either through pride or through arrogance are pernicious and disruptive of concord.

As some critics have appreciated, these are the virtues of neither classical republicanism nor active self-government and political participation.[81] They are moral virtues whose political relevance is satisfied by fitting subjects for peace, obedience, and concord. They teach subjects not to seek revenge, to pardon those who repent of past offenses, and to accommodate others. All of this is consistent with and supports Hobbes's political absolutism, an absolutism that tells him that prosperity and human flourishing will follow from obedience to government and not from the arrogant efforts to rework or reform its structure. But is Hobbes's science of virtue and vice for this reason merely an ideological construction of values whose purpose is instrumentally tied to the formation of dutiful subjects? In treating Hobbes's moral theory have we uncovered nothing more than a deceptive superstructure to a far more effective base of fear and self-interest?[82] Is this, in short, a moralized theory of prudence?

These are questions that raise two related but distinct issues: how we should evaluate the meaning and relevance of these moral virtues for assessing Hobbes's political theory, and how far we should take Hobbes's political vision to depend on these character traits or dispositions. I will address the latter question in the remainder of this section, and return to the matter of evaluating the consequences of this reading of Hobbes in the final section of the chapter.

80. *De cive*, 3.8.
81. See Mary G. Dietz, "Hobbes's Subject as Citizen," in Dietz, *Hobbes and Political Theory*, 107. While I agree with much of Dietz's analysis of Hobbes, I think it is ultimately a mistake to resolve Hobbes's science of virtue and vice into a "utilitarian measure directed toward strengthening allegiance to the sovereign and the commonwealth" (119n77). This type of reading owes itself, I think, to an unnecessary separation of Hobbes's ethical concerns from his political ones. A similar problem plagues Boonin-Vail's otherwise helpful analysis of Hobbes, *Hobbes and the Science of Moral Virtue*. In Boonin-Vail's case, however, the problem is reversed. Hobbes is read as a theorist of moral virtue, but the relevance of this for his political arguments is left undeveloped.
82. Using slightly different language, this is how Strauss characterized Hobbes's modernity: "Hobbes's political philosophy is nothing other than the progressive supplanting of aristocratic virtue by bourgeois virtue." *Political Philosophy of Hobbes*, 126. In Strauss's reading, it is the centrality of fear and the fear of violent death that secure Hobbes's political thought as modern and bourgeois.

The question at issue here is, why read Hobbes as a theorist of moral virtue? In seeking after the foundations and reputed stability of the Hobbesian commonwealth, most analyses have rested content with the traditional concepts of self-interest, coercion, and fear. Citizens will obey the commands of the sovereign because they will see in its dictates and in its continuance the means to their self-preservation and their long-term benefit or "delectation." Alternatively, because the passions of human beings and the temptations of avarice, ambition, and lust do not cease in political society, the laws will be observed and the stability of the regime secured through the power of the sword, that is, through the fear of the disciplinary consequences that will follow from violations of the civil law. It is certainly not my intention to discount these features of Hobbes's theory. To do so would, of course, be a gross and untenable distortion of both his view of human nature and his political outlook. But the combination of a strictly positivist perspective on Hobbes's theory of law, and an ethical subjectivist perspective on his moral theory, have left us in a distinctly compromised position from which it is nearly impossible to assess important features of Hobbes's writings. Hobbes gives us sufficient reason to suspect that he did not consider the engine of fear or the intoxicants of self-interest to be adequate resources for sustaining a commonwealth.

Instead, the answers to the above questions must also be sought in Hobbes's concern with the inculcation of habits, dispositions, and "manners" (morals) through education. Hobbes rejects altogether the notion that men have the necessary or sufficient resources, by nature, to live in political society. Hobbes's opposition to the Greek *zoon politikon* announces his modernity, but in a deceptive way it also makes clear that he does not think mere compacting enough for instituting and maintaining a government among men. This is a point to which I will return throughout this book, but for now what is important to establish is the centrality of the position that "man is made fit for society not by nature, but by education."[83] How can we explain Hobbes's concern with public education if we assume that self-interest and prudence, on one side, and coercion and the threat of punishment, on the other, are adequate for an understanding of Hobbesian civil association? How do we explain Hobbes's normative distinction between desiring to live in society and actually having the capacity or "fitness" to make good on what we desire, if prudential calculations of interest and happiness are the only qualities

83. *De cive*, 1.2n*.

necessary for political society?[84] The answer is that the commonwealth requires a leaven of an altogether different order from prudence or fear. By attending to Hobbes's concern with education we find a role and a political payoff for his science of virtue and vice and a deeper appreciation for the challenges of public reason.

The Public Educative Project: Love, Fidelity, and Habituation

In analyzing those "internal causes that tend to the dissolution" of governments, Hobbes organizes his treatment of this issue around three distinct problems. These include the "doctrines" and "passions" that he claims are contrary to peace, the qualities and conditions that predispose men to "quit their allegiance," and the nature of factions more generally. Foremost among the factors that destabilize a regime is the "perverse doctrine" that "the knowledge of good and evil belongs to each single man."[85] What we must recognize here is that this dangerous doctrine, which holds that each man, in his private capacity, is the rightful judge of good and evil, just and unjust, was Hobbes's own starting premise. As we saw earlier in relation to the authorization of public reason, within the confines of civil government this pernicious opinion must give way to the recognition that the civil laws are the rules of good and evil, just and unjust. In as clear a statement of moral conventionalism (and legal positivism) as one could hope to find, Hobbes declares that "legitimate kings therefore make the things they command just, by commanding them, and those which they forbid, unjust, by forbidding them."[86]

There are, of course, other doctrines "repugnant to civil society" that worry Hobbes, including the belief that all acts against conscience are sins (they are not sins if those acts are commanded by the sovereign); that the sovereign is subject to the civil laws (the sovereign cannot be

---

84. In the same note to *De cive* that I quoted above, Hobbes argues, "Manifest therefore it is, that all men, because they are born in infancy, are born unapt for society. Many also, perhaps most men, either through defect of mind or want of education, remain unfit during the whole course of their lives. . . . *Furthermore, although men were born in such a condition as to desire it [society], it follows not, that he therefore were born fit to enter into it. For it is one thing to desire, another to be in capacity fit for what we desire*" (1.2n*, emphasis added).

85. *De cive*, 12.1; see also *Leviathan*, chapter 29, pp. 238–39.

86. *De cive*, 12.1. It is important to note that this does not rule out the idea that subjects within a commonwealth still have liberty in those "infinite cases" that are not addressed by the civil laws. Hobbes believes that it is in the sovereign's best interest to leave men to dispose of their "harmless liberty" as they see fit. Ibid., 13.15–16.

subject to the laws it makes); that tyrannicide is lawful (tyrannicide does not exist, and *regicide* is always unlawful); and that subjects have absolute dominion over their property and goods (their propriety exists by the leave of the sovereign).[87] While Hobbes is equally concerned with replacing these ideas with his "true elements of civil doctrine," none of these other doctrines reflect positions that Hobbes at any time in his theoretical deductions actually endorsed. On the contrary, Hobbes begins with a psychological egoist and ethical subjectivist perspective that now threatens to unravel the state. The problem in this regard is that this "false doctrine" allows men to "dispute the commands of the commonwealth; and afterwards to obey, or disobey them, as in their private judgments they shall think fit; whereby the commonwealth is distracted and *weakened*."[88]

How does Hobbes propose to deal with these dangerous ingredients? In particular, are the customary tools of executive command and fear up to the task? Where the question is how to sustain a political commonwealth and make of it a "firm and lasting edifice," Hobbes explicitly argues that they are not. For the conservation of "inward peace," and to confront these unsettling beliefs, Hobbes concludes, "It is therefore the duty of those who have the chief authority, to root those [doctrines] out of the minds of men, *not by commanding, but by teaching; not by the terror of penalties, but by the perspicuity of reasons*."[89] Hence what Hobbes says about the nature of Christian faith can be applied in equal measure to the civic faith that public reason must teach: "faith hath no relation to, nor dependence at all upon compulsion or commandment; but only upon certainty or probability of arguments drawn from reason, or from something men believe already."[90]

Traditionally the question of human capacity or psychology has been taken as an inherent conceptual limitation in Hobbes's moral and political theory. The only way to secure trust, comity, safety, and a stable political order is not through man's inherent faculties of reason, consent, or will, but through the command and enforcement of a sovereign political power. Reason may point the way, and may instruct men in the path of peace, but until they transfer their rights and authorize an absolute authority to govern their actions, there can be no peace. While such a

---

87. This is a representative but not exhaustive list. See *De cive*, chapter 12, and *Leviathan*, chapter 29.
88. *Leviathan*, chapter 29.
89. *De cive*, 13.9 (emphasis added). See also *EL*, 2.28.8.
90. *Leviathan*, chapter 42, p. 362; see also chapter 47, pp. 499–500.

reading of Hobbes is supported by the text, it neither exhausts nor adequately covers his thought. Hobbes did not view human moral and political capacity as a fixed limit but rather saw it as a possibility, something that is always *in potentia*. To be sure, his occasionally jaundiced view of human nature has tended to overwhelm this more optimistic perspective. As a result, it has been relatively easy to overlook these features of his argument. This may in turn explain why scholars have put so much emphasis on the role of fear as the source of Hobbes's politics.

Yet citizens must be instructed in their duties and encouraged to find not just safety and protection in conforming to the laws but contentment and honor as well. Rewards and punishments will, of course, continue to be used as a means to choreograph men in the performance of their external obligations. Yet if governments were to rest satisfied with mere outward performance they would place assurances for the longevity of political society in very shallow roots indeed. Even here, however, we must note the educative function that Hobbes ascribes to punishment. Sanctions, or the threat of sanctions, do not work through fear alone. According to Hobbes, "the end of punishment is not to compel the will of man, but to fashion it, and to make it such as he would have it who hath set the penalty."[91] Since the will is always the last appetite or aversion that survives a subject's considerations before acting, punishments and rewards, to be truly effective, must reach deeper than the will. The will is not fully voluntary for Hobbes, and as such, the instruments of reward and sanction must find deeper sources with which to influence men's actions. They must actually "fashion," or reconstitute, the subject in ways conformable with peace and stability. There is evidence here to suggest that we accept a false (and perhaps anachronistic) division that is not part of Hobbes's understanding when we too readily separate enforcement and education in his political theory.

Hobbes leaves it as one of the fundamental rights of the sovereign to determine which opinions and doctrines are amenable or repugnant to peace. He also considers as one of the sovereign's principal duties an attention to "public instruction." This instruction, he makes plain, should be provided for by the "perspicuity of reasons," but it must also proceed by example.[92] While Hobbes does not spend a great deal of time detailing what the practical implications of instructing by example might involve,

91. *De cive*, 13.16.
92. *Leviathan*, chapter 30, p. 247.

he nonetheless raises the possibility that there are significant moral (not just strategic or prudential) limitations and positive moral duties on the sovereign. In *De homine* Hobbes gives us some insight into what this instruction by example might require of a political sovereign. Here Hobbes prevails upon fathers, teachers, and tutors that they must "imbue the minds of youths with precepts which are good and true, but [it must also be understood] how much they must bear themselves justly and in a righteous manner in their presence, for the dispositions of youths are not less, but much more disposed to bad habits by example than they are to good ones by precept."[93] (The emphasis on moral instruction through example is one with which Locke and Rousseau will heartily agree.) While no strict parallel can be offered here, Hobbes nonetheless claimed that the law of nature establishes as a precept for sovereigns that "they not only do righteousness themselves, but that they also by penalties cause the judges, by them appointed, to do the same."[94] All of this should remind us that Hobbes made an important distinction between the right of supreme authority, for which there were very few limits, and the actual exercise of that authority concerning which Hobbes acknowledged moral and political duties. The sovereign, in other words, should not only serve as the fount of the principled content of a regulative public reason but should provide a practical, embodied example of it.

Hobbes, of course, had his own thoughts on how the sovereign might meet these significant responsibilities. Indeed, he saw himself providing just this kind of moral counsel. As he declared in his epistle dedicatory to *The Elements of Law*, written in honor of William, the Earl of Newcastle (who would later become a royalist general at the beginning of the civil wars), "it would be an incomparable benefit to commonwealth, that every man held the opinions concerning law and policy, here delivered."[95] And again at the end of *Leviathan*, Hobbes allowed himself to imagine that were his deductions to be taught at the universities, "by that means the most men, knowing their duties, will be the less subject to serve the ambition of a few discontented persons, in their purposes against the state; and be less grieved with the contributions necessary for their peace and defense."[96] While the sovereign possesses the right (and duty) of public education, one of the significant roles that Hobbes's political theory

93. *De homine*, 13.7.
94. *De cive*, 13.17.
95. *EL*, epistle dedicatory, written in May 1640.
96. *Leviathan*, "Review, and Conclusion," p. 511.

assumes (in *De cive, Leviathan,* and *Behemoth*) is to instruct public right in the proper ("true") principles of civil science.[97]

One of the sovereign's most important duties, then, is to educate the people in the "grounds and reasons" of political right and, more practically, on the direct relationship between the sovereign's rights and the public's safety and contentment.[98] This in turn requires that the very foundations of political society and the nature and ends of political rule must be made transparent for all to see. In its own uniquely Hobbesian way, this represents an early version of what contemporary theorists of public reason call satisfying the publicity conditions for the regulative principles of society.[99] For Rawls this means that a political order does not depend on "historically accidental or established delusions, or other mistaken beliefs resting on the deceptive appearances of institutions that mislead us as to how they work."[100] Of course, by virtue of offering a contractarian account of political society, Hobbes has already revealed a commitment to the idea of publicity as an important feature for securing knowledge and acceptance of the basic institutions of society. Yet more can be said on this score if we take Hobbes's concern with education seriously. Other scholars who have considered Hobbes's commitment to public education, most notably Jeremy Waldron and S. A. Lloyd, have discerned in his account a liberal respect for individuals as reasoning

---

97. A similar hope for political theory may be detected in the following lines of Rousseau's *First Discourse:* "Therefore may Kings not disdain to allow into their councils the men most capable of advising them well; may they renounce the old prejudice, invented by the pride of the great, that the art of leading people is more difficult than that of enlightening them, as if it were easier to engage men to do good willingly than to constrain them to do it by force." *The First and Second Discourses,* ed. Roger D. Masters, trans. Roger D. Masters and Judith R. Masters (New York: St. Martin's Press, 1964), 63.

98. This is a relationship that is also asserted in Hobbes's *Dialogue Between a Philosopher and a Student of the Common Laws of England,* ed. Joseph Cropsey (Chicago: University of Chicago Press, 1971). In the short dialogue concerning the "Law of Reason," the lawyer argues that "Peace at home may then be expected durable, when the common people shall be made to see the benefit they shall receive by their Obedience and Adhesion to their own Sovereign, and the harm they must suffer by taking part with them, who by promises of Reformation, or change of Government deceive them" (57).

99. For the publicity conditions attached to public reason and regulative principles more generally, see Rawls, *Political Liberalism,* 66–71. I am in agreement with Waldron that Hobbes accepted a principle of publicity, even as I think that this principle requires a great deal more ethical work on and by subjects (in moral virtues in particular) to fully address questions of stability and allegiance. In other words, the recognition of a conventionalist account of justice on the part of citizens, while important for meeting a principle of publicity, does not on its own address the question of motivating citizens to abide by that publicly stipulated account of justice. See Waldron, "Hobbes and the Principle of Publicity."

100. Rawls, *Political Liberalism,* 68.

beings and a "proto-Enlightenment optimism" in the power of reason to secure the foundations of political order.[101] According to Lloyd, "Hobbes's system of education is not to be rejected as objectionably ideological, or as a coercive program of mind control, at least not under its formal description as a system of education in evident truths consonant with basic human interests by means of reasoned argument exposing their true grounds."[102]

These interpretations are quite valuable, and I think largely correct, but we should not press this point too far. Hobbes does not, in my view, satisfy (or strive to satisfy) what Rawls calls the "full publicity condition" for a well-ordered society. This is largely because, while the rights and obligations that citizens possess must be made publicly *known* by clear demonstrations, Hobbes is far less solicitous about ensuring that the basic political principles that are expressed through law and education are fully *acceptable* to everyone—in his own time, his metaphysical skepticism, his conventionalist account of truth and justice, as well as his Erastianism virtually assured that his substantive views and the formal methods that produced them would not find acceptance with most readers. Additionally, the separation that Hobbes's account produces between private conscience and public conduct, between individual faith and the freedoms of public expression and confession, should also give serious pause to any precommitment (on our part) to see Hobbes as a philosophical liberal.

The crucial point about Hobbes's case for public reason is that while the dictates of the sovereign authority are absolute, they are not on that account arbitrary. They are not arbitrary in the sense that the sovereign must be able to give reasons for its judgments about what conduces to the peace and felicity of the commonwealth. This means that the burdens of public justification are at the same time burdens of public education. Thus a good law, according to Hobbes, must satisfy two public requirements: it must be needed for securing the good of the people, and it must be "withal perspicuous."[103] This latter publicity condition is met "not so much in the words of the law itself, as in a declaration of the causes, and

---

101. Waldron, "Hobbes and the Principle of Publicity," 454, 469. For an even more vigorous treatment of Hobbes as a promoter of Enlightenment, see David Johnston, *Rhetoric of Leviathan,* chapter 5.

102. Lloyd continues by arguing, "Under these formal descriptions of the educational system and its background psychological and social assumptions, this looks like a system that even philosophical liberals could accept." "Coercion, Ideology, and Education," 59.

103. *Leviathan,* chapter 30, p. 255.

motives for which it was made."[104] So, while the legislative dictates are absolute, Hobbes's argument that the reasons for the law be made perspicuous to all citizens is both a stopgap on naked arbitrary rule making and expresses a commitment to public education that eschews "the illusions and delusions of ideology."[105] The sovereign's decrees are not arbitrary in the further sense that Hobbes thinks there are good moral, political, and prudential reasons for embracing his solutions to the problems of political order, especially in light of what he takes to be fundamental about human beings, both in "nature" and in history. Hobbes's aim is not progress in the full enlightenment of all, but to identify the reasonable and practical grounds upon which political stability and common political allegiance depend. In accordance with this, the rights that inhere in political sovereignty must be made public and "diligently, and truly taught." This is so, significantly, because the fundamental grounds for the rights of sovereignty "cannot be maintained by any civil law, or terror of legal punishment. For a civil law, that shall forbid rebellion, (and such is all resistance to the essential rights of the sovereignty), is not, as a civil law, any obligation, but by virtue only of the law of nature, that forbiddeth the violation of faith; which natural obligation, if men know not, they cannot know the right of any law the sovereign maketh."[106]

This is a complicated argument that reflects both the importance of public education in Hobbes's political theory as well as what seems to be a forthright acknowledgment of the limits of legal authority and political might in securing a lasting political society. The limits appear to be twofold. The first is the inherent limit laws and sanctions face in trying to supplant or uproot doctrines and opinion, where it is specifically the "errors" that need correcting, not the "persons erring."[107] Hobbes believed that opinion and the habits of men combine in such a way that, over time, the only way they might become susceptible to change is not by force but through a no less shortened commitment to habits, opinion, and education.[108] (As we will see in Chapter 3, this is also true for Locke.) In

---

104. Ibid., 256.

105. Rawls, *Political Liberalism*, 68–69n21.

106. *Leviathan*, chapter 30, p. 248.

107. See *De cive*, 13.9, for this language. Hobbes uses this same distinction to criticize the Catholic Church in *Behemoth*: "I think that neither the preaching of friars nor of monks, nor of parochial priests, tended to teach men what, but whom, to believe. . . . And the end which the Pope had in multiplying sermons, was no other but to prop and enlarge his own authority over all Christian Kings and States" (Dialogue 1, p. 16).

108. *EL*, 2.28.8.

Behemoth Hobbes seems to go even further in arguing that "a state can constrain obedience, but convince no error, nor alter the minds of them that believe they have the better reason."[109] The answer for the instruction of the people in their duties to the state cannot be sought in coercion or in the suppression of doctrine, but in the slow process of education from youth to adulthood.

The second limit we confront concerning the rights and executive powers of the sovereign relate to the more extensive boundary created by the idea that the civil laws themselves seem to depend on a more primary obligation and virtue of keeping faith, or trust. In the passage quoted above and others like it throughout Hobbes's corpus, there is some evidence to support the claim that Hobbes sought to ground civil authority upon the moral foundation of natural law. To consider this we must recognize that Hobbes is always careful to distinguish between law and contract. According to Hobbes, "contract is a promise, law is a command."[110] Contracts create self-imposed obligations, whereas laws impose obligations that are auto-justifying, as the precepts of that office that has sovereign authority. Hobbes marks the relevance of the distinction this way: "a man is obliged by his contracts, that is, that he ought to perform for his promise sake; but that the law ties him being obliged, that is to say, it compels him to make good his promise for fear of the punishment appointed by the law."[111] If a contract obliges of itself, and the law of nature imposes an obligation to keep faith, does the act of promising thereby ground the state and the citizen's duties to it? How should we understand this question in relation to the serious doubt Hobbes had about the human capacity to make and keep promises?

The first thing we must note is that there is an important sense in which covenants and the law of nature concerning fidelity to promises ground the subject's obligation to the civil laws. I have already quoted from *Leviathan* to this effect, but we also find in *De cive* the claim that "by virtue of the natural law which forbids breach of covenant, the law of nature commands us to keep all the civil laws."[112] Hence, if the sovereign

---

109. *Behemoth*, Dialogue 2, 62.

110. *De cive*, 14.2. This is a distinction that is also carefully drawn in Jean Bodin with great, and quite different, effect. *Six Books of the Commonwealth*, trans. M. J. Tooley (Oxford: Basil Blackwell, 1955), 1.8.

111. *De cive*, 1.2n*.

112. Ibid., 14.10; we might also add to this the argument from *The Elements of Law:* "A law obligeth no otherwise than by virtue of some covenant made by him who is subject thereunto" (2.29.2).

makes a law forbidding rebellion, that monarch or assembly has in fact effected nothing substantive and made a superfluous law. For unless we see that subjects were already obliged to obedience through their mutual covenant, and hence unable to rebel by virtue of this act, we will fail to understand how the civil law became valid and received its force in men's public lives in the first place. Men's obligations to civil obedience and the validity of civil laws have the same source: artificial covenants. The nature of Hobbes's commitment to popular consent, as all of this suggests, is quite extensive. Even under historical conditions in which sovereignty is acquired by conquest and force, a condition that Hobbes knows to be more frequent and empirically reliable than government by mutual covenant, the *right* of sovereignty is not established by possession or domination but by the "consent of the vanquished."[113] On these grounds we might turn a popular critique of Hobbes on its head. Covenant and promising are far from superfluous in Hobbes's political theory. Rather, positive civil law and state coercion are of no effect when it comes to influencing the basis of obligation and the fundamental legitimacy of the state. It is with this in mind that we can understand why treason, one of the more frightful political sins that Hobbes considers, is treated as a violation of natural law, not civil law.[114]

As clear as this might seem, we have not in fact retired the question regarding the priority of natural duties for establishing civil obligations in Hobbes. This is because, while there may be some evidence to suggest that the conceptual language of natural law grounds political right in Hobbes's theory, it is still the case that such "natural obligations," as he calls them, must be instilled and cultivated in men. That is, moral education and

---

113. Even conquest is contractual in Hobbes's political theory. This idea might justifiably strike modern readers as unduly cynical and apt to turn consent or contract into a mere ransom note for one's bodily survival. Along these lines we might feel compelled to ask how free or meaningful that consent can be which is obtained through the fear of losing one's life. This may be our question, but it is not Hobbes's. Sovereignty by institution is established through the fear that men have of one another, and sovereignty by acquisition is created through the fear that men have of those who wield power. In both cases fear is a determining factor in man's motivations. But this psychological state, at least for Hobbes, is not inconsistent with liberty. Fear in Hobbes is not a debilitating, negative condition but a condition in which a subject has taken "a certain foresight of future evil" (*De cive*, 1.2n†). The choice that sovereignty by acquisition may force upon citizens may be difficult, but for Hobbes the subject is nonetheless at liberty to submit or not. This is a position that trades on the meaning of liberty to establish the legitimacy of political authority under any conceivable circumstances. Yet we must also recognize that it articulates the important position that rights cannot be taken, only transferred or renounced.

114. *De cive*, 14.21; *Leviathan*, chapter 30, p. 248.

public persuasion play a definitive role here. While Hobbes argues that there is a natural law to keep covenants, he does not at the same time think (contra Hume's later critique) that this will in fact hold much sway over men, and his arguments concerning the generation and maintenance of the commonwealth do not depend on this as a law of nature. His argument does depend, however, on this law conceived as a virtue of fidelity and trust—a virtue, what is more, that needs to be taught, practiced, and habituated. In short, public justification is dangerously incomplete without a commitment to public education in the principles, rights, and qualities upon which the endurance of a regime depends.

In a manner of speaking, we might say that the Hobbesian social contract is something that the subjects who enter it must grow into. For what seems most distinctive about Hobbesian contractarianism is the lack of the necessary human characteristics or dispositions to support the social and political world Hobbes envisions. This is surely true if we compare him to Grotius, Pufendorf, or Locke, all of whom assumed some degree of inherent sociability among human beings. Yet we can evaluate Hobbes's achievements as more than the product of a skeptical figure who found a way to erect a commonwealth on sparse human resources and dour views of human motivation. Rather, Hobbes is a theorist who understood that to make civil society a lasting place for diverse human beings, an extensive amount of work would have to go into "framing" or educating subjects for citizenship. This is a position that, in the modern context, is most familiar to us in a thinker like Rousseau (who, as we shall see, confronted his own paradox at nearly the same point in his account of the social compact). But it is also present, assuredly in a different form, in Hobbes.

We can see the importance of forming or fashioning the will in Hobbes's account by observing that the sovereign is most vulnerable at the very point where it is provided its authority. Covenants and promises evoke a stable, unified, and faithful citizenry that is, as Rousseau would also appreciate, more frequently the effect than the cause of political institutions. The remedy to this situation for Hobbes is provided by public reason or, more specifically, public education. The intricate relationship between institutional vulnerability, consent, moral capacity, and education is expressed in the following passage from *Behemoth:*

> It is not the right of the sovereign, though granted to him by every man's express consent, that can enable him to do his office;

it is the obedience of the subject, which must do that. For what good is it to promise allegiance, and then by and by to cry out (as some ministers did in the pulpit) *To your tents, O Israel!?* Common people know nothing of right or wrong by their own mediation; they must therefore be taught the grounds of their duty, and the reasons why calamities ever follow from disobedience to their lawful sovereigns.[115]

When we look to those sections of his writings concerning instruction we find that Hobbes was rather sanguine about the powers of moral and political education. This may come as some surprise to readers who are less familiar with these aspects of Hobbes's theory and tend only to recall, reasonably enough, that Hobbes thought human beings a brutish, selfish, and nasty species. Indeed he continues to find them "ignorant of their duty to the public." This ignorance with respect to the foundational principles of political sovereignty and right is due in part to the fact that men either pay too much attention to their particular, private interests or take their lessons regarding public right from the erroneous doctrines declared from the pulpits.[116] Since the opinions that proceed from the pulpits are first hatched in the universities, Hobbes also held the schools responsible for leaving the mass of men ignorant with respect to their duties and the virtues necessary to sustain political society. The universities were the "handmaid to Roman religion," where the course of study was not philosophy but "Aristotelity."[117] While Hobbes leaves little doubt that England's civil wars were the result of a corrupt people seduced by the erroneous principles of rebellious clerics and unlearned divines, there is an important sense in which the public's failure to know their duties is also Charles's failure to properly regulate the schools and the churches. In all of this we can see Hobbes attacking a political culture that he holds culpable for generating the conditions in which rebellion and civil war could take place.[118]

---

115. *Behemoth*, Dialogue 3, p. 144.

116. Ibid., Dialogue 1, p. 39; see also Dialogue 4, where Hobbes declares that "the mischief [of the civil wars] proceeded wholly from the Presbyterian preachers, who, by a long and practiced histrionic faculty, preached up the rebellion powerfully" (p. 159).

117. *Leviathan*, chapter 46, p. 482; for the related charge that the universities of England were instituted to meet the theological and political designs of the pope, see *Behemoth*, Dialogue 1.

118. See in particular *Behemoth*, Dialogue 1, pp. 39–45. For a helpful discussion of the role that ambitious elites play in Hobbes's treatment of the Civil War, see Deborah Baumgold, "Hobbes's Political Sensibility: The Menace of Political Ambition," in Dietz, *Hobbes and Political*

Yet, despite having so much of his contemporary political and religious environment stacked against him, Hobbes deemed it both possible and practicable to turn all of this around. He would not countenance objections regarding the supposed incapacity of the masses (or the "vulgar"), nor did he pause very long to consider the dangers he imagined he would face if he continued to insist on these doctrines (particularly during the time of the Rump Parliament).[119] In *Behemoth* he asks, "Why may not men be taught their duty, that is, the science of just and unjust, as divers other sciences have been taught, from true principles and evident demonstration; and much more easily than any of those preachers and democratical gentlemen could teach rebellion and treason?"[120] Hobbes placed most of his faith in the prospects for more extensive moral and political education with the youth. In part this is because they enter the universities, Hobbes assumes, "void of prejudice, and [their] minds are yet as white paper."[121] They in turn will teach the "vulgar," as "the instruction of the people, dependeth wholly, on the right teaching of youth."[122] The young, Hobbes believes, will cherish and happily profess those doctrines that are clearly and methodically revealed to them. These principles will be accepted as truth in large part, Hobbes avers, owing to his method, but also because his doctrines will speak to their own experiences and understanding, and they will reflect the empirical "nature of things."[123] In all of this Hobbes's political theory envisions the reformation of a political culture through education in his science of virtue and vice.

This education, like his articulation of the moral virtues contained within the natural laws, concerns the inner life of the citizen. When we ask what exactly citizens are to be taught, we find, by considering the very language Hobbes uses, that it is an education of the heart rather than a

---

Theory, 74–90. See also Baumgold, *Hobbes's Political Theory* (Cambridge: Cambridge University Press, 1988).

119. See *Behemoth*, Dialogue 1, p. 39, where "B" asks, "But who can teach what none have learned? Or, if any man have been so singular, as to have studied the science of justice and equity; how can he teach it safely, when it is against the interest of those that are in possession of the power to hurt him?"

120. Ibid. See also *Leviathan*, chapter 30, where Hobbes asks pointedly whether the principles that he wants to have the common people trained in are more difficult to understand than the "great mysteries of the Christian religion, which are above reason, and millions of men be made to believe." He ends this line of questioning by asking, in typically self-confident manner, whether "any unprejudicated man, needs no more to learn it, than to hear it?" (p. 249).

121. *EL*, 2.28.8.

122. *Leviathan*, chapter 30, p. 253.

123. *De cive*, 13.9.

strict education in the codes, rules, and laws of public duties. In presenting his ideas on education, the language of desire and love, jealousy, covetousness, and fidelity abound. To see this we have to recognize that the framework for Hobbes's discussion of education in *Leviathan* is patterned after the Ten Commandments. And if the God of the Old Testament is a jealous God, so too is Hobbes's mortal God. For one of the first things the people are to be taught is "that they ought not to be in love with any form of government they see in their neighbour nations, more than with their own."[124] Indeed, love must transcend and render immaterial the question of regime type. The particular form of government is not in the last instance the ingredient that is instrumental in securing peace and concord among a diverse population, but the public's obedience, reverence, and love for their particular commonwealth. Hence, whether the people's covetousness issues from idealism, avarice, or a kind of political idolatry, the very desire for change is a breach of that love they are to have toward their sovereign. For this love to be mutual between sovereign and subject, the people must also be taught not to admire or honor any "popular men" more than is due their one true betrothed: "For that sovereign cannot be imagined to love his people as he ought, that is not jealous of them, but suffers them by the flattery of popular men, to be seduced from their loyalty."[125]

Hobbes's thoughts on civic education are one part reasoned justification of law and one part public romance; there are dry prescriptions for the training of subjects in their due obedience, and there are evocative appeals to the heart. Indeed, the very opportunity for so great an undertaking must come from men who have "become at last weary of irregular jostling, and hewing one another, and desire with all their hearts," to enter into these lasting bonds.[126] Of course, this education has its fair share of prosaic features, like instructing the people not to dispute the power of the sovereign, to abstain from doing injury to others, and so on. But Hobbes does not consider this education adequate if it is left as a set of simple prescriptions, drawn from scripture, relating to just or unjust acts. To ensure that the people across the generations learn their duties

---

124. *Leviathan*, chapter 30, p. 249. During the time in which Hobbes was writing, this meant the Dutch example. But he was equally concerned about the influence that the histories of the ancient Greeks and Romans were having on "young men" who "imagine their great prosperity, not to have proceeded from the emulation of particular men, but from the virtue of their popular form of government" (chapter 29, p. 241).

125. Ibid., chapter 30, 250.

126. Ibid., chapter 29, 237.

as expressed in the positive laws, Hobbes envisions a kind of political Sabbath day on which the congregants will have the laws read to them. Yet this education must go further, or rather deeper than this. For it is not the mere absence of unjust acts that this education hopes to produce, but the organization of man's affections and loyalties so that he may, in conforming with his duties, do so "sincerely from the heart."[127] Thus "the sum of the second table" of Hobbes's Civic Decalogue "is reduced to this one commandment of mutual charity, thou shalt love thy neighbor as thyself."[128]

Hobbes's moral and political education works to create the conditions necessary for the establishment of reciprocal love and fidelity, those qualities that mutual promises and covenants require but do not originate on their own. This leads to the curious idea that Hobbes's explicitly non-feudal understanding of political society had in some measure to seek recourse in the types of affective bonds that characterized the feudal world in order to bestow meaning on these artificial ties. As he argued in *De cive*, "Civil societies are not mere meetings, but bonds, to the making whereof faith and compacts are necessary."[129] If faith, trust, and love are necessary for the purposes of forging salient and lasting forms of political association, and we deny that these features either come naturally or are bestowed upon modernity by its progenitors, then a rather significant burden of responsibility falls upon the political theorist (and the contract theorist in particular) to account for these features in other ways. Hobbes's theory of public reason, which is essentially an account of education and the cultivation of moral virtue, is designed to meet this burden.

Thus I mean to insist on more than the simple idea that Hobbes thought it prudent to instruct the masses in their political duties.[130] Hobbes presents us with a project of civic-ethical transformation/habituation. That is, Hobbes's moral and political science should be understood as an attempt

---

127. Ibid., chapter 30, p. 252.
128. Ibid. See Hobbes's related discussion of the Ten Commandments in chapter 42, p. 377.
129. *De cive*, 1.2n*.
130. It should be added that Hobbes did not think that education alone was enough to secure the safety of the people and the long-term stability of political power. Hobbes was also concerned with the primary material conditions of the people, and so understood the role of economics and poverty in creating conditions ripe for rebellion or revolution. Thus he advised that the laws of the commonwealth be applied equally across all divisions of class, that the burden of taxation be administered equally according to what men consume, and that the sovereign not depend on the charity of "private persons" to provide for those who "by accident inevitable" cannot maintain themselves. Rather the sovereign should assist those in need through "public charity." See *Leviathan*, chapter 30, pp. 253–57.

to frame or fashion human character and the will, to change or instruct human endeavor through education in the natural laws (the moral virtues) in ways consistent with justice and political order. This can be described as the attempt to turn those "small beginnings of motion," which he calls endeavor, from physical, appetitive dispositions into manners (morals) that will sustain the commonwealth. As Hobbes made clear in *De homine*, "Dispositions, when they are so strengthened by habit that they beget their actions with ease and with reason unresisting, are called *manners*. Moreover, manners, if they be good, are called *virtues*, if evil, *vices*."[131] Hence this vocal critic of "Aristotelity" provides an understanding of virtue that holds resonant continuities with one side of Aristotelian moral philosophy; that is, moral virtues are established through habituated practices that reflect the specific principles that support a regime.[132]

Hobbes's political philosophy not only entails the project of transplanting man's body from the state of nature to a life in society, it also requires a transformation of his interior dispositions, will, and endeavor. As he argued, rather late in life, in *De homine*, "good dispositions are those which are suitable for entering into civil society; and good manners (that is, moral virtues) are those whereby what was entered upon can be best preserved."[133] In this way we can see that Hobbes acknowledges and applies himself to the immense moral and cultural work that must accompany a theory that holds that men are only made "fit" for society by education. As we shall see in subsequent chapters, this is a perspective that is also shared by Locke and Rousseau. When we pay attention to the moral-educational writings of contract theorists it becomes increasingly clear that one of the most important and "hazardous" steps in the course of their accounts is not from a state of nature to civil society but rather the passage from youth to adulthood and citizenship.[134] Indeed, the moral and civic transformations that are thought to transpire by virtue of the simple passage from a state of nature to a political state are belied by

131. *De homine*, 13.8.
132. Aristotle, *Politics*, 1276b15–1278b5.
133. *De homine*, 13.9.
134. See in this regard Locke, *Some Thoughts Concerning Education and Of the Conduct of the Understanding*, ed. Ruth W. Grant and Nathan Tarcov (Indianapolis: Hackett Publishing, 1996), §94. In Rousseau, this same passage is called a "crisis"; see *Émile, or on Education*, trans. Allan Bloom (New York: Basic Books, 1979), 416. Both texts will be discussed at length in subsequent chapters.

the attention they give to the cultivation of morals and manners. What the Greeks called *paideia,* the moderns call good breeding. In many respects, however, the object for the social contract theorists is the same: the formation of those citizens their theories of political order require but who are neither found in nature nor accrue through the accidents of history. Thus, alongside Hobbes's justly famous pessimism about the dangers to civil society that would likely arise from the recognition of full religious liberties and associational freedoms—those elements of his thought that keep him on the margins of the liberal tradition—we should also keep in mind Hobbes's less frequently appreciated optimism in the ability of public reason to fashion a substantive ideal of common citizenship out of anarchic pluralism.

The Social Contract and the Just Person

And when faith and works are separated, not only the faith is called dead, without works, but also works are called dead works, without faith.
—Hobbes, *Elements of Law*

Up to this point we have sought to establish the importance of certain virtues or states of character to Hobbes's political theory, but we have not yet disclosed their importance beyond the meaning they might have for consolidating a regime and forging obedient subjects. To what extent does Hobbes's political vision depend upon these moral virtues? Hobbes wants good (i.e., obedient) citizen-subjects, but does he also want, and intend to create, good (virtuous) persons? In what follows I will argue that Hobbes clearly wants to fashion loyal citizens, but he also wants to frame the will in accordance with justice and moral virtue. By this he means more than someone who will merely honor his contracts, for Hobbes considers it possible for someone to keep his promise and still be unjust. Hobbes has a more extensive understanding of justice than is fully captured in his strict definition of justice as the keeping of covenants, and this has important consequences for how we evaluate his moral and political theory. In short, the idea of order in Hobbes's theory is not exclusively legal or political, but also moral.

One of the ongoing difficulties in the study of Hobbes is the question of the fundamental sources for his theory of moral and political obligation. Critics of Hobbes frequently approach his writings with the view that to truly understand his theory we need to discern how and why obligations bind in the way that he claims.[135] In this search scholars have latched on to a host of legal, philosophical, and epistemological rudiments as a way to explain the function and force of obligation in Hobbes's theory. Many of these efforts, while informative, betray a desire to give Hobbes a monological voice and a philosophical consistency that he frankly does not have and that may not have been available to him at the time. There are prudential, moral, legal, theological, and even logical grounds (of noncontradiction) by which to view the basis of obligation in Hobbes's thought. Indeed, it is possible, at various points in Hobbes's writings, to find support for each of these positions. This fact alone has caused no small degree of consternation on the part of those readers who are anxious to sustain Hobbes's self-made image as a systematic philosopher. Hence, when confronted with contradictory features of his argument, critics seem to be left with a small number of interpretive moves. One can try to highlight certain dimensions of his thought at the expense of others, reinterpret the troubling aspects of the text in light of the interpreter's favored reading strategy, or split the differences and posit an esoteric/exoteric distinction in the content of Hobbes's account of obligation.[136]

As I have tried to show, a more fruitful way to approach the question of moral and political obligation in Hobbes is to read him as a theorist of virtue. In doing so the question that Hobbes confronts emerges not as a philosophical or epistemological one, concerning what can authoritatively ground moral and political obligations, but rather as a question concerning what must be done to make practical (or real) the belief that such obligations exist and are necessary for the civil (public) and moral (private) life of persons. The question, then, is how to instill justice, as a characterological fact or virtue within an extensive and diverse audience, not how to ground it as a matter of philosophy. In keeping with our

---

135. Or, in Kavka's case, the question is how to take Hobbes's account, as he understands it, and modify it for the purposes of forging an improved, more fully consistent Hobbesian theory of obligation. Gregory S. Kavka, *Hobbesian Moral and Political Theory* (Princeton: Princeton University Press, 1986).

136. The latter interpretive move is suggested by Oakeshott (see his introduction to *Leviathan*), among others. While such a reading has the virtue of acknowledging irreconcilable differences within Hobbes's account of moral and political obligation, it makes the mistake, in my view, of using the distinction Hobbes clearly makes between the mass of men and the few of "generous natures" to stabilize alternative accounts or sources of moral and civic duty. To read Hobbes this way is to all but rule out the possibility that he was concerned with a moral, educative project to make men just, not simply obedient. Thus, an esoteric/exoteric distinction may be descriptively useful, but it is normatively too restrictive.

concern about the constructive role that promising and compact play in the formation of civic identities, the covenant in Hobbes does not solve the problem of obligation, but it does point to the moral and political resources that must be created for a just polity to endure.

A position frequently attributed to Hobbes is the idea that human beings will conform to the laws of the state and abide by their agreements, in the last instance, by virtue of the power and threat of force marshaled by the sovereign. Hobbes gives us good reason to attribute this position to him. Yet he also argued, in several places, that those who follow the law and abide by their agreements from the fear of the consequences in failing to do so are "properly said to be unjust."[137] How can a subject who follows the law and keeps his promises still be "properly" considered unjust, and this by a thinker who is commonly taken (again for good reasons) as a legal/ethical positivist? Our answer to this question will not take the form of declaring Hobbes's "considered" or "true" opinion. Assertions like these are frequently as pretentious as they are erroneous and one-sided. Rather, I suggest that, as with his contending accounts of obligation, there are certain positions that probably cannot and should not be reconciled. But an examination of Hobbes's concern with the interior, with conscience, and with endeavor will allow us to confront important dimensions of his political theory.

What does it mean to say that Hobbes is concerned with justice as a question of human manners or character? By manners Hobbes means "those qualities of mankind, that concern their living together in peace, and unity."[138] For Hobbes there are certain features of the self as a social being, not by nature but by reason of the human passions and fears that drive people together, that can influence the overall felicity or difficulty of life in association with others. Hobbes famously took men's general inclinations and restless desires to place them at odds with one another, so that in the very chapter of *Leviathan* that introduces the idea that there are certain qualities of character that relate to the prospects of peace and unity, he goes on instead to list the numerous dispositions of men that render the possibility of a secure and contented life well nigh impossible without coercive state power.[139] If Hobbes's austere portrait of human

---

137. *De cive*, 3.5. See also, from the Latin variant of *Leviathan* (1688), chapter 15, where Hobbes argues that "an unjust man is one who neglects justice, even if, from fear or some other unworthy [*sinistra*] cause, he has never done any injury to anyone." *Leviathan*, ed. Edwin Curley (Indianapolis: Hackett Publishing, 1994), pp. 93–94.

138. *Leviathan*, chapter 11, p. 80.

139. Ibid.

psychology and the passions leads him to the conclusion that "men have no pleasure, but on the contrary a great deal of grief, in keeping company, where there is no power to over-awe them all,"[140] he does not for this reason reject the opinion that there are qualities, dispositions, or virtues that can bestow something noble upon human character and something just upon human association. When justice is understood as a virtue, and not identified solely with the narrow definition of keeping covenants or giving to each his own, justice concerns the inner qualities of character, or manner of life.

> These words, *just* and *unjust*, as also *justice* and *injustice*, are equivocal; for they signify one thing when they are attributed to persons, another when to actions. When they are attributed to actions, *just* signifies as much as what is done with right, and *unjust*, as what is done with injury. He who hath done some just thing, is not therefore said to be a *just* person, but *guiltless*; and he that hath done some unjust thing, we do not therefore say he is an *unjust*, but *guilty* man. But when the words are applied to persons, *to be just* signifies as much as to be delighted in just dealing, to study how to do righteousness, or to endeavour in all things to do that which is just; and *to be unjust* is to neglect righteous dealing, or to think it is to be measured not according to my contract, but some present benefit. So as the justice or injustice of the mind, the intention, or the man, is one thing, that of an action or omission another; and innumerable actions of a just man may be unjust, and of an unjust man, just. But that man is to be accounted just, who doth just things because the law commands it, unjust things only by reason of his infirmity; and he is properly said to be unjust, who doth righteousness for fear of the punishment annexed unto the law, and unrighteousness by reason of the iniquity in his mind.[141]

The distinction between just persons and just actions reveals once again Hobbes's abiding concern with the moral interior of the citizen. In

140. Ibid., chapter 13, p. 99.
141. *De cive*, 3.5. A similar passage, with some illuminating differences, can be found in *Leviathan*, chapter 15, p. 116. The only thing I will note here about the difference between these passages is that in *Leviathan* Hobbes tells us that the words *righteous* and *unrighteous* are equivalent to *just* and *unjust*.

making a distinction between justice as a dimension of human action and justice as a feature of human being, Hobbes signifies that justice is not only a category that pertains to legally enforceable behavior (the keeping of covenants) but also refers to a deeper strata of human character. "Where justice is called a virtue," Hobbes tells us, it means more than an outward conformity to law (civil or natural); it means that one endeavors, as a consistent feature of one's character (or "manner of life") to be just in one's relations with others. Virtue for Hobbes is a characteristic and habit of being, not reducible to or identifiable by actions alone. In making a distinction between the justice of actions and the justice of men, Hobbes recognizes that the relationship between action and character is often contingent, marked by misfires, mistakes, and, one supposes, luck—both good and bad. Thus in a single passage that mixes Hobbes's own disposition for charity and moral sternness he asserts that "a righteous man does not lose that title by one or a few unjust actions that proceed from sudden passion or mistake of things or persons; nor does an unrighteous man lose his character for such actions as he does or forbears to do for fear, because his will is not framed by the justice, but by the apparent benefit of what he is to do."[142] Neither fear nor self-interest, the most common elements stressed by readers of Hobbes for centuries, are sufficient sources for understanding what it means to have a will "framed by justice." And neither just nor unjust actions are sufficient signs for understanding the character or state of mind of one's fellow citizens.

In all of this, two errors in particular must be avoided. The first is to consider a guiltless man a just man and so confuse justice with the absence of injury. To do so is to depreciate both the value and the requirements Hobbes afforded the concept of justice. The second mistake is to count a man unjust on the basis of his actions. To do so is to risk condemning a righteous man on the basis of all too human frailties, passions, and errors.

The virtues, then, name the interior dimensions of personhood that,

142. *Leviathan*, chapter 15. See also *EL*, 2.25.10. In reference to the claim that the "righteous" person does not lose his character by one or a few unjust acts, Hobbes is not merely being charitable here. In the background is a further and I think significant insight for his time (and ours): that the individual conscience can err. What some people will claim as an act of conscience can be, for others, hideous monstrosities, and there is no reason to suppose that the assertion of conscience need bring critical judgment and public reasoning to a full stop. This is all the more worth recalling today insofar as Kant-inspired liberalism identifies the dictates of individual reason and conscience as an automatic conferral of dignity to the individual. There is no necessary reason to accept or assume this, and Hobbes certainly did not.

under the right conditions, enable the individual to get along well with diverse others.[143] Virtue so understood is not something directed to the natural, objective good of the individual, for of course Hobbes famously eschewed this Aristotelean/scholastic idea. Rather, as Hobbes makes clear, the end of virtue is peaceable, sociable, and comfortable living. These are qualities that both individuals and a political society must, as Hobbes makes plain, "taketh care" to bring about. As we have already seen, an easy way to comprehend the full meaning of what he means by this understanding of justice as a virtue is "reduced all to this one commandment of mutual charity: *Thou shalt love thy neighbor as thyself.*"

One of the more striking features of Hobbes's description of the unjust man is that this figure resembles the very subject that his political theory is frequently thought to produce. That is, the unjust man, according to Hobbes, is someone who performs just actions or abstains from unjust actions by virtue of the fear of punishment that is entailed by the law. Of course, fear is also the elementary form of human motivation that is so central to his theoretical account of political society. Nowhere does this seem clearer than in Hobbes's discussion of crime, in which he asserts that "of all passions, that which inclineth men least to break the laws, is fear. Nay, excepting some generous natures, it is the only thing, when there is appearance of profit or pleasure in breaking the laws, that makes them keep them."[144] And in the more moderate cases where men perform certain actions in conformity with the laws and do so because of the profit they think they will thereby receive, they can be called nothing more than guiltless.

We are forced then to ask how important the distinction between the just man and just actions is to Hobbes's political theory. What consequences, if any, does it hold for the way we understand his particular version of the social contract? The first thing we should acknowledge is that there does not seem to be any sense in Hobbes's theory that there

143. In this respect I agree with Peter Berkowitz about the significance of virtue in Hobbes's political theory, but I also want to indicate why we should go beyond the idea that "fear is the foundation of moral virtue" in Hobbes's account. See Berkowitz, *Virtue and the Making of Modern Liberalism* (Princeton: Princeton University Press, 1999), 53.

144. *Leviathan,* chapter 27, p. 221. There is yet another striking parallel to Aristotle in this passage. Both Hobbes and Aristotle recognize as worthy of particular distinction those "generous" beings who follow justice and moral principles without reference to the dictates and punishments of the laws. Further, they both recognize that their political arguments could not depend on these noble spirits. See *Nicomachean Ethics,* 10.9.1179b. For more detailed treatment of the relationship between Hobbes and Aristotle, see Thomas A. Spragens Jr., *The Politics of Motion: The World of Thomas Hobbes* (London: Croom Helm, 1973).

is an obligation to be a just person, whereas it is clear that there is an obligation to be guiltless—although, as we have noted, the sources of this obligation have been subject to notorious debate. The absence of any obligation to be just as a matter of character has frequently been taken as evidence that there is no salient distinction here, or it is one that in the end can be subsumed under any other (again highly variable) set of duties.[145] To deny any lasting significance to Hobbes's distinction on these grounds is a mistake. In the first instance, it makes very little sense to talk of obligations in relation to human conscience or disposition. Indeed, that there is no obligation to be just in Hobbes is fully consistent with his view that laws and commands can have no influence over human conscience. The coercion of laws is inconsistent with the meaning of the inner life or quality of the individual. In a rather dramatic example of this principle, Hobbes argued that even in cases of divine positive law, the only grounds upon which one can be bound to observe them is if one has undertaken to obey these laws. Hence Moses had no special status in relation to those at Mount Sinai who had no sure knowledge of the truth of his revelations.[146] Hobbes famously held that there can be no obligation on a subject if it does not come from his own actions.[147] Yet even here a subject is bound only to obey, but not to believe, "for men's belief, and interior cogitations, are not subject to commands, but only to the operation of God."[148]

Hobbes recognizes the limits and ultimate futility in trying to establish something like an obligation to be just. Such a position would amount to an effort to change human character or manners by fiat, to make men moral by dint of laws. In fact Hobbes points directly to the errors of those regimes that try to craft laws that will directly and imperiously govern human conscience. In doing so two things can happen: "men are either punished for answering the truth of their thoughts, or constrained to answer an untruth for fear of punishment."[149] Hobbes understands that the laws can govern only actions. Yet, as I have also sought to show, he nonetheless wants to speak to and influence human conscience and the moral interior. Internal faith and conscience are opaque and private for Hobbes, but they are not for this reason fixed or ineducable. Indeed,

---

145. See, for example, Howard Warrender, *The Political Philosophy of Hobbes* (Oxford: Clarendon Press, 1957), and Oakeshott's introduction to *Leviathan*.

146. See *Leviathan*, chapter 26, pp. 212–13.

147. Ibid., chapter 21, p. 164.

148. Ibid., chapter 26, p. 213; cf. Thomas Aquinas, *Summa Theologica*, 1a, 2ae, 100.9.

149. *Leviathan*, chapter 46, p. 491.

because conscience for Hobbes is the same as private judgment and private opinion, it can be in error. He wants to speak to this voice in human subjects not as a legislator but as a theorist of public reason and moral virtue. While there is no specifiable obligation to be a just person (for the reasons we have given), there is a consistent concern in Hobbes's political theory to create the conditions in which political society may generate just persons and not merely guiltless subjects.

In all of this Hobbes reveals some of the challenges that later, more fully liberal accounts of political society will have with the language of virtue. Hobbes acknowledges that a society made up of persons who abide by their commitments from immediate prudential calculations and/or fear is a society without just persons, although they may well be guiltless. Where the virtue of justice is absent, that is, where justice is not part of the interior complex of motivational dispositions in persons, society is going to be badly ordered and unstable. This is because Hobbes appreciates both the ease of breaking laws and the facility with which individuals (often lacking foresight) can rationalize their own violations. Hobbes considers both of these features of human nature in his famous "discussion" of the "fool": "The fool hath said in his heart, there is no such thing as justice; and sometimes also with his tongue; seriously alleging that every man's conservation, and contentment, being committed to his own care, there could be no reason, why every man might not do what he thought conduced thereunto: and therefore also to make, or not make; keep, or not keep covenants, was not against reason, when it conduced to one's benefit."[150]

What is most damaging about the place of the "fool" in society (or the attitudes of the fool within individual persons) is not just that he believes he may break his covenants when it conduces to his benefit, and so believes that he may lie to or deceive others when it suits his interests. With these criteria in mind we could only say that the fool does not have an "effective sense of justice," that is, a desire to abide by fair terms of cooperation (Rawls). More fundamentally, the fool has "said in his heart that: 'there is no such thing as justice.'" The problem, then, is not merely the fool's shortsightedness about what is necessary to his preservation (and by extension what is necessary to society's preservation, if he or his kind are received or retained among them), but that the fool has skeptically foreclosed the source of a deeper and more reliable (if still

150. Ibid., chapter 15, p. 114.

imperfect) conduit for justice: "the heart," or the interior sources and dispositions of virtue. To be sure, a "fool" who will respond only to appeals to self-interest or threats of force is not the worst thing that we can imagine—far worse is a political society that permits their number to grow by appealing only to people's self-interest or manipulating their fears.

Conclusion

It seems clear enough that enumerating the domains of law and right are primary for Hobbes, given his account of human nature and the concern for social peace in his thought. Yet there is little room to doubt that, left at this, much that is consequential for the long-term stability of a regime is left undone. To disclaim or forbear the transformative, cultivational possibilities of institutions and public culture (properly designed) would be a failure of political foresight, and one that would inevitably weaken and "tend to the dissolution of a commonwealth." We risk losing sight of this today by virtue of a fairly recent desire to conceive of liberal institutions as neutral toward pluralistic conceptions of the good. Hobbes recognized something that most of his contemporaries struggled with: there can be no strict or seamless uniformity of belief without the vain and illegitimate use of coercion. Yet Hobbes also recognized something that today's liberals still struggle with: political institutions and policies cannot remain neutral in relation to the need for faithful citizens.

Hobbes wants his readers to see that conscience and behavior, *in foro interno* and *in foro externo* obligations, are more likely to be at odds in a state of nature than in a life that is shared within the constraints of civil society. Now, to have shown this, or at least to have made a persuasive case for it, is surely not sufficient as a normative account of political society, even though it reveals Hobbes as one of modernity's first thinkers to have raised the general social-psychological dilemma of "civilization and its discontents." More important, by acknowledging that "there is scarce a commonwealth in the world whose beginnings can in conscience be justified," Hobbes initiated a form of contract thinking that did not simply presuppose a free, rational, and voluntarist will as the foundation of a legitimate regime (as per Kant), but presented a theory of compact, culture, and citizenship that registered the challenges and limits of fashioning a political society that could square with diverse, opaque, and free consciences. In this regard I have argued that public reason is clearly a doctrine of right (*ius*) in Hobbes's theory, an external constraint imposed by law as a condition for peace and stability. Yet public reason in Hobbes is also a doctrine of virtue, one that seeks to bring inner dispositions and manners under the influence of moral qualities as a further and more enduring condition for justice and mutual felicity. I have sought to sustain the essential and proper tension between conscience and commonwealth in Hobbes's thought, while simultaneously pressing the view that the most complete rendering of his moral and political theory is one that accords a central place to the idea that contract makes citizens, never simply the other way around. In contemporary terms this is to say that political justification always entails ethical and political transformation. Thus the proper question for moral and political theory is how best to conceptualize and undertake this complex task. In the next two chapters we turn to John Locke's "arts of government" with this same question in mind.

T W O

COMPACT BEFORE LIBERAL CONSTRUCTIVISM:
THE DIVINE POLITICS OF JOHN LOCKE

The taking away of God, tho but even in thought, dissolves all.
—Locke, *A Letter Concerning Toleration*

Late in his life John Locke offered the following distinction for those who might follow his approach to the study and practice of politics: "Politics contains two parts very different the one from the other. The one containing the original of societies, and the rise of and extent of political power, the other the art of governing men in society."[1] I propose to treat these two parts of politics, and these two dimensions of Locke's moral and political thought, in succession over the next two chapters. In this chapter I focus on the role of promising and consent in Locke's treatment of the "original" of political society and civic membership. In Chapter 3 I discuss Locke's theory of the natural law and analyze his educational writings in light of his overall political thought. Taken together, Locke's thoughtful attention to the rise and extent of political power as well as

1. John Locke, "Some Thoughts Concerning Reading and Study for a Gentleman," in Locke, *Political Essays*, ed. Mark Goldie (New York: Cambridge University Press, 1997) (major and minor essays from the Bodleain and British libraries) (hereafter *PE*), 351. All references to Locke's works are to the following editions: *Essays on the Law of Nature*, ed. W. von Leyden (Oxford: Clarendon Press, 1954) (hereafter *ELN*); *The Educational Writings of John Locke*, ed. James L. Axtell (New York: Cambridge University Press, 1968); *A Letter Concerning Toleration*, ed. James Tully (Indianapolis: Hackett, 1983); *Some Thoughts Concerning Education and Of the Conduct of the Understanding*, ed. Ruth W. Grant and Nathan Tarcov (Indianapolis: Hackett Publishing, 1996); *The Reasonableness of Christianity*, ed. George Ewing (Washington, D.C.: Regnery Gateway, 1965); *Two Treatises of Government*, student edition, ed. Peter Laslett (New York: Cambridge University Press, 1988) (hereafter *First Treatise* and *Second Treatise*, followed by paragraph number); *An Essay Concerning Human Understanding*, ed. Alexander Campbell Fraser (New York: Dover Publications, 1959) (hereafter *ECHU*); *The Works of John Locke*, 10 vols. (London, 1801); *The Life of John Locke, with Extracts from His Correspondence, Journals and Common-place Books*, ed. Peter King, 2 vols. (Bristol: Thoemmes Press, 1830).

the art of governing men in society is evidence of his recognition of the interdependent relationship between political justification and civic cultivation, a Lockean application of the central idea of this book that contract makes citizens, never simply the other way around.

This chapter and the next are written in the conviction that if we take Locke's *Essay Concerning Human Understanding* and his writings on politics, education, and religion together, we can discern the elements of a coherent and persuasive account of public reason that may be usefully compared to Hobbes and to later theorists of the social contract tradition.[2] In contrast to the Hobbesian account that I presented in Chapter 1, private judgment and human will play a wider, actionable role in Locke's moral and political thinking. According to Locke, the individual must freely and expressly consent to political society to be understood as a full and active member of that society. Yet, in contrast to Hobbes, this means that the individual must come to see himself as a *perpetual public judge* in the political and legal affairs of his civil association. The reasons for this, as we will see, are contained in Locke's understanding of the nature, extent, and limits of political power, on the one hand, and in his more general account of the natural law and the ontological limits that circumscribe human power, autonomy, and reason, on the other. With the need for perpetual public judges in mind, one of the central challenges for Locke, as for so much of contemporary politics, is to cultivate and sustain faithful *and* critically minded citizens. We might think of this as the dilemma of trust in Locke's political theory: how is it possible to entrust political authority to a representative few without breeding the social and political

---

2. It should be noted that this claim and the approach to the history of ideas (and to Locke in particular) that is expressed here is not uncontroversial. Indeed, there are at least three controversial points here. First, that we can and should read the *Second Treatise* alongside Locke's other writings. This is explicitly rejected by Laslett in his famous introduction to the *Two Treatises*. Second, that in pursuing this reading strategy we will find more coherence in Locke's thinking than is otherwise acknowledged by scholars. This is a position frequently rejected by other Locke interpreters, especially those influenced by Strauss. And third, that Locke is relevant for a reappraisal of the history of political ideas that both precede and follow him—an idea that cuts against the grain of some "contextualist" historians who see little merit in asking how Locke might be able to speak to us today. I hope that this chapter and the following one will provide an adequate defense of my overall approach to Locke and the contract tradition as a whole. In relation to and in support of the first point, see Ian Harris, *The Mind of John Locke: A Study of Political Theory in Its Intellectual Setting* (New York: Cambridge University Press, 1994); in relation to the second point, see Ruth W. Grant, *John Locke's Liberalism* (Chicago: University of Chicago Press, 1987), and Alex Tuckness, "The Coherence of a Mind: John Locke and the Law of Nature," *Journal of the History of Philosophy* 37, no. 1 (1999): 73–90; and in relation to the third, see Peter C. Myers, *Our Only Star and Compass: Locke and the Struggle for Political Rationality* (Lanham, Md.: Rowman and Littlefield, 1998).

conditions in which credulity and self-destructive passivity take hold? Can trust and critical attentiveness be brought together in practice without undermining the meaning and the value that each has for the life and endurance of a polity?

To be sure, the difficulties for Locke do not end here. Since consent to political society and the rule of law is a form of self-expression and self-identification, the simultaneous need for wary, attentive citizens who will keep ultimate (and sovereign) guard over the use and abuse of political power means that there is also an ongoing need for critical inward self-examination in any Lockean, liberal polity. This is another way of saying that the duties of man and citizen in Locke's moral and political thinking combine in such a way as to require a significant transformative ethos whose purpose is to shape the qualities of citizenship and ethics upon which the Lockean social compact relies.

In making this argument I mean to insist upon two further propositions that I will defend over the course of the following chapters: Locke was deeply aware of the difficulties inherent in the ideal of government by consent, and he offered some important (if underappreciated) ideas about how to meet (if never entirely resolve) the philosophical and practical challenges that the ideal of government by consent creates for citizens and leaders alike. Public reasoning (and the related idea of public judging) is one of the crucial means by which Locke aims to empower and shape the civic identities upon which a consensual free society depends. In Locke's case, the idea of public reason entails the education of public judgment in accordance with a set of natural law guidelines, standards that take moral and political primacy in Locke's theory. This latter task, of setting "the mind right, that on all occasions it may be disposed to consent to nothing but what may be suitable to the dignity and excellency of a rational creature," places Locke's thinking in tension with some dimensions of the liberal tradition that he is often thought to have sponsored.[3] While it is no longer possible for a *public* philosophy of citizenship and authority to be grounded in a comprehensive theistic account of the natural law (a point that Rousseau will underscore in the eighteenth century and Rawls will expand upon in the twentieth), Locke nonetheless provides an account that reveals the depths and the ongoing significance of a transformative ethos within the heart of modern liberalism. In my view this Lockean transformative ethos must remain a central feature

---

3. Locke, *Some Thoughts Concerning Education*, §31.

of any form of liberal political thinking that is oriented toward sustaining a liberal society of freedom amid diversity; yet at the same time, the deeply theistic (and Protestant) features of his account must be reworked and pluralized for the politics of the present day.[4] Still, more is alive than dead in Locke's political theory (with apologies to Professor Dunn), if we read him simultaneously as a theorist of political foundations and a moral artist of self/collective governance.

Contract, Virtue/Politics, and Morals: From Hobbes to Locke

In the previous chapter I established the centrality of moral virtues in Hobbes's political theory and with it the role that education and the cultivation of habits play in making the performance of these virtues possible. The presence of these virtues, like fidelity to promises, trust, and gratitude, are fundamental not only for securing a peaceful, orderly regime but in providing for a political society in which it can be said that citizens are not merely guiltless with respect to the law but just with respect to each other. I have presented a "thick," substantive, moral dimension to Hobbes's theory where other scholars have only found a cold mechanistic play of forces and an overwhelming *logos* of coercion, fear, and obedience. I have done so by discerning in Hobbes the self-conscious attempt to fashion beings with the "right"—the capacity and power—to make and keep promises, something his theory of politics both required and denied to human actors.

Hobbes's education in the habits of moral character can be fruitfully

---

4. Hence, while I agree with Jeremy Waldron about the deep significance of Christian (Protestant) religion to Locke's moral and political thought—and therewith a sizable dimension of our own intellectual inheritance in the West—I do not agree that a principle like human equality requires "some religious foundation." Waldron, *God, Locke, and Equality: Christian Foundations in Locke's Political Thought* (Cambridge: Cambridge University Press, 2002), 13–14, 240–43. Waldron means this last suggestion as a tentative, probing line of questioning rather than a bald assertion of religious/philosophical foundationalism, or at least so I should like to think. Be that as it may, I take an alternative tack to thinking about freedom and equality under moral pluralism in Chapter 5 that departs from Waldron's view. Nonetheless, in relation to Locke (and in agreement with Waldron), I don't believe that Locke's theism necessarily compromises his relevance for contemporary audiences (as John Dunn sometimes suggests), nor do I think that Locke's Christianity is an esoteric doctrine intended to cover modern rationalism (as many Straussians are wont to argue). For Dunn, see "What Is Living and What Is Dead in the Political Theory of John Locke?" in Dunn, *Interpreting Political Responsibility: Essays, 1981–1989* (Princeton: Princeton University Press, 1990), 9–25. For an excellent exposition and vigorous defense of the Straussian approach to Locke, see Michael P. Zuckert, *Launching Liberalism: On Lockean Political Philosophy* (Lawrence: University Press of Kansas, 2002), esp. chapters 1 and 3.

read in relation to the ominous "preparatory task" to which Nietzsche referred in analyzing the work that man performs upon himself in giving himself the capacity to promise.[5] This is a moral labor, according to Nietzsche, that establishes responsibility and a conscience, but it is also a form of moral education that fits man within a "social straitjacket," rendering him uniform, regular, and calculable. The infamous frontispiece to *Leviathan* is a powerfully provocative image of just this kind of social straitjacket, in which the moral and social norms that constitute and stabilize a regime also breed docile bodies and compliant subjects. Nietzsche's analysis of the role of promising and fidelity bears a striking resemblance to the type of political arguments Albert O. Hirschman has uncovered in the seventeenth and eighteenth centuries that were made in support of the role of self-interest in human behavior.[6] It seems that promising can do for the moral life of individuals what interest was expected to do for the economic: make men's actions predictable and their motives transparent. From the perspective of those political thinkers concerned with order and the long-term stability of regimes, the "discovery" of moral practices and principles that might generate constancy, predictability, and transparency in the lives of citizens could only be received as a great blessing. At any rate, what we are in a position to see now (and to which we will return in a later discussion) is the way in which the moral and cultural components of Hobbes's political thought are implicated in the type of stultifying, dehumanizing practices with which Nietzsche is concerned in his genealogy of moral practices and norms.

Of course it is not only from a Nietzschean perspective that we might raise critical questions concerning the Hobbesian formation of "just men." We might also seek an alternative use of promising and contract in the guise of John Locke. If Hobbes's theoretical-political interest in framing the moral interior of political subjects through the public injunctions of an absolutist regime is enough to make any self-respecting liberal blanch, perhaps Locke gives us a way to integrate promising/contract and the need for political order and stability with more extensive provisions for the freedom and equality of persons.

Indeed, Locke seems to identify some of the inherent limits and dangers involved in a Hobbesian system of education and subject formation.

---

5. Nietzsche, *The Genealogy of Morals*, trans. Walter Kaufmann and R. J. Hollingdale (New York: Vintage Books, 1967), second essay, 1–2.

6. Albert O. Hirschman, *The Passions and the Interests: Political Arguments for Capitalism Before Its Triumph* (Princeton: Princeton University Press, 1977).

In this case, however, it is not a question of whether, in authorizing the sovereign as Hobbes's theory requires, citizens flee polecats and foxes only to give themselves over to lions.[7] Rather, Locke should be read as a figure who provides an alternative perspective with respect to the question of the formation of political subjects. Public reason and a transformative ethos are constitutive dimensions in both Hobbes's and Locke's political theory; the important differences between them reside in the purposes and scope of this ethos. For example, in a critique of the "heathen philosophers" of antiquity Locke argues that these philosophers had in fact struck upon certain moral virtues that are consistent with the law of nature and had illuminated features of the moral self that Locke also wants to endorse. Yet there were significant limits concerning what these philosophers could provide as a sure guide for an individual's life and manners. In commenting upon these deficiencies, Locke's critique could also be taken as a commentary on our reading of Hobbes: "So much virtue as was necessary to hold societies together and to contribute to the quiet of governments, the civil laws of commonwealths taught and forced upon men who lived under magistrates. But these laws being for the most part made by such who had no other aims but their own power, reached no farther than those things that would serve to tie men together in subjection, or at most were directly to conduce to the prosperity and temporal happiness of any people."[8]

From Locke's perspective, neither the heathen nor the Hobbesian formulation had gone far enough in its account of the moral virtues. Neither had established morality upon its true foundation or shown how it could be taken as normative and universally obligatory for all. Previous moral philosophers and civil lawyers might have found ways to bind subjects together in obedience (by instruction or force), but they did not provide a persuasive account for why they were bound to any particular set of principles or virtues in the first place. This critique tells us some important things about Locke, foremost among which is that he seeks motivationally efficacious moral obligations, not merely prudential obedience; he wants self-conscious moral agents, not a credulous, law-abiding

---

7. Locke argues, by way of his continuing attack on Filmer in the *Second Treatise*, that absolute monarchies are "no Form of Civil Government at all" (§90). Absolutism may constitute a form of rule, but these regimes do not belong among true political societies as Locke understands them. In these instances a state of nature persists between the ruler and the ruled, where, that is, the monarch judges in his own case and in relation to the rest of society.

8. *Reasonableness of Christianity*, §241.

herd. The ancient philosophers (by which he usually means Aristotle and Cicero) had "showed the beauty of virtue; they set her off so, as drew men's eyes and approbation to her; but leaving her unendowed, very few were willing to espouse her. The generality could not refuse her their esteem and commendation, but still turned their backs on her and forsook her, as a match not for their turn."[9] By contrast, that which makes virtue and the performance of moral principles possible for the many, and obligatory for all, is the knowledge that these attributes are compelled by a superior law and derived from a superior source. For morality to have any force among men driven by the hedonic pursuit of pleasure and pain, it must be given a juridical and providential character.[10] In this way the ancients' "airy commendations" of virtue will be supplanted by an organizing moral frame with power to motivate and restrain the actions of free agents, body and mind.

> Open their eyes upon the endless, unspeakable joys of another life, and their hearts will find something solid and powerful to move them. The view of heaven and hell will cast a slight upon the short pleasures and pains of this present state, and give attractions and encouragements to virtue, which reason and interest and the care of ourselves cannot but allow and prefer. Upon this foundation, and upon this only, morality stands firm and will defy all competition. This makes it more than a name—a substantial good, worth all our aims and endeavors.[11]

One of the very few places in which Locke refers directly to Hobbes (or, a "Hobbist") is found in the *Essay Concerning Human Understanding*. In this context the question at issue is, most crucially for our present purposes, what explains the normative obligations created by promises and compacts. Locke's sardonic but not entirely inaccurate reply is that if a "Hobbist" is asked why compacts should be kept he will answer, "Because the public requires it, and the Leviathan will punish you if you do not."[12] If "one of the old philosophers" had been asked this same question, Locke suggests that they would answer, "Because it was dishonest,

9. Ibid., §245.
10. See "Of Ethic in General," in *PE*, 304.
11. *Reasonableness of Christianity*, §245; see also "Of Ethic in General."
12. *ECHU*, 1.2.5.

below the dignity of a man, and opposite to virtue, the highest perfection of human nature, to do otherwise."[13]

Given our reading of Hobbes, we can see that Locke is not dealing altogether fairly with Hobbes's argument. Of course, Locke is referring here to the caricature of a "Hobbist" and not to Hobbes himself. Yet, as we have seen, without addressing the ways in which Hobbes was concerned with virtue, "true endeavor," and the moral life of the subject, it is impossible to understand why, in fact, the individual who keeps his promise and abides by the compact for the reasons that Locke attributes to a "Hobbist" would, according to Hobbes, be "properly said to be unjust."[14] Hobbes's concern with the inculcation of certain virtues also makes the ancient-modern distinction that Locke employs to distinguish the "Hobbist" from the "old philosophers" less clear cut. Nonetheless, Locke's use of it here is designed to show the inadequacy of the ways in which morals and politics had been conjoined in the past. By comparison, Locke wants to bring morals and politics into what he thinks will be a more firm and lasting partnership, one that will have a different "relish" and greater efficacy for men during their "probationership" in this life.

This is a different kind of Locke from the one who has been canonized as the father of modern liberalism.[15] To be sure, Locke held that governments could play no legitimate role in legislating or governing virtues.[16] In *A Letter Concerning Toleration* Locke supports this position by making a clear separation between the City of Man and the City of God: "the power of Civil Government relates only to Mens Civil Interests, is confined to the care of the things of this World, and hath nothing to do with the World to come."[17] Likewise, the mutual compacts by which men enter into society with one another are pacts of assistance "for the defence of Temporal Goods," and as such these agreements leave every individual to the personal care of his or her own salvation and eternal happiness.[18]

---

13. Ibid.

14. Hobbes, *De cive*, 3.5.

15. In this respect I heartily agree with Nathan Tarcov: "Finding nothing decent or inspiring in the interpretations of Locke that are offered to them, students of our political culture have gone off seeking 'non-Lockean' elements in our heritage. They should discover, instead, the 'non-Lockean' elements in Locke." *Locke's Education for Liberty* (Lanham, Md.: Lexington Books, 1999), 210.

16. "Yet give me leave to say, however strange it may seem, that the lawmaker hath nothing to do with moral virtues and vices, nor ought to enjoin the duties of the second table any otherwise than barely as they are subservient to the good and preservation of mankind under government." "An Essay on Toleration," in *PE*, 144.

17. *Letter Concerning Toleration*, 28.

18. Ibid., 47.

This, of course, is a central axiom of modern liberalism, one that acknowledges human independence and difference and strictly excludes the use of the coercive arms of the state (or the church for that matter) from enforcing particular religious beliefs or observances. In his extensive exchange with Jonas Proast, Locke articulates a view of the limits of coercive authority that can be readily identified with the idea of public reason. In these letters Locke is at pains to argue that political authority (and the coercive forces of the state) should not be used in the promotion of religion because the result is always the rule of a particular interpretation of faith. The concept of a civil duty to promote religion (which Proast relentlessly defended) could not pass a standard of public reasonableness, and so would harm, not benefit, religion and the state.[19]

Yet for all of this Locke was far from indifferent with respect to the moral character of citizens, nor was he indifferent or neutral with respect to the greatest good, as he understood it, for all individuals—something the critics and defenders of "Lockean liberalism" frequently ignore. Indeed, as Locke claimed, "True politics I look on as part of moral philosophy, which is nothing but the art of conducting men right in society and supporting a community amongst its neighbors."[20] I want to explore in what follows the ways in which Lockean politics flows from his understanding of morality and the "art of conducting men right in society." In doing so we can gain a deeper appreciation for the ways in which Lockean contract theory is neither Hobbesian nor proto-Kantian but something uniquely valuable and challenging in its own right.

There are two central features of Locke's moral and political thought that I will focus on here. The first comes by way of an analysis of the normativity of promises in his theory. This provides us with a window through which we can discern an even more significant feature of Locke's theory, and that is the fundamental limits he understands to exist at an ontological level for individual sovereignty. Despite the frequent attributions to Locke and Lockean liberalism to the contrary, the self is not sovereign over significant areas of its moral and political life. By

---

19. See *A Second Letter Concerning Toleration* and *A Third Letter Concerning Toleration*, in *Works of Locke*, 6:92, 97, and 6:143, 213, 503–5, respectively. One of the best treatments of Locke's theory of toleration is provided by Ingrid Creppell, "Locke on Toleration: The Transformation of Constraint," *Political Theory* 24, no. 2 (1996): 200–240. See also Jeremy Waldron's provocative essay, "Locke, Toleration, and the Rationality of Persecution," in his *Liberal Rights: Collected Papers, 1981–1991* (Cambridge: Cambridge University Press, 1993), 88–114.

20. "Draft Letter to the Countess of Peterborough," MS Locke c. 24, fols. 196–97, in *Educational Writings of Locke*, 395–96.

nonsovereignty I mean that the self does not have legitimate authority or rightful power over politically and morally salient features of individual and—by extension—collective existence. This central claim, that the individual self is not fully sovereign in Locke's political and moral theory, has important consequences for the ways in which we understand his influential ideas about consent, trust, and political obligation.

The second element that I will focus on (in Chapter 3) is the tension between individual self-governance, or the proper "management of assent," and Locke's prescriptive thoughts on education. The question in this regard is whether Locke's extensive ideas about education support the kind of subject he deems necessary for civil society. I will suggest that there are sufficient reasons to doubt this. Nonetheless, the tensions in Locke's treatment of these issues can teach us a lot about the depth and complexity of this form of contract theory and the entailments and risks within an education for citizenship. As we have seen with respect to Hobbes, and as we will see in relation to Locke, Rousseau, and contemporary proponents of public reason, the tensions between autonomy and moral cultivation, individual liberty and political commitment, follow from a social compact that must shape the beings who make it.

In what follows I argue that to understand Locke—at least more immediately than do those who appropriate his name and certain fragmentary features of his political writings for celebrating or assailing "Lockean liberalism"—we must first forgo the concept of individual sovereignty and the idea that freedom and morals are purely voluntaristic and self-determining. In their place we need to consider the different meaning that temporal-political life has for Locke when understood (in rather Augustinian terms) as a necessary feature of man's brief "pilgrimage" or "probationership." Under these headings I will highlight the meaning, purpose, and consequences for what I take to be one of Locke's central concerns: the proper management or governance of individual assent in moral and political life.[21] To appreciate Locke's contribution to an understanding of the interplay of contract, culture, and citizenship, we must keep Kantian notions of autonomous practical reason from anachronistically shaping our reception of Locke. In general terms I want to show that Locke is no less a contract thinker for never allowing human will or free choice to be an autonomous or complete standard for political right. Instead we need

---

21. For the language of managing and governing assent, see *ECHU*, 4.14, 16–17, 20; and *Conduct of the Understanding*, §33, among other places.

to reconsider what contract theory can mean in relation to a thinker who put the natural law (God's will) at the center of his moral and political thought, while recognizing the practical limits of this perspective among beings who are more passionate than rational, more habitual and credulous than calculating and autonomous. I go on to argue in Chapter 3 that one of most pressing concerns for Locke is not the unlawful usurpations of magistrates or the dissolution of government, although this is obviously a matter of real, historical import. Rather, Locke's theory is animated by a more primary and extensive concern with the moral and political credulity of the public. In these terms Locke's moral and political thought is addressed to a public he fears is ill prepared to judge and act in ways consistent with the natural law and the conditions of their public trust when required to do so. These concerns animate Locke's contributions to the idea of public reason and his education in virtues, two underappreciated features of Lockean contractarianism that I aim to explore in what follows.

The "Original" of Political Society: Promising, Fidelity, and Moral Capacity

It might seem, on the surface at least, that Locke has a more adequate or internally coherent account of the social contract than Hobbes. We might claim this for Locke in part because the problem of the normativity of promises is removed from his analysis of the "original" of political society from the very beginning. Whereas we found that Hobbes's contract theory required the surreptitious formation of subjects who could become capable of promising and fidelity, Locke's account seems to presuppose both the capacity and the virtues entailed in promising as somehow natural to man. As we shall see, however, Locke has in fact opened new questions for his readers by visibly removing this as a problem of moral and epistemological discourse.

In his discussion of the state of nature Locke asserts that "Truth and keeping of Faith belongs to Men, as Men, and not as Members of Society."[22] Of course, it is of immense help in affording a degree of viability to this proposition that Locke's account of the state of nature is not asocial or presociological, nor does it lack a binding law by which to govern

---

22. *Second Treatise*, §14.

human relations. The idea that promises or compacts are obligatory and will be treated as such by individuals who are not, in reference to one another, members of a common "Body Politick," with a "common established Law and Judicature to appeal to," seems at once to invest the individual with a moral center and reflect an extensive degree of latent trust in and between human beings.[23] This might also reflect a degree of optimism about the powers of human rationality and reasonableness that shares more in common with the neo-Thomism of Suárez than it does with Hobbes.[24]

If this is Locke's position, or at least one part of it, then it is not strictly true, as Hume would later charge, that Locke has not given us any reasons for thinking that promises and the obligations they create are or can be more fundamental or primary for establishing political society than general interest, advantage, and necessity. For Hume, building an account of political obligations from the foundation of a duty to keep promises is a basic philosophical confusion, because political allegiance cannot be explained or justified in reference to fidelity where both of these traits are understood as inherently artificial or conventional moral duties. Hence such a move is, from Hume's vantage point, morally and epistemologically unsound, unnecessary, and dangerous. The reasons that Locke gives on this point, at this stage, may not be fully persuasive. Yet what Locke seems to refer to here as a natural capacity and immanent virtue is something that Hume wants to label conventional and manmade.[25] Of course this does not get us very far, for the philosophical debate about the sources of normativity within acts of promising is ongoing.[26] John Dunn has also

---

23. It should be noted that this condition of mutual trust and sociability is extended across racial lines in Locke's account. The example he gives to support the idea that promises are binding and effective for persons outside political society is drawn from his extensive readings in the travel literature of the seventeenth century: "The Promises and Bargains for Truck, &c. between the two Men in the Desert Island, mentioned by *Garcilasso De la vega*, in his History of *Peru*, or between a *Swiss* and an *Indian*, in the Woods of *America*, are binding to them, though they are perfectly in a State of Nature in reference to one another." *Second Treatise*, §14; see also Laslett's note.

24. For a useful discussion that relates certain features of Locke's consent theory to the neo-Thomism of Jesuit and Dominican writers, see Skinner, *The Foundations of Modern Political Thought*, vol. 2 (Cambridge: Cambridge University Press, 1978), chapters 5 and 6.

25. Hume, *A Treatise of Human Nature*, ed. L. A. Selby-Bigge, 2d ed. (Oxford: Clarendon Press, 1978), 542–43.

26. For advocates of the idea that promising is a conventional practice that requires a prior context of procedures or rules, see T. H. Green, *Lectures on the Principles of Political Obligation*, ed. Paul Harris and John Morrow (Cambridge: Cambridge University Press, 1986); H. L. A. Hart, "Legal and Moral Obligation," in *Essays in Moral Philosophy*, ed. A. I. Melden (Seattle: University of Washington Press, 1958); and John Rawls, "Two Concepts of Rules," *Philosophical*

identified the centrality of this position for Locke's politics, but when he claims, on Locke's behalf, that promising and fidelity simply are more fundamental than self-interest or utility, he has not extended our understanding on this crucial point very far.[27] Hence we might simply allow that the position Locke has staked out here is a matter of principle and perhaps even a logically necessary starting point for his theory that is just as reasonable or probable as its opposite, and one that constitutes a central moral feature of a distinctly Lockean politics—that is, that promising and fidelity are both available to individuals as intrinsic human capacities, and the duties they impose are rational and moral. If all thinking entails the acceptance of at least some ideas and principles that must be assumed for thinking to even be made possible, perhaps this is one of Locke's necessary but necessarily ungrounded grounds for his political and moral thought, a basic feature of a Lockean language game.[28]

While this acknowledgment may express something irreducibly true about the limits of human knowledge, and moral knowledge in particular, it is a strange and unsatisfactory conclusion to reach in relation to a thinker who spent so much of his intellectual life asking what it is possible for us to know and with what degree of certainty, a thinker who was concerned to search out and mark the boundaries between opinion and knowledge, faith and reason. We need to ask, then, how and in what sense trust or faith (*fides*), the virtue of promising, "belongs" to men, "as men." Does this virtue belong to men as property belongs to men, that is, through an admixture of labor, perhaps moral or discursive labor? Or does it "belong" to them as a natural right? Perhaps this is better understood as a power or capacity that men have by virtue of reason and language, one that is acquired with age and discretion. It is through an understanding of this question, and with it the theoretical and moral work that the concept of promising performs in Locke's thought, that we can

---

Review 64, no. 1 (1955). By contrast there is Thomas Scanlon's argument that promises create natural moral requirements; see his "Promises and Practices," *Philosophy and Public Affairs* 19, no. 3 (1990). See also Mark Tunick's useful discussion of this literature in *Practices and Principles: Approaches to Ethical and Legal Judgment* (Princeton: Princeton University Press, 1998).

27. John Dunn, "Contractualism" and "Trust," in Dunn, *The History of Political Theory and Other Essays* (Cambridge: Cambridge University Press, 1996), chapters 3 and 5; and Dunn, *The Political Thought of John Locke* (Cambridge: Cambridge University Press, 1969), chapter 10.

28. On this point, see Wittgenstein, *On Certainty*, ed. G. E. M. Anscombe and G. H. von Wright (New York: Harper and Row, 1969), §56. But also see Locke on this point, where he acknowledges that for "most men" it is "natural" and "almost unavoidable, to take up with some borrowed principles." *ECHU*, 1.2.26 and 4.16.4.

venture to understand other features of Locke's moral, epistemological, and political thinking.

Any reader of Locke's *Essay* might suspect that there is something quietly deceptive going on in Locke's description of the moral capacities of man by nature in the *Second Treatise*. Locke's claim that promising and the virtue of fidelity "belong" to men *qua* men seems to be all but ruled out by his treatment of what it is possible to understand or say about human beings in general. Human beings are understood, in part, as substances in Locke's philosophy. According to Locke, substances cannot be understood with certainty because they will always be partial ideas or reflections of real, material things. This is the epistemological problem of the general and the particular: "man" is a general, abstract category that necessarily glosses over the universal particularity of all things that exist.[29] The essence of any substance, and thus the essence of man, is a purely linguistic construction. Species beingness, to borrow a Marxian phrase (borrowed from Hegel), is an abstract artifice of human contrivance. It is not for this reason, however, totally arbitrary, for all of our ideas are reflections upon experience. Yet there can be no real or true essence conferred upon any substance, because the mind of man cannot discern such a quality in itself. Hence no "real" essence, whether deemed trust or faith, fallen or redeemed, can be granted to man as such. The most that can be attributed to human beings is a nominal and quite provisional essence. That is to say, the "real" simply is the nominal. So if promising, fidelity, and trust are going to be attributed to men, they can only be established through *a posteriori* reasoning, from observation and generalization, not from *a priori* claims of immanent moral capacity or knowledge.

There is further complexity here on the level of language as well. Our moral ideas and words are what Locke calls "mixed modes." As such, these ideas "are not looked upon to be characteristical marks of any real beings that have a steady existence, but scattered and independent ideas put together by the mind."[30] Locke's nominalism allows for the possibility that our moral languages are as potentially numerous and diverse as there are minds who put these ideas together, and do so "without reference to any real archetypes, or standing patterns, existing anywhere."[31] The only

---

29. *ECHU*, 3.3. While it is impossible for me to go into all of the complex issues that Locke's ideas on substance and essence entail, see W. von Leyden's helpful essay, "What Is a Nominal Essence the Essence Of?" in *John Locke: Problems and Perspectives*, ed. John W. Yolton (Cambridge: Cambridge University Press, 1969).

30. *ECHU*, 2.22.1.

31. Ibid., 2.31.3.

constraint in this regard, and what makes moral discourse possible, is "common usage" and the requirements of common dialogue. Yet this is precisely why moral discourse is so liable to what J. L. Austin called "infelicities," and why Locke acknowledges that these types of "misfires" are errors at the level of speaking and language, rather than "knowing right."[32] It is upon this same ground, the perfectly arbitrary condition of moral terms and ideas, that Locke famously thought he could show that morality was capable of scientific demonstration.[33]

Hence what appears to be a prediscursive and preconventional attribution of an innate moral essence for the individual self regarding faith and promising in the *Second Treatise* can only be taken as a nominal or logical essence. It is for this reason that Locke seems compelled to cite additional "evidence" from history and human experience to justify the attribution of virtues like trust and fidelity to man, for it is only on the basis of experience that we can know anything, according to Locke.[34] Hence, following Locke's epistemology, the most that can be said on this point is that promising and fidelity belong to men as a possibility, or as something they have done and can do. He is more true to this conception of things in his journal entry for May 16, 1681, when he owns that "it is true, that it is every man's duty to be just, whether there be any such thing as a just man in the world or no."[35]

Thus the attribution of an inherent moral quality in man, while it might suggest a logical necessity for his argument and one that would certainly, if true, go a long way toward securing the coherence and viability of his theory of the social compact, cannot, by the standards of Locke's own epistemology, stand as a secure ground for moral and political obligations. This crucial passage of the *Second Treatise*, while flattering the moral capacities of his readers, and distinguishing his contractarianism from some of his predecessors', can do no philosophical work. This is the same type of problem that Hobbes confronts in *Leviathan*, for the natural law, to perform promises, despite its centrality to the account he develops, cannot function in a foundational role for his moral or political

---

32. Ibid., 2.31.4; see also 3.10. See J. L. Austin, *How to Do Things with Words* (Cambridge: Harvard University Press, 1962), 14.

33. *ECHU*, 3.11.15–17.

34. See note 23 above.

35. Journal, in *Life of Locke*, 1:226. Notice that Locke, in contrast to Hobbes, claims an outright duty to be just while doubting that a just being exists. Hobbes asserts no such duty but fervently believes that there are at least a few men of noble and generous nature who deserve to be called just rather than merely guiltless.

theory. Yet, as we have seen, Hobbes provides a transformative account of civic membership that can be understood as a reflection on the idea that the social contract makes citizens, never simply the other way around.

What this means in Locke's case is that promises and the commitments they are thought to originate do not earn their normative or obligatory status from the mere fact that the individual has voluntarily willed them as self-imposed duties. Numerous commentators on Locke have seen in his contributions a more adequate version of contract because the will is thought to be morally self-obliging and politically self-determining in his theory. In contrast to Hobbes, where the will is determined by the last appetite or desire in the self's mechanistic response to pleasure and pain, the individual in Locke's theory is thought to be in full control of its undertakings, its present and future. I will address the role of the will in Locke's moral theory more extensively as part of my discussion of the governance of individual assent. For now we should note that after initially being defined as a power of directing individual action that is determined by our greatest present "uneasiness" of desire, Locke goes on to claim that the will is fundamentally about the power to suspend and examine the nature and objects of our desires.[36] What is at issue here is whether the human will or reason plays a sovereign, legislating, foundational role in forging the terms of one's obligations through something like a compact or promise. The question is whether the human will is a morally causal agent in Locke's theory, one that might constitute a voluntaristic metaphysic of morals.[37] It is this attribution that Locke's theory does not allow. This means that promissory obligations, what Locke consistently referred to as the bonds of human society, cannot come from man *qua* man.

The obligation to keep promises, and hence the very thing that makes such an act meaningful at all, can only come from the antecedent, binding authority of God and God's will. This is a position that is confirmed in more than one place in Locke's writings. In his *Essays on the Law of*

---

36. *ECHU*, 2.21.29–36, 48–53.

37. See Patrick Riley, *Will and Political Legitimacy* (Cambridge: Harvard University Press, 1982), chapters 3 and 7. I hasten to add that Riley does not read Locke's voluntarism in isolation from the constraints imposed by the natural law, but rather seeks an equilibrium between consent, natural law, and natural rights. Yet, to the extent that Riley understands the thrust of the social contract tradition as one that generates a voluntaristic metaphysics of morals, in which the "human will can be understood as a kind of moral causality that makes intelligible such notions as promise" (200), I find compelling reasons to demur in relation to both Locke and the contract "tradition" more generally.

Nature he argues that without the faithful fulfillment of contracts, one of the necessary supports for human society would be removed. Locke goes on to claim that "it is not to be expected that a man would abide by a compact because he has promised it, when better terms are offered elsewhere, unless the *obligation* to keep promises was derived from *nature*, and not from *human will*."[38] In his later *Essay Concerning Human Understanding* he argues in much the same way by asserting that compacts are binding for the Christian, as opposed to the "Hobbist" or ancient philosopher, because "God, who has the power of eternal life and death, requires it of us."[39] This position is in keeping with Locke's general understanding that all laws and obligations are derived from the natural law. Civil laws and private laws, such as contract, do not bind of themselves but only insofar as they are consistent with a larger and more extensive natural law.[40]

What we can understand by Locke's idea of a moral capacity "belonging" to man is that God has formed certain laws and obligations that it would be useless and absurd to think that men did not at least have the ability to perform. Strictly speaking, however, nothing belongs to man as man, nothing, that is, except moral duties and the latent capacities or potential to fulfill those duties. What man has, what he is, and what he is capable of becoming owe themselves to the existence and beneficence of God.[41] What looks like human moral interiority and essence, sovereignty, and independence are in fact their opposites. This predicate condition for all of Locke's political and moral thinking is made clear in the following extract from 1693: "The original and foundation of all law is dependency. A dependent intelligent being is under the power and direction and dominion of him on whom he depends and must be for the ends appointed him by that superior being. If man were independent he could have no law but his own will, no end but himself. He would be a god to himself, and the satisfaction of his own will the sole measure and end of all his actions."[42]

---

38. *ELN*, 1, p. 119 (emphasis added).

39. *ECHU*, 1.2.5.

40. This is a position that shares something in common with John Selden's understanding of the natural law. See John Selden, *Table-Talk* (1689), ed. Edward Arber (London: Westminister A. Contstable and Co, 1895), 66. See Richard Tuck for a helpful discussion of how this and other positions led Selden to an illiberal absolutist doctrine. Tuck, *Natural Rights Theories: Their Origin and Development* (New York: Cambridge University Press, 1979), chapter 4.

41. *ELN*, 6, pp. 181–87.

42. "Law," in *PE*, 328–29.

When contract theory is treated as an unambiguous species of consent theory, it is read as a doctrine that purports to establish the normative ideal that the legitimacy of governmental institutions depends upon the wills of individual persons who encompass and constitute them. In turn, the obligations that restrict the free and autonomous actions of the individual are justified in relation to those same voluntary, self-imposing acts of the will. To argue in this way is to assume something important, although not necessarily true, about individual rationality, prospective judgment, and the self's relationship to the things that it wills. More to the point, our ideas concerning what consent theory is and presupposes has a very tenuous relationship to the theory found in Locke. Indeed, the idea of a self-assumed obligation whose normative status as an obligation is thought to follow from the fact that it is a voluntary, self-imposed undertaking is foreign to Locke's moral and political theory: the obligation to keep promises derives from nature (God), not the human will. In a related way, the proposition that a rights discourse grounded in a theory of will and freedom as self-making is likely to unravel into a fragmentary individualism of venal acquisitiveness, absent a moral (divine) center by which to anchor, bind, and limit such a will, would surely have struck Locke as a nonstarter. That Locke can be read this way, against the grain of philosophical voluntarism and liberal constructivism, is due ultimately to the conditions of individual nonsovereignty in his theory. To help show this, I will briefly situate Locke's theory of obligation in relation to the critique provided by Hume—a critique that, at least since Bentham, has been taken as definitive in the rejection of modern social contract theory.

Hume's Critique of Contract

Hume's attack on the "fashionable" theory of contract is both epistemological and political in scope. As noted above, Hume sets his sights on the right target by questioning the meaning and status of the normativity of promises in social contract theory. In doing so he claims that fidelity is not a natural virtue and that promises are human inventions designed to serve human interests. For Hume, "interest is the *first* obligation to the performance of promises."[43] Moral sentiments may surround cultural

43. Hume, *Treatise of Human Nature*, 3.5, p. 523.

practices of promising and contract, and these sentiments may help explain why individuals take these acts to be obligatory, but general utility,
interest, and necessity are the ultimate grounds for these practices and
the reason why they are binding for human actors. Hume is willing to
concede that the first "ancient rude combinations of mankind" took place
by an "original contract," and that such an establishment would proceed
with reference to the laws of nature, and in particular the law concerning the performance of promise.[44] Yet these ancient sources hold no continuing relevance for the legitimacy or obligations that exist for present
political societies, and the argument that promise or consent is necessary
for the ongoing legitimacy and salience of political ties is, if not simply
the absurd position of a delirious (or ideological) mind, then at least
seditious.[45]

Hume's critique raises useful questions about the role and meaning
of promising in political theory, but it is a critique that depends for its
force—one that grew in popularity over the years—on misconstruing
the nature and object of contract and promise in Locke. Hume's critique
also entails a more problematic secularization of Locke's thinking, a secularization that in many ways anticipated the dispirited, prosaic Locke
conjured by later critics of modern liberalism.

Yet Hume fundamentally misconstrues Locke's position by failing to
recognize the proper object of the social compact. The compact or promise is an act taken within and for a community, not a particular government, regime, or prince. It is precisely because Hume takes this compact
as a promise *to* government that he does not recognize the degree of
stability provided by Locke's theory. Indeed, as I will argue further in
Chapter 3, the real problem for the Lockean theory of entrustment is
not instability but the opposite: the production of docile and credulous
subjects.

Hume reads Lockean contract as the imposition of a conditional promise between the people and a ruler. That is, he misreads Locke as providing
a conditional governmental contract rather than an unconditional social
compact. For Locke, once a member has entered into an actual promise
or compact and has thereby given his consent to the commonweal, he is
"perpetually and indispensably obliged to be and remain unalterably a

---

44. Ibid., 3.8, p. 541. See also Hume's essays "Of the Original Contract" and "Of the Coali-
tion of Parties," in Hume, *Essays: Moral, Political, and Literary*, ed. Eugene F. Miller (Indianapolis: Liberty Fund, 1985).
45. This language can be found in Hume, "Of the Original Contract," 470.

subject to it, and can never be again in the liberty of the state of Nature."[46]
Of course, Locke is most concerned in the *Second Treatise* to shore up
the right to resist tyrannical government. In that sense, a breach of *trust*,
not contract, by a usurping state authority would render one's obligations
to that power void. It is crucial to see in this that Locke makes a distinction between civil society and government. The act of promising or compacting indispensably weds one to a political community, not to a political
authority as such. As Locke explains, "the power that every individual
gave the society, when he entered into it, can never revert to the individual again, so long as the society lasts, but will always remain in the
Community."[47] The contract is as much an expression of a desire for society as it is a source for sustaining human sociability, not—as both Hume
and later critics of Lockean liberalism have supposed—a mechanism that
presupposes and reifies individualism (acquisitive or otherwise). Also crucial in this regard (and also confused by Hume) is the object of allegiance
in Locke. Subjects take oaths of allegiance and promises of fealty to executive rulers, but "'tis not to him as Supream Legislator, but as *Supream
Executor* of the Law . . . *Allegiance* being nothing but an *Obedience
according to Law.*"[48] Hence if the executive or legislative violates the community's standing laws, or flouts the antecedent natural law, there is no
obligation to that person or persons because they can no longer represent the public will. Nonetheless political or civil society continues; the
public will continues.

These are crucial distinctions to make given the historical context in
which Locke is writing. During the English civil wars, at the Restoration,
and again in the Glorious Revolution, good church men of scrupulous
conscience feared the moral consequences of violating their prior oaths
of allegiance, such as those engaged in the Solemn League and Covenant
under Charles I and the oaths of loyalty to James II.[49] Yet the relation
between governors and the governed is not contractual for Locke. Indeed,
these relationships are not contractual for most of the major contract

---

46. *Second Treatise*, §121.
47. Ibid., §243.
48. Ibid., §151.
49. A central figure in this context is Robert Sanderson, who contributed several tracts on
the sanctity of oaths and provided powerful counterarguments to the "de factoism" of writers
like Anthony Ascham during the years of the Commonwealth government. See Sanderson, *A
Resolution of Conscience* (1649), and his earlier *De Juramenti promissorii obligatione* (1646).
For a useful discussion of this general historical context, see Margaret A. Judson, *From Tradition to Political Reality* (Hamden, Conn.: Archon Books, 1980).

theorists of the modern period.[50] A government that is conceived as a party to a contract would have certain rights or claims against the rest of a political society. This is precisely what Locke (and Rousseau) want to deny. As we saw with Hobbes, a government that is party to a contract also means that the sovereign power would have specified, contractual duties that the people could in turn invoke against political power. And so, for opposite reasons, Hobbes is also anxious to deny a conditional governmental contract between ruler and ruled. The absence of a governmental contract (or *pactum subjectionis*) in Locke makes legislative and/ or executive powers revocable, but it does not lead to the instability of political order or civil society, for that is inviolable given the locus of obligation and its proper object. Hence even God is bound by his promises.[51]

More fundamentally, the difference between Locke and Hume on this point is that Hume does not consider Locke's theism and the way in which his religious perspective informs his theory. Hume imagines theorists of contract "embarrassed" by the question of why promises bind, or why one must keep his word. Yet Locke is far from embarrassed by such questions. Indeed, Locke and Hume share something of the same searching, critical attitude toward reigning cultural principles and standards of judgment. Both thinkers refuse to be taken off the trail of examination by the popularity, sacredness, or antiquity of received opinion. Hume would no doubt concur with what I think can be taken as the central Lockean

---

50. The *pactum subjectionis*, or contract of subjection (governmental contract), was more appropriate to medieval feudal conditions, where its central characteristic was the exchange of conditional oaths of allegiance and obligation between rulers and feudal magnates. See, for example, Manegold of Lautenbach, in *Medieval Political Ideas*, ed. Ewart Lewis (London: Routledge and Kegan Paul, 1954), 1:165. It is true, however, as Martyn P. Thompson has shown, that this understanding of contract did inform the writings of some of the English parliamentarians, like William Atwood and Robert Ferguson, in the context of 1689. See Thompson, *Ideas of Contract in English Political Thought in the Age of John Locke* (New York: Garland, 1987). But as far as the systematic theorists of contract are concerned, the governmental contract is conspicuous in its absence, for some of the reasons suggested above. It should be noted, however, that both a governmental and a social contract are present in Pufendorf's works on political theory, *De jure naturae et gentium* and *De officio hominis et civis*. As I noted in the Introduction, the social compact of the modern period has more in common with the Roman jurist Salamonio's definition of political community as *civilis societas*, where civil society is understood as a partnership among citizens created by a pact among themselves—the *pactio inter cives*. See *De principatu*, in Antony Black, "Juristic Origins of Social Contract Theory," *History of Political Thought* 14, no. 1 (1993): 69–70.

51. *First Treatise*, §6; *Second Treatise*, §195. This is a position also taken by Grotius in *Prolegomena to the Law of War and Peace*, trans. Francis W. Kelsey (New York: Liberal Arts Press, 1957), §§4, 11. The idea that *"Grants, Promises, and Oaths are bonds that hold the Almighty"* is an important source for those who take Locke to be a "traditional" moral rationalist or intellectualist.

mantra of public reason: "there cannot any one moral rule be proposed whereof a man may not justly demand a reason."[52] What might explain Hume's attack on Locke, then, is not that he lacks an answer to the question of the normativity of promises, or that it resides (at least from Locke's perspective) in an obtuse philosophical system, but that Hume cannot or will not treat seriously Locke's arguments from theology. Hence they can both identify the importance of a moral rule like keeping promises, just as the "Hobbist" or the heathen philosopher can. But from Locke's theistic vantage point, "several moral rules," like the injunction to keep promises, "may receive from mankind a very general approbation, without either knowing or admitting the true ground of morality; which can only be the will and law of God, who sees men in the dark, has in his hand rewards and punishments, and power enough to call to account the proudest offender."[53]

Where Locke and Hume disagree most clearly is on the question of the foundations for moral obligations and moral knowledge. There is a first-order difference here, between the rule of God and the role of interest in human relationships, that is never fully engaged. In contrast to Hume, utility can never be taken as an antecedent ground for moral or political obligations for Locke, although utility is frequently understood as a result of abiding by moral duties. Yet, to the extent that utility and general advantage coincide with our notions of right and wrong, virtue and vice, they do so again because God has framed this association for human beings, "God having, by an inseparable connexion, joined virtue and public happiness together, and made the practice thereof necessary to the preservation of society, and visibly beneficial to all with whom the virtuous man has to do."[54] Men may take utility as the standard by which to guide their actions in life, but underneath this is a more extensive, if unrecognized or underrecognized law.[55] Utility cannot be obligatory for individuals because it does not have the structure of a law. Utility may

---

52. *ECHU*, 1.2.4.

53. Ibid., 1.2.6.

54. Ibid. See also the following passage from *The Reasonableness of Christianity:* "The law of nature, is the law of convenience too: and it is no wonder that those men of parts, and studious of virtue . . . should, by meditation, light on the right even from the observable convenience and beauty of it; without making out its obligation from the true principles of the law of nature, and foundations of morality" (§242). This position, expressed in a slightly different way, can also be found in Grotius. See his *Prolegomena to the Law of War and Peace*, §15, where he argues that the law of nature is reinforced by, but not derived from, expediency.

55. *ECHU*, 2.28.11.

produce notions of good and evil, but not moral good and evil[56] (this is a line of argument that I develop further in Chapter 3). In this regard Hume has adopted a position that from Locke's vantage point shares something in common with the ancient morality and customs of heathen religion and philosophy, a body of ethics and a code of manners that left men in the "wild wood of uncertainty." As Locke argued, "Those just measures of right and wrong, which necessity had anywhere introduced, the civil laws prescribed, or philosophy recommended, stood on their true foundations. They were looked on as bonds of society, and conveniences of common life, and laudable practices. But where was it that their obligation was thoroughly known and allowed, and they received as precepts of a law—of the highest law, the law of nature?"[57]

Promises and the Bonds of Human Society

The central principle that comes out of this analysis is that promises and the mutual bonds they create come from us, but the obligations to keep them do not. Individual membership in political association, our obligations to them, and the moral purposes to which they are, or should be, directed, are substantially not our own. Men are given leave (under certain delimited conditions) to determine or designate to which political associations they will belong. But the "original" of these associations, the obligation to belong, and the limits concerning what the political powers constituted within these societies may legitimately do, and hence what individuals can confer upon such powers, are limited by a preexisting moral order. These constraints are formed by the superintending will and reason of God, and by the unique relationship of dependency that Locke conceives between the individual and the divine lawmaker.

As we have seen, Hobbes needs to produce beings who will become capable of mutual trust and faith. Locke holds that men are capable of faith as men. Yet the only way to understand this complimentary moral attribution is if we incorporate into this moral identity the fact for Locke that men are inextricably dependent upon God as God's creation. The sources or occasions of our commitments are particularistic, variable, and individualistic, but the obligations that exist in relation to those acts

---

56. Ibid., 2.28.5; see also *Reasonableness of Christianity*, §§241–42; and *ELN*, 8.
57. *Reasonableness of Christianity*, §243.

always already exist. Promises, then, always entail the solicitation of obligations that exceed, and in a sense await, the individual. Promises express a certain degree of human autonomy, for one makes a "choice" whether to make a promissory oath of allegiance. At the same time, however, one confronts the absence of individual sovereignty, for the rule or obligatoriness of those acts does not depend on the will of the individual or any customary cultural practice. It depends, as Locke says all obligations depend, on God.[58]

Promising and compacting in Locke are not the occasion for *de novo* political self-fashioning. Rather, promising represents the way in which an individual enters into a given context of moral and political duties that require his participation, but such participation is not a sufficient condition for the explanation of these obligations.[59] Such obligations are the more extensive ontological conditions that help to explain why, for example, even as the father's compact or promise cannot bind his son, nonetheless "the Son cannot ordinarily enjoy the possessions of his Father, but under the *same terms* his father did; by becoming a Member of the Society: whereby he puts himself presently under the Government, *he finds there established*, as much as any other Subject of the commonwealth."[60] The son must actively become a member of civil society through a promissory engagement, but such positive enactments do not in turn fashion or author the terms (positive) or moral standards (natural) that will govern his possessions or liberties, for such standards already exist. A further consequence of these limits, and with them the duties and rights of property inheritance, is that there is always more cross-generational stability within free political societies even as no one is naturally born a subject of a commonwealth, and even as no one is bound by the compacts of their ancestors.

The normative constraints we have disclosed in relation to what individuals actually unleash with respect to promises also bears upon the question of the obligatoriness of laws established by civil magistrates.[61]

58. *ELN*, 6, p. 183.

59. Locke uses almost the same language when he argues against the Grotian idea that universal consent establishes the terms of the natural law. In the *Essays on the Law of Nature* he argues that a "general agreement is by no means a sufficient reason for creating an obligation" (5, p. 177). He suggests that a universal act of consent, if possible, might point to a natural law, but it could not be mistaken for or prove a natural law, or, as a consequence, be taken as a binding obligation for every individual.

60. *Second Treatise*, §117 (emphasis added).

61. I am very much indebted to the work of John Dunn for my understanding of the nature of consent in Locke's political theory. See in particular his essay "Consent in the Political Theory

These laws are made possible by the fact that citizens have entrusted the power of making and executing laws on their behalf to public magistrates. But again, this act of entrustment is only the occasion for the conferral of that right to make laws, but neither this act nor the content of the laws constitutes the reason why they are obligatory. As long as these laws support and do not overturn the public good they will be followed with right, but their status as obligatory does not follow in the last instance from the initial condition of consent or from the fact that the authority or right to make these laws was conferred by a majoritarian act of entrustment. Rather, they are obligatory, assuming that these other necessary conditions have also been met, because they are derived from the natural law. Locke argued repeatedly and consistently along these lines throughout his political writings. In the early *Essays on the Law of Nature* he claimed that "positive civil laws are not binding by their own nature of force or in any other way than in virtue of the law of nature."[62] In the *Second Treatise* Locke argues with a slightly different purpose, but with the same effect, that the "Municipal Laws of Countries . . . are only so far right, as they are founded on the Law of Nature, by which they are to be regulated and interpreted."[63]

Given what has been argued so far, what kind of consent theory does Locke provide? Consent is a manifestation of and a reflection on human autonomy. This irreducible sense of individual autonomy cannot be denied in Locke's theory, either in the political realm or in the religious sphere. Obligation, however, is something that is attached to human beings by virtue of their unique character as human beings, that is, as beings that are rational, self-conscious, dependent, and capable of language. The first two of these human characteristics explain our obligations to God, and our mutual dependency and facility for language explain the source of our duties to human society. "God, having designed man for a sociable creature, made him not only with an inclination, and under a necessity to have fellowship with those of his kind, but furnished him also with language, which was to be the great instrument and common tie of

---

of John Locke," in *Political Obligation in Its Historical Context* (Cambridge: Cambridge University Press, 1980). See also his excellent *Political Thought of John Locke*, esp. 120–47. See also A. John Simmons, *On the Edge of Anarchy: Locke, Consent, and the Limits of Society* (Princeton: Princeton University Press, 1993), and Don Herzog, *Happy Slaves: A Critique of Consent Theory* (Chicago: University of Chicago Press, 1989), esp. chapter 6.

62. *ELN*, 1, p. 119, and 6, p. 189, where he argues that "the laws of the civil magistrate derive their whole force from the constraining power of natural law."

63. *Second Treatise*, §12; see also §135.

society."[64] Because we have consciousness of ourselves and can discern the faculties we have, we must accept, according to Locke, that we are not self-made. Similarly, we can, by using these faculties, identify order in the universe, an order that can only be attributed to a superior deity. On these bases we have a duty to worship God. Indeed, he allows in a commentary on Hooker that the very reason and purpose for entering society is "to own and worship God publicly in the world."[65]

Consent should be understood, then, as part of the ceaseless shifting that temporal, limited, and shortsighted beings perform during their "probationership" in the *saculem*. Consent situates us in certain specific civic relationships with other people. In a passage that reminds us of the Stoic and early Roman sources of the development of natural law thinking, Locke argues that it is by virtue of the law of nature that "*Mankind are one Community*, make up one Society distinct from all other Creatures. And were it not for the corruption, and vitiousness of degenerate Men, there would be no need for any other; no necessity that Men should separate from this great and natural Community, and by positive agreements combine into smaller and divided associations."[66] Nonetheless, express or tacit promise or consent does not explain the nature or status of the obligations that exist for human beings. To think of consent or the human will as actually justifying one's obligations to others is, for Locke, to set oneself impiously above or prior to the obligations that God has set for man. As Dunn has argued, "consent cannot simply be understood as a subjective fact, a fact about the psychology of the individual. It has to be understood primarily as a legal fact about the divine order of nature."[67]

Promises oblige not simply because we make them under voluntary conditions of choice but because there is a natural law, established by God's will, that commands the keeping of promises. The idea that promises are obligatory for human beings because they are self-assumed and hence a reflection of a voluntary will may be a desirable and even necessary moral

64. *ECHU,* 3.1.1.
65. "Ecclesia," in *PE,* 291–92.
66. *Second Treatise,* §128. In addition to reflecting the Roman origins of natural law theorizing, this passage also suggests a parallel to the social contract arguments of neo-Thomists like Suárez, for whom sin is the engine that drives men into political society. It is by reference to man's fallen status that Suárez can explain why men, who are free and equal and capable of reason, submit themselves to the laws of a commonwealth. See Suárez, *A Treatise on Laws and God the Lawgiver,* trans. Gwladys L. Williams, Ammi Brown, and John Waldron (Oxford: Clarendon Press, 1944), part 1, 160–69. For Roman origins, see *The Institutes of Justinian,* trans. J. B. Moyle (Oxford: Clarendon Press, 1913), 1.2.
67. Dunn, "Consent in the Political Theory of Locke," 32.

tenet for political liberalism (broadly understood), but it is not consistent with Locke's treatment and theoretical reliance on these acts. Such a position is tied to an understanding of freedom as radically self-determining and self-fashioning that is also not fully Locke's own. This places my reading of Locke in opposition to influential interpretations like that of Charles Taylor. Taylor argues that Locke's epistemology entails a radical disengagement from and objectification of the self in the interest of a more encompassing measure of self-control and a more radical form of self-making.[68] Yet, as I will argue further below in reference to Locke's discussion of opinion and habits, this type of rational disengagement from one's self and one's culture, while expressing one side of Locke's philosophy, is something that Locke ultimately recognized as a chimera. Further, it is only by recognizing the extensive limits that Locke attributes to disengaged, instrumental reason that we can begin to appreciate other central features of Locke's political writings and why, for example, he encourages the formation of habits and habituated virtues in his educational writings, rather than disengaged, rational analysis. Indeed, from a Lockean perspective, privileging the role of individual creation (or political constructivism, or ethical proceduralism) in this regard is a form of impiety. It shares in the kind of vanity and forgetfulness with which Locke charged Filmer in arguing that fathers create their children. Only God has the power of creation. As it is with children, so too is it with moral obligations: we "are but the occasions of their being,"[69] not their true source or progenitors.[70]

It is a serious theoretical confusion to claim, from a Lockean perspective, that individual agents "make" promises, insofar as a promise is the undertaking of an obligation. Human beings surely enunciate them, and participate in their verbal articulation, but we do not create or have any

---

68. See Charles Taylor, "Locke's Punctual Self," in *Sources of the Self* (Cambridge: Harvard University Press, 1989), 164–76.

69. *First Treatise*, §54; see also §§52–53.

70. There is another reasonable parallel here to the theory of Suárez. The kind of superintending obligations and limits that I am stressing are at work in Locke's political theory are also present in Suárez. For Suárez, a political community is created by the free consent of the individuals who constitute it, yet this did not mean that the community created the power by which they were to be governed and preserved. Such a power arises from the "very nature of things," and from "the providence of the author of Nature." *De legibus*, 3.3, pp. 377–80. This, of course, is no strict parallel, because in this context Suárez is concerned with political power, whereas Locke is discussing the ultimate sources of obligation. The moral and political effect are quite similar, however, insofar as we read these features of their texts as cautionary limits on the powers of human will and artifice within political theories dedicated to the idea of individual consent.

power over the obligations that they establish. Rather, promises and compacts in a very real sense make citizens, not the other way around. In promising, we enact or situate ourselves within an obligatory stream of actions that it is no longer within our power to control, stop, revoke, or annul. In addition, promising or contracting does not provide individuals with a proceduralist standard of justice by which to determine what is and what is not a morally legitimate field of action. This is not to depreciate the role of compact in Locke's political theory.[71] As he argues in the *First Treatise*, once we have done away with the idea that God creates or imposes positive political rule on men, "Governments must be left again to the old way of being made by contrivance, and the consent of Men . . . making use of their Reason to unite together into Society."[72] Yet promising, like reason and the will, is not a legislative instrument for Locke. It is a creative practice in the sense that promising and compacting can forge or contrive common associations (civil and religious), and can organize the distribution of power and offices, but cannot in turn effect the standards over which it should be guided and will be judged.[73] Reason is a faculty that is implanted in men by God.[74] Yet reason is a nonlegislating capacity; it does not create or will rules or laws for men. Rather, reason is a discerning faculty, one that seeks out and educates the self on the nature and content of divine natural laws but does not fashion or author those laws.

71. The necessity of compact has been questioned by interpreters who give more prominence to the role of natural law and right in Locke's political theory. This becomes a kind of overcorrection to the more familiar liberal Locke, to the extent that these critics have denied Locke the ability to explain how men can understand which particular regimes and laws they have a duty to obey. For a useful discussion, see Riley, *Will and Political Legitimacy*, chapter 3. For interpreters who question the status or primacy of contract in Locke, see Ernest Barker, "Introduction," in *Social Contract: Essays by Locke, Hume, and Rousseau*, ed. Ernest Barker (New York: Oxford University Press, 1962), xvi; John Plamenatz, *Man and Society* (New York: McGraw-Hill, 1963), 1:220–21; and Hanna Pitkin, "Obligation and Consent," *American Political Science Review* 59, no. 4 (1965) (part I), and 60, no. 1 (1966) (part II).

72. *First Treatise*, §6; see also Locke's defense of his *Letter Concerning Toleration*, where he challenges his critics to show their commission from God "if we are to accept the idea that Government's are instituted by God for specific spiritual ends which God has appointed." *Second Letter Concerning Toleration* and *Third Letter Concerning Toleration*, in *Works of Locke*, 6:120–21 and 6:212–13, respectively.

73. In the American setting, this is a position that can also be found in the work of New England Puritans like John Winthrop, and later in the eighteenth century in John Wise. See Winthrop, "A Model of Christian Charity," in *Puritan Political Ideas: 1558–1794*, ed. Edmund S. Morgan (Indianapolis: Bobbs-Merrill, 1965), 75–93; and John Wise's fascinating tract, *A Vindication of the Government of New England Churches*, in *Colonial American Writings*, ed. Roy Harvey Pearce (New York: Rinehart and Co., 1950), 318–45.

74. See *First Treatise*, §86.

Locke makes plain the limits on human reason by arguing that "nothing indeed is achieved by reason, that powerful faculty of arguing, unless there is first something posited and taken for granted."[75] Human reason must make use of elements of knowledge drawn from the senses, but reason cannot establish those elements. Reason "does not lay a foundation, although again and again it raises a most majestic building and lifts the summits of knowledge right into the sky."[76] Hence, we must constantly keep in mind the distinction between what human beings are at liberty to contrive and what they have the power to execute, on the one hand, and that which makes these acts normative and even necessary, on the other. To the extent that we lose sight of this distinction, and insofar as individual reason and the will are taken as the self-determining, self-authoring ground for either morals or politics in Locke, is the extent to which we have seemingly allowed Kant or neo-Kantian deontological liberalism to (mis)shape our reading.

If we are right about all of this, what are some of the consequences for so distinguishing the sources of obligation (mutual promising and consent) from the grounds of obligation (God's will, natural law)? The first thing we might note is that the social and political world is not as artificial, contingent, or as potentially capricious as we might be led to believe if we were to wrongly conflate the human will and consent with the reasons why the commitments they invoke are by right obligatory, or, which is much the same thing, to pridefully embellish the human capacity to settle viable, binding obligations for men in society with one another.

On the other hand, however, for the political world to have this kind of endurance we are compelled, with Locke, to see ourselves and the conditions for human action in a particular way. That is, we must accept that we are not sovereign over our own existence at the ontological level, and that this fact of dependency on a divine maker, to whom "we owe our body, soul, and life—whatever we are, whatever we have, and even whatever we can be"—comes with certain pregiven obligations.[77]

In addition to individual nonsovereignty, then, we must also acknowledge that even the bare possibility of a divine eternal being means that certain actions will be prescribed and others forbidden on the basis of this supreme will. This stands in contrast to the type of rationalism that Grotius playfully expresses in his *Prolegomena* to the *Law of War and*

75. *ELN*, 2, p. 125.
76. Ibid.
77. Ibid., 6, p. 187.

Peace: that the laws of nature "would have a degree of validity even if we should concede that which cannot be conceded without the utmost wickedness, that there is no God, or that the affairs of men are of no concern to him."[78] For Locke (and for Grotius as well) it is incumbent upon man, as God's creation, to discover those laws and follow them as the moral rules for life. This is the constrained but still significant and morally culpable space of individual autonomy in Locke's theory. Human moral autonomy is experienced within the palpable distance between human ignorance and that "twilight" of probability we have been given to know and follow God's will and laws. Moral autonomy and freedom is extended to man by virtue of the very limits of reason and human understanding. At the same time, this "state of mediocrity and probationership" is designed "to check our over-confidence and presumption" so that "we might, by every-day's experience, be made sensible of our short-sightedness and liableness to error; the sense whereof might be a constant admonition to us, to spend the days of this our pilgrimage with industry and care, in the search and following that way which might lead us to a state of greater perfection."[79] It is on the basis of how men use this autonomy and the moral freedom they have that they will be judged in the hereafter. This is a future juridical state that Locke thinks men have good reason to admit is at least possible, if not probable.

The duties of morality that Locke insists a "Hobbist" cannot admit might be understood as the difference between a conceptual framework that places God at its center and one in which there is no necessary or logical requirement that God exists. Further evidence for this can be adduced from the fact that self-preservation is conceived as a limitless amoral right in Hobbes, whereas the same concept of self-preservation is understood by Locke as a fundamental duty to God as man's divine creator, a duty that perpetually binds the individual to God's will. Self-preservation is a right, but it is derived from what Locke calls a "Fundamental, Sacred, and unalterable Law."[80] This same duty to self-preservation also has external obligations in relation to others. What we recognize in relation to others is not immediately their autonomy or their abstract rights, but that they are hewn from the same divine cloth that situates every individual in an irrevocable relationship of dependency to his creator. The same obligation to preserve oneself as God's creation entails duties to

78. Grotius, *Prolegomena to the Law of War and Peace*, §11.
79. *ECHU,* 4.14.2.
80. *Second Treatise,* §149.

preserve others as well (insofar as these are not in competition).[81] The mutual respect for persons in Locke's system does not issue in a final sense from the fact that individuals possess rights of freedom and property. Rather, mutual respect of persons flows from the duty of respecting that equality of condition that God saw fit to establish among men.

This also suggests why Locke argued that "those are not at all to be tolerated who deny the being of a God. Promises, covenants, and oaths, which are the bonds of human society, can have no hold upon an Atheist. The taking away of God, tho but even in thought, dissolves all."[82] Within a text dedicated to the wide extension of religious toleration and religious liberty Locke explicitly proscribes the extension of toleration to atheists. It is important to note that this limit on the trust and liberties that can be given to so-called atheists does not involve a precommitment to monotheism, or to a one true (Christian) religion. This is something that would be truly inconsistent with the rest of a tract that is at pains to argue for the wide extension of reciprocal religious liberties. Yet what is of central importance in the position Locke takes in the *Letter*, the *Essay*, and in the *Second Treatise* is the centrality and the moral force of compact and promise. Throughout these texts it is clear that Locke conceives the bonds of human civil and political society as promises, covenants, and oaths.[83]

From Locke's perspective the real problem of atheists is that they do not acknowledge their dependence on a divine creator, and hence think

---

81. Man also has ownership in himself, according to Locke, and it is on the basis of this idea that some have found a reason to reject the position expressed above. See Michael P. Zuckert, *Natural Rights and the New Republicanism* (Princeton: Princeton University Press, 1994), chapter 9. Laslett also sees a contradiction here; see his introduction to the *Two Treatises of Government*. Yet God's ownership as a divine maker who gives individual and collective life a purposive content is not inconsistent with a lesser power of self-preservation through property. Others have also argued that these are not contradictory positions. See John Colman, *John Locke's Moral Philosophy* (Edinburgh: Edinburgh University Press, 1983).

82. *Letter Concerning Toleration*, 51.

83. Kant presents an illuminating contrast on this point. In *The Metaphysics of Morals* Kant relates the following story from ancient times: "Protagoras of Abdera began his book with the words: '*As for whether there are gods or not, I do not know what to say.*' For this the Athenians drove him off his land and from the city and burned his books before the assembly. . . . In doing this the Athenian judges, as *human beings*, did him a *great wrong*. But as *officials of the state* and judges they proceeded quite *rightly* and consistently; for how could someone swear an oath unless it had been decreed publicly and lawfully, *on high authority (de par le Sénat)*, that there are gods?" Kant, *The Metaphysics of Morals*, ed. and trans. Mary Gregor (New York: Cambridge University Press, 1996), part 2, 229. By contrast, Locke would not allow for the kind of distinction that Kant makes here between private and public actors, or morals and politics. From a different perspective, neither would Hobbes; hence Hobbes rejects the value of oaths. See *Leviathan*, chapter 14, pp. 111–12.

of themselves as sovereign individualists, self-made and self-ruling. In his rejection of atheists from the right of toleration he suggests that they will have no reason to keep their promises, and that others can have no certainty that they will. In part this is because they will not fear the eternal sanctions that will follow upon the violation of promises. But this commitment—that "the taking away of God, tho but even in thought, dissolves all"—may reflect more than a concern with the dissolution of the fear of divine retribution and with it the psychological motivation for keeping promises. Further, what atheists will not acknowledge, according to Locke, is not just this "liability to punishment" but the more primary (and nonhedonistic) principle of a "liability to pay dutiful obedience."[84] This obligation refers to that wider form of duty that recognizes one's nonsovereignty, that is, the duty to "conform our actions to the rule imposed upon them, i.e., the will of a superior."[85] It is not just God's supreme power and will that makes his laws binding for men (as it would be in an extreme form of theological voluntarism); rather, God's laws are binding also because "we are rightly subject."[86] The obligatory force of God's laws are not limited to the fact that he has the authority of a supreme lawmaker with power to "coerce offenders and punish the wicked"; the obligation issues more immediately from the authority and dominion that exists by virtue of his natural right and the right of creation. As Locke puts it elsewhere, "who will deny that clay is subject to the potter's will?"[87]

We might also suggest that when Locke opposes Catholics (or at least the pope and certain Catholic theologians) on the grounds that they teach others that "Faith is not to be kept with Hereticks," part of what is involved (in addition to historical trouble for England, as between James I and Pope Paul V) is once again the dangerous assertion of a power that mortal beings do not possess. Of course, this is commonly understood as an illegitimate assertion of an ecclesiastical power over the political. And where popes have abrogated the allegiance of a king's subjects (although, in the interest of fairness, not without provocation),[88] from the standpoint of the differentiation that Locke (and others) made between religious and political societies, such an act is an illegitimate usurpation. But the power that is thereby asserted is not only political but also epistemological and

84. *ELN*, 6, p. 183.
85. Ibid.
86. Ibid., pp. 153–55.
87. Ibid., p. 157.
88. See Suárez's defense of the pope's actions against James I in *A Defense of the Catholic and Apostolic Faith Against the Errors of the Anglican Sect*.

moral. To teach that promises need not be kept with heretics of course presupposes that someone is in a position of moral and epistemological certainty from which it is possible to make clear distinctions between the heretical and the true or orthodox. Yet Locke denies this kind of knowledge or certainty to everyone. For this reason Locke's views on toleration issue, at least in part, from an enlightened but tempered form of moral skepticism.[89] What Catholics and atheists share in common, from Locke's perspective, is not just that promises, the bonds of society, are not safe with them. They are to be opposed because they assert a degree of sovereignty in and over this life that does not exist, and that degree of *soi-disant* sovereignty threatens to unravel the public reason by which political societies (and civic members) are to be governed.

Pilgrims and Servants:
Individual Nonsovereignty in Locke's Moral and Political Theory

As is well known, it is only through compact or consent that political society is established and a legislative authority is rendered legitimate for Locke. "The *Liberty of Man, in Society,* is to be under no other Legislative Power, but that established, by consent, in the Common-wealth, nor under the Dominion of any Will, or Restraint of any Law, but what the Legislative shall enact, according to the Trust put in it."[90] Locke claims that "Nothing can make any Man [a subject or member of a commonwealth] but his actually entering into it by positive Engagement, and express Promise and Compact."[91] By starting from the premise of the natural freedom and equality of individuals, the only way in which the authority of another can be rendered legitimate is if that power comes from the individual.[92] Political power, which Locke defines as "*a Right* of making Laws with penalties of Death, and consequently all less Penalties," is limited by the ends for which such a power was instituted among men, namely, the preservation of property (or "life, liberty, and estates") and, more broadly, the "Publick Good."[93]

In all of this Locke has given us a valuable frame that unites a basic

---

89. *Letter Concerning Toleration,* 36–37; *ECHU,* 4.16.4; see also Tully on this point in his introduction to the *Letter Concerning Toleration.*

90. *Second Treatise,* §22.

91. Ibid., §122.

92. See ibid., §§87, 95, 99, 102, 106, 119.

93. Ibid., §§3, 123.

form of moral and political individualism with popular sovereignty. This is a position that has inclined many interpreters to read Locke as a modern proponent of that form of contractual or procedural liberalism in which political right is subservient to the interests of property and aggregate forms of individual self-interest more generally, one in which a more substantive or extensive understanding of the "good" for man is simply excluded by definition. In what immediately follows, I want to argue that political power and legislative authority are, in the last instance, limited by the dependency and nonsovereignty of the individual. Political power is more extensively and ultimately circumscribed not by the dictates of individual rationality or self-interest, however general these claims might be among a certain population, but by the limits that surround each and every individual. As a result, there are moral (divine) limits and burdens, or ends for political power beyond what individual subjects might otherwise agree to in a contract or a majoritarian act of entrustment.[94]

One of the important connecting themes between Locke's first and second treatises is the fundamental distinction Locke is at pains to make, contra Filmer, between political power and other relationships, like the paternal or the conjugal. The important premise here, and one that reflected and helped solidify revolutionary politics, is that no one is rightly subjected to the will or authority of any other person unless and until one has consented to that power. Locke understood, of course, that we are all born "weak and helpless."[95] As long as one is in a state of immaturity, without the full use of reason or understanding by which to "direct one's will," one is properly governed by the will and prescriptions of the father and/or mother. So, according to Locke, natural freedom and subjection to parents (not necessarily the father) "consist together, and are founded on the same principle."[96] That principle is that a person attains the state of equal natural freedom when he or she has the capacity of knowing the law (the natural law) by which individuals are to govern themselves and their actions.

Hence, in contrast to Filmer, one cannot generalize from the rule of the father to political relationships because the supremacy of fathers (or mothers, or guardians) is fleeting. What is more, the paternal (or parental)

---

94. For a related treatment of Locke that emphasizes the significance of a hierarchical divine design in much of his thought, see Kirstie M. McClure, *Judging Rights: Lockean Politics and the Limits of Consent* (Ithaca: Cornell University Press, 1996).

95. *Second Treatise*, §56.

96. Ibid., §61.

relationship is more accurately characterized according to Locke as one in which the parents are under an obligation, from God, to preserve, nourish, and educate their children. This is because it is not the parents but God who has created them: "*Adam* and *Eve*, and after them all *Parents* were, by the Law of Nature, *under an obligation to preserve, nourish, and educate the Children*, they had begotten, not as their own Workmanship, but the Workmanship of their own Maker, the Almighty, to whom they were to be accountable for them."[97] Likewise, children have this care as their right or privilege.[98] Parents do not have sovereignty, or ultimate, arbitrary power over their children. It should also be added that husbands do not have sovereignty over their wives.[99] The failure to recognize the ontological limits of power and sovereignty for the individual, and hence the constraints that operate on all levels of human relationships (familial, conjugal, and political), is the source of some confusion in Carole Pateman's influential reading of Locke.[100] The exclusion of women from the Lockean political sphere are clear, but the idea that classical Filmerian patriarchalism is exchanged via the social contract for a modern form of patriarchal power ("sex-right") based upon conjugal relations is inconsistent with Locke's acknowledgment of the limits in all forms of human power. For the ends of the artificial, negotiable, and revocable marriage contract, which include procreation and mutual support in the care of children, entail no political power and no measure of absolute or sovereign power. "If it were otherwise," Locke argues, "and that absolute *Sovereignty* and Power of Life and Death naturally belong'd to the Husband, and were *necessary to the society between Man and Wife*, there could be no Matrimony in any of those Countries where the Husband is allowed no such absolute Authority. But the ends of Matrimony requiring no such Power in the Husband, the Condition of *Conjugal Society* put it not in him, it being not necessary to that State."[101] Thus one of the more

---

97. Ibid., §56.

98. Children also have duties. These include honor and gratitude toward the parents. See ibid., §§56, 66–68, and *First Treatise*, §§52–53, 56.

99. *Second Treatise*, §83.

100. See Carole Pateman, *The Sexual Contract* (Stanford: Stanford University Press, 1988), 52–53.

101. *Second Treatise*, §83; see also §82. Mary Lyndon Shanley gives a sophisticated treatment of the important differences between the marriage contract and the social contract in Locke's political theory. See her "Marriage Contract and Social Contract in Seventeenth-Century English Political Thought," in *The Family in Political Thought*, ed. Jean Bethke Elshtain (Amherst: University of Massachusetts Press, 1982). See also Melissa A. Butler, "Early Liberal Roots of Feminism: John Locke and the Attack on Patriarchy," *American Political Science Review* 72, no. 1 (1978): 135–50.

fundamental arguments against Filmer is not provided by the selectivity of his biblical exegesis or the trouble of tracing the rightful descendants of Adam's authority, but rather the so-called sovereignty of Adam, upon which absolute monarchy is grounded, is itself a chimera. Adam was not sovereign over anything.[102] Indeed, the very category of sovereignty is misplaced when dealing with human beings and the relationships and governments they contrive.

With age comes the capacity to reason and therewith one's natural equal freedom. Indeed, it is probably more accurate to say that it is not nature but what Locke calls "discretion" that makes one free. By nature we are potentially free; with age and the maturity, reason, and discretion that come with it—under the proper guidance and management—we are substantively free. Lockean freedom is always necessarily a discretionary, mature, reasoning freedom. Against Filmer's contention that the idea of natural freedom involves a liberty to do whatever one likes, Locke insists throughout his writings that liberty does not mean individual license but is that which is left to the individual where a standing rule or law does not speak. The rub is that for Locke there is always a standing law, for the law of nature is perpetual and universal.[103] And where there is government and positive civil laws, individual liberty consists in the freedom to "dispose, and order, as he lists, his Person, Actions, Possessions, and his whole Property, within the Allowance of those Laws under which he is."[104]

Freedom is dependent for its meaning and place in human life upon the prior existence of law, not its absence or silence: "*where there is no Law there is no Freedom.*"[105] This is true for Locke in a double sense. The first sense, as suggested above, is that freedom is a right one earns by virtue of certain capacities of reason and understanding that must first be developed and sustained in order to merit such a station (much more will be said about this developmental process below). The second sense or reason why freedom and law are understood to be codependent and coterminous is that this effectively rules out the permissibility of absolute or arbitrary rule. What freedom and the law conjoin, no arbitrary human will may dissolve.

102. *First Treatise*, §§15, 41, 51–55.
103. *Second Treatise*, §6; *ELN*, 7, p. 191.
104. *Second Treatise*, §57.
105. Ibid. This is a political view, it should be added, that is as out of tune with those who today recognize in nearly all governmental actions a usurpation of private liberty as it was with those good Anglicans in Locke's time who would not risk making claims of liberty for fear of chastising established powers.

Despite everything we have said concerning the place of reason and freedom in human life, the discretionary autonomous self is not sovereign in Locke's moral and political theory. Locke's central axiom of individual nonsovereignty, invoked repeatedly in the *Second Treatise*, is that "no body can give more power than he has himself."[106] This statement should lead us to ask what are those things over which individuals do not have power and which, as a result, they are unable to confer upon others, in particular, upon political rulers? First, more affirmatively, individuals have two powers in the state of nature: to do whatever they deem fit to preserve themselves and others within the confines of the natural law, and to punish the crimes committed by others against that law.[107] This second power turns out to be ineffective, susceptible to abuse and self-interested partiality, and helps explain, in large measure, why individuals leave the state of nature. Hence this is a power each individual "wholly gives up" by entering political society. The power (although not the right or the duty) concerning self-preservation and the preservation of others is also transferred, "to be regulated by Laws made by the Society." That these promulgated positive laws will now determine this fundamental matter of preservation is something that Locke admits "in many things confine the liberty he had by the Law of Nature."[108] Yet man's condition within civil society cannot be understood as one that is devoid of individual sovereignty in contrast to a "state of nature" in which the individual is sovereign. For even within the state of nature, the individual is only a "Judge, Interpreter, and Executioner" of those standards (the laws of nature) by which he will regulate—albeit poorly—his relationships with others.[109] He does not have sovereign authority or political power, which according to Locke concerns the right to make laws.

The absence of individual sovereignty in Locke's theory means that there is a substantive lack of legitimate power and authority over specific areas of moral and political life. This lack of individual sovereignty, which is coextensive with the appearance of individual life on earth, that is, within and without the "state of nature," generates an economy of political and moral power. In this economy, as in all economies, relative scarcity fixes the value of its terms. In this moral and political economy no one has absolute or arbitrary power over her own life. We do not make

---

106. Ibid., §23; see also §§135, 137, 149, 164, 172.
107. Ibid., §128.
108. Ibid., §129.
109. Ibid., §§136, 7, 13.

ourselves and as a result we cannot unmake ourselves or end our own lives.[110] Neither can we give up this life to be ruled absolutely or arbitrarily by others, for "he that cannot take away his own Life, cannot give another power over it."[111] The absence of power over our own lives in this respect means that any actions that seek to assert or lay claim to this power, as well as any similar undertaking that may be self-imposed, is illegitimate—more, it is against God's will and law. Political absolutism and slavery in the political sphere and suicide in the private moral sphere are alike rendered illegitimate and impious by the very absence of individual sovereignty. No individual or group of individuals is free to select these as forms of being or nonbeing.

Individuals lack sovereignty at a basic ontological level because they are, as Locke describes it, "servants of one Sovereign Master."[112] The individual self's appearance in the world, as well as the subject's purpose in the world, do not derive from the will or desire of the individual. As servants they are "sent into the World by his order and about his business, they are his Property, whose Workmanship they are, made to last during his, not one anothers Pleasure." Individual existence is best understood in Locke's theory as an office or, as he calls it, a "Station," one that comes with certain fixed roles and constitutive duties. One of the most fundamental of such duties is to maintain and preserve one's office, and "when his own Preservation comes not in competition, ought he, as much as he can, to preserve the rest of Mankind."[113] I have already noted the Augustinian resemblances here, despite the lack of evidence that Locke ever read the Bishop of Hippo.[114] Yet this is something other than a model of two cities, God and man, or two objects of love. Rather, this is a theologically centered conception of politics in which the vertical distribution of power and sovereignty emanates from the highest conceivable point. This is a view in which the right object of one's life, pursuits, and judgments is provided by one's dependent status as a being with ascriptive duties and proscriptive interdictions. But within this order, limited horizontal modes of relating and associating are possible; indeed, God requires it of men.[115]

Nor are we sovereign over our spiritual or religious life. Individuals

110. Ibid., §6.
111. Ibid., §23.
112. Ibid., §6.
113. Ibid.
114. See J. R. Harrison and Peter Laslett, *The Library of John Locke*, 2d ed. (Oxford: Clarendon Press, 1971).
115. *Second Treatise*, §77; *ELN*, 4, pp. 156–57.

do not have the power to give up or entrust the determination of their souls to others. That is, no one can fix our beliefs for us. This is not simply because individual belief is an intrinsically private matter, although it surely is for Locke. Rather, we cannot confer the care for our souls and the matter of our beliefs to religious or secular authorities, because faith and belief are not within our powers; again, we are not sovereign over this dimension of our lives. Instead, according to Locke, belief or nonbelief is a feature of God's divine grace.[116]

Locke's argument for toleration puts stress on the idea that conscience and faith cannot be coerced. The "Care of Souls is not committed to the Civil Magistrate, any more than to other men." The reason is once again the lack of sovereignty in this respect, for "it appears not that God has ever given any such authority to one man over another."[117] There are clear limits concerning what secular or religious authorities can do in relation to religious beliefs, because faith cannot be compelled. There are also significant constraints on how far one can persuade or make use of arguments to "draw the Heterodox into the way of Truth"—which Locke grants—because there are limits on how far the individual can direct the bearings of his or her private soul. "It is absurd," Locke says, "that things should be enjoyned by laws, which are not in mens power to perform. And to believe this or that to be true, does not depend on our will."[118] This is a significant position that Locke articulated consistently throughout his life.[119]

Individual nonsovereignty, the extent to which the individual lacks both a power and a right to rule over certain features of his life, is best interpreted as providentially proscribed limits on human agency and self-determination. Yet this same lack of sovereignty holds a generative,

---

116. *Letter Concerning Toleration*, 26–27, 46.
117. Ibid., 26.
118. Ibid., 46.
119. For example, see his early *First Tract on Government*, where Locke argues that since the nature of religious beliefs are not in one's power, "'twould be as irrational for men to engage to be of the same religion or persuasion with their magistrate, as to promise to have the same looks or constitution" (in *PE*, 15). One wonders why Locke did not extend the logic of this position to atheists: if this or that belief is not in one's power, why isn't the presence or absence of belief also correspondingly not in one's power and, as a consequence, a condition that merits the same measure of toleration granted to every other reasonable, fallible, and nonsovereign creature? Any answer to this question would have to turn to the nature and structure of Locke's natural law philosophy, something I undertake in Chapter 3. Still, I mean to suggest that there is a possible avenue of argumentation here by which one could use Lockean reasoning to open up and render more generous Lockean politics. Points like this one testify to how Locke could be used to address shortcomings in our own contemporary practices of toleration and mutual respect.

positive quality by establishing a fixed limit against which no instituted human powers may legitimately transgress. Absolute, arbitrary political rule is prohibited not because it violates the principle of consent (for it need not violate such a procedural rule), but more fundamentally because it claims a power that does not exist among men and that no procedure of consensual agreement can produce without offending God's laws. Such ontological limits on political power mark a key difference between Locke and Hobbes (as well as Grotius).[120] Paradoxically, in the very denial of individual sovereignty, a measure of subjective individual freedom is secured. More positively, individual nonsovereignty and the epistemological limits of human reasoning concentrate and organize man's purposive pursuits in relation to his greatest concern: the right standards of moral judgment and action. As Locke argues in the *Essay*:

> Since our faculties are not fitted to penetrate into the internal fabric and real essences of bodies; but yet plainly discover to us the being of a God, and the knowledge of ourselves, enough to lead us into a full and clear discovery of our duty and great concernment; it will become us, as rational creatures, to employ those faculties we have about what they are most adapted to, and follow the direction of nature, where it seems to point us out the way. For it is rational to conclude, that our proper employment lies in those inquiries, and in that sort of knowledge which is most suited to our natural capacities, and carries in it our greatest interest, i.e. the condition of our eternal estate. Hence I think I may conclude that *morality* is *the proper science and business of mankind in general*, (who are both concerned and fitted to search out their *summum bonum*).[121]

We must make one cautionary note here about the argument I am putting forward. The claim that there is no principle of individual sovereignty in Locke's moral and political theory must be distinguished from his *individualist* account of *popular* sovereignty.[122] Locke argued that within a

120. See, for example, Grotius's discussion of engaging in or consenting to servitude. *De Jure Belli ac Pacis*, trans. Francis W. Kelsey (Indianapolis: Bobbs-Merrill, 1925), 1.3.8.
121. *ECHU*, 4.12.11.
122. For discussions of Locke's theory of popular sovereignty, see Julian H. Franklin, *John Locke and the Theory of Sovereignty: Mixed Monarchy and the Right of Resistance in the Political Thought of the English Revolution* (New York: Cambridge University Press, 1978), and J. W. Gough, *John Locke's Political Philosophy: Eight Studies* (Oxford: Clarendon Press, 1950).

constitutional regime the legislative power will be supreme. Nonetheless, "the Legislative being only a Fiduciary Power to act for certain ends, there remains still *in the People a Supream Power* to remove or alter the Legislative, when they find the Legislative act contrary to the trust reposed in them."[123] Locke also famously argues that the people (and even each individual) shall be the judge whether their trust has been broken.[124] Yet this is a power that can only appear once government is dissolved. Lockean popular sovereignty always (or only) exists as a power *in potentia*, only becomes actual or practical when "foolish" and "wicked" legislators violate their trust or exert an authority that no human being may rightly claim. Popular sovereignty (or "supream power") is a stopgap for the inevitable power vacuum created by the illegal actions of rulers, that is, where there is already no longer a government or magistrate but a lawless individual or group of individuals.

This is surely a limited understanding of *popular* sovereignty—as we shall see further in comparison to Rousseau.[125] Yet, even more to the point, Locke's thoughts concerning the "supream power" of the people is grounded in the very limits of personal/political power we have already explicated. Hence the occasion for the appearance or expression of popular sovereignty is morally justifiable because under such conditions the people are *restoring* political power to its proper relationship within a more extensive ontological order, as expressed by the law of nature. "For no Man, or Society of Men, having Power to deliver up their *Preservation*, or consequently the means of it, to the Absolute Will and arbitrary Dominion of another; whenever any one shall go about to bring them into such

---

123. *Second Treatise*, §§149, 243.
124. Ibid., §§240, 241.
125. Nonetheless, Richard Ashcraft has provided a crucial counterpoint to this by showing how the Lockean notion that political power devolves or "reverts" to the people (ibid., §242) was in fact a position far too radical for most of the English Whigs during his lifetime and for a good while after. Ashcraft, *Revolutionary Politics and Locke's Two Treatises of Government* (Princeton: Princeton University Press, 1986). That Locke's writings were on the radical fringe of the political debates in 1689–90 has also been confirmed by other scholars. See Mark Goldie, "The Revolution of 1689 and the Structure of Political Argument," *Bulletin of Research in the Humanities* 83 (1980). For a sympathetic but critical response to Ashcraft's contextualist account, see Martyn P. Thompson, "Locke's Contract in Context," in *The Social Contract from Hobbes to Rawls*, ed. David Boucher and Paul Kelly (New York: Routledge, 1994). We should always remember that these interpretive disagreements possessed real material consequences for those who employed these Lockean ideas within specific historical circumstances of political instability. For just one of many examples of this, see James Otis's tract, written during the American Revolutionary period, "The Rights of the British Colonies Asserted and Proved" (1764) in *Pamphlets of the American Revolution*, vol. 1, *1750–1765*, ed. Bernard Bailyn (Cambridge: Harvard University Press, 1965).

a Slavish Condition, they will always have a right to preserve what they have not a Power to part with; and to rid themselves of those who invade this Fundamental, Sacred, and unalterable Law of *Self-Preservation*, for which they enter'd into Society."[126] In relation to these natural (divine) limits, the expression of popular sovereignty, when needed, is as much a duty weighing on society "to preserve what they have not a Power to part with" as it is a right to their lives, liberties, and estates. It is for this reason that Locke can provide a consistent political perspective that denies sovereignty to the individual while allowing for expressions of popular sovereignty when conditions warrant.

Conclusion

A commitment to liberal principles of freedom and equality generally entails an appeal to a political voluntarist scheme to explain and justify civic obligations. Locke has traditionally been taken as one of the core theorists of a voluntarist account of political obligation. Yet, as I have argued, the dual occurrence of individual nonsovereignty and the derivative (theological) source of the obligations of promises reveals a substantial degree of political nonvoluntarism in his account. Our political obligations do not simply follow from the fact that we have undertaken or willed them in a context of uncoerced free choice—although such conditions, along with maturity and rational discretion, are fundamentally necessary. The problem with the voluntarist formulation is that it ascribes too much originating, Promethean power to the individual. Such a conception tears the Lockean subject from the divine, juridical context in relation to which and for the sake of which human beings exist, falsely "unencumbering" them and thereby misconstruing an important source of later modern liberalism.[127] If the historicist critique of contract theory has not given its proponents their due, then the voluntarist appropriation of Lockean consent theory has loaded it with more political and philosophical freight than it can withstand. That is, the voluntarist account has ascribed a secular conception of rational, procedural agreement and willful self-fashioning that cannot stand up to close scrutiny of what

---

126. *Second Treatise*, §149.
127. See Michael Sandel, "The Procedural Republic and the Unencumbered Self," *Political Theory* 12, no. 1 (1984): 81–96, and Sandel, *Liberalism and the Limits of Justice* (Cambridge: Cambridge University Press, 1982). See also Taylor, *Sources of the Self*, chapter 9.

makes political obligations and civic memberships normative and truly binding for Locke. Modern voluntarist theories of political obligation elide distinctions that Locke's theory simply does not allow: for example, the distinction between the occasion of undertaking an obligation, the moment of making a promise, or giving consent, and the separate question of what makes that undertaking obligatory. Voluntarist theories of obligation want to collapse these two features and argue that the obligations that exist for individuals are binding and obligatory because they are self-imposed. As I have tried to show, this is precisely what Locke rejected as specious and impious.

We can see more generally that nature (*physis*) and convention (*nomos/nomoi*) are never fully or clearly separated in Locke. Locke seems to have known that between the act of making a promise and keeping it, a whole world of endless and unpredictable possibilities are opened that threaten to render individual or collective endeavors null and void, or just absurd and tragic. What keeps these enactments from becoming another entirely forgettable portion of the scrapheap of human artifice is that they are not entirely our own. "He that, with Archelaus, shall lay it down as a principle, that right and wrong, honest and dishonest, are defined only by laws, and not by nature, will have other measures of moral rectitude and pravity, than those who take it for granted that we are under obligations antecedent to all human constitutions."[128] The promises and compacts citizens make, and the obligations they articulate, do not receive their force or value from the idea (or outward appearance) that they are human inventions. Their rightful obligatory force and value derive from a divine will. But this force is not simply disciplinarian, although this is one of its key components. Rather, "all obligation binds conscience and lays a bond on the mind itself, so that not fear of punishment, but a rational apprehension of what is right, puts us under an obligation, and conscience passes judgment on morals, and, if we are guilty of a crime, declares that we deserve punishment."[129]

128. *ECHU*, 4.12.4. Archelaus was a pupil of Anaxagoras, a sophist. Locke seems to have selected his target of criticism very well. According to Ernest Barker, Archelaus was the first philosopher to draw the fundamental distinction between *physis* and *nomos*, arguing that the noble and the base are determined by convention and not by nature. See Barker, *Greek Political Theory* (London: University Paperbacks, 1918), 61. This section of the *Essay* is also intriguing for the short but favorable reference Locke makes to Plato: "he who, with Plato, shall place beatitude in the knowledge of God, will have his thoughts raised to other contemplations than those who look not beyond this spot of earth, and those perishing things which are to be had in it."

129. *ELN*, 6, p. 185.

The act of making a promise removes the possibility or permissibility of appealing to self-interest or utility as legitimate claims for keeping or breaking that promise.[130] Locke's moral theory does, of course, partake of a degree of psychological hedonism, in that the essential motives for man are directed toward human happiness and the aversion of pain. Yet it is not for this reason a theory that assumes that the natural law dictates that man's first duty is to his own interest or utility, but the reverse. "Utility is not the basis of the law or the ground of obligation, but the consequence of obedience to it."[131] Promises must be kept even though they may be a hindrance to one's utility or immediate happiness. This is true despite the fact that morality aims toward man's happiness. Hedonism and ultimate moral rectitude are not in conflict for Locke—but here again the reason is provided by a religious perspective that sees God's laws providing the general archetype for men's hedonic calculations: heaven and hell. Thus, in the next chapter I provide an analysis of Locke's natural law theory for the purposes of highlighting and considering critically both the transformative dimensions of Lockean contractarianism and the distinctive version of public reason that follows from his philosophical corpus.

130. See also "Morality," MS Locke, c 28, in PE, 267–69.
131. ELN, 8, p. 215.

THREE

Governing Subjects and Breeding Citizens:
Dilemmas of Public Reasoning and Public Judgment in Locke

> Our main care should be about the inside.
> —Locke, *Some Thoughts Concerning Education*

In the previous chapter we saw how Locke addressed the "original" of societies, that is, "the rise of and extent of political power." In this chapter we will be concerned with that other dimension of politics that Locke emphasized but that has been given far less critical consideration in the scholarship dedicated to his political theory: "the art of governing men in society."[1] In turning to what Locke thinks is necessary in relation to the art of governing men (something Michel Foucault would later call the "conduct of conduct"), we will be in a far better position to understand the deep interconnections between contract, culture, and citizenship in Locke's political thought. Again, one of the primary reasons for attending to these features of Locke's thinking, or indeed to those of any of the contract theorists of the modern period, is to appreciate the extent to which contract makes citizens, never simply the other way around.

In the case of Locke, the idea that contract makes citizens means, among other things, that political theory is never solely a juristic exercise concerned with fixing rights and obligations.[2] Political theory is also dedicated to contributing, both philosophically and practically, to the ethical and

---

1. There are, of course, some important exceptions here. See James Tully, *An Approach to Political Philosophy: Locke in Contexts* (Cambridge: Cambridge University Press, 1993), esp. chapter 6; Duncan Ivison, *The Self at Liberty: Political Argument and the Arts of Government* (Ithaca: Cornell University Press, 1997); and Nathan Tarcov, *Locke's Education for Liberty* (Lanham, Md.: Lexington Books, 1999).

2. For a reading of Locke along these lines, see J. G. A. Pocock, "A Discourse of Sovereignty: Observations on the Work in Progress," in *Political Discourse in Early Modern Britain*, ed. Nicholas Phillipson and Quentin Skinner (Cambridge: Cambridge University Press, 1993), 377–428.

cultural conditions upon which the endurance of a reasonable regime of law and right depend. This is an understanding of the nature and purposes of political theory that is not often attributed to social contract theorists of the past, nor is it one that finds much of a home in contemporary contractarian philosophy.[3] By uncovering the extent to which this vision of moral and political reflection animates the social contract tradition and Locke in particular, we may be able to shift our attention toward this broad body of thought in ways both more useful and more challenging for the present age.

Specifically, if he is read as I am advocating here, Locke imparts an unnerving lesson to the modern reader: the ideal of government by consent and of a society of, by, and for the people is almost always in jeopardy. Indeed, Locke understood better than most that the ideal of government by consent is enormously difficult to sustain, in theory and in practice. In what follows I hope to make good on this claim by addressing the multiple challenges that Locke discerned in the ideal of free self-government. But I also want to argue that Locke offered some important (if underappreciated) ideas about how to attend to the difficulties that a government by consent creates for both citizens and leaders, ideas that repay thoughtful reconsideration today. One of the questions that Locke's political thought should raise for us—once we see the extent to which the transformative ethos of social contractarianism is present in his writings—is how well these transformative commitments honor other ethical and political attachments with which they are always in tension, attachments to goods such as individual liberty, autonomy, and moral pluralism. In the end I will suggest that the internal problems of Lockean public reason serve as a forceful reminder today of the limits of human reason and the essential tensions between liberty and virtue. Public reason in Locke does not aim to supplant or coerce individual reason; it aims to do something far more significant and more difficult. Lockean public reason aims to shape and govern individual judgment from the inside out in accordance with the guidelines of the natural law. For Locke, political self-rule, understood as a civic virtue, is intimately connected to, in fact presupposes, the rule of self as a moral virtue. With these ideas in mind, we first turn to Locke's treatment of the law of nature and then to his writings on education.

---

3. For example, David Gauthier largely eschews the transformative aims that I am discussing here. See in particular his classic work *Morals by Agreement* (Oxford: Clarendon Press, 1986).

Seeking the Natural Law

The role of the natural law in Locke's moral and political theory has been the subject of a great deal of astute scholarly debate. This controversy shows no signs of abating. In large measure, the question at issue here is (a) to what extent Locke should be counted among the theological voluntarists with respect to the natural law, (b) whether he should be understood as providing a modulated version of natural law rationalism or intellectualism, and (c) whether one can even speak of a coherent natural law theory in Locke's writings. On the first count, Locke is fully entrenched within modernity; on the second count, he provides a decayed form of traditional (or perhaps neo-Thomistic) natural law morality.[4] Alternatively, there is the esoteric escape route suggested by Strauss, according to which Locke follows Hobbes's lead and consequently holds no recognizable theory of natural law at all and should be read outside the classical Christian tradition altogether.[5]

The general contours of this debate within the tradition of natural jurisprudence itself is very old, going back at least to William of Ockham's

4. Francis Oakley and Elliot Urdang have provided an invaluable service to these debates by showing how the voluntarist/intellectualist split in the philosophy of the natural law has animated this tradition from the start. Hence these differences cannot in turn be used to label a thinker "modern" or "traditionalist" unless one is willing to ignore the diversity that has long existed within these accounts. See Oakley and Urdang, "Locke, Natural Law, and God," *Natural Law Forum* 11 (1966); Oakley, "Locke, Natural Law, and God—Again," *History of Political Thought* 18, no. 4 (1997). This has consequences for the way in which we understand figures like Grotius, whom many scholars label the father of modern natural law, but it also clearly affects the way we assess Locke. For other contributions to these disputes, see W. von Leyden, "John Locke and Natural Law," *Philosophy* 31, no. 116 (1956); Martin Seliger, "Locke's Natural Law and the Foundation of Politics," *Journal of the History of Ideas* 24, no. 3 (1963): 337–54; John W. Yolton, ed., *John Locke: Problems and Perspectives* (Cambridge: Cambridge University Press, 1969); Richard Tuck, "The 'Modern' Theory of Natural Law," in *The Languages of Political Theory in Early-Modern Europe*, ed. Anthony Pagden (New York: Cambridge University Press, 1987); Knud Haakonssen, *Natural Law and Moral Philosophy: From Grotius to the Scottish Enlightenment* (New York: Cambridge University Press, 1996); John Colman, *John Locke's Moral Philosophy* (Edinburgh: Edinburgh University Press, 1983); David Wooten, "John Locke: Socinian or Natural Law Theorist?" in *Religion, Secularization, and Political Thought: Thomas Hobbes to J. S. Mill*, ed. James E. Crimmins (London: Routledge, 1989); John Marshall, *John Locke: Resistance, Religion, and Responsibility* (Cambridge: Cambridge University Press, 1994); and Alex Tuckness, "The Coherence of a Mind: John Locke and the Law of Nature," *Journal of the History of Philosophy* 37, no. 1 (1999): 73–90.

5. Leo Strauss, *Natural Right and History* (Chicago: University of Chicago Press, 1953), 202–51. See also Strauss, "Locke's Doctrine of Natural Law," in *What Is Political Philosophy? And Other Studies* (Westport, Conn.: Greenwood Press, 1959). For a useful reply to Strauss, see John W. Yolton, "Locke on the Law of Nature," *Philosophical Review* 67, no. 4 (1958). A more recent Straussian interpretation of Locke and the natural law is provided by Steven Forde, "Natural Law, Theology, and Morality in Locke," *American Journal of Political Science* 45, no. 2 (2001): 396–409.

separation from Aquinas.[6] At the extreme and recriminating limits of this division, God is either a tyrant for whom there are no limits on what he may will as good or evil for man by divine fiat, or God is superfluous, because there is an independent, eternal, and natural standard of law that binds God's will. Pufendorf and Leibniz provide a telling opposition in this regard, but some of Locke's earliest critics, like Thomas Burnet, charged him with locating the standards of moral good and evil in the arbitrary will of God.[7] David Wooten has more recently summarized this reading as follows: "Where Hobbes had made his sovereign a 'mortal God,' Locke had made his God a Hobbist sovereign, whose commands were to be obeyed out of fear of pain and hope of pleasure."[8]

On one level it is at least surprising, if not a bit odd, that so many people would worry for so long about whether the natural law is a law *because* God wills it so, or whether the natural law is good and just and *hence* a wise and benevolent God considers it to be a law for men and supervises or guides them accordingly. Such disputes, as prominent and intellectually charged as they are, cannot help but strike many a modern reader as hopelessly tendentious. With the battle lines drawn in this way, we might never have got around to considering the effects that any form of natural law theorizing, irrespective of its presumed source or autonomy, will have on the way in which we understand human moral capacities and the scope of human agency.

While most of what Locke has to say about the natural law suggests, to me at least, that he is best understood as a critically minded theological voluntarist,[9] I want to redirect the discussion of natural law in Locke

6. The most famous source of a discussion of these matters is found in an extended footnote by Otto von Gierke in *Political Theories of the Middle Age*, trans. F. W. Maitland (Bristol: Thoemmes Press, 1996), 172n256. For a very useful critical assessment of this note, see Oakley and Urdang, "Locke, Natural Law, and God."

7. See, for example, the following argument from Leibniz's critique of Pufendorf: "God is praised because he is just. . . . Neither the norm of conduct itself, nor the essence of the just, depends on his free decision, but rather on eternal truths, objects of the divine intellect, which constitute, so to speak, the essence of divinity itself; and it is right that our author [Pufendorf] is reproached by theologians when he maintains the contrary; because, I believe, he had not seen the wicked consequences which arise from it. Justice, indeed, would not be an essential attribute of God, if he himself established justice and law by his free will." Leibniz, "Opinion on the Principles of Pufendorf," in *Political Writings*, trans. and ed. Patrick Riley (New York: Cambridge University Press, 1972), 71. For Thomas Burnet, see his "Remarks upon *An Essay Concerning Human Understanding:* In a Letter Addres'd to the Author" (1697).

8. Wooten, "John Locke: Socinian or Natural Law Theorist?" 42.

9. I say a critically minded voluntarist because, while Locke's stresses the role of God's will in determining what is right and obligatory for man, he nonetheless holds on to the idea that all moral imperatives can and must be questioned, even those that we receive as divine revelation

and ask about the consequences of his natural law theory and his psychological hedonism for moral and political agency. In what follows I argue that one of the more important features of Locke's theory of the natural law is not its voluntarism and/or intellectualism but what I will call its transformative, developmental, or "process character" in the moral life of the individual. This in turn carries valuable insights into the way in which Locke conceives and normatively works to instill the necessary skills and virtues for active membership in political society.

Locke's moral philosophy has, for good reason, been understood as one that is essentially hedonistic. As he argues in the *Essay*, "Good and evil . . . are nothing but pleasure or pain, or that which occasions or procures pleasure or pain to us."[10] Insofar as Locke's theory of morality is rooted in the hedonic pursuit of pleasure and aversion to pain, his conception of the moral life, like his political contractarianism, can be understood as an instrumentalist, thin, unsatisfactory, and perhaps unworkable vision of collective existence. To see how and why this is in fact not the case, we have to seek out the nature of the complex relationship between hedonism, theism, and the natural law in his writings.

By stressing Locke's hedonism outside the context of his theocentric perspective, we get the common notion that Locke denies the relevance of discussing the *summum bonum* for man. Read in this way, Locke equates an individual's greatest happiness with what brings him the greatest pleasure. Since this calculation will vary from one individual to the next, "the philosophers of old did in vain inquire, whether *summum bonum* consisted in riches, or bodily delights, or virtue, or contemplation."[11] Yet Locke rejects the discussion of a more extensive, substantive good for man only if we (wrongly) suppose that "all the concerns of man

---

(*ECHU*, 4.18.10). Indeed, for Locke, God expects or wants man to engage in this kind of questioning; it is in fact part of man's duty to God: "I think it may not be amiss to take notice, that, however faith be opposed to reason, faith is nothing but a firm assent of the mind: which, if it be regulated, as is our duty, cannot be afforded to anything but upon good reason; and so cannot be opposite to it. He that believes without having any reason for believing, may be in love with his own fancies; but neither seeks truth as he ought, nor pays the obedience due to his Maker, who would have him use those discerning faculties he has given him, to keep him out of mistake and error" (ibid., 4.17.24). If Protestantism and modern natural law theorizing combined in such a way as to make the standards for a rational account of morality more remote, at least in comparison to earlier scholasticism, Locke seized upon this intellectual and religious climate not as a path to skepticism or secular rationalism but as a way to encourage a particular form of individual moral self-examination and collective political striving.

10. Ibid., 2.28.5; see also 2.20.2 and 2.21.43.
11. Ibid., 2.21.56.

terminated in this life."[12] If there were no prospects of life beyond the grave, the proposition that men's greatest pleasures and pains define for them their individual good and evil would be right, and it would be fruitless to inquire into an individual or human *summum bonum*. Under this impious supposition, it would be right to argue, "'Let us eat and drink,' let us enjoy what we delight in, 'for tomorrow we shall die.'"[13] But if men accept even the "bare possibility" of the existence of God, which Locke claims no one with reason may deny, then men cannot be thought to live in the manner of insects, beetles, and bees, with their various delights that are only meant to last for one season and then "exist no more forever." Rather, they are beings who have telic purposes, a greatest good, and greatest concernment—their future eternal happiness. "The rewards and punishments of another life, which the Almighty has established, as the enforcements of his law, are of weight enough to determine the choice, against whatever pleasure or pain this life can show, when the eternal state is considered but in its bare possibility, which nobody can make any doubt of."[14]

Lockean psychological hedonism, then, is not the basis for a rejection of a substantive conception of freedom (liberty in the pursuit of our "true felicity") or the rejection of a *summum bonum* for man,[15] but is a way of conceiving the internal operations of human motivation that are themselves a reflection of, or consistent with, God's workmanship. How else, Locke asks, does one explain the probable existence of heaven and hell, if not because God understands that men are motivated by the pursuit of pleasures and rewards and by the aversion to pain and punishment. For Locke, God himself acknowledges a basic distinction among men between what moral rectitude requires in and of itself as moral goodness (for example, love and charity toward others), and what is needed to motivate human beings to act in ways consistent with the morally good and virtuous. Thus we cannot confuse psychological hedonism with ethical hedonism, cannot wrongly conflate moral good and evil with a utilitarian calculus of pleasure and pain.

Obligations and the factors that motivate men to fulfill them must be clearly distinguished. Locke suggests that the failure to distinguish a rule

12. Ibid. See also "Understanding," in Locke, *Political Essays*, ed. Mark Goldie (New York: Cambridge University Press, 1997) (hereafter *PE*), 260–65.

13. *ECHU*, 2.21.56.

14. Ibid., 2.21.72.

15. For this argument, see Strauss, *Natural Right and History*; but also J. B. Schneewind, *The Invention of Autonomy* (New York: Cambridge University Press, 1998), chapter 8.

from the motives to follow the rule will only equip us with a moralistic language, one that is bound to "evaporate" into "words and dispute and niceties."[16] We will not possess an obligatory or efficacious moral law unless such a law has sanctions attached to it that compel beings who are motivated by pleasure and pain. Without addressing the motivational sources for moral behavior, philosophers can give us only verbal moralisms, not effective guides for judgment and action. "The moral rectitude of [an action] considered barely in itself is not good or evil nor [in] any way moves the will, but as pleasure and pain either accompanies the action itself or is looked on to be a consequence of it. Which is evident from the punishments and rewards which God has annexed to moral rectitude or pravity as proper motives to the will, which would be needless if moral rectitude were in itself good and moral pravity evil."[17]

From all of this we can see that Locke's is a divinely inspired hedonism, or, put differently, that man's psychological hedonism is conferred by a providential source. Surely hedonism has never sounded so pious as it does in Locke. To the extent that man's moral life and his standards of judgment are taken over by a concern with heaven and hell we might conclude that Locke's moral theory is (despite the cues he claims to take from scripture) ultimately self-regarding, if not selfish and greedy.[18] But we cannot conclude that human life is for that reason without moral purpose and a greater end.

---

16. See "Of Ethic in General," in *PE*, 302. This is how Locke reads the "Ethics of the schools" and Aristotle in particular. "The end and use of morality being to direct our lives, and by showing us what actions are good, and what bad, prepare us to do the one and avoid the other; those that pretend to teach morals mistake their business, and become only language masters where they do not do this; when they teach us only to talk and dispute, [and] call actions by the names they prescribe, when they do not show the inferments that may draw us to virtue and deter us from vice" (300).

17. "Voluntas," in *PE*, 321.

18. This too can be easily overstated. We should not underestimate the fact that, while Locke puts stress upon the hedonic motivations for moral actions, he nonetheless believes in the independent moral status of those laws and obligations. This is particularly clear in the *ELN*, and in the old distinction he adopts between the "liability to punishment" and the "liability to pay dutiful obedience" (6, p. 183). On the other hand, notice how the language of the market, of interest, advantage, and bargain, enter into Locke's discussion of Christian virtue. The ancient philosophers, according to Locke, had shown the beauty of virtue, and while most men "could not refuse her their esteem and commendation, very few were willing to espouse her." But with the appearance of Christ, his death and resurrection, and the promise of immortal life, piety is given an "advantage . . . over all that could tempt or deter men from it!" Locke continues: "But now there being put into the scales on her side, 'an exceeding and immortal weight of glory;' interest is come about to her, and virtue now is visibly the most enriching purchase, and by much the best bargain." *The Reasonableness of Christianity*, ed. George Ewing (Washington, D.C.: Regnery Gateway, 1965), §245.

We might also conclude from what we have seen so far that Locke offers us a strictly juridical moral theory, one that is defined above all by God as a sovereign lawmaker with the power to reward the virtuous and, more centrally, the power to punish the aberrant. We would not be wrong, per se, in doing so. But this type of description can be easily exaggerated, and when we leave it at this, we have surely not gone far enough. For what seems most valuable to Locke is that this hierarchical juridical frame (divine, natural, and civil) establishes duties and rights, penalties and rewards, that form an ontological context whose defining feature is the dynamic character of life in which individuals seek outwardly and question themselves inwardly concerning the nature and ends of their judgments and actions, beliefs and conduct. This is what free moral agency means for Locke: suspending and examining one's desires and inclinations in relation to a moral code or guide. "That, in this state of ignorance we shortsighted creatures might not mistake true felicity, we are endowed with a power to suspend any particular desire, and keep it from determining the will, and engaging us in action. This is standing still, where we are not sufficiently assured of the way: examination is consulting a guide."[19] Through such "suspension" and fair examination we have true moral liberty and become capable of experiencing "real happiness."

Most human errors and faults can be traced to the failure to use this power of judgment correctly. "If the neglect or abuse of the liberty he had, to examine what would really and truly make for his happiness, misleads him, the miscarriages that follow on it must be imputed to his own election."[20] We are still, of course, liable to failures even when we engage our powers of volition and nonvolition in the prescribed way. Locke does not suppose that the individual is completely transparent to the self, as "we are not masters enough of our minds." Yet, as he argues in *An Essay Concerning Human Understanding*: "God, who knows our frailty, pities our weakness, and requires of us no more than we are able to do, and sees what was and what was not in our power, will judge us as a kind and merciful Father."[21] Rather than "enlightened" self-interest, or self-interest rightly understood, we might call this liberty and self-interest divinely understood.

Locke appreciates that this understanding of the will and judgment places a heavy emphasis on the standards by which men are to examine

19. *ECHU*, 2.21.51.
20. Ibid., 2.21.57.
21. Ibid., 2.21.54; see also 4.27.24.

and regulate their passions. Of course he is also well aware that far from being rational, self-interested actors who pursue their understanding of the good with knowledge and foresight, men are for the most part feeble, passionate, desirous beings who are more prone to self-delusion and hasty choices than to critical self-examination, forbearance, and deferred gratification. "Blind precipitancy," whether from acquired dispositions, habits, or momentary ill-ordered passions, more often than not defines how men act in relation to what they perceive to be their good.

The disjunction between how men judge and act and how they should judge and act is a central concern throughout Locke's political and moral writings. Locke argued consistently over the course of his life that there is a law of nature, decreed by the will of God, that determines what is and is not to be done and is knowable to man by the "light of nature" alone.[22] Many years before his famous attack on innatism in the *Essay Concerning Human Understanding*, Locke argued in the *Essays on the Law of Nature* that the law of nature is neither innate nor the result of a universal consensus among men, as per Grotius, nor can it be learned from custom or tradition. The natural law is not in men, nor does it come from men as a dictate of reason (or so-called right reason) or as the product of consensual will formation.[23] The human faculty of reason is too weak and limited for these purposes and can only search for the natural law. Indeed, Locke is at pains to caution men against confusing the search and discovery of the natural law with its actual authorship, for in doing so they fundamentally misconstrue the status of the moral obligations that always already exist for them. According to Locke reason is not "so much the maker of [the natural] law as its interpreter, unless violating the dignity of the supreme legislator, we wish to make reason responsible for that received law which it merely investigates; *nor indeed can reason*

22. See *ELN*, 1, pp. 109–13; *ECHU*, 4.14; *Second Treatise*, §12; "Understanding," in *PE*, 262–63.

23. I am aware, of course, that in the *Second Treatise* Locke seems to equate the laws of nature with reason (§6) and even suggests that the law of nature is "writ in the Hearts of all Mankind" (§11). Others have tried to explain, excuse, and/or resolve these apparent contradictions in Locke; see Laslett's introduction and see also von Leyden's introduction to the *Essays on the Law of Nature*. There are indeed many different ways of accounting for these differences, from the biographical development of the author to the changing circumstances and audiences that constitute the historical conditions for the *Second Treatise* and the *Essays on the Law of Nature*, or the *Essay Concerning Human Understanding*, respectively. I will make no contribution to these efforts here apart from noting that when Locke entered into the "particulars" of the law of nature (which he infamously disclaimed in the *Second Treatise*, §12), there is more consistency and substantive moral and political depth to these accounts than is often supposed.

give us laws, since it is only a faculty of our mind and part of us."[24] No statement better captures the difference between Locke, and whatever form of liberalism we may wish to derive from his authority, and a Kantian-inspired constructivist liberalism.[25]

For Locke, the natural law is the one and only true "touchstone" for judging between moral right and wrong, virtue and vice.[26] But that this law exists, that it has all the requisite qualities of a law and is obligatory over conduct, and that men can know it by reason alone and follow it, does not of course mean that all men universally do so. Locke can make sense of the diversity of moral principles and customs throughout the world (without succumbing to moral relativism or skepticism) by observing how men make actual use of their faculties. "God having fitted men with faculties and means to discover, receive, and retain truths, according as they are employed. The great difference that is to be found in the notions of mankind is, from the different use they put their faculties to."[27] In fact, what seems most valuable about Locke's writings on the law of nature is precisely the distance between what he takes to be the eternal and unalterable rules of moral judgment, on the one hand, and the standards, customs, impulses, and passions that men actually use in relation to their actions (and what they label "virtue" and "vice"), on the other. The locus of Locke's moral arguments concerning the natural law is not to be found in the law's content but in the moral inferences he makes from human faculties and the obligations and the substantive value he attributes to the process of searching for the law of nature.

For Locke, our human faculties—for example, reason, intellect, and will—have intrinsic moral purposes or ends. By virtue of the fact that we are made, and made the way we are, by an omnipotent God who could

---

24. *ELN,* 1, p. 111 (emphasis added).

25. There is one further point to make concerning this passage. It is a long, unnecessary, and unwarranted leap to argue on this basis that Locke thereby rejects moral autonomy, as Gauthier claims. This is doubtless a different form of autonomy from the Kantian variety, according to which the individual is a law unto himself. Locke's considered views on the will and the powers of suspension and examination allow for an extensive degree of autonomous self-direction, unconstrained by heteronomous desires and interests, even as Locke's analysis suggests that this occurs in fewer cases than he might prefer. Yet, even within the parameters of an obligatory natural law context, individual moral autonomy has powerful resonance in Locke's writings. But here I would suggest that individual moral autonomy is as much a duty, an independent moral requirement, as it is a privilege of a willful agent. Cf. David Gauthier, "Why Ought One Obey God?" in *The Social Contract Theorists,* ed. Christopher W. Morris (Lanham, Md.: Rowman and Littlefield, 1999), 88–89.

26. *ECHU,* "Epistle to the Reader," 18–19, and 2.28.8.

27. Ibid., 1.3.23; see also *ELN,* 2, p. 133.

have fashioned us in any way he saw fit, the distinctly human faculties that we do possess hold moral content for us.[28] The first defining feature of the self and of an individual's identity is a self-consciousness of himself as a unique being. This self-consciousness, according to Locke, leads directly to an awareness of the existence of God and of humanity's dependence on God. "For knowing God to be a wise agent he cannot but conclude that he has that knowledge [knowledge of himself as a self] and those faculties which he finds in himself above the other creatures given him for some use and end."[29] By virtue of the faculties that men possess (an agile mind, reason, and a body which is quick and easy to move), Locke infers that "God intends man to do something."[30] Men's ends principally are two: to show gratitude and reverence toward the "author of their being," and to assist and preserve one another in mutual society.

Not only do our peculiar faculties have moral content, like the fingerprint of God on his workmanship, we are under an additional and more extensive obligation to understand and perfect these faculties as far as is possible for limited, shortsighted creatures. In a moving passage Locke argues that it is "highly rational to think, even were revelation silent in the case, that, as men employ those talents God has given them here, they shall accordingly receive their rewards at the close of the day, when their sun shall set, and night shall put an end to their labours."[31] Additionally, the very limits of our faculties, the insufficiency of human knowledge, also have moral content and betray divine purposes. These limits should teach men humility by revealing the extent of their shortsightedness and their congenital liability to error. Yet these limits should also "excite in us a desire and endeavour after a better state."[32] Our ideas of human or social perfection will always outstrip our individual and collective capacities (a point that is deeply relevant to Rousseau as well). Yet Locke's moral inferences from human faculties suggests that what we have, although it falls short of what we can imagine, is good enough to obtain knowledge sufficient for guidance in this life, "if we will but confine it within those purposes and direct it to those ends which the constitution of our nature and the circumstances of our being point out to us."[33]

28. *ELN*, 7, p. 199; *ECHU*, 4.12.11.
29. "Law of Nature," in *PE*, 270.
30. *ELN*, 4, p. 157.
31. *ECHU*, 4.14.2.
32. Ibid.
33. "Understanding," in *PE*, 260.

Locke is at pains to show the moral content and purpose of human faculties because he wants to argue that men can attain knowledge of God and an understanding of their duties without relying upon the false crutch of innate ideas or dispositions. Moral judgments and actions based upon principles thought to be innate, according to Locke, follow from nothing more than custom, education, and habit. More damning still, those who take things on trust (and this is the majority, in Locke's view) "misemploy their power of assent, by lazily enslaving their minds to the dictates and dominion of others, in doctrines which it is their duty carefully to examine, and not blindly, with an implicit faith, to swallow."[34] To be sure, this is a condition that concerns the actions and interests of religious and political elites as much as it does the majority of men. Locke comes as close as one can to arguing that innatism is a kind of political and religious conspiracy designed to render men more governable on the grounds "that principles must not be questioned."[35] Innatism naturalizes and sacralizes that which is conventional and arbitrary by dint of repetition, custom, and education, taking root in men "before their memory began to keep a register of their actions."[36] Further, those principles that are introduced to the "unwary" and "unprejudiced" (Locke's famous *tabula rasa*) by those who "affect" to be teachers and masters become self-perpetuating with time.

A motley and debilitating mixture of pride, mental laziness, absence of leisure, fear, and shame keep "innate" principles from being questioned. The result is a docile and credulous citizenry wherein the individual will "take up, from his education and the fashions of his country, any absurdity for innate principles; and by long poring on the same objects, so dim his sight as to take monsters lodged in his own brain for the images of the Deity, and the workmanship of his hands."[37] The problem is not so much the loss of any rational ground for moral principles, or that the rule of custom and tradition will lead to complete moral relativism and vice. Even under these conditions, "what we take over from other people's talk, if we embrace it only because others have insisted that it is good, may perhaps direct our morals well enough and keep them within the bounds of dutiful action."[38] Rather, the problem posed by innatism and

---

34. *ECHU*, 1.3.23.
35. Ibid., 1.3.25.
36. Ibid., 1.2.23.
37. Ibid., 1.2.26.
38. *ELN*, 2, p. 129; see also *ECHU*, 2.28.11.

the religious and political elites that espouse it is the cultural production of subjects who lack the critical discerning faculties necessary to properly regulate their assent to any "truths," religious or political. As we will see further below, this constitutes one of the central dilemmas for the ideal of government by consent and for the role that public reason and proper public judgment should play in political society.

When Locke argues that human beings have the "natural light" of reason to know the natural law, he does not mean to suggest that such a law is innate or that such knowledge will come easily to men, or that all or even most men will come to this knowledge and its true foundations. Instead, this is a kind of knowledge that a man can attain for himself, without the help of others, "if he makes proper use of the faculties he is endowed with by nature."[39] Locke provides a telling analogy by comparing the search for the natural law with mining for silver and gold. Like the veins of gold that lie concealed in the earth, Locke refers to this treasure trove as the "hidden and secret laws of nature."[40] As with mining, the pursuit of man's duty in the natural law requires a similar kind of toil and perseverance: "First they have to equip themselves; and it is with great labour that those resources which lie hidden in darkness are to be brought to the light of day. They do not present themselves to idle and listless people, nor indeed to all those who search for them, since we notice some also who are toiling in vain."[41] The pursuit of the natural law is itself a preparatory task that entails the formation of a particular kind of subject. It is only through a form of moral labor, by which we mix ourselves with the created universe, that the individual may potentially fashion a self capable of reasoning, judging, and acting properly in the *saculem*. Such a person will worship God, seek out and observe the laws of nature, enter and preserve society with others, and regulate his assent according to the standards of divine (natural) law. We do not come to possess the natural law as a natural right through this process, but (as with Locke's labor theory of property) we do come to own this natural law as something of us, not just for us. The mining work that is being done here is an inward work on ourselves.

While the natural law is the same as God's divine positive law (scripture) and its obligatory conditions are the same—coming from a supreme lawgiver—its method of promulgation and the manner by which one

---

39. *ELN*, 2, p. 123.
40. Ibid., 1, p. 115, 2, p. 135.
41. Ibid., 2, p. 135.

comes to know this law are different from divine positive law.[42] It is precisely because of its different "method of promulgation" that there is something we might call content in the form of Lockean natural law. This content is what I am calling the developmental or ethical process character of the natural law. Positive divine law is apprehended by faith. The natural law is known "by the light of nature" (reason). The very process of seeking it, and the labor employed in trying to discover and interpret it among beings who can have no certain knowledge and who must instead rely on probabilistic judgments, is a process of critical engagement with one's culture and traditions, and, more specifically, a reflective examination of what one has swallowed from that culture. The process character of the natural law sets the context within which it becomes possible for the individual to pursue the good life, the value of which is independent of the individual will. The discursive interaction of reason with nature is necessary for both the "direction of life" and the "formation of character."[43]

It is of vital importance to Locke that each individual learn that there is a natural law, which is God's will, knowable by reason, universal, and eternally obligatory. What is more, it is a duty for man to seek this law—this is the import of Locke's moral inferences from the faculties. Men will obtain God's truths and laws in accordance with and insofar as each person employs those critical, discerning, reasoning faculties that God has given them for this very purpose. As he argues in *A Letter Concerning Toleration*, "Those things that every man ought sincerely to enquire into himself, and by Meditation, Study, Search, and his own Endeavours, attain the Knowledge of, cannot be looked upon as the Peculiar Possession of any one sort of Men."[44] If we were to reject or become lackadaisical about pursuing the natural law (God's will), as when we accept cultural standards or the opinions of others on trust, or presume certain principles to be innate, and so fail to question or examine those principles that inform our actions, we diminish the very faculties that God intended us to use and perfect (as far as possible) and thereby fall further away from him and our primary moral duties. We would consequently not only judge wrongly, according to the wrong standards, but would enervate our moral capacities, short-circuit the pathways of our proper development, and

42. Ibid., 6, p. 189. See also *A Second Vindication of the Reasonableness of Christianity*, in *Works of Locke*, 7:229.

43. *ELN*, 4, p. 149.

44. *Letter Concerning Toleration*, 36. This might well be taken as the basic principle of the Protestant Reformation.

potentially jeopardize our greatest concernment (eternal life). We would give up on a necessary feature of man's pilgrimage in this life. Innatism in religion and patriarchalism in politics both commit significant errors in this regard. They inure the individual and his reason from becoming capable of seeking the proper foundations of morals and politics by instructing the subject, from earliest childhood, to accept as tradition that which it is everyone's moral and political responsibility to scrutinize.[45]

Thus, in my reading, the natural law is about getting narrow, desirous, habitual creatures to lift their eyes above their immediate pleasures and the conditions of their cultural constitution as selves. Locke plays the moralist in all of this by seeking to redefine the public's conception of the good and their standards of judgment alongside a commitment to individual moral freedom and religious liberty. "To him, I say, who hath a prospect of the different state of perfect happiness or misery that attends men after this life, depending on their behaviour here, the measures of good and evil that govern his choice are mightily changed."[46] Lockean freedom is given moral, substantive purpose by virtue of such changes in the standards of men's moral judgments. Each individual will seek the natural law as an individual moral and epistemological responsibility. In doing so the individual will not simply possess an essentially Christian moral code (which Locke admits the rule of custom and opinion more or less provide), but will have become the kind of subject who might more properly govern his assent in relation to his greatest end. Hence, one of the telic functions of the natural law, as a transformative practice, is to breed beings capable of public reasoning and public judgment.

It is central to Locke's ethical purpose to argue that the failure to search for and follow the natural law is not due to a lack of capacity, despite the extensive limits that exist for human understanding. Rather, such a failure is always one of will, or bad, hasty choice.[47]

45. I take this to be part of Locke's purpose when he argues in the *Second Treatise*, contra Filmer, that "the law that was to govern *Adam*, was the same that was to govern all his Posterity, the *Law of Reason*. But his Off-spring having another way of entrance into the World, different from him, by a natural birth, that produced them ignorant and without the use of *Reason*, they were not presently *under that Law*" (§57). The method of promulgation, or the means by which individuals come to learn the law of nature after the Fall, is different for Adam's descendants. A failure to note this difference is not only to misunderstand the relationship between human freedom and the moral law but also to fail to see or fulfill man's preexisting moral duties to seek out the natural law.

46. *ECHU,* 2.21.62.

47. See "Understanding," in *PE*, 263–64: "I think one may safely say that amidst the greati gnorance that is so justly complained of amongst mankind, where anyone endeavored to know his duty sincerely with a design to do it scarce ever anyone miscarried for want of knowledge."

There are, however, serious difficulties here. Locke seems caught, in a self-conscious way, between a theistic perspective that makes temporal human pleasures pale in comparison to eternal bliss, and a sociological analysis from which it is clear that nothing could be more ineffectual for the instruction of human willing or judging than to insist upon cloudy and remote incentives. And given the history of religious wars, Locke is not unfamiliar with the ways in which arguments grounded in theological commitments have been used in illegitimate ways to coerce and repress dissenters. Locke has in mind a single measure of moral value and a teleological conception of man's greatest end. Of course, he rules out the use of force or coercion with respect to individual standards of the good, and he rejects natural or dispositional knowledge or motivation in relation to their true ends. Instead, Locke wants to believe that if the benefits of virtue and religion were set next to the fleeting pleasures of the present, men could not help but choose the path that would lead to the former: "were the satisfaction of a lust and the joys of heaven offered at once to any one's present possession, he would not balance, or err in the determination of his choice."[48] And while there are moments in Locke's writing that suggest a penchant for moral determinism of this type, Locke recognizes that this position is both normatively weak and psychologically/sociologically overwrought. A host of factors, both personal and cultural, intervene to disrupt the proper conduct of judgment. From the combination of man's "narrow scantling of capacity" to his passionate nature and the "fallacy of a little difference in time," men are more inclined to pursue immediate pleasures than seek their greater future good. Ignorance, inadvertency, and bad habits, by themselves or in combination, allow a shallow presentism to gain a disproportionate influence in men's judgments and actions.

In more general terms, there are three standards by which men judge their voluntary actions and regulate their assent. These standards, which Locke terms "moral relations," are the natural law, the civil law, and the law of opinion or fashion. Each law has its own principles and powers of enforcement. The divine law judges whether human actions are sins or duties, the civil law determines whether our actions are criminal or innocent, and the laws of opinion attribute virtue or vice to our deeds. What is crucial about these distinctions is that while Locke views the divine (or natural) law as the only true guide for moral rectitude, and although the

48. *ECHU,* 2.21.60.

civil law has all the powers of the commonwealth behind it, the real, effective force guiding men's everyday judgments and actions is the rule of fashion or custom. It is not sin or crime that men fear most but disrepute, shame, and public censure. Hence men "do that which keeps them in reputation with their company, little regard the laws of God, or the magistrate."[49]

For Locke, nothing could be more morally perilous, "since there is much more falsehood and error among men than truth and knowledge."[50] Devoid of true or certain knowledge, all human beings have to go on for the proper regulation of their assent to moral principles is probability. For beings without demonstrable knowledge who must nonetheless judge and act in relation to questions of great concern for their present and future lives, the grounds of probability become the foundations upon which assent must be built.[51] Probabilistic judgments share in the same kind of process character as the pursuit of the natural law, insofar as its proper mode of engagement will produce critical, examining subjects who will not assent to any proposition that the evidence will not bear.[52] Locke enumerates the grounds of probability only to find that the majority of men do not assess the principles they assent to by the standards of critical, rational inquiry, but give up their assent to "common received opinions, either of our friends or party, neighbourhood or country."[53]

If Locke recognizes that most men do not properly regulate their assent or their actions according to the natural (divine) law or by the terms of probabilistic reasoning, and instead dangerously pin their ideas on the opinion of others (even while supposing that they will be reconciled with God at the final judgment), then the idea that compacts and promises will be performed because God wills it and has sanctions to enforce his

---

49. Ibid., 2.28.12.
50. Ibid., 4.15.6.
51. Ibid., 4.16.
52. This is also one of Locke's criteria for determining who is an earnest "lover of truth." See the chapter on "Enthusiasm" he added to the fourth edition of the *Essay*. *ECHU*, 4.19.1. Locke's argument that the search for truth requires that one "first prepare his mind for the love of it" suggests a comparison to the ancients. But while Socrates and Locke both speak of the lovers of truth, their understandings of this love are quite different. For Locke, the love of truth means loving truth for "truth's sake." Such a love does not give more credit or assent to truth than what the proofs (from sense and reflection) can show. Love of truth is shown by remaining indifferent to its propositions until one has properly examined and balanced its claims. For Socrates, the love of truth is an erotic love. The idea that one reveals oneself to be a lover of truth by remaining steadfast in one's indifference could not have sounded more strange to Socrates.
53. Ibid., 4.20.17.

will is as causally deficient to order men's motives toward civil society as the rest of the natural law's dictates turn out to be in practice.[54] In the case of mutual promising and compact, however, we are dealing not only with the relative standing of the individual to God but with what Locke repeatedly refers to as the very bonds of society.[55] Those bonds now appear to be subject to the laws of fashion and what most men in a society deem praiseworthy or blameworthy, rather than an independent theological source that will fix the standards of the good and the measures of individual right.

Locke approaches the discussion of moral relations with a great deal of practical realism. The common measures by which men distinguish between virtue and vice and deem their actions morally good or bad is not what Locke thinks it can or should be. Yet he does not for this reason think that human society is damned or without moral direction. The reign of fashion and opinion means that the measures of virtue and vice will vary according to different cultural standards: "what was thought praiseworthy in one place, escaped not censure in another."[56] Nonetheless, this does not generate problems of relativism because Locke finds a significant overlap in the moral standards that receive cultural and temporally specific expression in practice. This prodigious overlap (one that makes cross-cultural moral and political judgments possible from within a Lockean frame) is provided by the ontological conditions of man and his dependency on God: "it is no wonder that esteem and discredit, virtue and vice, should, in a great measure, everywhere correspond with the unchangeable rule of right and wrong, which the law of God hath established; there being nothing that so directly and visibly secures and advances the general good of mankind in this world, as obedience to the laws he has set them, and nothing breeds such mischiefs and confusion, as the neglect of them."[57]

According to Locke there are two parts to ethics. The first is the "rule" of ethics, "which men are generally in the right in, though perhaps they

---

54. Locke's sensitive discussion of the ways in which individuals regulate their assent and moral beliefs is part of a development of his thinking (over the many revisions of the *Essay*) that contrasts with his willingness at times to argue that God's laws and justice act in a deterministic fashion on men's judgments and actions. See *ECHU*, 2.21.72. For a useful discussion of this development over the course of Locke's many revisions to the *Essay*, see Tully, *Approach to Political Philosophy*, chapter 6.

55. *Letter Concerning Toleration*, 51; *ELN*, 8, p. 213.

56. *ECHU*, 2.28.11.

57. Ibid.

have not deduced them as they should from their true principles."[58] As we have seen, the overlap in moral standards that obtains among different societies at different times is something that ties utility and the standards of virtue and vice together. This overlap produces stability and regularity and provides moral direction, even though most men fail to see that it has its true source in providence.[59] This introduces the second part of ethics, which is the "true motives" to practice these standards of right. And, as we might have anticipated, Locke argues that this part of ethics is "generally either not well known or not rightly applied."[60] More must be done to guide men in the regulation of their assent and the governance of their actions than can be provided by autonomous willing, individual searching, or private judging. As we have seen, of the three moral relations that men judge and act by, the most powerful and most immediately persuasive is the law of fashion and opinion. "The principal spring from which the actions of men take their rise, the rule they conduct them by, and the end to which they direct them, seems to be credit and reputation, and that which at any rate they avoid, is in the greatest part shame and disgrace."[61]

If, as Locke argues, commendation and shame are among the strongest human motives and have governed the actions of the greatest part of the "history of mankind,"[62] then a moral and political theory that hopes to persuade and shape men's judgments and actions must concern itself with the fashions, opinions, and habits of a society. Indeed, this is precisely what Locke counsels: "He therefore that would govern the world well, had need consider rather what fashions he makes, than what laws; and to bring anything into use he need only give it reputation."[63] We must turn, then, to the transformative work that Locke considers necessary to shape subjects who will become capable of properly governing their assent, morally and politically. This will in turn introduce us to Locke's education in virtue, which is organized around the techniques of cultivating and sustaining the proper habits of self-governance. As we will see, the social compact and Lockean politics in general presuppose this kind of moral and civic

58. "Ethica B," in *PE*, 319–20.
59. Locke argues that this was also true of the ancient philosophers who had stumbled upon the laws of nature but could not give adequate reasons for why these laws were obligatory for men. See *Reasonableness of Christianity*, §§242–43.
60. "Ethica B," 319–20.
61. "Reputation," in *PE*, 271.
62. *ECHU*, 2.28.12.
63. "Reputation," 272.

education. Nonetheless, this is an education that inevitably raises other questions concerning individual autonomy and moral freedom in Locke's theory, and therewith much of modern liberal theory inspired by Locke.

Governing Assent:
The Crisis of Credulity and the Politics of Judgment

In what follows I provide an analysis of the unique preparatory work that goes into forming subjects who might sustain the Lockean compact. The politically salient point here is that the trust citizens put in their government is a trust that refers to and is regulated, first and foremost, according to the law of nature that it is government's minimal purpose to uphold (i.e., to preserve society).[64] Governments (the legislative and executive powers of political society) must be regulated according to this standard, and so it becomes a fundamental duty for every citizen to become familiar with these natural guides and to learn how to reason, judge, and act in relation to them and the principles they reflect. An individualist politics of entrustment creates individual duties concerning the proper regulation of assent to moral beliefs and practices. But "in the whole conduct of the understanding, there is nothing of more moment than to know when, and where, and how far to give assent, and possibly there is nothing harder."[65] Locke expresses here a profound appreciation for what Allen Buchanan calls our "ineliminable social epistemic dependency," and with this dependency comes our exposure to a variety of prudential and moral risks.[66] Lockean judgment and the regulation of assent is both a social-political question concerning the common good and the preservation of property (life, liberty, and estates), and a moral duty antecedent to the positive laws of the state. If the people are to judge whether their government acts in conformity with the public good, consistent with their trust and the fixed parameters of the law of nature, then they must be taught how to reason and judge well.[67] For the aim is not simply to comply with the law and the moral principles it articulates but to reason, judge,

---

64. *Second Treatise*, §§12, 134, 135.

65. *Conduct of the Understanding*, §33.

66. See Allen Buchanan, "Political Liberalism and Social Epistemology," *Philosophy and Public Affairs* 32, no. 2 (2004): 95–130. My thanks to Stephen Macedo for suggesting this essay to me.

67. See also Kirstie McClure, *Judging Rights: Lockean Politics and the Limits of Consent* (Ithaca: Cornell University Press, 1996), esp. chapters 5 and 6.

and act from them in relation to the deliberations that citizens undertake during the course of their shared political lives—especially in relation to fundamental questions that touch on the continuation or dissolution of government.

Recall that the idea of public reason expresses a commitment to public reasonableness as a necessary standard for the morally legitimate exercise of political power. If contract makes citizens, public reason is one of the central modes by which this moral and civic formation takes place. In Locke's case, the idea of public reason entails the education of public judgment in accordance with a set of natural law guidelines, standards that take moral and political primacy in Locke's theory. This task of setting "the mind right, that on all occasions it may be disposed to consent to nothing but what may be suitable to the dignity and excellency of a rational creature," places Locke's thinking in tension with some dimensions of the liberal tradition that he is often thought to have spawned.[68] At the same time, Locke must confront some basic internal challenges that his natural law account faces in shaping the citizens who would make and, more important, sustain a social compact over time. I turn first to a discussion of these internal difficulties and then consider the instructive tensions that Locke's transformative politics poses for other values within the liberal tradition.

We must acknowledge that it is to Locke's eternal credit that he understood the practical limits of his own theistic arguments from the natural law and the near powerlessness of probability for determining moral first principles and guiding human action. Indeed, he was rather pessimistic about these standards of judgment gaining a secure foothold among men, such as they are. As he avers in the *Second Treatise*, "though the Law of Nature be plain and intelligible to all rational Creatures; yet Men being biassed by their Interest, as well as ignorant for the want of study of it, are not apt to allow of it as a Law binding to them in the application of it to their particular Cases."[69] The natural law may be potentially "plain and intelligible," but it still requires study and constant endeavor, a form of moral labor that constitutes a particular form of moral character. Yet Locke is fully aware of the self's resistance to these standards, however good they may be both in themselves and for the individual's present and future happiness. Locke acknowledges in the *Second Treatise* and elsewhere that

68. Locke, *Some Thoughts Concerning Education*, §31.
69. *Second Treatise*, §124.

this standard, while containing the authoritative principles of moral and political right, is motivationally weak in guiding men's judgments and actions. The law of nature fails to persuade the majority of men because it directs them toward an absent future good that, while incomparably greater than the paltry joys of this world, is unable to counterbalance the uneasiness that surrounds present pleasures or pains.[70] By contrast, the law that men cannot avoid and that never fails to persuade is the law of opinion or fashion: "no man escapes the punishment of their censure and dislike, who offends against the fashion and opinion of the company he keeps, and would recommend himself to."[71]

If the divine law (whether discerned by revelation, scripture, or the light of nature) is unable to guide men's moral relations and judgments, perhaps the standards of rational probability will provide a more accessible or causally efficient means by which to regulate men's assent to moral and political principles. According to Locke, God granted human beings the faculty of judgment to compensate for their lack of clear and certain knowledge. Given the absence of demonstrative evidence or certainty, human judgment and action must proceed according to the standards and degrees of probability. Probability as such "induces" the mind to accept as true those propositions that have the support of proofs or clear arguments.[72] Locke argues that the grounds of probability provide us with the only sure foundations by which to regulate assent. At times he goes as far as the deterministic claim that where manifest probability lies on one side of a proposition, we are not free ("it is not in our choice") not to assent to that position with the greater probability.[73] While Locke's enumeration of these epistemological standards might suggest a "science" of morals, or the rational foundations for common agreement on matters of general concern, his sensitive analysis of the rampant and persistent errors of judgment and "wrong assent" reveal both the limits of reason and the more general force of custom, habits, and opinion.

The problem, again, is that men are to judge in life on the basis of probabilistic reasoning, not as a mode of reasoning that is good in itself but because this is the best they can do. Yet the majority of men instead follow the pull of present passions, immediate interests, and, most powerfully, public opinion and what they have been accustomed to believe since

70. See *ECHU*, 2.21.64–69.
71. Ibid., 2.28.12.
72. Ibid., 4.15.1–4.
73. Ibid., 4.20.16.

time out of mind. The individual so understood is not a self-conscious, autonomous being of reason guided by the light of self-interest alone—the caricature of modern liberalism. Rather, a host of nonvolitional, non-rational factors influence the scale of values by which everything else in an individual's life is measured. The lesson Locke draws from this is not that men do not love truth the way they should—he acknowledges and accepts that most men are not philosophers.[74] Instead, the problem is a political-cultural and epistemological-moral one wherein "fashion and the common opinion having settled wrong notions, and education and custom ill habits, the just values of things are misplaced, and the palates of men corrupted."[75] As we have seen, Locke makes moral inferences about the true and proper ends of man on the basis of human faculties such as reason, language, and self-consciousness. Still, that human beings have these capacities does not entail that they will be used or developed as they should, a fact that can also be seen in Locke's account of the state of nature, a moral and sociable condition that is capable of peace but also suscepti-ble to uncertainty, grave disorder, and cycles of illegitimate violence.

When it comes to diagnosing those features of life that distort and pull men away from the right use of their judgment and the proper use of their liberty, Locke unites a focused moral outlook that reminds one of St. Augustine (wherein it is the wrong objects of love that lead men astray), with a keen psychological/sociological analysis that might only be rivaled by Tocqueville or Durkheim. For Locke, most people are so caught up in the day-to-day pressures of life and work that they lack the time and leisure to make proper inquiries into their principles of belief. Some simply lack the skills necessary to "carry a train of consequences in their head," while others, out of laziness or the fear of an internal dis-sonance that might follow from a fair examination of those opinions that serve their "prejudices, lives, and designs," lack the necessary will.[76]

What is most telling about Locke's discussion of the errors of wrong

---

74. See *Reasonableness of Christianity*, §243. Even if all men were philosophers, the forces of conformity and credulity, crafted in the schools, would hardly provide them with any reli-able form of cultural exemption in this regard. See, for example, Locke's sensitive discussion of precisely this problem in *ECHU*, 4.20.11.

75. *ECHU*, 2.21.71.

76. Ibid., 4.20.1–6. These constraints also become the basis for Locke's emphasis on the value of the scriptures in teaching men their moral duties. "Hearing plain commands is the sure and only course to bring them to obedience and practice. The greatest part cannot *know*, and there-fore they must *believe*." For this, Christ and the gospels are necessary. See *Reasonableness of Christianity*, §243.

assent is that these errors are themselves quite reasonable. That is, Locke acknowledges the difficulty of actually persuading men to change the standards or the scale of values by which they regulate their assent. "If he be one who takes his opinions upon trust, how can we imagine that he should renounce those tenets which time and custom have so settled in his mind, that he thinks them self-evident, and of an unquestionable certainty; or which he takes to be impressions he has received from God himself, or from men sent by him?"[77] In fact the very limits of reason and the weakness of probability suggest additional grounds for tolerance in relation to the diversity of opinions. "It would, methinks, become all men to maintain peace, and the common offices of humanity, and friendship, in the diversity of opinions; since we cannot reasonably expect that any one should readily and obsequiously quit his own opinion, and embrace ours, with a blind resignation to an authority which the understanding of man acknowledges not."[78] This set of commitments not only expresses some of the values that Locke finds in a standard of public reasonableness, it also indicates a more generous Locke than the one that placed atheists outside the pale of toleration (discussed in Chapter 2).

Opinion and beliefs, "insinuated" into "unwary" and "unbiased" minds from the time of the nursery, stick with the individual; such principles are indeed "beyond all possibility of being pulled out again."[79] What fashion and opinion settle, custom and habit solidify. As a result, men are not only led astray but their "taste" for virtue, their willingness to examine what they have swallowed from their culture, is corrupted. The mind is not open and impartial but always already holds certain culturally imbued commitments and personal psychic investments. Reason and probability cannot hope to persuade those who have been bred according to certain principles that have become sacred and natural, where to question such principles is to profane them. Locke's rule of probabilistic reason, to regulate assent according to "the evidence which things carry with them," and his moral injunction that every individual should strictly examine every principle he admits as true, could not be more ineffectual or powerless.

No one is so open or so candid, so disengaged from his culture and time, as to be capable of the kind of self-scrutiny that Locke recommends. The empirical self, indifferent and permanently open to what sense, experience, and the preponderance of evidence can prove is a chimera of

---

77. *ECHU,* 4.16.4. This is a point also developed in Aristotle, *Ethics,* 10.1179a35–b26.
78. *ECHU,* 4.16.4.
79. Ibid., 4.20.9. See also *Conduct of the Understanding,* §33, and "Study," in *PE,* 369–72.

philosophy. Locke knows this. While he stresses again and again that there is nothing more dangerous than accepting principles without questioning or examination, nothing, it seems, could be more difficult, unnerving, or painful.[80] The barriers to such critical examination are both individual and cultural. "Men will disbelieve their own eyes, renounce the evidence of their senses, and give their own experience the lie, rather than admit of anything disagreeing with [their] sacred tenets."[81] So much for Lockean empiricism. Self-interest, passion, pride, and the overwhelming force of cultural tradition and education combine to render reason and probability extraordinarily weak. What makes all this even harder for Locke to take is that most people refer the determination of their assent to the authority or opinion of others. Hence the majority is not so much in error as it holds what social scientists today call nonsalient opinions. What Locke finds in his analysis of the regulation of assent is interest, power, and party zeal or faction, without a corresponding awareness, let alone an examination or understanding, of the principles for which they contend.[82]

The way in which individuals regulate their assent to moral principles is thus of central concern to Locke. This is an issue that concerns the moral life and the nature of religious belief—the traditional context for the discussion of assent—but it is also an issue that has enormous political consequences. The limits of the natural law, reason, and probability in relation to the powerfully seductive but crushing forces of opinion, fashion, and education are not only moral and epistemological but political as well. If we situate Locke's concerns with the problems of the management of assent and the forces of habit and tradition in relation to the *Second Treatise*, we can begin to discern a consistent and deep concern with what I will call the crisis of credulity: a problem that is characterized by excessive or misplaced trust in the current structure and authority of a political order.

80. "Study," 371.
81. *ECHU*, 4.20.10.
82. See ibid., 4.20.18: "If any one should a little catechise the greatest part of the partizans of most of the sects in the world, he would not find, concerning those matters they are so zealous for, that they have any opinions of their own: much less would he have reason to think that they took them upon the examination of arguments and appearance of probability. They are resolved to stick to a party that education or interest has engaged them in; and there, like the common soldiers of an army, show their courage and warmth as their leaders direct, without ever examining, or so much as knowing, the cause they contend for." Such conformity might make for good soldiers, but for Locke it clearly makes for bad citizens and spells an even greater moral disaster.

It has long been a matter of some interpretive controversy whether there is any internal coherence in Locke's diverse writings such that we can speak of an integrated moral, epistemological, and political purpose.[83] I cannot offer any definitive response to this question here, but if we situate the *Second Treatise* in relation to the issues I have discussed thus far, we can illuminate an important subterranean problem that runs throughout his explicitly political works. If I am right about the substantive link between the problems posed by innatism, custom, and education in the moral life of the individual and the problems of credulity and trust in the body politic, then this surely brings a certain measure of unity and coherence to Locke's political and epistemological writings. However, I take this latter point to be a matter of far less significance than what we can actually learn about the nature and scope of Locke's arguments by reading his works together.

The *Second Treatise of Government* quietly narrates a problem for political society that is exactly the opposite of the one Filmer (and later Hegel) identified in relation to governments founded upon consent. The trouble here is not that governments will be weak and unstable for having been lodged in the will and private judgments of individuals. Rather, political memberships forged through promise and consent, and a government of laws empowered by the trust of the governed, seem to generate new forms of docility and credulity. The problem of credulity in the political sphere both reflects and bolsters the nonrational and nonvolitional forces of custom and habit that characterize Locke's more extensive cultural/epistemological critique.

When Locke argues that "people are not so easily got out of their old Forms, as some are apt to suggest,"[84] he is meeting the objection that a government based upon the trust of the people will entail frequent disruptions and instabilities. (Indeed, this is a problem that Locke confronts in his political writings of 1690.)[85] The idea that political society is based upon an agreement of the people was an old Leveller position, and depending on how one configured the "people," it was a radical and unnerving position for most men in power. By arguing with similar purposes but

---

83. See, for example, Ruth W. Grant's helpful discussion of these issues in the secondary literature in *John Locke's Liberalism* (Chicago: University of Chicago Press, 1987), 9–11.

84. *Second Treatise*, §223.

85. See James Farr and Clayton Roberts, "John Locke on the Glorious Revolution: A Rediscovered Document," *Historical Journal* 28, no. 2 (1995): 385–98. In this article Farr and Roberts provide us with a copy of Locke's thoughts on the events of 1688–89 (Bodleian MS Locke e. 18).

with more subtlety and different emphasis, Locke registers a qualitatively different kind of problem for politics. That is, the people are inordinately patient, slow, and averse to change, "hardly to be prevailed with to amend the acknowledg'd Faults, in the Frame they have been accustom'd to."[86] Here Locke signals a different kind of problem for his vision of politics from the one that preoccupied other radicals in his time concerning the justification of resistance, rebellion, or revolution. He discusses this problem at length in the *Essay* and elsewhere—that individuals will hold on to their tenets in the face of overwhelming evidence to the contrary, from passion, interest, long custom, and corrupt habits. As Locke argues in the *Essay,* "Habits have powerful charms." In the *Second Treatise* we see the particularly difficult social and political consequences that follow from the idea that the people are congenitally averse to changing what they have been "accustom'd to," even when, as Locke puts it, "all the World sees there is an opportunity for it." Here it is the political problem of a people "more disposed to suffer, than right themselves by Resistance."[87]

I think we may justifiably read these sections of the *Second Treatise* as the adverse political consequences that follow from the fact that "all the world are born to orthodoxy."[88] A regime and the customs, traditions, and opinions that surround and support it are part of what Locke calls "inherited local truths." Unlike property, there is very little choice about whether one wants to accept this inheritance. In large measure this is because the language of choice has lost all coherence. Individuals are born into and imbibe these "local truths," which "not one of a hundred ever examines," indeed never thinks to examine as is their duty.[89] As we have seen, this is a grave moral dilemma for Locke, because under such conditions the faculties of men are "disabled" and they lose all sight of and motivation for the proper searches they were designed to undertake. Their capacities for such examinations may still exist, but in being "disabled" they risk serious atrophy. Under certain conditions, as when a governor makes his arbitrary will the rule of law, this becomes a political crisis as well. For however ill disposed or unprepared the people may be to examine the actions of governors, over and against the pretenses and arts they use to color their usurpations, the people are not free not to oppose such developments (recall from Chapter 2 that they are not sovereign over

---

86. *Second Treatise,* §223.
87. Ibid., §230.
88. *Conduct of the Understanding,* §34.
89. Ibid., and see §41.

these matters). As Locke puts it, "*trust* must necessarily be *forfeited*" under certain conditions.[90] Such necessary conditions of forfeiture obtain when the ends for which political power was entrusted in the hands of the legislative or executive are manifestly neglected or opposed.

The failure to revoke such a trust, or to see it as already forsaken, in the face of such evidence is practically speaking to confer a power on governors that no one in fact possesses. The evasion or neglect of judgment in these cases is not within men's legitimate scope of choices: "it being out of Man's power so to submit himself to another, as to give him a liberty to destroy him; God and nature never allowing a Man so to abandon himself, as to neglect his own preservation."[91] The natural law, the limits of individual or collective sovereignty, and the nonvoluntaristic and antecedent conditions of trust mean that citizens, under certain conditions, are compelled to see that whether by "ambition, fear, folly, or corruption" their obligation to magistrates has already ended. The breach of public trust, say, by endeavoring to destroy the property of the people, brings of necessity a forfeiture of power.[92] The rub, of course, is that the people who "are not apt to stir" must still be brought along, for ultimately (exempting, of course, God's ultimate judgment) "the people shall be judge."[93]

Recent historiographic work has provided strong evidence to show that Locke composed the *Second Treatise* during the exclusion crisis and designed it as a justification for radical Whig activity during this period. Its belated publication in 1689 represented the continuation of a radical political position that, in comparison to the convention debates and the revolutionary settlement, was quite out of tune with the governing political views (both Tory and Whig) of its time.[94] In this context we might be inclined to think that Locke's repeated efforts in the *Second Treatise* to downplay the extent to which the people will seek, in an anarchic way, to constantly overturn government if they were to become mobilized by his theories of freedom and consent was designed to undercut the

90. *Second Treatise*, §149.
91. Ibid., §168; see also §§149 and 131.
92. In providing a correction to Barclay, Locke argues that under such conditions a "King has Dethron'd himself." Ibid., §239.
93. Ibid., §§230, 240–43.
94. See, among others, Ashcraft, *Revolutionary Politics and Locke's Two Treatises of Government* (Princeton: Princeton University Press, 1986), and Mark Goldie, "The Revolution of 1689 and the Structure of Political Argument," *Bulletin of Research in the Humanities* 83 (1980). See also Gordon J. Schochet, "Radical Politics and Ashcraft's Treatise on Locke," *Journal of the History of Ideas* 50, no. 3 (1989): 491–510, and Lois G. Schwoerer, "Locke, Lockean Ideas, and the Glorious Revolution," *Journal of the History of Ideas* 51, no. 4 (1990): 531–48.

prevalent arguments that such ideas can only spell disorder, anarchy, and confusion.[95]

Yet if we situate those moments in the *Second Treatise* where Locke loudly demurs on the broader political consequences of his ideas alongside his epistemological, psychological, and sociological analyses of the ways in which men regulate their assent, we can see that the general drift of these sections reflects a different kind of problem for his more explicitly political theory. To wit, the argument that the people will find it difficult to "rouze" themselves is not simply a matter of meeting preexisting Whig and Tory objections to radical arguments about the popular basis of political power, or heeding the Anglican Church's doctrine of passive nonresistance, although it surely encompasses these historical purposes. Rather, the conditions or facts of credulity and servility are a more extensive problem, if not the central problem, for his moral and political theory—one that he confronts throughout his writings. By situating the *Second Treatise* in relation to his moral and epistemological writings, we can begin to see how great a problem it is that the masses of men are more inclined to accept faults (errors) than trouble themselves with correcting them, although natural right, natural obligation, and the clearest probability are on their side.

It is crucial to see that the underlying problem of credulity in the *Second Treatise* is no simple attack on the minds of men, or the natural capacities of the masses, or the possibility of democracy. Locke explicitly rejects such arguments.[96] Locke's is a far more radical and self-consciously unsettling attack on a culture that produces this type of subject—a critique encompassing the Anglican Church, the Whig gentry, public teachers, parents, and private tutors. This is a critique that encompasses both "designing leaders" who profit from public servility and the "following herd."[97] Political and ecclesiastical elites induce and encourage the public to accept principles on trust and "take them off from the use of their reason and judgment, and put them upon trust without further examination: in which posture of blind credulity, they might be more easily governed by."[98]

To argue that the people are prone to accept unthinkingly and on faith

95. See Locke's repeated efforts to put to rest the idea that his "*Hypothesis* lays a *ferment* for frequent *Rebellion*." *Second Treatise*, §§168, 203, 207–9, 223–25, 230, 240–43.
96. See for example, *Conduct of the Understanding*, §11.
97. See *Reasonableness of Christianity*, §241.
98. *ECHU*, 1.3.25.

the principles and institutions to which they have been accustomed is, then, no simple rhetorical strategy by which to comfort his more conservative and battle-weary readers. Nor is it merely about locating the responsibility for the dissolution of government in the ambitions and usurpations of magistrates—the true rebels in Locke's account.[99] Rather, given the way the dynamic of credulity constitutes a central problem in nearly all of Locke's writings, from the *Essays on the Law of Nature* to the *Essay Concerning Human Understanding*, the *Second Treatise* provides a subtle political turn on this moral and cultural dilemma. This is a political and moral crisis that receives its most strident attack in the *Conduct of the Understanding*: "We take our principles at haphazard upon trust, and without ever having examined them, and then believe a whole system, upon a presumption that they are true and solid; and what is all this but childish, shameful, senseless credulity?"[100] Locke is attacking the organized institutional forces of habituation, acculturation, and socialization, and illuminating what he takes to be the serious moral, social, and political consequences of such personal and institutional rigidity. Locke's fear is that what people accept on trust, whether in the form of principles or institutions, generates a vicious, self-perpetuating spiral of ill-ordered choices and bad judgments, solidified by habits that enervate the mind, domesticate us politically, and damn us morally.

The rhetorical and textual dynamic of the *Second Treatise* is to downplay the threat of revolutionary activity on the part of the masses. But what is also registered here, in relation to the rest of Locke's moral and epistemological writings, is that such rigidity and cultural recalcitrance is a real problem. The very regularity, necessity, and calculability that Nietzsche would later identify as the necessary precursors to acts of promising (and morals more generally) seem to be anticipated by Locke. In contrast to Nietzsche, however, the problem in Locke is not one concerning

---

99. *Second Treatise,* §226. We might also note here that the public's reputed unwillingness to acknowledge or amend the errors and faults of government gives further coherence, and slightly different meaning, to Locke's claim that there is nothing more easily avoided, on the part of governors, than the inconveniences of public resistance (§209). We might read this against the grain and suggest that this makes up part of Locke's counsel to magistrates (i.e., William III). We should also note that part of Locke's defense of prerogative (wisely employed) is that it allows the executive to act in ways contrary to custom and fashion when reason and the public good require it, as, for example, in the terms and boundaries of representation. Executive prerogative is a necessary governmental power (when used for the public good) to counteract the general problems of custom, habit, and public docility or conformity, which are prone to "gross absurdities" (§§157–58).

100. *Conduct of the Understanding,* §12.

memory, or the task of breeding a memory in a human animal who needs forgetfulness, who needs, as Nietzsche puts it, "a little quietness, a little *tabula rasa*."[101] The cultural-political dilemma of credulity seems even less rational than this in Locke's account. For here it is a matter of fixed, acculturated habits of belief and belonging, a mode of being that does not invite or need the activity of memory.

To the extent that Locke's immediate audience is not the aristocracy and landed classes but the "urban merchants, tradesmen, artisans, and independent small gentry who constituted the social foundations for any radical political theory—including Locke's—in the seventeenth century,"[102] we might also read these features of the *Second Treatise* as positive spurs to the kind of critical examination and moral investigation he consistently advocates in his works. We might then read Locke's *Second Treatise* as a text that endeavors to reveal to its readers the moral, intellectual, and political labor they must undertake—a participatory labor they are right to undertake, more, one that it is their duty to perform, but concerning which most are unready, unwilling, and increasingly unable to start for cultural and ideological reasons.

Lockean politics faces a problem precisely because it situates the legitimate transfer of authoritative decision making and political power in the trust of the people. Locke is concerned with sustaining social and political stability, but at the same time he recognizes that cultural and political objects of trust have a tendency to become the engines of their own reification. What individuals choose or assent to, often in haste and without undertaking a fair and just examination, has a tendency to stick to them. Or, as Aristotle put it, "states of character arise out of like activities."[103] Our moral and political judgments have consequences for all our future choices, and more specifically, the standards according to which all future choices and actions will be made. Indeed, the language of choice begins to lose some of its coherence in Locke's analysis because what we are really talking about is the force of habit and custom, incumbent upon ill-ordered choice and bad judgment: "For, though his will be always determined by that which is judged good by his understanding, yet it excuses him not; because, by a too hasty choice of his own making, he has imposed on himself wrong measures of good and evil; which, however false and

101. Friedrich Nietzsche, *The Genealogy of Morals*, trans. Walter Kaufmann and R. J. Hollingdale (New York: Vintage Books, 1967), second essay, 1–4.

102. Ashcraft, *Revolutionary Politics*, 578–79.

103. *Nichomachean Ethics*, 2.1103a33–b25.

fallacious, have the same influence on all his future conduct, as if they were true and right. He has vitiated his own palate, and must be answerable to himself for the sickness and death that follows from it."[104]

It is important to distinguish between what people accept on trust or faith as moral principles and what they lodge their trust in as a matter of political empowerment. The first is an epistemological and religious question, the second is a political-constitutional decision. In both cases, however, what individuals put their trust in often has the effect of reflecting upon the truster in powerful and distorting ways. The politically consequential point is to know how to distinguish between putting the necessary trust in political rulers and taking the governance they provide on trust. For Locke, to take anything on trust is to "misemploy [the] power of assent."[105] But it is even more troubling when these standards are adopted as commitments that cannot be questioned, when they come to stand as part of one's identity and are naturalized as somehow a part of who one is, or who one has always been. Hence the problem of preventing or even responding to the usurpations of a tyrannical regime is not simply a contingent matter of history and circumstance but a problem intrinsic to his theory. Promising, compact, and fidelity will provide social stability, and entrustment will provide the conditional grounds of political authority and obligation. But where trust and faith (*fides*) slide into credulity and docility, as it seems they are congenitally prone to do, citizens are transformed into the docile playthings of their own inventions.

In order to generate a citizenry that will be capable of judging properly about true rebellion, and to know when and how to "rouze themselves," a people must know how to properly govern their assent to political rule and authority. They must be capable of seeing beyond "ancient Names" and "specious Forms," that is, they must be willing to look beyond appearances—something that since Plato has been a crucial political virtue. They must be capable of looking into the future, of using prospective judgment. They must be candid, sincere, and courageous with themselves; willing to accept whatever ill statement this makes about their previous choices. In this way the people will be able to unite the prospective rights that Locke affords them to *prevent* tyranny, with the prospective judgment of identifying the overarching designs of "a long train of Abuses, Prevarications, and Artifices."[106]

104. *ECHU*, 2.21.57.
105. Ibid., 1.3.23.
106. *Second Treatise*, §§220, 225.

As I have stressed, the problem of credulity in Locke's theory is no mere psychological trait, or inherent human liability, but a political-cultural product. Of course, it should not go unnoticed that public credulity and servility are always good for political order and stability—a point well appreciated by both Locke and the targets of his critique in the *Essay*. And of course some measure of epistemic deference is both necessary and useful for any modern state with a reasonably advanced social division of labor. Yet credulity or unwarranted and unreasonable deference is a problem for morals and religious belief because "no man can so far abandon the care of his own Salvation, as blindly to leave it to the choice of any other, whether Prince or Subject."[107] But as we have seen in relation to the *Second Treatise*, credulity is no less a political sin as well. Under these conditions what people accept on faith or trust is no longer subject to critical self-examination. As a result, individuals not only mistake falsehood for truth, tyranny for lawful government, but the human faculties it is their constant duty to develop in the endless pursuit of the laws of nature are left fallow. The problem of credulity is that trust, the central concept in Lockean politics, can drain the very springs of political agency and future political mobilization. To avoid this loss, and to avoid the problem of political subjects giving or accepting standards of political rule that violate the minimum standards of the law of nature, citizens must be taught to govern their assent properly.

Education in the Habits of Virtue

It makes no small difference, then, whether we form habits of one kind
or of another from our very youth; it makes a very great
difference, or rather *all* the difference.
—Aristotle, *Nichomachean Ethics*

We have now come to the point where we can ask how Locke's thoughts on education fit into his overall project of "governing men in society." How does he seek to produce the kind of subject who will be capable of entering and sustaining the social compact, and so respect the duties of fidelity and trust, without at the same time undoing the critical faculties of reason, examination, and moral-political judgment? In what ways are Locke's ideas for education consistent with the requirements of his moral

---

107. *Letter Concerning Toleration*, 26.

and political theory? How adequate is Locke's social epistemology for creating a culture of reasonable citizenship?

It may come as some surprise, given Locke's scathing critique of custom, habit, and tradition—forces that seem to have rendered men all but ineducable—that Locke's ideas for education are largely organized around the formation of habits, not beliefs. Indeed, he acknowledges that "it will be possibly entertained as a paradox," but the paradox for Locke is not that he turns to the subject of men's habits but rather the idea that "men can *make* things or actions more or less pleasing to themselves; and thereby remedy that, to which one may justly impute a great deal of their wandering."[108] For Locke, habits, custom, and opinion are necessary features of political society, just as human passions constitute a necessary feature of the individual life. With respect to the passions, the question is not one of "having or not having appetites, but [whether we have] the power to govern and deny ourselves in them."[109] Likewise, his more extensive reply to the conditions of habits and custom is not an inquiry into how these extrarational features might be extirpated from the calculus of social and political order but, more pragmatically, how these necessary characteristics of political society might be given a different structure and a different purpose. Habits are conditioning factors in the moral life of individuals that seem to preexist and await the self, but they are also flexible and adaptable sources for the self, if "managed" properly.

Locke's prescriptive education in virtue is one that elides the customary divisions of *physis* and *nomos* to get inside the subject, "correct the palate," and with contrary habits change our pleasures and give men a relish for virtue.[110] Since "the great thing to be minded in education is what habits you settle," Locke's concept of education is less directed toward reason, memory, reflection, or instruction in rules or principles than toward reiterated practices. By focusing upon the practice and reiterated exercise of certain actions, the tutor (or "governor") who follows Locke's advice will instill in his students (that is, male members of the gentry) certain habits that will come to be "woven into the very principles of [their] nature."[111]

---

108. *ECHU*, 2.21.71.

109. *Some Thoughts Concerning Education*, §36.

110. See "Ethica B," in *PE*, 319–29; *ECHU*, 2.21.71; *Some Thoughts Concerning Education*, §§2, 18, 42.

111. *Some Thoughts Concerning Education*, §§18, 42, and see §§64, 66. The emphasis in Locke's educational plans is on the formation of habits, but this does not entirely preclude "reasoning" with children under certain conditions. See §§80–81. This is also the source of one of Rousseau's critiques of Locke.

Habits transmute convention and artifice into nature through daily practices. Yet, given everything that we have seen so far, why should this be considered a normative good in Locke's theory?

Locke's interest in the education of youth was announced rather early in his philosophical career. As can be see in the *Essays on the Law of Nature*, his concern with education was directed at the kind of habits that traditional forms of moral instruction, wittingly or unwittingly, produced among the young. In the *Essays* and in the *Essay Concerning Human Understanding* Locke is more concerned with showing the limits and problems of organized instruction (primarily from churches) than with providing an alternative scheme of education. For Locke, no instruction was needed to learn the one thing it was most necessary for everyone to know: the law of nature. Indeed, education and instruction, at least of the traditional variety, was a significant hindrance in this respect. While certain precepts of the law of nature (like love for God, fidelity to promises, and purity of character) could be transmitted to individuals through moral education, such a process is not the "primary" or "certain" way of knowing the law of nature. I have already discussed the importance of this point in relation to learning or knowing the law of nature in Locke's moral theory. In the context of the present discussion, what is even more troubling for Locke is that people embrace these precepts on the basis of the purported authority of the instructors and grow content with these "second hand rules of conduct," building their "morals after the manner and belief of those among whom they happen to be born and educated, and . . . have no other rule of what is right and good than the customs of their society and the common opinion of the people with whom they live."[112] Traditional moral education, even when informed by the precepts of the law of nature, can sap the individual of the strength, capacity, desire, and will to seek and examine the law of nature, as is his duty. The acceptance of what custom, education, and tradition instruct, because others have insisted that it is good, may of course make for dutiful subjects (as Hobbes recognized), but it is also the source of serious moral and political error: "for this reason they least of all strive to derive the law of nature from its very fountainhead and to investigate on what principles the ground of their duty rests, in what manner it creates obligations, and what its first origin is; for they are, after all, guided by belief and approval, not by

112. *ELN*, 2, p. 129.

the law of nature."[113] Even though we should keep in mind the distinction that Hobbes made between profession and belief, from Locke's vantage point, Hobbesian subjects are simply badly educated citizens.[114]

The alternative for Locke is an education whose purpose is to promote virtue. By this Locke means an education in self-governance or, better, self-mastery. Virtue for Locke is about controlling human passions and judging our interests and desires before the tribunal of reason. "The great principle and foundation of all virtue and worth is placed in this, that a man is able to *deny himself* his own desires, cross his inclination, and purely follow what reason directs as best though the appetite lean the other way."[115] This kind of stoical self-discipline concerns both the body and the mind. And of course what "reason directs," left open here, is a question that I have argued must be answered with respect to the natural law. At issue here is how men come to develop the skills or dispositions necessary to fulfill this duty—one with moral and political purchase for the individual *cum* citizen. For Locke this capacity or power is not brought about through reason, or discourse, but through the formation of habits. Locke's emphasis on the *practice* of virtue is quite telling. It points to his consistent recognition of the limits of language (or, we might say, moralisms) in matters of personal conduct and belief, and a practical, prudent response to the very problems he had identified in relation to the motivational weakness of both the natural law and probability.

Yet the practical effect of Locke's focus on habit is to reintroduce the mechanisms of the "law of fashion," that is, shame and credit. While critical of the effects that reputation, opinion, and custom can have on the direction that men take in their moral and political lives—usually with the effect of tying them to distorted worldly interests and immediate pleasures—Locke also has hopes of using these same mechanisms for an education in virtue. In fact, Locke refers to the use of esteem and disgrace, credit and shame as "the great secret of education."[116] For a tutor to bring his pupils around to the practice of certain virtues it is necessary

113. Ibid.

114. This differs quite fundamentally from scholars who want to treat Locke's writings on education as in continuity with Hobbes. Compare my treatment with that of Thomas L. Pangle, *The Spirit of Modern Republicanism: The Moral Vision of the American Founders and the Philosophy of Locke* (Chicago: University of Chicago Press, 1988), 215–29, and Joseph Carring, "Liberal Impediments to Liberal Education: The Assent to Locke," *Review of Politics* 63, no. 1 (2001): 41–76.

115. *Some Thoughts Concerning Education*, §33.

116. Ibid., §56.

to instill a love of credit and a fear of shame. In this way he will provide the necessary incentives for virtuous conduct and a corresponding disincentive that will "shame them out of their faults."[117]

Is there a tension in Locke's thinking between the right "governing of assent" and the habituation in virtues to which his thoughts on education are directed? The question we need to ask is: what are the consequences of Locke's turn to habits for his theory of moral freedom? Can an education in the habits of virtue, "woven into the very principles of his nature" and backed by the powers of shame and reputation, generate citizens who will critically examine the principles and institutions to which they are asked to assent? Will they be capable, interested, or committed to Locke's own calls for the fair and balanced governance of individual assent? Or have the problems of innatism surreptitiously reappeared within Locke's theory—new habits, incorporating new principles, fashioned by designing tutors, and enforced by the opinions and fashions of the company one keeps? How much more epistemically reliable is Locke's education for citizenship than what he is opposing? The error of innatism was to confuse customary moral conventions for intrinsic natural truths. Locke's concept of education plays a rather fast and loose game with these same distinctions in order to produce virtuous, self-governing men. While the crucial difference in this respect is that Locke is quite self-conscious about these manipulations and does not attribute their operation to providential design, the effect (if successful) looks like innatism by different means—practice and habits rather than principles and memory. To the extent that reflection and reason are taken out of the process, we might justifiably conclude that there is a problem for individual moral autonomy here.

Perhaps the real paradox with which Locke leaves us is how, or whether, an education in habits and custom, governed by the mechanisms of praise and shame, will produce citizens capable of critical self-examination, public reasoning, and the proper governance of assent and public reason. Locke has a vision of the kind of populace he thinks is necessary to sustain the right kind of relations between men, between man and God, and between governors and the governed. The question we must now confront is whether Locke has provided an effective or successful means of bringing this about.

I think it is safe to conclude that there is a basic tension here between

117. Ibid., §58.

the habituation in virtues and the morality of individual self-government directed by the light of reason alone. If the human capacity for virtue is perfected by a process of habituation that naturalizes individual choice and actions, those capacities and the ends to which they are directed may well remain at a level below individual reason or self-consciousness. The value of habits, for Locke, is that they do not depend upon reflection, thought, or memory. Yet to the extent that the reiterated practice of virtue "settle[s] the habit of doing without reflecting on the rule," the power or "charm" of habits may be too great ever to allow for the mature flowering of the reason this education was ostensibly designed to make possible. Additionally, there is room to doubt how far an ingrained and acute sensitivity to credit and shame will provide the "proper stock" where, upon adulthood, the "true principles of morality and religion" may be grafted.[118] Such an education may only make men all the more sensitive to the laws of fashion and opinion, sowing the seeds for docility, conformity, and credulity. While Locke acknowledges that the passage from youth to manhood (and citizenship) is "the most hazardous step in the whole course of life," we might also wonder whether this passage may not prove tragic for the ideal of government by consent.

A more optimistic outlook is suggested if we allow for the idea that Locke's concept of education is oriented toward habits of critical examination rather than habits of rote performance or belief. That is, habits and individual moral autonomy need not be understood as contradictory features of the self. The habits Locke has in mind are those that will create dispositions toward the rational regulation of passions and interests, habits of self-governance and self-examination. In this sense, Locke's education is one that is designed to make individuals lifelong learners, that is, critically minded, questioning, examining citizens. "The business whereof in respect of knowledge is not, as I think, to perfect a learner in all or any one of the sciences, but to give his mind that freedom, that disposition, and those habits that may enable him to attain any part of knowledge he shall apply himself to, or stand in need of, in the future course of his life."[119]

As we have found with respect to promising and the natural law, the proper governance of assent is something that "belongs" to human beings, but not as an interior moral quality or dispositional knowledge. Rather,

118. Ibid., §200.
119. *Conduct of the Understanding,* §12.

these practices belong to men first of all as a duty, and second as forms of moral character that are within the reach of every individual who employs his critical reasoning faculties as he should. Locke's keen if slightly overstated sociological analysis suggests that this human potential is rotting beneath the weight of cultural traditions and habits that have little more to support them than power and interest. Locke's highly practical response is to insist on new habits, manners, and customs. There are tensions here, but ones that help inform us of the full measure of Locke's contributions to moral and political theory.

The tension in Locke between self-governance and the empire of opinion, between individual moral autonomy and the force of cultural and religious norms, is a tension at the heart of modern political theory from the Reformation on. The mistake that is frequently made with respect to Locke is to overlook this tension in his own thinking and see him as a one-sided Enlightenment figure who put all his stock in the unfettered use of reason for moral and political life.[120] Of course, there are strands in Locke's thinking to suggest just this type of reading. In the *First Treatise* he argues that men are carried to a level below that of beasts, where they quit the very faculty that places them on a plane "almost equal to Angels." "Fancy and passion must needs run him into strange courses, if reason, which is his only Star and compass, be not that he steers by."[121] Yet we have also seen the extent to which Locke wants to use the laws of reputation, of credit and disrepute, praise and shame, to mold human character (or at least that of the gentleman class) for virtue and citizenship. Not, of course, that he was unaware of the problems that exist when the laws of fashion and reputation have taken a foothold among nations. "When Fashion hath once Established, what Folly or craft began, Custom makes it Sacred, and 'twill be thought impudence or madness, to contradict or question it."[122]

Locke is in a good position to understand the problem of the cultural critic who is charged with "impudence or madness" because his own attack on innatism was turned into charges, alternatively, of deism and atheism. There was a good measure of both "folly and craft" in innatism, according to Locke. But he also respected the responsibility of the cultural critic,

---

120. See, for example, Peter A. Schouls, *Reasoned Freedom: John Locke and Enlightenment* (Ithaca: Cornell University Press, 1992), esp. chapter 7.

121. *First Treatise*, §58.

122. Ibid.

for although he pulled up the foundations of what he understood as erroneous and self-serving principles, he provided a series of alternative organizing frames, some more practical and some more tension ridden than others.

Conclusion

I began this discussion of Locke with the question of whether Lockean contractarianism, in contrast to the Hobbesian variety, provides an alternative account of political order and stability that, while relying on the moral language of promising and the otherworldly sanctions this entails, might sustain a meaningful commitment to individual freedom and moral autonomy. As we have seen, the absence of individual sovereignty with respect to the normative force and status of promissory/compactual obligations (in contrast to their expression), alongside a commitment to the natural law as the one and only true guide to man's greatest good, generates more tensions for Locke's approach to political society than is appreciated by those who read him strictly as a theorist of voluntaristic, rational self-determination, or "will and artifice." In Locke's case this tension is understood as one that arises between the demands of God's will, and the proper standards of judgment and action which that law represents, and the freedom of the individual. Locke described his understanding of this problem in a famous letter to his friend William Molyneux: "though it be unquestionable, that there is omnipotence and omniscience in God, our maker, and I cannot have a clearer perception of any thing, than that I am free; yet I cannot make freedom in man consistent with omnipotence and omniscience in God, though I am as fully persuaded of both, as of any truths I most firmly assent to."[123]

While Locke may not have found a way to bring coherence to these principles in thought, I have argued that both the process/developmental character of the natural law and his advocacy of education in the habits of virtue can be read as attempts to make this tension politically and morally productive, livable, and legitimate. By analyzing these features of Locke's writings we find powerful streams of nonvoluntarism in his account of political obligation and nonrationalism in his concept of education in virtue. These currents do not foreclose the ideas of individual

123. Letter to Molyneux, January 20, 1693, *Works of Locke*, 9:305.

moral autonomy or freedom in Locke's theory, any more than do promises under conditions of nonsovereignty, or basic human dependency. But these strands of Locke's thinking situate these modern values within a more extensive and limiting context that it behooves us to recognize for a more complete understanding of modern social contract theory.

FOUR

ROUSSEAU'S CONTRACTARIAN REPUBLIC:
THE CULTURE OF CONSTITUTIONAL SELF-GOVERNMENT

> There is no use in distinguishing between the mores [*moeurs*]
> of a nation and the objects of its esteem.
> —Rousseau, *The Social Contract*

Despite the enduring fame of Rousseau's great work, *The Social Contract*, Rousseau's place within the social contract tradition proper, as with his relationship to natural jurisprudence more generally, has long been plagued by interpretive and philosophical difficulties. In this chapter I provide a reading of Rousseau that seeks to take seriously and unite both his contractarianism and his substantive republican conception of politics and ethics. I argue that the means of connecting these otherwise discontinuous features of his (and therewith modern) political thought is provided by paying attention to the ways in which Rousseau speaks to the motivational bases of a public-spirited society within the limits created by man's private passions and self-interest. By highlighting the underlying connections between contract and culture, the will and social mores, I want to show how Rousseau offers a practical way of reappraising the relationship between private vices and public virtues. Yet, unlike some of his contemporaries—such Adam Smith, David Hume, and Bernard Mandeville—who were also engaged in critical discussions concerning the relationship between private vices and public goods, Rousseau draws upon private passions and interests not to defend the conventions and morality of commercial society but to transmute those passions (like *amour propre*, or vanity) toward virtuous civic ends.

Rousseau appreciates that the "homeland cannot subsist without freedom," but also that freedom cannot subsist without virtue, "nor virtue without citizens." To "train citizens," they must "feel themselves to be members of the homeland; to love it with that delicate sentiment that any isolated man feels only for himself; to elevate the soul perpetually toward this great object; and thereby transform into a sublime virtue this dangerous disposition from which all our vices arise."[1] One of the remarkable and perhaps incongruous features of Rousseau's political thought is that he aims to do this, in part, through the language of contract and promise—a language that is often taken as a mode of thinking that abandons and is opposed to any personal, transformative project in politics or ethics.[2] Hence, to piece these features together I begin with a discussion of the ethics of commitment and promising in Rousseau's social contract, and then turn to an analysis of the role of culture and *moeurs* (manners) in Rousseau's moral and political work. The goal throughout is to combine two features of his thinking that seem not to belong together: his contractarianism and his civic republicanism. When these two features of his thought are properly united, Rousseau is no longer the strident, inhospitable, austere voice of ancient virtue but a modern thinker who can be usefully appreciated as a realistic and culturally sensitive Madisonian constitutionalist.

By this I mean that Rousseau, like Madison, believed that "it is reason, alone, of the public, that ought to control and regulate government."[3] And yet, like Madison, Rousseau had serious doubts about the prospects

---

1. Jean-Jacques Rousseau, *The Social Contract*, with *Geneva Manuscript* and *Political Economy*, ed. Roger D. Masters, trans. Judith R. Masters (New York: St. Martin's Press, 1978) (hereafter *SC*, followed by book, chapter, and page number); the citation here is to *Political Economy*, 222. Other references to Rousseau's major works are to the following editions: *The First and Second Discourses*, ed. Roger D. Masters, trans. Roger D. Masters and Judith R. Masters (New York: St. Martin's Press, 1964); *Émile, or on Education*, trans. Allan Bloom (New York: Basic Books, 1979); *The Government of Poland*, trans. Willmoore Kendall (Indianapolis: Hackett Publishing, 1985); *Politics and the Arts: Letter to M. D'Alembert on the Theatre*, trans. Allan Bloom (Ithaca: Cornell University Press, 1960); *La Nouvelle Héloïse*, trans. Judith McDowell (University Park: Pennsylvania State University Press, 1968); "Preface to *Narcissus*," in *The Discourses and Other Early Writings*, ed. and trans. Victor Gourevitch (Cambridge: Cambridge University Press, 1997). I have also consulted additional translations from the Pléiade edition of the *Oeuvres complètes*, including *Rousseau—Political Writings*, trans. Frederick Watkins (New York: Nelson, 1953); and Victor Gourevitch's translations, *The Social Contract and Other Later Political Writings* (New York: Cambridge University Press, 1997), and *The First and Second Discourses and Essay on the Origin of Languages* (New York: Harper and Row, 1986). For previously unavailable English translations of Rousseau's *Dialogues* and valuable political fragments, I have consulted *The Collected Writings of Rousseau*, ed. Roger D. Masters and Christopher Kelly, 12 vols. (Hanover: University Press of New England, 1994), vols. 1–4.

2. For a recent treatment of social contract theory along these lines, see Ronald Dworkin, "Foundations of Liberal Equality," in *Equal Freedom: Selected Tanner Lectures in Human Values*, ed. Stephen Darwall (Ann Arbor: University of Michigan Press, 1995).

3. Madison, Federalist no. 49, in *The Federalist*, ed. Clinton Rossiter (New York: Mentor Books, 1961), 317.

of a viable, regulative public reason because, when empowered to judge publicly on matters of foundational, constitutional significance, "the *passions*, not the *reason*, of the public, would sit in judgment."[4] In contrast to Madison, however, the answer to this dilemma did not require precluding the public from considerations of constitutional essentials (as far as possible) in order to "control and regulate" the passions of the crowd and maintain political stability. Instead, while sharing in Madison's concern for the sustainability of a constitutional-republican equilibrium, Rousseau offers us a political theory that seeks to secure a wide role for public reasoning about constitutional questions, while simultaneously providing for the endurance of a free and stable governmental regime across generations. In analyzing these (admittedly paradoxical) aims, we will see that Rousseau's controversial notion of the general will shares in many of the basic features that have come to define the ideal of public reason in contemporary liberalism.[5] Indeed, I will suggest that some features of Rousseau's conception of general willing/public reasoning need to be recovered today in order to help provide a stable balance to the always agonistic, but interdependent, claims of individual liberty and civic virtue within liberal societies. Crucial among these Rousseauian features is what I will refer to as an ethos of political revisability—an ethos that emphasizes the moral and civic importance of collective political self-examination. Rousseau has a unique theory of constitutional order that integrates an idea of public reasoning as a reiterative practice of collective self-reflexivity with a cultural-civic concern for the preconditions of stability that makes his thought highly relevant for large, complex, and increasingly interdependent political regimes.

Promising: Subject and Sovereign in the Social Contract Tradition

Moral and philosophical discussions concerning the normative force of promising, and questions concerning the kind of obligations promises

---

4. Ibid. For a provocative discussion of these ideas in Madison, see Stephen Holmes, *Passions and Constraint: On the Theory of Liberal Democracy* (Chicago: University of Chicago Press, 1995), 152–58, 271–74.

5. Rawls makes this connection explicit in *Political Liberalism* (New York: Columbia University Press, 1996), 219–20. I mean to develop this connection further throughout this chapter, and to consider what might be gained by drawing Rousseau into contemporary debates about public reason and political stability. See also on this point Gerald F. Gaus, *Contemporary Theories of Liberalism: Public Reason as a Post-Enlightenment Project* (Thousand Oaks, Calif.: Sage, 2003), 131–33, 150–52.

create, are given valuable political expression in Rousseau's social and political theory. Indeed, there is perhaps no thinker within the general orbit of the social contract "tradition" who feels the tensions between the enabling and disabling functions of future-oriented commitments, between promising and the will, between the foundational social compact and the fluxuating life of the polity and the self, more acutely than Rousseau. It is his unique combination of a concern for stability, law, and order and his radical political commitment to an ethos of revisability that makes Rousseau such an intriguing and difficult figure. In attempting to understand him in this way, however, we are afforded an opportunity to bring together his contractarianism and his civic republicanism. We can thus, I believe, locate more coherence and more political realism than is generally acknowledged within a thinker who is justifiably known for his many paradoxes.

As we move from Hobbes to Locke to Rousseau within the social contract tradition it is important to see that political sovereignty, conceptually and politically speaking, is shifted both downward and outward within the body of the polity. As political sovereignty is reconceived within this tradition, a one-time perpetual covenant that alienates political power (Hobbes) becomes a perpetual social compact attached to a conditional delegation of political trust (Locke), and then a social compact that is itself conditional and perpetually, or at least always potentially, revisable (Rousseau). As Rousseau makes clear, "there is not, nor can there be, any kind of fundamental law that is obligatory for the body of the people, not even the social contract."[6] We can further clarify these differences in the various contractarian schemes we have so far considered by making a distinction between subject and citizen, or client and participant, in their theories of politics.

The Hobbesian citizen is a subject, loyal and properly quiescent except where basic self-preservation is at stake. The Lockean citizen is also a subject, but one who may need to exert his ultimately "supream power," along with his fellows, under appropriately dire circumstances—specifically, when the government or legislative power has already been "forfeited" or dissolved. In contrast, the Rousseauian citizen is always simultaneously subject and sovereign.[7] In this sense the self is always double: a subject with duties and bound to the laws, and a citizen with rights who is the

---

6. *SC*, 1.7, p. 54.
7. Ibid., 3.13, p. 100.

author of the laws. It is precisely this internal dualism that makes a social contract possible for Rousseau, and the social contract—the political relation itself—is responsible for this doubling of the self.

Promises make individuals subjects, and they are bound to their promises as subjects; but in their double capacity as sovereign citizens, individuals are always potentially free, in principle, to undo, remake, or revise the social compact in common agreement with others. Men are bound as subjects (as per the rest of the contract tradition), and free as sovereign (as per Hobbes or Bodin). As a consequence, men are also always "doubly engaged": toward private individuals as a member of sovereign authority, and toward the sovereign as a private subject. Moral and political duties toward other private subjects are at the same time the rights that individual citizens also want to claim for themselves, which is why Rousseau thinks it is impossible for sovereign authority to do anything detrimental, unnecessary, or odious to the individual. Hence an important dimension of "negative liberty" is contained within Rousseau's theory of sovereignty. This idea corresponds not only to the moral law, *pacta sunt servanda*, but also to the legitimating supposition that gives inherent and fundamental protections to the individual, *volenti non fit iniuria*, or no one willingly consents to harm himself. Thus, if promises always entail the transfer or exchange of rights and duties, that exchange is in a powerful sense always simultaneously an intrinsic, personal one, and a shared, political engagement. The contract is an act of mutual, reciprocal engagement between individuals who are always double, and at the same time each individual contracts with himself, "so to speak." As a result, the traditional principle that one is not obliged to promises one makes with oneself (something Rousseau calls a "maxim of civil right") does not apply in this case precisely because the act of promising in the formation of the body politic has rendered men no longer singular, unitary beings, but double. This multiplicity within the self is both the condition and the product of the social compact and must be sustained, for the essence of the body politic lies in the harmony between subject and sovereign, not their conflation or unity.[8]

These reflections might seem only to add the trouble and weight of internal dissonance to moments of political conflict in which the private will of the individual comes into conflict with the public will and public

8. Ibid.

reasoning of the citizen, a circumstance Rousseau accepts as both inevitable and productive of the entire field of the political.[9] If so, then we might conclude that democratic subjectivity of the Rousseauian variety is unworkable because it escapes the political division of labor (representation) only at the price of dividing the individual in a schizophrenic fashion. Yet the internal dissonance that is the inevitable by-product of Rousseau's social contract, distinguishing and uniting subject and sovereign within and between each person, is the necessary condition for the development of both political freedom and moral autonomy in his political theory.

The fundamental requirement of reciprocity and equality in the act of political association entails the idea that the terms of the contract must come from each and apply to all equally. Owing to these requirements, among others, Rousseau claims that "the sovereign power has no need of a guarantee toward the subjects."[10] The only way interpreters can thereby discount the inherent limits that exist to protect individual subjects in their rights, freedoms, and goods is to refuse to take seriously Rousseau's complex theory of sovereignty. While the sovereign does not need to assure the subject of his freedoms—because "no one is unjust to himself"[11]—the opposite is not true. That is, the sovereign (and by this we must again emphasize both the body politic and one's own public persona or civic role) needs guarantees of the veracity of the subjects' (and its own) words. Despite the common interests that bring a body of people together, form the basis of their social bond, and become the sole ground for their collective decision making, Rousseau argues that the sovereign "would have no guarantee of the subjects' engagements if it did not find

9. As Rousseau makes clear, "each individual can, as a man, have a private will contrary to or differing from the general will he has as a citizen. His private interest can speak to him quite differently from the common interest." Ibid., 1.7, p. 55, and 2.1, p. 59. For the idea that such differences in fact produce politics, see his frequently ignored claim: "If there were no different interests, the common interest, which would never encounter an obstacle, would scarcely be felt. Everything would run smoothly by itself and politics would no longer be an art" (2.3, p. 61n). See also *Second Discourse*, 193–94, note i; and *Political Economy*, 214.

10. *SC*, 1.7, p. 55.

11. The idea that no one is willingly unjust to himself is less Platonic in this context than it might otherwise sound. This is a principle, in my view, that corresponds more closely to the role of *amour propre* and self-interest in human motivation and behavior and, as I suggested above, incorporates a standard of "negative liberty" into Rousseau's theory of sovereignty. This can perhaps be seen most clearly in the following passage: "Why is the general will always right and why do all constantly want the happiness of each, if not because there is no one who does not apply this word *each* to himself, and does not think of himself as he votes for all? Which proves that the equality of right, and the concept of justice it produces, are derived from each man's preference for himself and consequently from the nature of man." Ibid., 2.4, p. 62.

ways to be assured of their fidelity."[12] The moral and political problem for Rousseau, as for Hobbes and Locke, is not simply to provide an account of obligation via a backward-looking contract. Instead, the fundamental challenge is to consider both the political-institutional and the personal-ethical conditions from which a certain kind of civic fidelity may come to flourish.

The importance of all this is that it makes possible a distinctly different way of accounting for and understanding the role and importance of contractarianism in Rousseau's political theory. We must recall that the relationship between subject and sovereign is always, in part, an intrapolitical and intrapersonal association, and one, as we have noted, that is not inherently or naturally harmonious. Keeping this in mind, the act of making the social contract generates a promise of fidelity on the part of individuals (and the private, subjective side within each individual) that no subject can have complete confidence in either meaning or knowing fully what it does or will entail, or whether he shall be able to continue to abide by and keep such a promise in the future. The social contract, in other words, engages individuals in the promise to become what they are not either by nature or by history: citizens of an always specific and limited polity.

Rousseau appreciates, as do Hobbes and Locke, that making citizens of men is not the labor of a single day or the product of a singular, magical act.[13] Mutual promising and contract are fundamental to enacting the "remarkable change in man" that Rousseau avers takes place in the passage from the "state of nature" to the civil state, because such an act makes men, first, compelled to keep trust, and by dint of practice, habituation, and internal struggle, actually trustworthy. This progressive, developmental quality of the contractual relationship, and the challenges it entails, can also be seen in a crucial stage of Émile's education. In this instance, the tutor and his pupil make a mutual promise or "contract" and so ground the tutor's authority on Émile's will rather than the (temporary) conditions imposed by his immaturity. In this context the problem for the tutor is to show Émile the dangers of making promises and undertaking difficult commitments without sufficient examination or deliberation.

---

12. Ibid., 1.7, p. 55. Recall that Spinoza also saw the basic stability of a regime as dependent on the virtue of fidelity.

13. See Rousseau, *Political Economy*, 222–24. A very good treatment of this is provided by Zev M. Trachtenberg, *Making Citizens: Rousseau's Political Theory of Culture* (London: Routledge, 1993).

In a passage that captures the need for foresight, the positive role of constraints, and the ineluctable problems that the passions and human mutability pose for fashioning and maintaining stable commitments, Rousseau's tutor exclaims:

> Young man, you make difficult commitments lightly. You would have to know what they mean in order to have the right to undertake them. You do not know the fury with which the senses, by the lure of pleasure, drag young men like you into the abyss of the vices. I know that you do not have an abject soul. You will never break faith, but how often you will repent having given it! . . . Just as Ulysses, moved by the Sirens' song and seduced by the lure of the pleasures, cried to his crew to unchain him, so you will want to break the bonds which hinder you.[14]

Passages like this help to convey that promising is not a simple expression of autonomy, or what Rousseau calls moral freedom, that is, obeying laws we have prescribed to ourselves. We might be inclined to read Rousseau this way (as so many others have since Kant) because his description of moral freedom could be taken as an account of what it means to make a promise, that is, to form a voluntary self-binding commitment that places limits on liberty (or the "impulse of appetites") and that consequently presupposes the capacity to govern ourselves. Yet the social contract exists, I am arguing, precisely because these capacities cannot be assumed to exist, and, what is only modestly paradoxical, the fidelity or commitment of citizens needs to be pledged before it can be honored. That is, contract and promise produce citizens, not simply the other way around. For Rousseau this means that autonomy and moral and civil freedom are won only through the ongoing practice of political self-governance.[15]

14. *Émile*, 326. For a strikingly similar though assuredly more positive evaluation of the role of self-binding as a response to the role of human passions, see Jon Elster's most recent treatment of these issues in *Ulysses Unbound: Studies in Rationality, Precommitment, and Constraints* (New York: Cambridge University Press, 2000), chapter 1.

15. This idea seems to be conveyed in later discourse-theoretic accounts of democracy, such as that provided by Habermas: "It is only participation in the practice of politically autonomous lawmaking that makes it possible for the addressees of law to have a correct understanding of the legal order as created by themselves." *Between Facts and Norms: Contributions to a Discourse Theory of Law and Democracy*, trans. William Rehg (Cambridge: MIT Press, 1998), 121. It seems worthwhile to note that Rousseau's first formulation of these ideas, in his *Geneva Manuscript*, entailed a discussion of oath taking as the "ordinary" means of guaranteeing the

Being compelled to keep a promise once made is not, in this sense, the burden of a particular moment of crisis. Instead, it will be the very difficulty of trying to live with and among others, and to live with oneself, where subjects are always being pulled by the partiality of the private will and the generality and equality of the general will and public reason. Virtue, which for Rousseau always has a distinctly political meaning, is defined as the conformity of the private will to the general will.[16] Given the reading of the contract that we are encouraging here, this makes virtue a process rather than an end, a matter of civic becoming rather than a simple product of laws. And, as we shall see further below, virtue and fidelity to the social compact depends far more on *moeurs*, culture, and habits than on private or even public willing.

In this reading of Rousseau, the notion of "being forced to be free," however paradoxical and unfortunate in its locution, recognizes the simple idea that promises create obligations and expectations on the part of others that cannot justifiably be evaded or revoked on private utilitarian grounds. Hence Rousseau's controversial claim can be rather easily connected to the Rawlsian notion that the obligation to keep promises is an obligation of fairness.[17] Still, more than a duty of fairness is at issue here, and the reason for this is that the problem that being "forced to be free" serves to redress is potentially more extensive and intractable than a matter of reaping benefits and shirking responsibilities. The immediate context of this unduly contentious phrase is a condition in which a subject "wishes to enjoy the rights of the citizen without wanting to fulfill the duties of a subject."[18] As Aristotle might put it, this is someone who aims to disrupt the very meaning of citizenship (and a city) by seeking to rule, without being ruled in turn. Within the frame of the reading we are

---

fidelity of subjects' engagements to a sovereign authority. Rousseau's rejection of this idea, excluded from the final version of *The Social Contract*, helps illuminate the idea that he is seeking a form of commitment and a guarantee of human veracity that are both "independent of the consent of private individuals" and do not rely on the supposition of a transcendental order to ground political obligations. See *Geneva Manuscript*, 1.3, p. 165. Yet when Rousseau went about writing a plan of government for the island of Corsica, "the first act in the establishment of the projected system," he recommended, "should be a solemn oath sworn by all Corsicans twenty years old or older." The oath was a necessary but not a sufficient condition for becoming a citizen. See Rousseau's *Constitutional Project for Corsica*, in *Rousseau—Political Writings*, 302–3. Compare Thomas Paine's discussion of oaths in *Rights of Man* (New York: Penguin Books, 1984), 206–7.

16. See *Political Economy*, 217.
17. See Rawls, *A Theory of Justice* (Cambridge: Harvard University Press, 1971), 111–12.
18. *SC*, 1.7, p. 55.

proposing here, then, the issue at stake is not only a simple matter of fairness, or of a free rider (what Rousseau would call a de jure liar—one who makes a promise with no intention of keeping it.)[19] Rather, the problem is one in which a subject wants to play the part and is prepared to assume the role of the political tyrant, that is, one who is all sovereign and not also subject, and is thereby free (in his mind) to make or unmake promises at will.

Hence being "forced to be free" announces a problem internal to Rousseau's theory that he seeks to confront. The challenge is about checking the internal sources of political despotism within a political culture, and checking the graspingness and the desire for a disproportionate amount of power to which ambitious and vain creatures always aspire. Being "forced to be free" is not a threat to individuals but a warning to political societies that fancy their origins in the consent of citizens; it is an institutional reminder that citizens of and by contract are always subject and sovereign, and that these qualities, requirements, and roles will always be difficult to reconcile. Like young Émile, they may want (at some point in their lives) to break the bonds that constrain them. And if no safe or moral course for the revision and reconsideration of these commitments is provided, those ties will be experienced as coercive fetters rather than meaningful, reciprocal bonds. And if, like Émile, citizens of the compact "repent" of their commitments but do not break them outright, then resentment and disaffection will take root where love and fidelity were supposed to flower. In what immediately follows, I consider how Rousseau confronts this political-ethical dilemma, and what we might still learn from it today.

Passion, Foresight, and Constitutional Foundations

For Rousseau, the body politic derives its existence "solely from the sanctity of the contract."[20] There are, nonetheless, several significant problems with respect to the role, possibility, and meaning of promising in Rousseau's social and political theory. On the one hand, following a long line of moral/psychological thinking on the continent (from Descartes to Pascal), Rousseau conceives of human beings as creatures who are driven

19. *Émile*, 101.
20. *SC*, 1.7, p. 55.

more by passion and desire than by reason and interest. In a telling passage from a letter to the physiocrat Mirabeau, Rousseau reveals how extensively he thinks the passions rule the actions of men. The following passage also reveals what he shares with natural law thinkers like Hobbes, Locke, and Spinoza, for whom the influence of the passions and desires was precisely part of the problem of fashioning a stable political order:

> But let us assume this whole theory of natural laws to be always perfectly evident, even in its applications, and of clarity that adjusts the eyes. How can philosophers who know the human heart grant so much authority over men's actions to this evidence, as if they did not know that one very rarely acts by one's lights, and very frequently by one's passions? One proves that the despot's most genuine interest is to govern legally; this has been recognized at all times: but who conducts himself according to his truest interests? only the wise man, if he exists. . . . What is the use of reason's enlightening us, when passion leads us?[21]

This and countless other passages detailing the force of the passions raises the problem of foresight in the moral and political life of the self.[22] Foresight is, of course, a quality that is in high demand in the modern period, where political rule is increasingly detached from inherited frames of reference. The word *promise* itself has an etymological association with the act and implied capacity of foresight—*pro-mittere*, or sending forth into the future.[23] As we have seen, the difficulty of meeting the need for stability across generations amid the all too human insufficiencies of foresight and fidelity was a problem for Hobbes as well, owing in large part to his theory of human nature and the close proximity of appetite to the will. The lack of foresight (and the related problem of credulity this breeds)

21. Rousseau to Mirabeau, July 26, 1767, in *Social Contract and Other Later Political Writings*, 268–71.

22. Spinoza is sensitive to the problems of human foresight in much the same way as Rousseau. Given Spinoza's understanding of the power of the passions and the relative weakness of human reason, he argued that "every one, indeed, seeks his own interest, but does not do so in accordance with the dictates of sound reason, for most of men's ideas of desirability and usefulness are guided by their fleshly instincts and emotions, which take no thought beyond the present and immediate object." *A Theological-Political Treatise*, trans. R. H. M. Elwes (New York: Dover Publications, 1951), chapter 5, p. 73.

23. For a discussion, see William Vitek, *Promising* (Philadelphia: Temple University Press, 1993), 21, and Michael Robins, *Promising, Intending, and Moral Autonomy* (Cambridge: Cambridge University Press, 1984).

is also a serious concern for Locke, given his understanding of human beings as passionate, shortsighted, and habitual creatures. We might further suggest that in the absence of a Hobbesian natural war between men, and in the absence of the kind of fear that this generates, there is no immediate motivational or psychological urgency for the development of foresight. In Hobbes's theory fear is itself a form of foresight, and it generates a psychological condition that helps organize and concentrate the mind on principles it seems rational and reasonable to agree upon.[24] The crisis of foresight, aggravated by beings who are driven by needs that are more frequently the result of cupidity than of weakness and who are more prone to follow their passions than their reason, is the immediate precondition for the role of a founding, lawgiving legislator in Rousseau's political theory.[25]

On the other hand, just as foresight is needed for politics, and in particular for acts of political founding, promising raises the problem of forming and sustaining meaningful commitments in the political lives of citizens. This problem sets the stage for a crisis of meaning insofar as the expressions of and ties to the past slide into cultural petrification, routinization, and political or legal despotism. So, while foresight is a necessary virtue during moments of political founding, it can easily overstep the bounds that make a shared civic life meaningful as it attempts to orchestrate that future in full, perhaps with the hope of evading politics altogether.[26] As Rousseau remarks in reference to the *Institutes* of Justinian, "by wanting to foresee everything, Justinian produced a useless work."[27] For Rousseau, then, not only is the potential scope of collective self-governance usurped to the extent that the laws endeavor to settle the political in advance, the very meaning and salience of laws in the lives of citizens can be compromised as well. While Hobbes also lamented the relative absence of foresight among men, he too appreciated its dangers. Those who look too far ahead are, for Hobbes, "over provident," and he likens them to Prometheus, who "hath his heart all the day long, gnawed on by fear of death, poverty, or other calamity; and has no repose, nor pause of his anxiety, but in sleep."[28]

24. See *De cive*, 1.2n†.
25. *SC*, 2.6, p. 67; this is even more clear in the *Geneva Manuscript*, 1.7, pp. 177–78.
26. For an insightful study of this last theme in the history of modern political thought, see Bonnie Honig, *Political Theory and the Displacement of Politics* (Ithaca: Cornell University Press, 1993).
27. "On Laws," in *Collected Writings*, 4:29.
28. *Leviathan*, chapter 12, pp. 87–88.

Likewise for Rousseau, foresight "takes us ceaselessly beyond ourselves and often places us where we shall never arrive. This is the true source for all our miseries."[29] On this score, Rousseau was as concerned with how people can be legitimately released from promissory obligations and the laws they give themselves as he was with what makes these obligations normative and binding in the first place. While Rousseau's theory of sovereignty gives his conception of politics a sense of mutability and contingency that is distinct from that of Grotius, Hobbes, Pufendorf, or Locke, he cannot for that reason be taken as someone who has left us with no way to think about the place, source, or value of political commitments. Yet there is no denying that his peculiarly democratic contractarianism poses a rather difficult set of questions for his political theory. Consider, for example, the following propositions, which, however paradoxical, are always maintained in the same breath: there are no fundamental laws, *and* the laws should be thought holy, venerable, and sacred; yesterday's laws have no binding force today, *and* the laws should be respected because of their antiquity; citizens are both sovereign and subject and must have the right and opportunity to change and revise their laws, *and* the surest sign of a regime's health is that it doesn't need many laws, and that one that doesn't change them often, if at all.[30]

To consider how we might bring these features together, and what this can illuminate about Rousseau's political theory, we must first ask a more basic question: does his theory in fact allow for the kind of obligations and political commitments that are raised by mutual promises or compacts? After all, Rousseau argued powerfully that "it is absurd for the will to tie itself down for the future."[31] If the will cannot be tied to a future, then it would seem rather perverse to speak of promissory obligations in Rousseau's moral and political thought. According to Nietzsche, promises require, or surreptitiously breed where absent, a "memory of the will."[32] Yet in Rousseau's account, the will has neither memory nor future. The will is sheer performance and expression or it is nothing, for "willing and doing are the same for every free being."[33] Ultimately the will cannot bind itself to any future because the will "has no dominion over itself."[34]

29. *Émile*, 82.

30. For these claims, see in particular Rousseau's "Dedication to the Republic of Geneva," in the *Second Discourse;* see also *SC*, 3.11, pp. 98–99; and his "Preface to *Narcissus*," §34.

31. *SC*, 2.1, p. 59.

32. Nietzsche, *Genealogy of Morals*, second essay, 1–2.

33. *Geneva Manuscript*, 1.4, p. 168.

34. Ibid., 2.2, p. 181.

There is a strong sense in which Rousseau's theory of the will is more unstable, more unpredictable, and eminently more perishable than even Hobbes's identification of the will with appetites, for at least Hobbes claimed that covenants "are an act of will" and are always concerned with future performance.[35] In Rousseau, the will cannot be attached to any future-tensed words without losing its performative quality as will. For these same reasons the will cannot be transferred or alienated, for where it is, one is really no longer referring to the human will, and one is no longer speaking of a human being, for "taking away all his freedom of will is taking away all morality of his actions."[36]

This conception of the will likewise corresponds to a theory of the self in which human beings are understood as essentially inconstant creatures who are always in the process of becoming. Thus, given such a theory of the self and the will, "it would be foolhardy to affirm that one will want tomorrow what one wants today."[37] The past is never really *our* past because no subject and no generation is ever the same from one moment to the next (a proposition Heraclitus, but few others, could have agreed with).[38] Given the relationship between subject and citizen that we have described as being central to Rousseau's contractarianism, one might conclude that his theory of sovereignty is built not only on sand but on quicksand.[39] It is little wonder, then, that an artful critic like Bertrand de Jouvenal would claim that "'social contract' theories are views of childless men who must have forgotten their own childhood."[40]

Additional problems arise in Rousseau's account because political sovereignty is conceived on the model of a single moral entity or person. The traditional principle that individuals are not bound by the promises they

35. *Leviathan*, chapter 14.
36. *SC*, 1.4, p. 50.
37. *Geneva Manuscript*, 1.4, pp. 167–68.
38. But see Nietzsche's positive estimation of pre-Socratics like Heraclitus in *The Will to Power*, trans. Walter Kaufmann and R. J. Hollingdale (New York: Vintage Books, 1967), §419.
39. Arendt criticizes Rousseau's conception of the will and its relationship to sovereignty in these terms. See Arendt's essay "What Is Freedom?" in *Between Past and Future* (New York: Penguin Books, 1968), 163–64.
40. Bertrand de Jouvenal, *The Pure Theory of Politics* (Indianapolis: Liberty Fund, 1963), 60. This wonderfully acrid passage (which I owe to Gordon Schochet) has the unintended effect of pointing to precisely why it cannot hold for Rousseau. As I argue below, it is in the cultural transmission of standards, norms, manners, and habits (in large part through parents) that a commonwealth is secured from the vagaries and rationalism of a theory of politics located in the will. What I would call stories of cultural transmission, concerning, for example, the love of *la patrie*, are stories that Rousseau himself says he learned from his father. See, for example, "Dedication to the Republic of Geneva," in *Second Discourse*, 86–87; and *Letter to M. D'Alembert*, 135–136n.

make with themselves means that "it is contrary to the nature of the body politic for the sovereign to impose on itself a law it cannot break." Rousseau's apparent point here is to show that "there is not, nor can there be, any kind of fundamental law that is obligatory for the body of the people, not even the social contract."[41] In this sense, a regime is potentially never done with anything. Again, for Nietzsche, this could only be understood as a kind of dyspeptic illness. One of the central limits on a self-governing political body in Rousseau's theory is that it can forge no commitments that are off limits to change or revision. But what are the consequences of limiting political sovereignty in this way? Shall we, for example, conclude with Hegel that a politics so conceived could only provide guarantees of permanent impermanence and perpetual arbitrariness?[42]

One significant consequence of this type of questioning is that we seem prohibited from treating Rousseau as a theorist of political commitment, public reason, or constitutionalism, let alone as a theorist of social contract.[43] But this would be a mistake, and in what follows I will try to show why. Ultimately, what we need to understand in Rousseau are the tensions that exist between acts of promising, or mutual political foundation, and the irrepressible contingencies of associated political existence. To do so, we need to give more weight to Rousseau's distinction between the maxims of politics (prudence or *phronesis*) and the rule of right (or moral standards) and to understand what is at stake in the distinction for Rousseau. This distinction provides the necessary background for a more complete assessment of Rousseau's political theory. In particular, it allows for a critical understanding of his effort to fashion a workable relationship between law and morals, and between *amour propre*, autonomy, and civic virtue. Rousseau is an institutionalist and, I believe, a constitutional thinker, but one who may best be described as a cultural Madisonian. Where Jefferson or Paine or d'Alembert could be described as rationalists with respect to law and morality (as per Oakeshott),[44] Rousseau is more appropriately understood as a theorist of civic culture whose democratic principles are prudently tempered by a concern for the *moeurs*, manners, habits, and opinions that ultimately sustain a political order.

41. *SC*, 1.7, p. 54.
42. See Hegel, *Philosophy of Right*, trans. T. M. Knox (New York: Oxford University Press, 1967), §§29, 75, 258, and "Additions," §47.
43. For doubts along these lines, see Holmes, *Passions and Constraint*, chapter 5.
44. See Oakeshott's insightful essay, "Rationalism in Politics," in *Rationalism in Politics and Other Essays* (Indianapolis: Liberty Press, 1991), 5–42.

Promising, Law, and the Ethos of Revisability

Despite all of the difficulties that Rousseau's concept of the will seems to create for any coherent account of promise or contract in his political theory, Rousseau did not for this reason exclude the possibility of making and keeping promises. As he makes clear in the *Geneva Manuscript*, "One can obligate oneself to do, but not to will; and there is a great difference between executing what one has promised, because one has promised it, and continuing to will it, even when one has not previously promised to do so."[45] This distinction between promising an action and continuing to will the performance of the same action helps to preserve the possibility of self-binding, future-oriented commitments. At the same time, however, the will is still precluded from making any such commitments, so the quality that makes us most distinctly human (according to Rousseau) is not addressed, or rather is challenged both by the presence of any such future commitments or duties and by the dichotomy such bonds create within the subject between doing (and being obliged) and willing (and being a fully autonomous moral creature).

This highly perishable conception of the will has a distinctly democratic political purpose for Rousseau. It shows, he claims, that "today's laws should not be an act of yesterday's general will, but of today's, and we have engaged ourselves to do not what everyone has willed, but what everyone now wills, on the understanding that the sovereign, whose resolutions as sovereign concern only itself, is always free to change them."[46] This democratic conception of the will makes frequent assemblies and the public freedom to reconsider the laws—or at least the uncoerced acceptance of existing laws—matters of central moral and political importance. This is so because fear, or the use of state-based coercion to prop up existing laws or institutions, means that silence can never be interpreted as the continuing or tacit consent of a people to its laws. Rather, silence under coercive or corrupt conditions, in which the public cannot form or articulate its shared reason about its "constitutional essentials," announces more loudly than any rebellion the illegitimacy of a regime.[47]

The institutions and ethos of revisability in Rousseau are the central features that make laws and willing—otherwise mutually contradictory actions—compatible—for again, laws and promises are always of the past

---

45. *Geneva Manuscript*, 2.2, p. 181.
46. Ibid.
47. See ibid., 1.5, esp. 173–74.

the instant they are expressed, whereas the will can exist only in the moment of its expression and still be free. This ethos of revisability is given institutional form within the periodic assemblies that Rousseau advocates. In these assemblies citizens are asked to consider both whether they want to preserve their present form of government and whether they want to continue to entrust the offices of that government to those incumbents who are at present responsible for the duties of executive administration. The sole object of these assemblies, Rousseau tells us, is the "maintenance of the social treaty." That is to say, the social compact can be maintained and renewed only through the public activity and public reasoning of citizens. In large measure Rousseau encourages these channels of democratic accountability to prevent the usurpations of government—something that he thinks is as inevitable as the death of every living thing. Yet, so long as these institutions and this spirit of revisability persist, the proper relationship between sovereign authority, public reason, and government will be sustained. As Rousseau makes clear (inverting Hobbes and radicalizing Locke), a magistrate's "own reason should be suspect to him, and he should follow no other rule than the public reason, which is the law."[48]

These institutionalized forms of participation, public reasoning, and revisability may well prevent two of the greatest ills that can befall a polity, the indifference of citizens to the laws of a regime and the ambitions of magistrates to shape the laws to their desires.[49] More generally, the institutionalized capacity to revisit past agreements, promises, and laws, and the sense of open-endedness this creates, free and empower individuals to act in a world without certainty and allow them to undertake collective decisions in which one can never know or foretell the full consequences of one's actions. The opportunity to revisit past agreements means that one's past need not dictate the shape of one's future. Accordingly, the institutionalization of revisability respects the essential contingency and mutability of the self and the polity. With spaces of negotiation institutionalized within the practices of promising and compacting, commitments that come to grief or breed regret need not end in tragedy. The

---

48. *Political Economy*, 211. Further on in the same work Rousseau argues, "It is to law alone that men owe justice and freedom. It is this healthy instrument of the will of all that reestablishes, as a right, the natural equality among men. *It is this celestial voice that tells each citizen the precepts of public reason*, and teaches him to act according to the maxims of his own judgment and not to be in contradiction with himself" (214, emphasis added).

49. Ibid., 224.

ethos of revisability, then, does not foreclose future-oriented commitments but rather makes them tolerable for beings who must always live in the present and who often have cause to rue the past.

Even as Rousseau provides for this extensive (and unparalleled) measure of political power to citizens, in effect rendering every popular assembly an abbreviated constitutional convention or political interregnum, the problem that needs to be explained, according to Rousseau, is not ceaseless change and political instability but why "so much respect [is] accorded to ancient laws."[50] Rousseau goes further, claiming that laws, "far from weakening, continually acquire new force in every well-constituted State." And this, it turns out, is as it should be, for an "established government must never be touched until it becomes incompatible with the public good."[51] In contrast to democratic willing and political revisability, this is a more cautious, Lockean form of political counsel, one that does not rest the grounds for regime change on the mood, interests, or fleeting will of periodic assemblies (about which Madison had so many justifiable concerns)[52] but on the violations of public trust.[53] Indeed, Rousseau is willing to go even further and claim that the moral health of a regime is evinced by the degree of respect the people have for the laws and in their being "free of any desire to improve on its traditional ways."[54] How then do we reconcile, if at all, these two features of Rousseau's thinking?

We can do so, first, by observing that there is an important difference for Rousseau between learning the kind of political prudence required in collective decision making through the participation of citizens in their own self-governance, on the one hand, and living by those same principles through the acceptance of a priori principles that constituted powers should not be opposed (as in Kant) or can only be opposed when governmental powers usurp the public trust (as in Locke), on the other. Rousseau wants to agree with thinkers like Locke, Madison, and Burke that fundamental changes to a polity are "always dangerous." In Madison's words, such constitutional "experiments are of too ticklish a nature to be

50. *SC*, 3.11, p. 99.

51. Ibid., 3.18, p. 106.

52. For Madison's concerns with frequent constitutional conventions, as called for by Jefferson—in both the Virginia Plan and in private correspondence—see Federalist no. 49, and his letter to Jefferson, February 4, 1790, in Madison, *Writings* (New York: Library of America, 1999), 473–77.

53. Cf. Locke, *Second Treatise of Government*, §149.

54. "Preface to *Narcissus*," §34.

unnecessarily multiplied."[55] But the crucial claim here is that for Rousseau this necessary "circumspection" is a "*maxim* of politics and not a *rule of right*."[56] Citizens cannot be prohibited from such fundamental reconsiderations just because there is a chance that the use of such powers may end up badly. Rousseau agrees with other modern contract theorists that governments are not instituted by or through contracts but rather through an act of law (public reason) undertaken by sovereign authority, that is, by the body of citizens. And, as he claims throughout *The Social Contract*, "a people is always the master to change its laws." This principle applies even to the best laws of a regime: "for if it wishes to do itself harm, who has the right to prevent it from doing so?"[57]

We should recognize in this argument a fundamental feature of that antiperfectionist strand of the liberal tradition, represented by figures like John Stuart Mill and more recently by Jeremy Waldron, which places significant value on the principle and right of autonomy.[58] Here of course we are dealing with a question of collective right, political self-determination, and a rather vague sense of the harm principle, yet the linkages to an antiperfectionist conception of politics are so frequently ignored or denied in Rousseau's thinking that they are worth highlighting in this context. A moral "rule of right" that would prohibit citizens from altering or revoking the governmental forms of a regime, or by common agreement dissolving the social compact itself, would make it impossible to reenact or maintain the terms of the social treaty, and with it the primary conditions for political allegiance. It is this very reenactment that provides an education in the "maxim of politics" that teaches citizens to approach the ills of a regime with caution and prudence. Whereas a writer like Paine argued that government by precedent, "without any regard to the principle of the precedent, is one of the vilest systems that can be set up,"[59] Rousseau argues that political rule, without reference to the reiterated practices that makes power personally salient, is bound to inure citizens to passivity and ultimately delegitimize governmental authority.

55. Madison, Federalist no. 49, 315.

56. *SC,* 3.18, p. 106 (emphasis added).

57. Ibid., 2.12, p. 76.

58. There is a large body of literature that deals with the proposition that one has a "moral right to do moral wrong." See Ronald Dworkin, *A Matter of Principle* (Cambridge: Harvard University Press, 1985); Jeremy Waldron, "A Right to Do Wrong," *Ethics* 92, no. 1 (1981): 21–39; and Robert P. George, *Making Men Moral: Civil Liberties and Public Morality* (Oxford: Clarendon Press, 1993), chapter 4.

59. Paine, *Rights of Man,* 196.

In accordance with the interpretation I am offering here, we can also work through one of Rousseau's more famous paradoxes—a paradox that is also present in Hobbes and Locke. This is the problem that the "healthy maxims of politics" and "fundamental rules of statecraft" are necessary for a people to have prior to the formation of a political society, but that they can only acquire these things by means of the laws and the practice of public reasoning about the terms of their association. That is to say, citizens must have certain types of virtues or qualities of character to make associated living, common willing, and public reasoning possible.[60] This is one of the principal reasons why a founding legislator is necessary in Rousseau's theory. Yet, as we have seen, the ethos of revisability and the institutions of periodic reevaluation are the schools not only for political and moral freedom but for practical wisdom and public reasoning as well. At the same time, these institutions express ideas that rely on and dovetail with traditionally liberal concerns about rights and autonomy. Rousseau's argument here is that the attempt to foreclose this type of political participation through principles or procedures that make it difficult or impossible entails not only an immanent threat of legal despotism but a more immediate violation of political autonomy and moral freedom.

From Revisability to Recalcitrance: "The True Constitution of the State"

Given all of this, is the past (including our own freely chosen collective past) always to be understood as a constraint on the present? Is there a way to make such constraints legitimate? Political thinkers like Paine, Jefferson, and Kant have all provided compelling arguments that one generation cannot legitimately bind the next to specific doctrines or arrangements without usurping from beyond the grave the rights and freedoms of the present. Self-binding future-oriented commitments and the benefits of mutual coordination and reliability, as well as the augmented freedoms that come from those limitations that allow individuals to "have done" with certain concerns and thus "make room for new things,"[61] are seriously challenged by these critics. Constitutions should not be treated

---

60. Once again, this is a position shared by Rawls. See *Political Liberalism*, 205–6.
61. Nietzsche, *Genealogy of Morals*, second essay, 1.

with sanctimonious awe, according to Jefferson, not only because the "dead have no rights" and each generation is independent of the one preceding it but because an uncritical reverence for ancient forms cripples the progress of the mind, reason, and experience.[62] In a similar vein, Kant argued that "one age cannot enter into an alliance on oath to put the next age in a position where it would be impossible for it to extend and correct its knowledge . . . or to make any progress whatsoever in its enlightenment."[63]

Despite Rousseau's rejection of the underlying conceptions of history, progress, and enlightenment that constitute such an important feature of the Jeffersonian and Kantian prohibitions against cross-generational commitments, the positions Kant and Jefferson take on the question of political precommitment nonetheless seem consistent with important features of Rousseau's thinking. In particular, Kant's and Jefferson's arguments seem consistent with Rousseau's theory of the will, in which political expressions and public duties are either of the present or are no longer a manifestation of the sovereign general will. And since the only thing that can bind an individual to a political society is the observance of the general will, the extent to which that will is compromised by an attempt to make perpetual what can only be provisional becomes the avenue by which citizens are freed from any binding moral or political obligations. The political consequence of this, as we have seen, is the idea that "yesterday's laws do not obligate today." Yet unless or until we are willing to view human beings and each new generation on the order of "silk-worms and butterflies," appearing and receding from the historical stage in unison and neither dependent on those who preceded them nor obliged to consider those who will follow after them, such an understanding, as Hume argued, seems to offer no hope for stability in politics or reliability in social relationships.[64] Rousseau may have feared the prospect of flattering human pride by thinking it possible to give political institutions a durability and solidity that "human things do not allow."[65] Yet we might ask to what extent his democratic humility slid too far in the

62. Jefferson to Samuel Kercheval, July 12, 1816, in *The Portable Thomas Jefferson*, ed. Merrill D. Peterson (New York: Penguin Books, 1975), 559–60. For similar arguments see Paine, *Rights of Man*, 41–45.

63. Kant, "An Answer to the Question: 'What Is Enlightenment?'" in Kant, *Political Writings*, ed. Hans Reiss, trans. H. B. Nisbet (New York: Cambridge University Press, 1991), 57.

64. Hume, "Of the Original Contract," in Hume, *Essays Moral, Political, and Literary*, ed. Eugene F. Miller (Indianapolis: Liberty Fund, 1985), 476–77.

65. *SC*, 3.11, p. 98.

other direction and so jeopardized the necessary stability and reliability that mutual self-binding promises and laws make possible for coordinated action and living in common.

By observing all of the ways in which Rousseau's theory of the subject and the human will, as well as his institutional configurations of revisability, seem to foreclose the possibility of constitutional or self-binding commitments, we have made a toughest-case scenario for treating Rousseau as a constitutionalist. Thus, if we can show that despite these features, or indeed with the aid of them, Rousseau does indeed provide a way to account for the endurance of commitments and political bonds across time, then we may have identified a productive way to bring together his contractarianism and his sociocultural theory of civic belonging and virtue, while acknowledging why such a reading might initially cut against the grain.

With all the necessary cautions that must attend even the most modest attempts to connect a thinker as unique and perplexing as Rousseau to modes of thought and discourse that seem distinct from his own intellectual context, I want to move this reading of Rousseau's political theory— on the question of the value of self-binding political commitments— closer to Burke than to Paine, closer to Madison than to Jefferson. In doing so I will argue that political sovereignty of the Rousseauian variety is compatible with self-binding restrictions and generational continuity when we situate the general will within the proper sociocultural context—when, that is, we see that the legal expressions of the general will (which otherwise seem so inherently perishable) are themselves embedded within a cultural context of morals and habits that are inherently recalcitrant, conservative and conserving, and socially and epistemologically prior to and determinative of the legal. The normative bonds of promises and the meaning of civic commitments are not derived from a higher code of natural duties, nor are they derived from the private will alone. The engagements that bind citizens to the social body are obligatory not simply because they are mutual but because they are mutual within an embedded moral context of manners, customs, and habits that give these bonds meaning and permanence.

To follow this line of argument, we must ask how Rousseau thinks it possible, within the frame of his peculiar version of the contract and the institutions we have described, to generate an enduring and stable polity, and indeed one that will produce habits, customs, and a "prejudice favoring antiquity"—a republic, what is more, that will consolidate a mode of common living and general willing that will "render the laws more venerable each day."[66] We know that Rousseau wanted to find a legitimate and reliable form of political association that would reconcile right with interest and justice with utility, but how does he seek to secure ongoing public commitment to willful artifice? It is one thing to say that such commitments are politically and socially necessary, and that the "people must believe that only the excellence" of the laws could have preserved their institutions over time. It is another to show how and why, within the context of Rousseau's willful contractarianism, such a thing is possible.

If Rousseau's claim to take "men as they are" and "laws as they might be" were accepted at face value, one might think that Rousseau understood the law as the primary agent in the moral and political lives of men. Likewise, one might suspect that the laws, whether fundamental, civil, or criminal, are the key mechanisms in shaping, educating, and fashioning men for citizenship. Finally, one might accept the critical perspective that Rousseau thinks it possible (and desirable) to "denature" men or take them out of themselves through the force of the law, and thereby give them an entirely different (artificial) nature that is more consistent with his vision of political order and so make durable political commitments possible. Such a view finds support in passages like the following from *Émile*:

> Dependence on men, since it is without order, engenders all the vices, and by it master and slave are mutually corrupted. If there is any means of remedying this ill in society, it is to substitute law for man and to arm the general wills with a real strength superior to the action of every particular will. If the laws of nations could, like those of nature, have an inflexibility that no human force could ever conquer, dependence on men would then become dependence on things again; in the republic all of the advantages of the natural state would be united with those of the civil state, and freedom which keeps man exempt from vices would be joined to morality which raises him to virtue.[67]

66. Ibid., p. 99.

67. *Émile*, 85. See also the following from *Émile*: "Good social institutions are those that best know how to denature man, to take his absolute existence from him in order to give him a relative one and transport the *I* into the common unity, with the result that each individual believes himself no longer one but a part of the unity and no longer feels except within the whole" (40). See also *SC*, 2.7, p. 69, and *Political Economy*, 216, 222. For an extensive and illuminating discussion of the ideas contained in this passage, see Judith Shklar, *Men and Citizens: A Study of Rousseau's Social Theory* (Cambridge: Cambridge University Press, 1969).

Yet this passage suggests at least two kinds of relationships that Rousseau otherwise rejects. The first is a mimetic or foundationalist relationship between the laws of nature and artificial civil-political laws. If the positive laws of human societies were capable of being grounded in this kind of natural-eternal standard, Rousseau would be offering something more than a complex form of constitutionalism; he would be providing an antipolitics of law removed from human beings and the will altogether. Since such a standard is not admissible for "the children of Adam," a natural, "thing-like" quality and inflexibility for the law is impossible. Hence human interrelationships cannot take this form. The chains of human interdependency cannot be returned to a premoral or amoral condition, but they can be made legitimate and the source of lasting civic bonds rather than the occasion for deception, betrayal, and cruelty.

The law cannot have an ordering or normalizing control over the moral life of individuals because ultimately it is not law, but *moeurs*, custom, and opinion that govern men. Like Hobbes, Rousseau repeatedly and consistently stressed that laws can judge and regulate actions but cannot penetrate to the will or the interior of the person.[68] In this sense the will might be taken as a protected, autonomous force in the private life of the individual and in the public, political lives of citizens. For those who treat Rousseau as an anticonstitutionalist and find little but inconstancy and perishability in his theory of politics and sovereignty, the will is afforded this kind of autonomous status. Yet this is a mistake, because it ultimately decontextualizes the general will from the cultural moorings that give Rousseau's contractarian republic its stability and endurance. The will, both private and public, subjective and general, is not an autonomous, self-justifying force in Rousseau's political thought but is regulated and mediated by a prior and more extensive, if amorphous and double-edged, power: public opinion and the *moeurs*, customs, habits, and manners of society.[69]

Men are not ultimately governed or changed by laws but by other human beings acting within a specific set of cultural standards and norms.

---

68. See *SC*, 4.7, pp. 123–24; *Second Discourse*, 227, note s; "Preface to *Narcissus*," §34; *Letter to M. D'Alembert*, 66–67; "On Laws"; and *Government of Poland*, 18.

69. For a very helpful discussion of the trouble in translating *moeurs*, see Bloom's translation of the *Letter to M. D'Alembert*, 149n3. As Bloom explains, "*Moeurs* are morals as they express themselves in the way of life or the customs of men and nations; they are akin to what we would call character." See also Gourevitch's very helpful discussion, which supports the idea that Rousseau generally distinguishes between *moeurs* (morals) and laws, in *Social Contract and Other Later Political Writings*, xlv.

If the most powerful force in the life of individuals is not government or laws, and thus not even their own self-willed laws, but rather *moeurs* and public opinion, then we need to try and understand how these forces relate to Rousseau's political theory and to his version of the social compact. Rousseau tries to explain his sense of the formative primacy of *moeurs* in a variety of ways. In *The Social Contract* he argues that mores, custom, and opinion form the "true constitution of the state." This is the "unshakable keystone" that preserves "a people in the spirit of its institution, and imperceptibly substitutes the force of habit for that of authority."[70] In *Political Economy* Rousseau argues repeatedly that "the greatest wellspring of public authority lies in the hearts of citizens, and that for the maintenance of the government, nothing can replace good mores."[71]

These ideas were common enough in the seventeenth and eighteenth centuries. As Burke claimed, "Manners are of more importance than laws. Upon them, in a great measure, the laws depend."[72] And according to Montesquieu, "a people invariably knows, loves, and defends its morals more than its laws."[73] Other examples could be drawn from Adam Smith, David Hume, and other political philosophers of the era. Yet for Rousseau the centrality of opinion corresponds in large part to the idea that human beings are uniquely driven by *amour propre*, or the desire for the recognition, esteem, and approval of others. Living in and for the opinion of others takes men out of themselves. And "when we do not live in ourselves but in others, it is their judgments which guide everything."[74]

Amour propre is the central motivational engine in the life of man, by which he seeks social and cultural self-preferment.[75] It is a "relative sentiment," which means that an individual's vanity is gratified only so long as and to the extent that he is afforded a greater measure of esteem than others. Hence *amour propre* often carries along with it a passion

---

70. *SC*, 2.12, p. 77.

71. *Political Economy*, 217.

72. Edmund Burke, *Letters on a Regicide Peace*, in *Selected Works of Edmund Burke* (Indianapolis: Liberty Fund, 1999), 3:126 (letter no. 1).

73. Montesquieu, *Spirit of the Laws*, 10.11, quoted in Gourevitch's introduction to *Social Contract and Other Later Political Writings*, xlv.

74. *Letter to M. D'Alembert*, 67.

75. One of the best treatments of this concept of which I am aware is provided by N. J. H. Dent, *Rousseau: An Introduction to His Psychological, Social, and Political Theory* (New York: Basil Blackwell, 1988). See also Joshua Cohen, "Reflections on Rousseau: Autonomy and Democracy," *Philosophy and Public Affairs* 15, no. 3 (1986): 275–97, and Laurence D. Cooper's excellent discussion in *Rousseau and Nature: The Problem of the Good Life* (University Park: Pennsylvania State University Press, 1999), chapter 4.

for domination. Men "prize the things they enjoy only insofar as the others are deprived of them."[76] So long as his vision of political society continually heeds this central motivation, Rousseau believes that he has found a way to take men as they are and to generate a polity that will be more than the sum of its private, self-regarding, and morally suspect parts. It seems, then, a particularly grievous mistake to separate Rousseau's ideas about civic virtue from his understanding of *amour propre*. When Rousseauian virtue is discussed without reference to the primary psychological and motivational sources that make it both necessary and possible, his theory of virtue accordingly looks Spartan, austere, and coercive. Virtue might lose its loveliness in the disclosure of what it owes to man's vanity, but without paying attention to what makes it necessary or indeed possible, virtue loses everything that makes it human.

What we should recognize in all of this is that Rousseau's treatment of *amour propre* is no mere rebuke to the psychological proclivities of men—although it is, in part, a critique of the modern bourgeois, who in living for the opinion of others is a disordered cipher; he is one who would perhaps be less dangerous if it weren't necessary for him to color his bad faith with the affected language of civility and politeness.[77] Yet Rousseau's analysis can also be read as a cultural-institutionalist account that modulates and conditions the role of contract and will in his theory, because "there is no use in distinguishing between the mores of a nation and the objects of its esteem."[78] While Rousseau thinks it possible gradually to have an effect on the nature of these objects, and with them the quality and condition of a people, there are nevertheless cultural conditions, like *moeurs*, that set fundamental limits on the laws and the general will and accordingly provide an important source of independent and cross-generational stability in his political theory.

This is because these cultural practices and institutions are fundamentally recalcitrant—slow, averse to change, and conservative or conserving forces in the political life of men. "Most peoples, like men, are docile in their youth. They become incorrigible as they grow older. Once customs are established and prejudices have taken root, it is a dangerous and foolhardy undertaking to want to reform them. The people cannot even

76. *Second Discourse*, 175.
77. See *First Discourse*, 37–39; *Second Discourse*, 179, 193–95, note i. For an effective discussion, see Ruth W. Grant, *Hypocrisy and Integrity: Machiavelli, Rousseau, and the Ethics of Politics* (Chicago: University of Chicago Press, 1997), chapter 5.
78. *SC*, 4.7.

tolerate having their ills touched for the purposes of destroying them."[79] The problem of mass opinion and the credulity it breeds is, as we have seen, a central concern in Locke's moral and political theory as well. A significant motivation in Locke's education in the habits of virtue is an attempt to cultivate a subject who will be capable of examining those culturally accrued principles by the light of reason. Rousseau, by contrast, is less concerned with the epistemological conditions of public opinion and whether the principles and tastes that it expresses are consistent with the standards of rational self-governance.[80] Instead, Rousseau is willing to grant more autonomy to the role of custom, taste, and prejudice in the life of a polity. This is because Rousseau, for the most part, does not admit a natural jurisprudential standard of judgment against which to assess the rationality of the morals (manners) of a people and, perhaps more important, because he locates the very source of stability and political-institutional longevity in the cultural autonomy of a people.

This of course does not mean that any set of cultural practices or forms of public opinion can support a stable regime. Public opinion is primary because of man's *amour propre*—but this desire for approval and relative standing can be fulfilled in different ways. In large part this has to do with the particular objects of esteem that a culture values. As a moral critic of modernity, Rousseau pours scorn on the nature of the objects that most regimes and cultures seem to cherish. "That which is the object of public admiration is always the object of individual desire, and where a man must be rich in order to shine, the governing passion will be that of getting rich."[81] Of course, he stresses time and again that the governing passion ought to be love of country. The standards according to which a people's judgments are made and the common objects of their esteem should be directed at public goods and civic service. This is in contrast to the feverish pursuit of commercial or luxury goods, which will prove both hard for a regime to sustain over the long haul and which does little, on its own, to produce citizens. Underlying this moral critique is a more extensive understanding of the mutually constitutive traffic that goes on between the individual—and the individual's sense of self—and the cultural and social institutions (both formal and informal) that surround, support, shape, constrain, debase, frustrate, and ennoble the individual.

---

79. Ibid., 2.8.
80. For a related argument, see Shklar, *Men and Citizens*, chapter 3.
81. *Government of Poland*, 17.

"The soul gradually adapts itself to the objects that occupy it," for good and ill.[82]

To hope to have some effect on the nature of these objects, and to try and shape or educate opinion, one must begin by following opinion. Rousseau might well oppose the practice of dueling, for example, as he certainly did, but neither reason, nor moral homilies, nor laws will have any sway over the prejudices, tastes, and parochialism of a culture. As he puts it, "the law's disapproval is never efficacious except as it reinforces disapproval on the part of the citizens' own judgment."[83] Thus, "to change the actions of which public esteem is the object, the judgments that are made about them must be changed beforehand."[84] Law is less a pedagogical force in the life of human beings than it is a belated product that reflects upon the primary and constitutive education that one receives through a life in common with others. In this sense changes in the law are relatively powerless over the conditions and qualities of a people's morals (manners). The same, however, cannot be said of changes to a people's social and cultural way of life. This, for Rousseau, was the fatal oversight that the rationalist d'Alembert (and by extension Voltaire) made in proposing a theater for Geneva. M. d'Alembert, it must be recognized, was sensitive to the question of context and custom in his original proposal in the *Encyclopédie*. D'Alembert thought it possible to introduce the theater to Geneva and offset any potential ill consequences to the tastes and manners of its people with the use of "severe and well administered laws," and so combine "the prudence of Lacedaemon" with the "urbanity of Athens." Rousseau famously demurred. He did so because in his view d'Alembert had both overestimated the power of laws to influence a

---

82. *First Discourse*, 63.

83. *Government of Poland*, 18.

84. *Letter to M. D'Alembert*, 71. This also introduces, according to Rousseau, the particular role of women in his moral and political thought. As he goes on to say, "I am convinced that we will never succeed in working these changes without bringing about the intervention of women, on whom men's way of thinking in large measure depends" (71–72). There is a fundamental tension here, because Rousseau had argued at length in *Émile* that women are more prone to a life mediated by the forces of public opinion and reputation, whereas here they are called upon to determine and regulate the life of men through the same cultural forces that are responsible for their domestication and political exclusion. This is less a paradox than a matter of Rousseau pushing the contradictions in his own thinking upon a subject who, precisely because she is theorized outside of politics, cannot fight back. For a very helpful discussion of these issues in Rousseau's political theory, see Linda M. G. Zerilli, *Signifying Woman: Culture and Chaos in Rousseau, Burke, and Mill* (Ithaca: Cornell University Press, 1994), chapter 2. See also Nicole Fermon, *Domesticating Passions: Rousseau, Woman, and Nation* (Hanover: Wesleyan University Press, 1997).

culture and underestimated the effects that are bound to follow from even modest changes to a people's manners and habits. The stakes of such changes are presented even more powerfully in Rousseau's *Preface to Narcissus*. There he argues that "the slightest change in customs, even if it is in some respect advantageous, invariably proves prejudicial to morals. For customs are the morality of a people; and as soon as it ceases to respect them, it is left with no rule but its passions, and no curb but the laws, which can sometimes keep the wicked in check, but can never make them good."[85]

Contract, Culture, and Citizenship in Rousseau

The thrust of this discussion has been an effort to contextualize the general will, Rousseau's version of public reason, so as to appreciate the degree to which it is embedded within a cultural and spatiotemporal condition in which the morals (manners) and opinions of a people are always prior to any legal expression of sovereignty. If the laws have any sway over the shape of a people's morals, it is when the laws have drawn their relevance and force from this prior and more fundamental base of human motivation and existence.[86] To think that one can significantly shape or influence a culture and its beliefs and practices through rational tinkering with policy is to set the cart before the horse—as a means of conveyance, sociologically and morally speaking, one will not get far at all. What this means is that laws are always the last and nearly retrospective expression of changes that have already shaped the life of a polity. With morals (manners) and social change theorized in this way, general willing—the public expression of law—is the least dramatic and least necessary thing a sovereign body does. "Never do good laws change the nature of things; they only follow it, and only such laws are obeyed."[87]

---

85. "Preface to *Narcissus*," §34. It should be noted that Rousseau encourages the theater and other distracting spectacles among a people who were already morally corrupt. For Rousseau this meant that the theater had an important palliative role to play in Paris. But this position is entirely consistent with the argument I am making here, because Rousseau's prescriptions still flow from a prior consideration of the qualities and characteristics of a particular culture, in this case one that he diagnoses as "bad," "wicked," and "corrupt." Under these conditions the question at stake is "no longer a matter of getting people to do good, but only of distracting them from doing evil." See ibid., §§36–37; *Letter to M. D'Alembert*, 65.

86. See *Letter to M. D'Alembert*, 66.

87. Ibid., 79.

Rousseau's theory of contract, then, does not, as Burke and others would later charge, impose changes out of "present conveniency" and "momentary opinion."[88] And the reason, as we have seen, is that opinion and *moeurs* more generally do not operate in that way. Critics like Hegel (or, from a different perspective, de Maistre) surely have a logical point to make in arguing that what the will can impose the will can just as easily annul. But if the will is situated within the cultural context that Rousseau thought was its necessary and constitutive breeding ground, then it is no longer possible to accord these criticisms any substantial interpretive weight.

Rousseau's cultural constitutionalism, indeed the whole of his social and political theory, cannot be understood without a full recognition of the manner in which the general will grows out of a situated cultural condition that slows, conserves, and stabilizes the ship of state. Thus appearances and long-standing interpretations to the contrary notwithstanding, one generation *can* bind the next in Rousseau's political theory. But this does not principally take place through the laws but through a more powerful force: the manners, customs, and habits that ultimately shape the laws. The general will of any given generation does not exist outside of, or prior to, the cultural context that makes that expression possible. While Rousseau's theory of contract eschews any remnants of a medieval or organic conception that are found in Burke's notion of "great primaeval contract of eternal society . . . connecting the visible and invisible world," its moral-cultural moorings bring it far closer to a partnership between generations than to a rationalist rule of right.[89]

The role of culture and public opinion in Rousseau's moral and political theory, it must be acknowledged, raises the specter of heteronomous forces of judgment and authority, especially for those who insist on reading Rousseau through the crystalline prism of Kant.[90] Indeed, it seems that the only (semi)autonomous moral and political force in Rousseau's theory is opinion, *moeurs*, and custom. If so, the question we face is how

---

88. Burke, *Reflections on the Revolution in France*, ed. L. G. Mitchell (Oxford: Oxford University Press, 1993), 88, 95–97.

89. Ibid., 96–97.

90. See, for example, Ernst Cassirer, *The Question of Jean-Jacques Rousseau*, trans. Peter Gay (New York: Columbia University Press, 1954); Andrew Levine, *The Politics of Autonomy: A Kantian Reading of Rousseau's Social Contract* (Amherst: University of Massachusetts Press, 1976); and William Galston, *Kant and the Problem of History* (Chicago: University of Chicago Press, 1975).

to evaluate these formative cultural conditions. To claim that *moeurs,* habits, and opinion make compact, promising, and self-binding commitments possible and enduring may only open Rousseau to new attacks. For sympathetic critics like Patrick Riley, qualities like the ones we have discussed generate a paradox of "willed nonvoluntarism."[91] This is the idea that Rousseau holds a voluntarist theory of the will in order to account for the legitimate origins of political society and obligation, but incorporates a vision of ancient republican unity and generality that ultimately imposes standards that negate the voluntarist will. For other critics, like Lester Crocker, the influence of these cultural forces reveals the affinities between Rousseau and totalitarianism.[92] Although it is not my purpose to defend Rousseau from such charges—to do so would only require that we note all of the ways in which Rousseau's thinking begins with and preserves a concern for individual liberty[93]—what I want to insist upon instead is that a consideration of the relationship between laws and morals—with culture/*moeurs* as the central, mediating term—not only shields Rousseau from such charges but, more to the present point, provides the necessary background from which to appreciate the place and value of self-binding, future-oriented commitments in Rousseau's political theory.

Contract alone, and even contract within the institutions and ethos of revisability that serve to keep obligations salient and purposeful, is insufficient in accounting for the source and meaning of civic commitments in Rousseau. What the law commands, even where that command is the expression of the general will and the product of public reasoning, has no necessary relationship to the motivational life of men, and in particular to the deeper recesses within the self that could make the prescriptions of the laws truly salient. There is always a palpable disjunction in

91. Patrick Riley, *Will and Political Legitimacy* (Cambridge: Harvard University Press, 1982), chapter 4. For a different but related reply to Riley, see Cohen, "Reflections on Rousseau."

92. Lester G. Crocker, "Rousseau's *soi-disant* Liberty," in *Rousseau and Liberty,* ed. Robert Wokler (Manchester: Manchester University Press, 1995), 244–66.

93. Consider, for example, the following powerful argument from Rousseau's *Political Economy:* "If someone tells us it is good that a single man should perish for all, I shall admire this adage from the lips of a worthy and virtuous patriot who consecrates himself willingly and out of duty to die for the safety of his country. But if this means that the government is allowed to sacrifice an innocent man for the safety of the multitude, I hold this maxim to be one of the most execrable that tyranny ever invented, the most false that might be proposed, the most dangerous that might be accepted, and the most directly opposed to the fundamental laws of society" (220).

Rousseau's political theory between what the laws require, the normative obligations of civic duties, and what men actually do or desire to get away with. The general will on its own cannot meet the problem of human motivation and private willing. Thus Rousseau makes repeated arguments to the effect that a regime of laws without reference to the heart, habits, and mores of a people is doomed to perpetual instability. "If you want the laws to be obeyed, make them beloved, so that for men to do what they should, they need only think they ought to do it."[94] To argue that the problem of human motivation in morals and politics can be addressed through the organization of love and desire is not, on its face, much help in trying to get a handle on how a political order is going to be stabilized within the structure of Rousseau's contractarianism.

We can try to supply such an understanding by noting that the project of forming citizens is, for Rousseau, about giving them the proper objects of love and esteem. The real problem for Rousseau's social and political theory is not the will as such—which is typically treated as epiphenomenal, fleeting, and partial—but the objects of the will. Those objects are in large part determined by forces that are beyond the control of the private or public will, as well as the dictates of rulers and legislators (although wise legislators will "attend" to them "in secret"). "Opinion, queen of the world, is not subject to the power of kings; they are themselves her first slaves."[95]

Without the right kind of objects, individuals caught within the rush of an increasingly commercial society will exist as isolated beings and consumers, but not as citizens. The increasing specialization within the division of labor that is such a conspicuous feature of modern society has produced "physicists, geometers, chemists, astronomers, poets, musicians, painters"; but, Rousseau always adds, "we no longer have citizens."[96] As a result, the human passions turn to concupiscence, greed, and luxury, not to virtue and patriotism. There can be no denying the fact of so-called heteronomy in Rousseau's social and political theory. There are certain qualities and actions it is good and right that people should undertake, and it is even better if they should will them in an autonomous fashion. Yet "if it is good to know how to use men as they are, it is better still to make them what one needs them to be."[97]

94. Ibid., 217.
95. *Letter to M. D'Alembert*, 73–74.
96. *First Discourse*, 59.
97. *Political Economy*, 216.

Conclusion

Passages like this last one have always quite rightly raised the eyebrows of those concerned with the freedom and autonomy of the individual in Rousseau's political theory. Prescribing an object, standard, or principle that it is right or necessary for an individual to will is at the very least a challenge to personal autonomy and a voluntarist conception of the will, if not their negation.[98] But, as I have also argued, the sources of heteronomy (or what some, following Foucault, might call disciplinary power and normalization) must be placed within the context of both Rousseau's understanding of the private motivational factors in the life of men and the recalcitrant cultural forces that set limits on how far a people can be governed and remade in the image of different moral and political objects. What each of these features reveals is that Rousseau thought it necessary to speak to the personal and passionate sources of human motivation and action (*amour propre*), and at the same time he understood that there were significant limits on how far the cultivation of persons could extend. In these terms, the self should be understood as prior to his or her ends, and as capable of reevaluating and modifying those ends for objects of greater fulfillment. In this spirit Rousseau echoed the eminently liberal principles of the Marquis d'Argenson to the effect that, "in the Republic . . . each person is perfectly free with regard to everything that does not harm others."[99] At the same time, practically and politically speaking, the self is an embodied, situated being that is shaped in powerful ways by the morals (manners) of its time and place—forces that are not open to the easy manipulation of philosophers, legislators, or "dexterous

---

98. It should be noted that Rousseau holds no illusions about the difficulties of conjoining respect for individual freedom and autonomy with a normative account that aims to "train" men into what they need to be. Passages like the following from *Political Economy* should be kept in mind as we try to assess the relationship between Rousseau's contractarianism and his republicanism: "Someone may tell me that anyone who has men to govern should not seek, outside of their nature, a perfection of which they are not capable; that he should not want to destroy their passions, and that the execution of such a project would not be any more desirable than it is possible. I will agree the more strongly with all this because a man who had no passions would certainly be a very bad citizen. But it must also be agreed that although men cannot be taught to love nothing, it is not impossible to teach them to love one thing rather than another, and what is truly beautiful rather than what is deformed" (222). The double negative in the last sentence of this passage is a telling expression of the difficulty and circumspection with which Rousseau introduces his positive political theory. And, like the rest of the passage quoted here, it registers a humility, caution, and concern for the limits of normative thought and practice that are not typically accorded to Rousseau.

99. *SC*, 4.8n, p. 130.

politicians" (as per Mandeville).[100] Likewise, the vain desires for relative
standing and individual preferment can be gratified only through an economy that transcends the purview or skills of most governments and
laws.[101] Indeed, I think it is possible to see the role of *moeurs,* custom,
and opinion acting as powerful cultural checks on the ambitions and interests of rulers, operating in a more subtle and less (or pre-) rational
way, but toward the same ultimate purposes as Madisonian constitutional
constraints. In this sense, opinion and the habits of a people may temper
the otherwise more dangerously heteronomous force of legislators and
rulers, while simultaneously mitigating the plasticity and rationalism of
modern politics.

100. See Bernard Mandeville, *The Fable of the Bees: Or, Private Vices, Publick Benefits*
(1714), ed. Phillip Harth (New York: Penguin Books, 1970), 87. Yet Mandeville may have been
closer to Rousseau on these matters than he might otherwise seem, for within the body of
Mandeville's writings far more significance is placed on the role of time and custom in the
development of moral standards than upon the cynical (and I think satirical) notion of the flattery of skilful politicians.

101. I say "most" regimes because Rousseau is full of advice concerning how regimes like
Poland, Corsica, and Geneva might be able to structure their laws and institutions in ways that
will slowly shape the nature of public esteem and approval by moderating the objects of desire
within a culture. See *Government of Poland,* chapters 3–4, and *Constitutional Project for Corsica,* in *Rousseau—Political Writings,* 325–27.

FIVE

JOHN RAWLS, PUBLIC REASON,
AND TRANSFORMATIVE LIBERALISM TODAY

In previous chapters I have shown the important role that public reason plays within a broad tradition of moral and political reflection in the seventeenth and eighteenth centuries that understood the multiple ways in which "contract makes citizens," never simply the other way around. As we have seen, the transformative purposes of the modern social contract, despite important differences within this tradition, entail a form of ethical and political work that tracks back and forth between the individual (individual belief, conscience, and opinion) and the broader culture and social institutions of which individual members are a part. Contract makes citizens by embedding and educating subjects, over time, into particular sociocultural systems of civic self-understanding and collective identity. At times this form of ethical-political work is undertaken in subtle and indirect ways (Locke and Rousseau), and at other times the ethics of civic formation is more directly interventionist and paternalistic (Hobbes and Rousseau). As we have also recognized, in no case does this cultural-civic project come to fruition without its own internal challenges, limitations, and failures. Yet to claim that contract makes citizens is to emphasize the central point that a concern for political justification—symbolized and addressed by the idea of a mutual compact, promise, or agreement—sponsors a range of ethical-civic transformative practices in order to make good on the idea of political society as grounded in a mutual promise and, most important, to sustain such an understanding of self and society over time. The central question of this chapter is: to what extent does this continue to hold true in the political thought of John Rawls and contemporary liberalism more broadly? To what extent does contemporary political liberalism presuppose and contribute to a transformative ethic whose aim is not only to justify law and civic bonds but to shape and constitute moral pluralism in accordance with the perceived demands of securing liberty and stability amid diversity?

To answer these questions we must first appreciate some of the important factors that distinguish Rawls and contemporary liberals from the rest of the contract theorists I have discussed so far. In this context, the move from Hobbes to Rawls entails, in moral terms, a gradual secretion in the substantive content of public reason, from one of maximal meaning with telic purposes to a more minimal and strictly political doctrine; in political terms, this is a move away from the conflation of a sovereign/ruler's reason (human or divine) with public reason, to a concept that is "free standing" of any one comprehensive set of interests or values. In brief, a stronger effort is made in contemporary liberalism to erect distinctions between political and personal ideals and to solidify distinctions between political and metaphysical foundations.

As contemporary liberalism tries to adopt a stance of political persuasion and moral justification through public reason alone, two significant moves take place. First, liberalism becomes more modest, circumspect, and chastened in its claims. Specifically, if political liberalism is capable of justification to diverse others, it can only be justified in and for the public political domain, not as a comprehensive moral account, a telos, or an account of ethical self-flourishing as such. Hence, as much as Kant and Mill may continue to inspire contemporary liberals, each of these accounts—but especially Kant's—has to be tailored to fit within the political-moral constraints incumbent upon the acknowledgment of "reasonable pluralism."[1] Second, at the same time that contemporary political liberals assume a more modest tone about the proper aims and ends of politics given the "fact of reasonable pluralism," the political domain itself is correspondingly narrowed as well. The political domain as such is self-consciously viewed as the thin skein of a minimal "overlapping consensus," and is carefully distinguished from the background culture of civil society and the variety of "nonpublic" forms of reasoning found therein. Crucial here is the idea that public reason has its limits, or scope conditions. Thus public reason is only meant to apply and to regulate public

---

1. For a critical discussion of this in relation to Kantian aspirations for public reason, see Onora O'Neill, "Political Liberalism and Public Reason: A Critical Notice of John Rawls, *Political Liberalism*," *Philosophical Review* 106, no. 3 (1997): 411–28.

political discussion in relation to "constitutional essentials" and matters of basic justice.[2]

Taken together, do these developments mean that the transformative aims that have been so central to the contract tradition (in my reading) can be held off or avoided by contemporary liberalism? I think the answer is no, and this constitutes an important if underappreciated link between contemporary liberalism and the past thinkers I have examined. For here, as in Hobbes, Locke, and Rousseau, a doctrine of right and a doctrine of virtue (to invoke Kant) meet in the idea and the practice of public reason. To separate these interdependent features of politics and ethics, or to hope to have one without the other, would require that we either foreclose moral and political concerns about the justification of law or naively assume that we will always have citizens and leaders who possess the skills, dispositions, and virtues necessary to undertake the challenges of democratic self-governance under conditions of moral pluralism. The central question, then, is not whether the "arts of government" and the formation of civic subjects still holds relevance for the present but, rather, how has the "conduct of conduct" (Foucault) changed and developed in light of the past and in relation to the challenges of sustaining a liberal democratic society in the present? And, more pointedly, does liberal public reason provide the best means of honoring our commitments to moral pluralism and democratic openness, while meeting our concerns for political stability? Or are other virtues and moral qualities necessary to supplement and make good on the liberal values of reciprocity, civility, and tolerance?

These questions are worth attending to because one of the overriding aims of Rawlsian liberalism is to illuminate a form of reasoning and judging that is exclusively concerned with the proper exercise of political power within a diverse democratic society. Given the fact of reasonable pluralism, the central question for liberal democratic theory is: "How is it possible that there may exist over time a stable and just society of free and equal citizens profoundly divided by reasonable though incompatible religious, philosophical, and moral doctrine?"[3] Public reason represents

---

2. "Constitutional essentials" refer to questions that deal with the general structure of government and the political process, and specify the equal basic rights and liberties of citizens. For a discussion, see Rawls, *Political Liberalism* (New York: Columbia University Press, 1996), 227–30. Matters of "basic justice" relate to questions of economic and social justice that are not covered by a constitution. See Rawls, "The Idea of Public Reason Revisited," in Rawls, *The Law of Peoples* (Cambridge: Harvard University Press, 1999), 133n7.

3. Rawls, *Political Liberalism*, xviii.

both the means to and the substance of a form of moral and political consensus—covering language, ideals, and virtues—that is otherwise unavailable, without coercion, to a diverse liberal society. Liberal public reason provides the possibility for such a consensus because it is focused on political values (principles that apply to basic political and social institutions, principles that can be presented independently from "comprehensive doctrines"), and applies only to the "public political forum," and then only with respect to questions about constitutional essentials and matters of basic economic and social justice.

Nonetheless, as much as public reason is concerned with meeting the reciprocal conditions necessary for establishing morally legitimate law, Rawlsian political liberalism also seeks "wholehearted members of a democratic society," citizens who possess a "firm allegiance to a democratic society's political (moral) ideals and values."[4] As is true of all the thinkers explored in this book, Rawls wants political stability grounded in the "right reasons," that is, not in the form of a political compromise or a mere *modus vivendi* (where a balance of powers creates, at least for a time, political order and a recognition of rights).[5] This means that public reason serves not only to provide the guidelines in accordance with which citizens should reason with one another in making arguments about law and public policy. Public reason is also, crucially, about how citizens are to conceive of themselves as liberal democratic citizens as such, and how they are to properly understand their political and moral relationships to others. For Rawls, "understanding how to conduct oneself as a democratic citizen includes understanding an ideal of public reason."[6] And even more broadly, "a well-ordered society publicly and effectively regulated by a recognized political conception fashions a climate within which its citizens acquire a sense of justice inclining them to meet their duty of civility and without generating strong interests to the contrary."[7]

With this in view, public reason in Rawls and contemporary political

---

4. Rawls, "Idea of Public Reason Revisited," 149–50.

5. There is, of course, significant disagreement today about whether we are justified (in accordance with liberal standards) in seeking for something "more" than a *modus vivendi*. For important challenges along these lines, see Chandran Kukathas, *The Liberal Archipelago: A Theory of Diversity and Freedom* (Oxford: Oxford University Press, 2003); John Gray, *Two Faces of Liberalism* (New York: New Press, 2000), chapter 4; and Andrew Murphy, *Conscience and Community* (University Park: Pennsylvania State University Press, 2001), chapter 8. Also helpful here is Richard Flathman's discussion in *Reflections of a Would-Be Anarchist: Ideals and Institutions of Liberalism* (Minneapolis: University of Minnesota, 1988), chapter 3.

6. Rawls, *Political Liberalism*, 218.

7. Ibid., 252.

liberalism more broadly is as much about the ethical cultivation of democratic citizens as it is about meeting the public justificatory requirements that attend the use of political power under pluralistic social conditions. Here, as with the rest of the earlier contract tradition to which Rawls saw himself contributing, public justification entails a necessary measure of moral-civic (trans)formation in order to fulfill the requirements of political stability. Indeed, I want to argue that the kind of political-ethical cultivation to which public reason is dedicated makes the standard of liberal legitimacy possible to conceive in the first place. This is another way of saying that *contract continues to make citizens in contemporary political liberalism.* Public reason in Rawls is not "Hobbesian" supplanting of private judgment in accordance with the standards of authorized sovereign reason, but more like a liberalized version of the Hobbesian account I presented in Chapter 1. Indeed, Rawlsian public reason is more like a synthesis of the contract theories we have explored, drawing on Hobbesian concerns for the virtues of justice, Lockean guidelines of moral and political inquiry, all working in such a way as to realize the Rousseauist ideal of separate persons reasoning and judging as citizens of a distinct political-cultural system over generations. As I will show in the first part of this chapter, Rawlsian public reason is fundamentally mischaracterized when is thought to express "epistemic abstinence" or "ethical indifference" toward the subjects that constitute a liberal democratic society.[8]

The central normative question that arises from this analysis is not *whether* but *how* liberal political societies should properly understand the nature and the aims of the ethical-transformative influences they have on the character, identity, and self-understanding of the members that constitute these regimes. I turn to this discussion in the second part of this chapter. If it is simply no longer possible to ignore or deny the influence that liberal institutions have—by design—on the character and self-understanding of citizens, then what is increasingly needed today is a greater measure of critical self-consciousness about the nature and direction of liberalism's transformative ethos. The point is not simply that a liberal transformative ethos is bound to generate unequal burdens and disproportionate constraints on certain groups and forms of life within a

---

8. See, respectively, Joseph Raz, "Facing Diversity: The Case of Epistemic Abstinence," *Philosophy and Public Affairs* 19, no. 1 (1990): 3–46, and Jeffrey C. Isaac, Matthew F. Filner, and Jason C. Bivins, "American Democracy and the New Christian Right: A Critique of Apolitical Liberalism," in *Democracy's Edges,* ed. Ian Shapiro and Casiano Hacker-Cordón (Cambridge: Cambridge University Press, 1999), 222–64.

diverse polity (that is after all part of its political purpose).[9] Rather, what is needed is a greater appreciation for the *mutually transformative possibilities* that can arise in any public encounter between citizens in a pluralistic democratic society. Yet, as I will show, public reason's educative, disciplinary features are a one-way street of civic cultivation in contemporary political liberalism. As long as this remains true, the idea of public reason (as it currently stands) cannot serve as an adequate source for securing reciprocity and mutual respect within diverse liberal regimes. Thus, at the end of this chapter I offer an account of democratic humility as a critical supplement to public reason. The aim here is to offer some ideas for a reconstruction of the ways in which we understand and approach the relationship between moral pluralism and democratic citizenship today. In my view, the transformative dimensions of liberalism need to be reconceived as a reciprocal condition of democratic life under pluralistic conditions. In previous chapters we saw how liberal political theory strives to shape its audience in accordance with the virtues of fidelity and allegiance; toward the end of this chapter I consider the qualities through which contemporary liberalism might be transformed by those whose conduct and self-understanding it hopes to govern.

Political Justification and Moral Allegiance in Contemporary Liberalism

The idea of public reason in contemporary liberal philosophy is substantially a continuation of forms of thought and practice that have been present in modern political theory going back at least to Hobbes. Today public reason represents an effort to forge a common language and a proper mode of arguing and reasoning about public things under conditions of diffuse and persistent moral pluralism. In light of the "fact of reasonable pluralism"—the fact that a plurality of reasonable yet incompatible comprehensive doctrines is the normal and expected result of life under free institutions—citizens of liberal democratic societies "need to consider

---

9. Stephen Macedo has been one of the most candid and vigorous defenders of the value of public reason on just this point. See his "Liberal Civic Education and Religious Fundamentalism: The Case of God v. John Rawls?" *Ethics* 105, no. 3 (1995): 468–96; "Transformative Constitutionalism and the Case of Religion: Defending the Moderate Hegemony of Liberalism," *Political Theory* 26 (1998): 56–80; and *Diversity and Distrust: Civic Education in a Multicultural Democracy* (Cambridge: Harvard University Press, 2000).

what kinds of reason they may reasonably give one another when fundamental political questions are at stake."[10] Briefly stated, democratic self-
governance under conditions of moral pluralism requires us to "replace"
comprehensive doctrines of truth and right (drawn from religion and
philosophy) with a standard of political reasonableness.[11] The central
normative idea here is that when citizens and leaders deliberate on questions of constitutional essentials and matters of basic justice, public political reasoning and justification must meet a "criterion of reciprocity":
we must sincerely believe that the reasons and terms that we propose
could be reasonably accepted by other citizens who are free and equal.

Contemporary liberals, like their historical forebears, hold the view
that the exercise of political power should be capable of being justified to
diverse others through reference to a general and widely acceptable public language and widely acceptable political values. Rawls refers to this
as meeting the "full publicity condition" for a well-ordered society. Thus
the theoretical defense of public reason is first and foremost an effort to
answer the ongoing problem of political justification under diverse social
conditions where citizens are conceived as free and equal. The very idea of
a social contract has long offered an interpretive/normative framework
for confronting the problem of political justification. This is especially
true of contract theory within a Kantian-constructivist frame like Rawls's.
As with the earlier social contract tradition, to which so much of Rawls's
thought is indebted, the central question for contemporary public reason
is the following: under what conditions can the exercise of political power
and the enforcement of coercive laws be morally legitimate for otherwise
free and equal persons? To this question, public reason and the liberal
standard of legitimacy (based on the criterion of reciprocity) answers,
"our exercise of political power is proper and hence justifiable only when
it is exercised in accordance with a constitution the essentials of which
all citizens may reasonably be expected to endorse in the light of principles and ideals acceptable to them as reasonable and rational."[12]

The idea of public reason, then, is an idea whose goal is to help citizens and leaders of diverse democratic societies find a common public basis
of moral and political justification. If successful, the adoption of such an
ideal will not lead to a general agreement on any or all political matters,

10. Rawls, "Idea of Public Reason Revisited," 131–32.
11. Ibid., 132, 171–72.
12. Rawls, *Political Liberalism,* 217.

but it will, Rawls argues, secure the legitimacy and morally binding status of those laws or policies that have been enacted in accordance with the criterion of reciprocity. The idea of public reason, as so far described, holds important moral and political resources for meeting requirements of justice and legitimacy under conditions of persistent moral disagreement. Yet the idea of public reason not only seeks to provide normative guidelines for the conduct of public deliberation and judgment concerning essential questions of social and political justice. Public reason also offers a more far-reaching moral conception about the very meaning of democratic citizenship under moral pluralism. "The idea of public reason specifies at the deepest level the basic moral and political values that are to determine a constitutional democratic government's relation to its citizens and to one another. In short, it concerns how the political relation is to be understood."[13] In what immediately follows I provide an analysis of public reason as it relates to both of these dimensions: its discursive/linguistic features, and its hermeneutic-formative aims.

Grammar and Identity in Liberal Public Reason[14]

Given what has been said so far, it is easy to see why Rawls's argument is frequently interpreted as seeking to exclude or otherwise constrain religious or other comprehensive moral and philosophical views from politics.[15] Recall that the exercise of political power within a pluralistic social environment must meet a criterion of reciprocity, requiring that citizens replace comprehensive views with a standard of political reasonableness. Yet it is not accurate, in my view, to refer to public reason as an effort to privatize or "bracket" religious or other comprehensive modes of expression, and this is because far more is involved here. Rawls's last contributions to these questions show that he sought to expand his view of public

13. Rawls, "Idea of Public Reason Revisited," 132.

14. Portions of this section draw upon my essay "Arendt, Rawls, and Public Reason," *Social Theory and Practice* 31, no. 2 (2005): 257–80.

15. See in this respect the arguments of Jeremy Waldron, "Religious Contributions in Public Deliberation," *San Diego Law Review* 30, no. 4 (1993): 817–48; David Hollenbach, "Public Reason/Private Religion? A Response to Paul J. Weithman," *Journal of Religious Ethics* 22, no. 1 (1994): 39–46; Nicholas Wolterstorff and Robert Audi, *Religion in the Public Square: The Place of Religious Convictions in Political Debate* (Lanham, Md.: Rowman and Littlefield, 1997); and Andrew Murphy, "Rawls and the Shrinking Liberty of Conscience," *Review of Politics* 60, no. 2 (1998): 247–76. A similar critique is also presented by Seyla Benhabib, "Liberal Dialogue Versus a Critical Theory of Discursive Legitimation," in *Liberalism and the Moral Life*, ed. Nancy Rosenblum (Cambridge: Harvard University Press, 1989), 143–56.

reason to allow for the inclusion of comprehensive doctrines in public argument. The crucial "proviso" that he attached to this liberalization (or widening) of public reason is that "reasonable [comprehensive] doctrines may be introduced in public reason at any time, provided that in due course public reasons, given by a reasonable political conception, are presented sufficient to support whatever the comprehensive doctrines are introduced to support."[16] By putting it in just this way Rawls shows on the one hand that he is concerned to have public discourse reflect a commitment to general accessibility for all citizens in a pluralistic society even as the modes of public argument are diversified. On the other hand, this proviso also suggests that the real argumentative weight in public deliberations must be carried by liberal public reason, since this stipulated limitation strives to make redundant (or politically superfluous) the religious/comprehensive views whose content must be fully accounted for by nonreligious (or noncomprehensive) values in order to stand up to liberal scrutiny—that is, to be deemed reasonable and publicly justifiable. The reason for this type of moral and political weighing is that there "are many nonpublic reasons but only one public reason."[17] The nonpublic status of "comprehensive doctrines" does not mean that they are essentially private, but their presumed nongeneralizability (and/or nonaccessibility) renders the public political employment of such views deeply problematic, and absent certain liberal impediments and constraints (i.e., the proviso), these claims are judged potentially coercive.

At its core, then, the idea of public reason claims to provide a moral standard of reciprocity and mutual respect that instructs citizens of a pluralistic democracy to eschew those forms of reasoning and modes of argument they cannot reasonably and sincerely expect that others could endorse or assent to; or, in accordance with Rawls's proviso, one should always be ready and able to supplement those claims or "grounding reasons" with nontheistic, nonsectarian public reasons.[18] This is how contemporary liberalism understands what respect for persons requires; this is what civility means. If a stable political society under conditions of ethical and philosophical pluralism is the goal, then (shadowing Rawls's own move away from "metaphysics") public dialogue (and political philosophy)

---

16. Rawls, *Political Liberalism*, li–liii; and Rawls, *Justice as Fairness: A Restatement*, ed. Erin Kelly (Cambridge: Belknap Press of Harvard University Press, 2001), 90.

17. Rawls, *Political Liberalism*, 220.

18. See also Amy Gutmann and Dennis Thompson, *Democracy and Disagreement* (Cambridge: Belknap Press of Harvard University Press, 1996), chapter 2.

should avoid or seek to minimize long-standing philosophical controversies.[19] As Rawls makes plain, this criterion "imposes very considerable discipline on public discussion"[20]—a point many of Rawls's defenders seem to have overlooked, with a few notable exceptions.[21] The idea of public reason applies not only to institutions like the U.S. Supreme Court (which Rawls calls an "exemplar of public reason") but also to citizens in a wide range of public political activities, such as advocacy, campaigning, voting, and so on. Additionally, while Rawls is most concerned to establish the operation of public reason on matters of "constitutional essentials," where basic issues of rights and liberties are at stake he is admirably forthright in acknowledging that "it is usually highly desirable to settle political questions by invoking the values of public reason."[22]

One useful way to understand public reason, or at least one side of this important idea, is to view it as a kind of language requirement for liberal citizenship. To adopt and practice the moral duty of citizenship that is conveyed by public reason is to "adopt a certain form of discourse."[23] Public reason, then, is to become the official language for the public political domain. It is not the only language you will hear in politics, of course, but it should of right be the dominant one at the end of the day. Not everyone will be a native speaker, but everyone will be expected to learn it and use it, "in due course." In this respect the Rawlsian proviso is a requirement that imposes a moral duty on citizens who would draw on comprehensive doctrines in public argument to be fluent in more than one language. More generally, liberal public reason is a kind of political Esperanto that aims to help citizens live on "the surface" of their political relations with one another, providing a necessary second tongue for properly public (i.e., moral and civil) engagement. Other "nonpublic" languages, drawn, for example, from churches, sacred texts, or moral philosophy, must either be set aside or readily translated in the public domain according to the moral rules of liberal grammar. But political (that is,

19. Rawls, "The Idea of an Overlapping Consensus," in *John Rawls: Collected Papers*, ed. Samuel Freeman (Cambridge: Harvard University Press, 1999), 429.

20. Rawls, *Political Liberalism*, 227.

21. See, for example, Paul J. Weithman, "Rawlsian Liberalism and the Privatization of Religion: Three Theological Objections Considered," *Journal of Religious Ethics* 22 (1994): 3–28, and Weithman, *Religion and the Obligations of Citizenship* (Cambridge: Cambridge University Press, 2002), chapter 7. See also Macedo, *Diversity and Distrust*.

22. Rawls, *Political Liberalism*, 215. For an informative critical discussion of the limits of public reason, see Kent Greenawalt, *Private Consciences and Public Reasons* (New York: Oxford University Press, 1995).

23. Rawls, *Political Liberalism*, 242.

nonsectarian and noncomprehensive) translation itself is a moral duty of citizenship, not a task that can be sloughed off on others, at least if one wants to be judged a reasonable and civil person. Since no language is ever separable from the broader culture of which it is an integral part, public reason represents more than just the kind of reasons and arguments that are employed in public; it also highlights a specific way in which citizens are to understand themselves and relate to one another over time.[24]

It is important to stress here that Rawls and other contemporary liberals encourage the adoption of standards of public reason and a form of liberal bilingualism because it not only addresses the essential question of how to justify coercive laws in a pluralistic social environment under various "burdens of judgment" but also casts the political relation of citizens in a constitutional democratic regime as one of "civic friendship."[25] The "civic" side of this "civic friendship" is expressed by public reason's injunction to appeal only to political values (not comprehensive philosophic or religious values, or at least not exclusively) when it comes to public political deliberations. The rather surprising notion of "friendship" here comes from the norms of reciprocity, civility, and trust that Rawls believes will proliferate with the exercise and cultivation of liberal public reason over time. Public reason, then, is not just a matter of specifying the legitimate (epistemic) grounds for arguments that address questions of basic justice or the use of coercive power, it is a normative (moral) model of citizenship that seeks to shape the contours and dimensions of the public political sphere, the language and arguments heard therein, and the dispositions, character, and identity of all those who participate in democratic political argument. To understand and comport oneself as a democratic citizen, in accordance with this liberal frame, means that one has absorbed the values and procedures of public reason. In this sense, learning the arts of public reasoning is itself a project of civic formation, a project of political and moral assimilation for all citizens.

In sum, public reason is a device of representation that offers a normative account of legitimate law, as well as a deeper sociocultural interpretation of the nature of citizenship and civic bonds as such. Thus it is inaccurate and not a little misleading to think, as Kwame Appiah does, that "Rawlsian strictures about the ideal of public reason are perhaps best interpreted as debating tips: as rhetorical advice about how best, within

24. See Rawls, "Idea of Public Reason Revisited," 132.
25. Rawls, *Political Liberalism*, li.

a plural polity, to win adherents and influence policies."[26] While it is surely correct to say that there is nothing explicitly coercive in the idea of public reason (since it is a moral and not a legal duty of citizenship), it is quite misleading to equate public reason with "debating tips," since to do so requires that we reduce this standard from one of moral principle to one of political prudence. Such an interpretation also misses the full extent to which Rawlsian public reason is morally and politically invested in the formation of civic identity, intervening in the processes by which civic self-understandings are made, shaping moral pluralism and identity as it goes. If we hold these dual dimensions of public reason together— its normative-discursive guidelines and its cultural-hermeneutic and formative aims—the critical question we should be asking about public reason and political liberalism is the following: what is the relationship between political and moral justification, on the one hand, and the ethical-civic formation of liberal subjects, on the other? Specifically, does the former presuppose and require the latter? If so, is public reason justificatory, or does it point in the direction of rationalization or normalization?

The Virtues of Persons, or Let's Be Reasonable

To appreciate the full measure and one-way directional flow of public reason's transformative aspirations it is necessary to establish a few additional features of Rawls's thought. Rawls accords two central moral powers to all persons as citizens, powers that he refers to as the reasonable and the rational. The first relates to a person's capacity for a "sense of justice" and the second pertains to a person's capacity for a conception of the good. Of particular interest here is Rawls's idea of the virtue of reasonableness. Persons are reasonable, according to Rawls, "when they are ready to propose principles and standards as fair terms of cooperation and to abide by them willingly, given the assurance that others will likewise do so."[27] Reasonable people may not be altruistic beings or moved by the general good as such, but they are ready and able to abide by a principle of reciprocity, so long as others are willing to do the same. Rawls notes that this distinction between the reasonable and the rational goes back to Kant's distinction between the categorical and the hypothetical

26. Kwame Anthony Appiah, *The Ethics of Identity* (Princeton: Princeton University Press, 2005), 81.
27. Rawls, *Political Liberalism*, 49.

imperative in the *Foundations*, but the general idea here also bears a striking resemblance to Hobbes's second law of nature: "That a man be willing,
when others are so too, as far-forth, as for peace, and defence of himself
he shall think it necessary, to lay down this right to all things; and be
contented with so much liberty against other men, as he would allow other
men against himself."[28] In both cases this capacity for a sense of justice
(even if only an *in foro interno* obligation) makes it possible to conceive
of political society as a fair system of social cooperation over time.[29]

Added to the idea that persons possess a sense of justice and are ready
and willing to propose and abide by fair terms of cooperation, a second
aspect of reasonableness is a "willingness to recognize the burdens of
judgment and to accept their consequences for the use of public reason
in directing the legitimate exercise of political power in a constitutional
regime."[30] The burdens of judgment, as Rawls has enumerated them, help
to give us an account of why free institutions lead to "reasonable pluralism." The burdens of judgment also give us a standard against which
to judge between reasonable and unreasonable doctrines or persons. The
burdens of judgment include considerations of the following type: (1)
the evidence bearing on specific issues is complex, often conflicting, and
hard to assess; (2) even when we agree about the considerations that are
relevant, we may disagree about their weight; (3) the way we assess evidence and weigh moral and political values is shaped to some extent by
our life experiences, which in complex modern societies are bound to differ from individual to individual; (4) often there are normative considerations on both sides of an issue; and (5) difficult decisions have to be
made within a system of social institutions that is limited in the total
range of values it can realize.[31]

Reasonable persons and groups (or doctrines) recognize that the burdens of judgment set important limits on what can be justified to others
who are free and equal. Thus "reasonable persons will think it unreasonable to use political power, should they possess it, to repress comprehensive views that are not unreasonable, though different from their
own. This is because, given the fact of reasonable pluralism, a public and

28. Hobbes, *Leviathan*, chapter 14, p. 104.
29. And, as I argued in Chapter 1, Hobbes should not be seen as trying to derive the reasonable from the rational. Rawls also insists on this separation in his theory, in contrast to the
type of contractual account provided by Gauthier in *Morals by Agreement* (Oxford: Clarendon Press, 1986).
30. Rawls, *Political Liberalism*, 54.
31. Ibid., 56–57.

shared basis of justification that applies to comprehensive doctrines is lacking in the public culture of a democratic society."[32] Finally, not only do people possess this form of moral sensibility, they further want to be, and to be recognized by others as, fully cooperating and reasonable members. "This supports their self-respect as citizens."[33]

I have provided this brief account of the moral powers of persons in Rawls's theory because many of his critics have accused him of smuggling into his definition of the person the capacities that are necessary to make his account of public reason work. For critics like Duncan Ivison and others (e.g., David Gauthier), Rawls has simply presupposed, in his definition of a person, the very qualities that are required for public reason to operate as a meaningful guideline in public life. If these critics are right, then Rawls has not provided a sufficient answer as to why citizens should accept the constraints of public reason, especially if people do not possess a "higher-order motivation to act for public reasons" as presupposed by this theory (a critique that also applies to Scanlon).[34] And if there is more than one way to draw a distinction between public and nonpublic reason, as seems likely, then the Rawlsian account fails to provide sufficient motivation for the acceptance of this particular, singular construal of public reason. Indeed, why should we accept the idea that the "fact of reasonable pluralism," with which Rawls and political liberalism begin, does not itself imperil the boundaries of public reason that Rawls believes it is possible for diverse citizens to agree upon?[35]

While I think this critique is on to something valuable, it also misses something very important about the Rawlsian account—a feature that connects Rawls to the other thinkers I have examined here. Indeed, I think this critique has gotten the challenge of public reason in Rawls exactly backward. For Rawls, as for Hobbes, Locke, and Rousseau, the ultimate challenge of confronting the problem of freedom and stability amid pluralism cannot be securely addressed through analytic distinctions and

32. Ibid., 60–61.
33. Ibid., 81–82.
34. See Duncan Ivison, "The Secret History of Public Reason: Hobbes to Rawls," *History of Political Thought* 18, no. 1 (1997): 143. A similar critique is made by those who claim that a commitment to tolerance is as controversial as any other comprehensive commitment that political liberals otherwise seek to bracket from their political account. See Thomas Christiano, "Is There Any Basis for Rawls' Duty of Civility?" *Modern Schoolmen* 78 (2001): 151–61. See also Allen Buchanan, "Political Liberalism and Social Epistemology," *Philosophy and Public Affairs* 32, no. 2 (2004): 95–130.
35. See also William Galston, "Pluralism and Social Unity," *Ethics* 99, no. 4 (1989): 711–26.

perspicuous definitions of persons, moral capacities, and principles of justice. Instead, Rawls, like his predecessors, acknowledges that a significant
amount of cultural/civic self-fashioning is required if a liberal society is
going to be "well ordered" in the way that he thinks is both possible and
desirable. In other words, the central question is not: what must be true
about human beings in order for a standard like public reason (and its
values of reciprocity and civility) to function in a reliable way? Rather,
the central question (a twist on "Rousseau's paradox")[36] is: what kind of
moral and ethical work can be performed, consistent with the view of
persons as free and equal, such that a widespread and stable recognition
may take hold concerning the overriding weight of political virtues and
the values they express? How is it possible that free and equal persons,
with their own conceptions of the good, will not only act in accordance
with these civic qualities but act from them as a consistent and stable
feature of their character as citizens?

From Justice to Virtue: Rawlsian Sentimental Education

To see how this might be possible it is necessary to consider how a political society might move from a *modus vivendi* agreement, to a constitutional consensus, to what Rawls refers to as an overlapping consensus.
The transformative linkages that unite contract, culture, and citizenship
are especially clear in relation to how Rawls imagines liberal principles
of justice gaining firm moral allegiance. It is also in this setting that we
can begin to gauge the manner in which public reason comes to shape
moral pluralism in accordance with the virtue requirements of sustaining a system of social cooperation over generations.

   A constitutional consensus is a form of agreement that establishes certain basic principles that govern electoral procedures and helps to moderate political rivalries within society. A constitutional consensus, in Rawls's
view, is neither very deep nor very wide. The initial stages in the acceptance of such a consensus might come about in a manner not unlike the

---

36. Rousseau's paradox, addressed in Chapter 4, is stated by Rousseau in this way: "In
order for an emerging people to appreciate the healthy maxims of politics, and follow the fundamental rules of statecraft, the effect would have to become the cause; the social spirit, which
should be the result of the institution, would have to preside over the founding of the institution itself; and men would have to be prior to the laws what they ought to become by means
of laws." *SC*, 2.7, p. 69.

modus vivendi following the Reformation: "at first reluctantly, but nevertheless as providing the only workable alternative to endless and destructive civil strife."[37] A distinctive feature of Rawls's political liberalism is that such a chastened, pragmatic version of political consensus is not a sufficient basis for either conceiving the nature of political society or appreciating the full conditions upon which the endurance and stability of a regime depend.[38] In the field of comparative politics, a similar point is made in distinguishing between periods of democratic transition and the full conditions (economic, political, and cultural) that are necessary for the consolidation of a democratic state. In this respect Rawls's concern is to ask how a firm (moral) allegiance to liberal principles might develop over time. The first elements that are needed to move toward this type of consolidation are provided by liberal principles that "meet the urgent political requirement to fix, once and for all, the content of certain political basic rights and liberties, and to assign to them special priority."[39]

Rawls imagines that citizens will first come to affirm the principles of justice incorporated into a democratic constitution out of the recognition of the good that those principles will accomplish for themselves and those they care for. Here a commitment to democratic institutions and the principles that regulate them may be based on long-term self-interest and/or group interests. If, however, a conflict is seen to arise between a society's regulative principles and a citizen's comprehensive beliefs or doctrines, Rawls posits that citizens will, over time, adjust or revise their doctrines rather than reject these principles.[40] This is, to my mind, a crucial claim. Is it a groundless one? I don't believe so. Rawls is not only taking advantage of a "certain looseness" in people's comprehensive views of the good that leaves some room for those perspectives to cohere with a society's principles of justice; he is also banking on the idea that public reason will serve as a broadly educative device in the formation of civic/self-identity. A stable constitutional consensus not only depends upon a

---

37. Rawls, *Political Liberalism*, 159.
38. In so arguing I believe that Rawls sustains an important link with a more classic understanding of political theory as a branch of moral philosophy. Despite some of my concerns about Rawls's political liberalism, I think that this is still the best way to envision the nature of political theory as a field today.
39. Rawls, *Political Liberalism*, 161.
40. Ibid., 162–63, 208–9. Stephen Macedo argues this point even more forcefully: "It is to be hoped that in a healthy liberal democracy beliefs in tension with fundamental liberal democratic commitments will gradually be diminished in importance." *Diversity and Distrust*, 137. See also 134: "Assimilation is not to be despised; it is rather to be embraced—if we assimilate in nonoppressive ways and toward justifiable values."

familiar scheme of rights and legal protections but further requires the incorporation of an idea of public reason. "For it is through citizens using and following this reason that they can see that their political institutions and democratic procedures are willingly recognized. It is on that recognition—on that evident intention—that so much depends."[41] So much depends on this, surely, because to accept a constraint like public reason (as a moral duty) where others may not do likewise is, as Hobbes would have appreciated, to make one a prey to others. That is, the acceptance of a moral constraint to show mutual respect to others in matters of deep political significance, if not widely shared as a firm and reliable political-moral ethos, is to willfully place oneself at a distinct disadvantage.

Given all of this, public reason in Rawls is an effort to work on and to shape the moral sensibilities of diverse citizens who share a social scheme of cooperation backed by coercive laws. Political stability for the "right reasons" requires citizens with the right dispositions. What is noteworthy about this is that Rawls's own Kantian inheritance holds that persons are rational and reasonable as such. Especially important here is the idea that as reasonable persons we are "moved by an effective desire to act from [and not merely in accordance with] the principles of justice." What Rawls seems to have come around to, without specifying it as such, is that this moral power is not in fact something that can be safely assumed or relied upon without active cultivation, discipline, and encouragement. Hence, as a political society strives to meet the full publicity conditions for the principles that will govern its basic political institutions, Rawls stresses the idea that such a political conception will take on a wide role as part of the public culture. "In this way," Rawls argues, "citizens are made aware of and educated to this conception. They are presented with a way of regarding themselves that otherwise they would most likely never be able to entertain. To realize the full publicity condition is to realize a social world within which the ideal of citizenship can be learned and may elicit an effective desire to be that kind of person."[42]

Thus the best way to interpret public reason in Rawls's thought is to situate it in a way that is structurally parallel to the way it works in the rest of the contract tradition: forming the very citizens who are presupposed by the contract or a "constitutional consensus." In Rawls's case this means enabling the civic qualities and second-order desires that make

41. Rawls, *Political Liberalism*, 163.
42. Ibid., 71.

justice as fairness possible and stable over time. In these terms, the criterion of reciprocity at the center of public reason is a necessary cultural-political embodiment of the idea of fairness that is at the heart of Rawls's contractarianism (expressed by the original position and the two principles of justice). Public reason is a principle whose purpose is to structure and mediate the relationship between contract (the formation of principles of justice) and the broader political culture through which citizens are cultivated. Hence it is substantially correct to say that Rawls's conception of political justification is, in the end, "more Rousseauian than Kantian."[43] Public reason in Rawls is more Rousseauian than Kantian because it is less concerned with the universal or epistemic status of public justification, and more concerned with showing how any workable or motivationally efficacious conception of public justification will depend upon a prior culture of civic attachment.

The Obstinacy of Reason

While it is still true to say that the central concern to which public reason provides an answer is the issue of coercion and the need to make coercive laws morally legitimate, public reason also addresses the deeper issue that we have seen animating the entire contract tradition: the endurance of political society and the need for faithful citizens—citizens who will accept the "strains of commitment" because they have learned to place political values and political virtues above other considerations when deliberating and judging about matters of fundamental political importance.[44] Citizens will have become capable of this kind of weighing of values because they have come to see themselves and the political relation as a whole in a very distinctive way. Under the sway of public reason (as is also true under Rousseau's general will) the question of politics is not how to gain influence, form winning coalitions, or force effective bargains but to show how the use of political power may be justified to all citizens who are understood as free and equal.[45] The best way to view public reason, then, is as an idea whose full import is only to be gauged

43. O'Neill, "Constructivism in Rawls and Kant," in *The Cambridge Companion to Rawls*, ed. Samuel Freeman (Cambridge: Cambridge University Press, 2003), 353.
44. For Rawls's discussion of the strains of commitment, see his *Theory of Justice*.
45. Rawls makes this connection to Rousseau explicitly: "public reason with its duty of civility gives a view about voting on fundamental questions in some ways reminiscent of Rousseau's *Social Contract*. He saw voting as ideally expressing our opinion as to which of the alternatives best advances the common good." *Political Liberalism*, 219–20.

by recognizing its central role in the establishment of a political-cultural pattern of citizen formation. As a "technology of self-formation" (and a hermeneutics of civic self-understanding) public reason not only checks and constrains "unreasonableness" in oneself and others, it seeks to form and normalize "political reasonableness" as a central moral value for democratic citizens under conditions of moral pluralism. This is not a critique of public reason, as such (not yet). It seems to me that there is no use in denying the ways in which every political society makes certain forms of being possible, while limiting, constraining, or criminalizing others. Indeed, a political society that failed to generate citizens in accordance with its basic principles of justice would not long subsist as a specific regime type (Plato, Aristotle, Montesquieu, and Mill, to name a few, are all in agreement here); this is true even as these forms always need to be further pluralized and renegotiated over time—a point I return to below.[46] Rawls and contemporary liberals are no doubt correct to insist that a liberal state should not seek to favor any one conception of the good over another (this is what Rawls means by applying the principle of toleration to philosophy itself). Yet the liberal state, as this discussion of public reason attests, cannot be "neutral" about the qualities, characteristics, and civic identities of liberal democratic subjects who share in the responsibility for the exercise of political power.[47] To the extent that Rawls hoped to sustain a distinction between neutrality of aim and neutrality of effect (embracing the former but rejecting the later), this discussion of public reason shows such a distinction to be one without a practical difference. For public reason's aim and its intended effects are all one: the formation of a particular type of liberal democratic citizen. Political justification and civic formation are mutually dependent features that meet in the idea of public reason.

In light of this, one of the more important questions that we should be asking is: how well do a political society's organizing principles and patterns of civic formation sustain critical self-reflection in relation to the

---

46. There are two relevant factors for consideration here, one empirical and one normative. In the first case, as Rawls rightly acknowledges, "it is surely impossible for the basic structure of a just constitutional regime not to have important effects and influences as to which comprehensive doctrines endure and gain adherents over time. We must accept the facts of commonsense political sociology." On the normative dimension of this influence, Rawls argues that a constitutional regime that seeks to strengthen certain civic virtues need not be seen as a perfectionist state. "Rather, it is taking reasonable measures to strengthen the forms of thought and feeling that sustain fair social cooperation between its citizens regarded as free and equal." Ibid., 193–95.

47. See William Galston, *Liberal Purposes: Goods, Virtues, and Diversity in the Liberal State* (Cambridge: Cambridge University Press, 1991), esp. part 2.

transformative features of its laws and public ethos? Given the fact that the transformative dimensions within every political society are always distributed unequally and have disproportionate effects on different citizens and groups, the presence and the health of institutions and dispositions of critical self-reflexivity should never be taken for granted, or their value for democratic inclusion and justice underestimated. By self-reflexivity I mean the disposition and practice of thinking reflectively and self-critically about a society's basic institutions and the patterns of life they encourage or restrict.[48] This is a quality that is worth taking seriously because there are always "nonpublics" or "counter-publics"[49] seeking to cross the threshold of recognition and respect that comes with public status, and a regulative standard of proper reason giving, from the perspective of those who are not yet acknowledged as equal members of the public, may serve as another means of their marginalization.[50] As the critical work of scholars like Pateman, Mills, and others attests, this has long been a central concern in relation to the social contract tradition.[51] If some "nonpublic" reasons are defined out of court from the beginning, how do these groups and interests receive a hearing? How might voices defined as "private," groups labeled as "sectarian," or identities and practices categorized as "abnormal" or "perverse" challenge the public reasons and "commonsense" views that define them thus? These questions not only point to some of the limits in the Rawlsian "conduct of conduct" encompassed by public reason but, given the one-directional structure of public reason and its conception of public culture—always shaping, educating, and assimilating but seemingly never influenced by the "nonpublics" that are its object—these questions also highlight an internal

48. For an illuminating set of case studies that reveal (among other things) the moral and political value of critical self-reflexivity in practice, see Paul Lichterman, *Elusive Togetherness* (Princeton: Princeton University Press, 2005).

49. For the language and idea of "counterpublics," see Michael Warner, *Publics and Counterpublics* (New York: Zone Books, 2002).

50. See Anne Philips, "Dealing with Difference: A Politics of Ideas, or a Politics of Presence?"; and Iris Marion Young, "Communication and the Other: Beyond Deliberative Democracy," both in *Democracy and Difference: Contesting the Boundaries of the Political*, ed. Seyla Benhabib (Princeton: Princeton University Press, 1996).

51. Carole Pateman, *The Sexual Contract* (Stanford: Stanford University Press, 1988); Charles W. Mills, *The Racial Contract* (Ithaca: Cornell University Press, 1997). Also relevant here is the work of Don Herzog, *Happy Slaves: A Critique of Consent Theory* (Chicago: University of Chicago Press, 1989), as well as the earlier work of Jean Bethke Elshtain, *Public Man, Private Woman: Women in Social and Political Thought* (Princeton: Princeton University Press, 1981), and Susan Moller Okin, *Women in Western Political Thought* (Princeton: Princeton University Press, 1979).

challenge for contemporary liberalism: is an operative standard of public reason likely to generate "wholehearted" citizens or to aggravate and deepen sources of collective resentment, polarization, and totalistic forms of opposition?

Now, a recent expression of contemporary liberalism, one that is refreshingly self-conscious about its own partisanship, bids us to get tough about these persistent worries: if there are groups that refuse to abide by the principles and norms of liberal public reason and its traveling companions of mutual respect and civility, so much the worse for those groups—"we" (reasonable political liberals) should not lose a great deal of sleep over this fact.[52] As Macedo has forcefully argued, "Not every form of cultural and religious diversity is to be celebrated, and not all forms of what can be labeled 'marginalization' and 'exclusion' are to be regretted or apologized for. Profound forms of sameness and convergence should not only be prayed for but planned for without embarrassment."[53] At one level, these defenders are making a valid and important point: all political societies, associations of willful artifice, impose necessary constraints on their members and make moral judgments in accordance with the substantive values upon which a political order is thought to rest. As Isaiah Berlin famously put it, "The world we encounter in ordinary experience is one in which we are faced with choices between ends equally ultimate, and claims equally absolute, the realization of some of which must inevitably involve the sacrifice of others."[54] There is a valuable, self-consciously tragic sensibility in this idea.[55] Yet public reason isn't offered as a way of keeping citizens or leaders attuned to the full political and moral (if tragic) consequences that attend every institution or constitutional settlement. Instead, it is a way of shoring up self-confidence in the moral legitimacy of those necessarily incomplete judgments and of

52. See Macedo, "Transformative Constitutionalism and the Case of Religion," as well as Brian Barry, *Culture and Equality: An Egalitarian Critique of Multiculturalism* (Cambridge: Harvard University Press, 2001); Richard Sinopoli, "Thick-Skinned Liberalism: Redefining Civility," *American Political Science Review* 89, no. 3 (1995): 612–20; and Amy Gutmann and Dennis Thompson, "Moral Conflict and Political Consensus," *Ethics* 101, no. 1 (1990): 64–88.

53. Macedo, *Diversity and Distrust*, 2. Isaac et al. have discerned an element of "Hobbesianism" in Macedo. Depending on what they mean by Hobbesianism, I am inclined to agree— if we have in view the Hobbes I have presented in Chapter 1. For Macedo's own appreciation of and critical response to Hobbes, see ibid., 167–69.

54. Berlin, "Two Concepts of Liberty," in Berlin, *Four Essays on Liberty* (Oxford: Oxford University Press, 1969), 168.

55. See also the valuable work of J. Donald Moon, *Constructing Community: Moral Pluralism and Tragic Conflict* (Princeton: Princeton University Press, 1993), esp. chapters 3 and 9.

fostering the conditions for their social consolidation over time. There is a potentially significant problem here. For in my view liberalism does not lack for self-confidence in the regulative powers of reason; what it lacks is a built-in attentiveness to its own moral and political limitations; what it does not provide for is a sensibility or ethos in accordance with which its own principles and values (like public reason) might be periodically reexamined in light of the unequal burdens that are generated by every political settlement.[56] Indeed, we can press this point further by asking, does liberal public reason hope to do away with this sensibility? In my view it may do so, by pushing diverse citizens into a tough and unnecessary corner: one either accepts something like the necessary operative standards of public reason or risks being defined as a bad citizen, that is, uncivil, disrespectful, unfriendly, and so on. Likewise, "the liberal hope is that politicians who violate these liberal norms [of public reason] will be punished, not by the government, but by commentators and voters. If, in response to these judgments about appropriate political argument, people feel 'censored' or marginalized, they have nothing but their own hypersensitivity to blame."[57] Thus, in addition to a one-directional construal of public culture, the ascendancy of public reason will mean that the burdens of justificatory proof will fall on those groups or ways of life that find themselves outside its regulative norms, not (as per an important stream of the liberal tradition represented by Mill, Humboldt, Shklar, and Flathman) on those who punish and discipline in accordance with a set of normative criteria, however "reasonable" they may seem to the coinsurers of this variety of liberalism.

What other options do we have? If political wisdom is always found in the active avoidance of zero-sum conflicts,[58] how might we reap the valuable political and moral goods of public reason while sustaining a more generous and self-reflexive attitude toward the mutually constitutive relationship between diversity and democratic self-governance? In other words, while tapping into and seeking to encourage practices and qualities that are necessary to facilitate collective political endeavors, how might we also sustain critical sensitivity to the ways in which those enterprises frequently entail their own forms of exclusion and marginalization?

56. I am reminded here of Oakeshott's famous line that the rationalist is essentially ineducable: how true is this of the defenders of public reason today? That is, how educable is public reason?

57. Macedo, "Transformative Constitutionalism and the Case of Religion," 71.

58. To invoke Machiavelli.

If, as I have argued throughout, political justification always entails and calls forth ethical (trans)formation, the relevant question for theory and practice is: how might this relationship best be conceived such that it can simultaneously honor our commitments to liberalism, reasonable moral pluralism, and democratic stability? I want to stress that my concern is not with the presence of a transformative ethos in political liberalism but with its normative structure: a structure that is too one-directional to be endorsed as is stands for mediating the complex relationships between democracy, liberalism, and moral pluralism. In the second part of this chapter I introduce the idea of democratic humility as a potentially useful supplement to liberal public reason.

Democratic Humility: An Old Virtue for Late Modern Times

The case for democratic humility begins with the question: how are meaningful dialogue and mutual understanding between plural beings possible? Related to this question, I am also interested in asking how a plural citizenry can navigate the tensions that arise between commitments to a diversity of incommensurable fundamental values and beliefs, on the one hand, and the fluid, rapidly changing, and interdependent conditions of contemporary political life and culture, on the other. What qualities and dispositions are necessary for citizens and leaders to be fully alive and attentive to the diversity and contingency of contemporary pluralistic democracies, and in a manner that will foster mutual learning, respect, and the positive embrace of revisability? The general intimation that I want to explore here is the sense that contemporary ethical-political conditions, both within and between territorial states, have made humility, properly reworked, relevant once again. In what follows I present humility as a window through which we allow what is outside the self or group to enter in and work upon us, at least for a time. Specifically, I define *democratic* humility as a cultivated sensitivity toward the limitations, incompleteness, and contingency of both one's personal moral powers and commitments and the particular forms, laws, and institutions that structure one's political and social life with others.

As we have seen, the burdens of judgment, as Rawls has enumerated them, help to give us an account of why free institutions lead to "reasonable pluralism." Yet the burdens of judgment also provide some of the basic conditions in which a public ethos of humility might take on

renewed value today. For Rawls, the burdens of judgment and the irreconcilable disagreements they generate establish the conditions that make
the operation of public reason necessary, at least on fundamental issues of
justice. By contrast, I want to suggest that the burdens of judgment, along
with a more general recognition of the incompleteness and partiality of
human knowing and judging, should not prompt us to fashion a deraci-
nated mode of discourse—one that would "only appeal to presently accepted general beliefs and forms of reasoning found in common sense."[59]
Rather, contemporary conditions for political judgment and action should
spur us to first cultivate forms of civic attentiveness that can help maximize the possibilities for reciprocal learning and moral growth from our
mutual interactions with others, even when (or especially when) our democratic entanglements are themselves the outgrowth of deeper moral or
religious disagreements. To the extent that an ethos of democratic humility can be effectively cultivated among a diverse array of citizens and
leaders, we might find that our civic lives and what we are willing to label
just and reasonable will be complicated and expanded not by prior orchestrations of public reason but by forms of political expression and action
moderated by and received in humility. Why should this be so, and why
should it be considered desirable?

With humility in place we can make a virtue of our necessary limitations and political burdens by cultivating a disposition that inclines us
to remain open to the multiple (and unpredictable) potentialities that
exist for the self or group in every meaningful political encounter. As
others have acknowledged, the fact of incommensurable value pluralism
alone cannot make one "alive" to the plurality of values, or to the contingency and potential revisability of one's own commitments.[60] If we
further acknowledge that contemporary conditions of cultural and ethical pluralism and substantive, agonistic strife are just as likely to produce
greater degrees of mistrust, cultural polarization, and resentment as they
are to generate an ethic of attentiveness and mutual respect, a crucial
challenge becomes how to connect the ontological and political conditions

59. Rawls, *Political Liberalism*, 224. In a related way Jürgen Habermas argues in support
of "the moral point of view . . . which compels the participants to *transcend* the social and historical context of their particular form of life and particular community." Habermas, "Remarks
on Discourse Ethics," in *Justification and Application*, trans. Ciaran Cronin (Cambridge: MIT
Press, 1993), 24.

60. See the useful discussions in Macedo, *Liberal Virtues*, 234–40, and George Crowder, *Liberalism and Value Pluralism* (London: Continuum, 2002), chapter 8.

of contemporary life to the formation of a more positive political ethic and a more inclusive democratic culture. What I am claiming is that this possibility can be more effectively realized when a prior supporting disposition opens one to those differences and prompts a critical attentiveness to their potential value. On this point, one feature of the Christian notion of humility retains its significance, and that is the importance of critical reflection and contemplation of self as an integral art in the cultivation of a self and in fostering generous and sympathetic relationships with others.

Sources of Democratic Humility

An ethos of democratic humility, as I am imagining it here, is one way of orienting us to a more general range of existential realities for human being: on the one hand, the incompleteness, boundedness, and contingency of the self and its identity, and on the other our capacity for development, moral growth, and natality.[61] These dual features of human incompleteness and becoming, of boundedness and the capacity for novelty, have a historical corollary in the paradox of democratic politics: between democratic energies that represent periodic forces of disturbance, pluralization, and revision and those that seek order, stability, and closure.[62] If in addition to these features we further take hold of the idea that late modernity is marked by the acceleration and intensification of these strains for both the self and pluralistic societies,[63] we might come to see value in new forms of ethical cultivation adapted to these specific characteristics of being, even if, as is partially the case here, such a project involves "uncovering buried goods through rearticulation."[64] In my view, democratic humility is best understood as a quality that is rooted in the recognition that we are in need of ethical dispositions in accordance with which we can live within the multiple and increasingly heightened tensions of our ontological-historical condition without striving or

61. Thanks to Stephen White for helpful correspondence on the arguments of this section. I am drawing here on the language of natality from Hannah Arendt, *The Human Condition* (Chicago: University of Chicago Press, 1958), chapter 5.

62. On these points, see Hannah Arendt, *On Revolution* (New York: Viking Press, 1965), chapter 6, and, more recently, Alan Keenan, *Democracy in Question: Democratic Openness in a Time of Political Closure* (Stanford: Stanford University Press, 2003), 9–20.

63. See William Connolly, *Identity/Difference: Democratic Negotiations of Political Paradox* (Ithaca: Cornell University Press, 1991), 25–26. See, more recently, Connolly, *Neuropolitics: Thinking, Culture, Speed* (Minneapolis: University of Minnesota Press, 2002), chapter 6.

64. Charles Taylor, *Sources of the Self* (Cambridge: Harvard University Press, 1989), 520.

believing it necessary, desirable, or possible to either resolve or detach ourselves from these challenges.[65]

It is against this general backdrop, what one might call a late modern ontology of democratic selves and society, that a reworked ethos of humility gains its value and motivational force for contemporary politics and ethics. For a cultivated sensibility of civic humility may offer a practical means of affirming the relational and contingent features of one's identity without inciting resentment, either toward the limits or differences in relation to which the self is constituted or in relation to the necessary revisability of the laws and institutions that house one's social and political life with others. An ethos of democratic humility may increase the likelihood that one's agonistic political engagements with diverse others will be an occasion for reciprocal learning and moral growth, insofar as participants in a shared public culture come to acknowledge that these onto-political features, unchosen and indeterminate, reveal that there is always something worthy they can learn from others, if only because these "others" are (like themselves) in a constant process of relational becoming and self-definition. By exercising this virtue in their reciprocal political engagements, participants not only "articulate" an awareness of the incompleteness and fundamental contingencies of self and society, as both an ontological source of identity and an essential condition for pluralistic democracies, but in doing so they also express willingness to critically attend to, listen to, and learn from diverse others.[66] By awakening a mutual appreciation for the limitations and contingencies of self and society, this conception of humility may make a little room for new voices within and/or without the self, or alternatively, may make older and long repressed voices more audible, and perhaps also more capable of being understood and included within the penumbra of rights and justice.

It should be acknowledged that the same dimensions of being and history in reference to which an ethos of democratic humility takes its value might foster passivity, deferential resignation, and/or resentment, if unaccompanied by the specific type of ethical cultivation toward which this sensibility is directed. In the view being offered here, one is not humble

---

65. In Stephen G. Salkaver's apt phrase, this means coming to embrace democracy as something that is "morally indefinite." See Salkaver, *Finding the Mean: Theory and Practice in Aristotelian Political Philosophy* (Princeton: Princeton University Press, 1990), 208.

66. See Taylor, *Sources of the Self*, 88–89, 95–96, for a discussion of both the importance of and the limitations embedded in the "articulacy" of the moral sources.

before some other agent but rather exercises humility, as an adverbial virtue, in relation to an identity whose solidity is provided by relations of mutual dependency with differences that are often ignored, slighted, or denied. One is not humble before the law (secular) but exercises humility in relation to extant institutions whose "necessity" or "naturalness" often occludes ongoing forms of marginalization and humiliation. In the first case one critically reflects upon the self/identity as a way of opening pathways of attentiveness and receptivity to differences that may already be constitutive of what one is; in doing so, new or better understood relations of mutual dependency may take hold. In the second case, one is alive to the possibility that long accepted ideas about basic institutions (marriage, family, the nation-state) may need to be reconceived in light of new or more clearly recognized forms of diverse human being.

While the movement from the ontological to the political-ethical is neither direct nor easy,[67] this conception of humility is oriented toward important democratic ideals of mutual attentiveness, political inclusion, reciprocal learning, and moral growth. In my view, these last qualities are more likely to come about in a substantively meaningful way if diverse participants engage more directly the differences in the moral and religious sources they honor. Once that problematic ideal is entertained, the question of the manner or sensibility in accordance with which such pluralistic engagements will occur takes on central ethical significance. In this respect, democratic humility is grounded in the ideal of a more attentive and inclusive form of political dialogue that it also seeks to cultivate and shape.

Democratic Humility and Political Liberalism

According to Rawls, the "burdens of judgment are of first significance for a democratic idea of toleration."[68] I have argued that these same burdens of judgment are among some of the basic conditions for a democratic conception of humility. I now want to consider more directly the relationship between humility and liberal virtues like tolerance and reciprocity. I have already indicated the ways in which humility draws on important features of contemporary political liberalism, especially in relation to its

---

67. See Stephen White's discussion of this point in *Sustaining Affirmation: The Strengths of Weak Ontology in Political Theory* (Princeton: Princeton University Press, 2000), 10–12, 118–22.
68. Rawls, *Political Liberalism*, 58.

construal of the sources of disagreement for pluralistic societies.[69] Yet the generosity, fairness, and open-mindedness that are often taken as hallmarks of liberal citizenship might be given more effective motivation if, as an ethos of humility would suggest, intrinsic and instrumental goods can be expected to flow from a more active mode of attentiveness to others. Whereas virtues like tolerance, civility, and reciprocity provide necessary qualities for making judgments under conditions of plural and incommensurable values, civic humility promises to perform some additional ethical and political work that may help vivify political liberalism's affirmation of diversity and inclusion.

First, where a cultivated disposition of civic humility is effectively in play, political actors may be more open to the possibility that their views, perspectives, and moral horizons (including basic categories of justice, reason, and "common sense") may need to be questioned and potentially expanded if they are to deal fairly with others. Alternatively, democratic humility may soften the harder edges of identity, belief, and preunderstanding enough to acknowledge those circumstances when our customary defenses, in the name of long-held political settlements and principles ("walls" of separation, "neutral" justice, "normal" sexuality), may need to be reconceived in the light of new challenges, or better understood challenges. Without a self-conscious effort to cultivate such an ethos, I fear that important virtues like tolerance, forbearance, and civility may become shallow, formal performances that prematurely close off the possibilities for a mutually enriching and transformative mode of political and ethical engagement across multiple forms of difference. The risk is that tolerance and forbearance constitute an ethical response to difference that renders the moral and substantive nature of those differences inaudible/irrelevant to already established identities.

An ethos of democratic humility can help offset this danger because it works on and through us in a manner that is amenable to and yet distinct from acts of tolerance and civility.[70] If tolerance and civility require that we practice forbearance and restraint in our relations with others, democratic humility entails ethical work that can facilitate a critical attentiveness

69. I might also note here that liberalism's historical acknowledgment of political artifice and conventionality provides another connecting link to democratic humility and the reflexive sensibility it strives to cultivate toward preexisting institutions.

70. For an insightful account of civility as a virtue of dialogic citizenship, and one that takes seriously the challenges and limits of virtue for diverse liberal regimes, see Mark Kingwell, *A Civil Tongue: Justice, Dialogue, and the Politics of Pluralism* (University Park: Pennsylvania State University Press, 1995), esp. chapter 6.

toward those differences that may have only been tolerated before. What democratic humility requires, from citizens and leaders alike, is the recognition that we are all shaped, enabled, but also constrained by our specific (but also fluid) moral, cultural, and cognitive horizons, even if we cannot specify the nature or limits of those horizons in advance.[71] When this recognition is brought to bear on public questions that are ineluctably constrained by the burdens of judgment, democratic humility holds out both the intrinsic value and motivating promise of deeper forms of understanding and self-knowledge, and recalls us to the fact that one's standing in a community radically depends on the reciprocal willingness of others to give one's own claims a serious hearing. Against the ontological and historical backdrop I mentioned earlier, these forms of attentiveness and critical listening may not only indicate important reservoirs of meaning and value within democratic selves but may facilitate new modes of social and political alliance within democratic societies as well.

Second, democratic humility may improve the fairness of political judgments by encouraging citizens and leaders to attend, with as much openness, care, and foresight as possible, to the lived experiences and ways of knowing and seeing that characterize all those who might be affected by a particular public policy or judgment. This clearly connects democratic humility to the conditions necessary for meeting important liberal standards of equal respect, reciprocity, and moral justification.[72] Yet here too democratic humility does not stress the ability to justify one's perspective or actions to others on grounds that they could accept (or not "reasonably reject"), but instead works on the initial motivation to actively attend to those others in the first place. If reciprocal reason giving is going to form an effective or stable basis for the moral validity of agreements in a pluralistic society, then it seems that this kind of exchange depends not only on a will to justify one's position to others but on a prior willingness to actively engage, listen, and learn from diverse others. For it seems that only then can the more general liberal principles of reciprocal reason giving and moral justification really get off the ground or indeed travel very far.[73]

---

71. I am drawing on the language of horizons from Hans-Georg Gadamer, *Truth and Method*, trans. Joel Weinsheimer and Donald G. Marshall (New York: Continuum, 1994), 304–7.

72. I have been influenced on the importance of these points by J. Donald Moon. See, for example, his response to William Connolly in "Engaging Plurality: Reflections on *The Ethos of Pluralization*," *Philosophy and Social Criticism* 24, no. 1 (1998): 63–71.

73. For an insightful study that takes the question of the conditions of listening seriously, see Susan Bickford, *The Dissonance of Democracy* (Ithaca: Cornell University Press, 1996).

Finally, unless and until we are collectively engaged in the task of understanding the nature and ground of the values and beliefs that others honor, we are not in a position to critically reconsider how contemporary practices and institutions are often complicit in their own forms of repression, silencing, exclusion, and humiliation. Without a cultivated ethical and political orientation characterized by humility, citizens and leaders may have a difficult time appreciating the moral and political significance of these moments of sociocultural reevaluation. This affirmation might take shape as an open, prospective alertness to the ways in which our ever-changing social and political interdependencies require a congruent willingness to return to and renegotiate our practices from time to time. Political liberals are sensitive about the ability and willingness to reexamine previous judgments and long-held convictions.[74] Yet this capacity can be facilitated and rendered less onerous by the acknowledgment, at the outset, that any decision under the contingent and pluralizing dynamics of contemporary democratic societies is a necessary but also temporary settlement, never a closure. By fostering an active sense of the limits and contingencies that inhere in all of our social and political enactments, and by folding this into our various collective identities and practices, democratic humility may help to generate a "pathos of distance" (Nietzsche) out of which a critical attentiveness and self-reflexive appraisal of identity, institutions, and actions may take hold. And when *phronesis* and foresight fail us, as they are bound to do, democratic humility may help us to acknowledge those circumstances in which the best that we can do is grant or seek forgiveness.[75]

74. Rawls has referred to this as one of the basic moral powers in reference to which citizens are to be regarded as free and equal persons. See *Political Liberalism*, 18–19. See also Rawls, "Reply to Habermas," in *Political Liberalism*, 372–434.

75. I have been influenced on this last point by Arendt's treatment of forgiveness in *The Human Condition*, 236–43. More recently, P. E. Digeser has provided a very thoughtful treatment of forgiveness that, among other things, considers how forgiveness could "swing free" of resentment. See Digeser, *Political Forgiveness* (Ithaca: Cornell University Press, 2001).

CONCLUSION:
THE POLITICS OF NOT SETTLING DOWN

As I have suggested throughout this book, there are better and worse ways of addressing the central questions that have structured social contract theory from the seventeenth century to the present. In what follows, I offer my own contestable response to the institutional, cultural, and civic questions that continue to vex contemporary liberal societies.

Recall that the first question to which the idea of contract responds is how to shape political institutions that are legitimate, stable, and capable of eliciting the voluntary and affectional attachments of their diverse members. We can now offer the view that as a matter of design those institutions will meet these challenges best that seek to maximize democratic forms of public reasoning and common judging while providing for the widest possible extension of political learning and judgment. In short, those institutions that facilitate democratic deliberation alongside the extension of practical wisdom will offer the best means of combining legitimacy with affectional allegiances. Rousseau's brief for frequent assemblies and periodic constitutional revision—reflecting what I referred to in Chapter 4 as a moral and political ethos of revisability—remains deeply relevant for our time.

The second question I have posed concerns the disciplines of cultural and self-fashioning required for sustaining political order and equal freedom amid pluralism. I have argued that diverse liberal societies must acknowledge that disciplines of civic and self-cultivation are a necessary feature of their own perpetuation over time. At the same time we must recognize that this also generates an ineliminable paradox for freedom within diversity. This is something that Locke, at his best, can still reveal to us. If this paradox isn't taken seriously and incorporated into the critical self-awareness of liberal citizens and leaders, it will not be the source of enabling tensions with a diverse liberal society but the occasion for humiliation, marginalization, and resentment.

Thus our third question—how to undertake projects of civic cultivation while sustaining commitments to autonomy, freedom, and diversity—becomes the definitive if troubled terrain for contemporary politics and ethics, as it has been since the time of Hobbes. In response we may offer the idea that the transformative project at the heart of modern theory and politics needs to be conducted with a spirit of critical attentiveness, ethical pluralism, and democratic humility, one in which our answers to all three of these questions are sustained by a commitment to mutual justifiability, revisability, and cultural and self-examination. These specific qualities are necessary because the institutional and cultural consolidations that are provided by every substantive response to these questions are likely to result in the marginalization of a range of constituencies, concerns, or interests that liberal democratic societies must be made mindful of and be willing to reconsider (whether these concerns are, for example, ecological and international or religious and domestic). These specific traits are necessary because there is an abiding sense within the contract tradition and modern political thought generally—especially noteworthy in the case of Hobbes, but also in Rawls—that one of the central purposes of political theory is to make it possible to "settle," "once and for all," basic questions of obligation and principles of justice. There is a desire to be done with politics, at least in relation to certain types of concerns (Rawls calls them "constitutional essentials"). One interesting feature of considering Rawls in relation to Hobbes in this respect is that Hobbes would suggest that just about every public question has the potential to become a "constitutional essential" and thus must be secured from perpetual political struggle for the sake of peace and felicity. Locke creates an ambivalent wedge on this issue that Rousseau radically opens, if only to reseal it through more subtle cultural means. And in the case of "communitarian critics" of this tradition, a similar logic is at work: by "revealing" certain historical and cultural preconceptions already at work within a given political society, public life itself is made discernible only by the recognition of a unique chain of interdependencies. In seeking to "settle" certain basic features of politics, liberals and their critics have sought to wrestle the contingencies and fluidity of public life into a corner—and call that corner the prepolitical. What one comes to recognize through a reexamination of this tradition is the very strong temptation—still operative today—to naturalize, and thus remove from public questioning and political contestation, the terms of civic identity and the aims of public life.

We are in need a political ethic of civic and self-cultivation shorn of the rigidities and excesses of disciplinary normalization. There is no way to deny the interdependencies of institutions, culture, and identity, short of willful blindness. The question instead is how, given these ambiguous relationships, the transformative energies within any political society can be, first, opened to critical self-reflection and examination; second, rendered more attentive to the differential force that these formative disciplines have in the lives of persons and groups in positions of vulnerability and inequality; and third, made more receptive to the need to renegotiate the terms of civic identity and purpose from time to time, accepting as an affirmative feature of pluralistic liberal societies the idea that in politics, there can be no permanent settlements.

BIBLIOGRAPHY

PRIMARY SOURCES

Althusius, Johannes. *Politica: Politics Methodically Set Forth and Illustrated with Sacred and Profane Examples*. Edited and translated by Frederick S. Carney. Indianapolis: Liberty Fund, 1995.

Aquinas, Saint Thomas. *On Law, Morality, and Politics*. Edited by William P. Baumgarth and Richard J. Regan. Indianapolis: Hackett Publishing, 1988.

———. *Summa Theologica*. Translated by Fathers of the English Dominican Province. London: Burns, Oates and Washbourne, 1935.

Aristotle. *The Nichomachean Ethics*. Translated by David Ross, revised by J. L. Ackrill and J. O. Urmson. Oxford: Oxford University Press, 1980.

———. *The Politics*. Translated by Carnes Lord. Chicago: University of Chicago Press, 1984.

Ascham, Anthony. *Of the Confusions and Revolutions of Government*. London, 1649.

Bentham, Jeremy. *A Comment on the Commentaries and A Fragment of Government*. Edited by J. H. Burns and H. L. A. Hart. Atlantic Highlands, N.J.: Humanities Press, 1977.

Blackstone, William. *Commentaries on the Laws of England*. A facsimile of the first edition of 1765–1789. Chicago: University of Chicago Press, 1979.

Bodin, Jean. *On Sovereignty*. Edited and translated by Julian H. Franklin. New York: Cambridge University Press, 1992.

———. *Six Books of the Commonwealth*. Translated by M. J. Tooley. Oxford: Basil Blackwell, 1955.

Bramhall, John. *The Catching of Leviathan, or the Great Whale*. 1658. In *Leviathan: Contemporary Responses to the Political Theory of Thomas Hobbes*, ed. G. A. J. Rogers, 115–79. Bristol: Thoemmes Press, 1995.

Buchanan, George. *De jure regni apud Scotos*. 1630.

Burke, Edmund. *Reflections on the Revolution in France*. Edited by L. G. Mitchell. Oxford: Oxford University Press, 1993.

———. *Select Works of Edmund Burke*. 3 vols. Indianapolis: Liberty Fund, 1999.

Burnet, Thomas. *Remarks upon An Essay Concerning Human Understanding: In a Letter Addres'd to the Author*. N.p., 1697.

Cicero. *De officiis*. Translated by Walter Miller. Cambridge: Harvard University Press, 1921.

Clarendon, Edward, Earl of. *A Brief View and Survey of the Dangerous and Pernicious Errors to Church and State in Mr. Hobbes's Book, Entitled Leviathan. 1676.* In *Leviathan: Contemporary Responses to the Political Theory of Thomas Hobbes,* ed. G. A. J. Rogers, 180–300. Bristol: Thoemmes Press, 1995.

Commager, Henry Steele, ed. *Documents of American History.* New York: Appleton-Century-Crofts, 1958.

Constant, Benjamin. *Political Writings.* Translated and edited by Biancamaria Fontana. Cambridge: Cambridge University Press, 1988.

Filmer, Robert. *Patriarcha and Other Writings.* New York: Cambridge University Press, 1991.

Franklin, Julian H., ed. and trans. *Constitutionalism and Resistance in the Sixteenth Century: Three Treatises by Hotman, Beza, and Mornay.* New York: Pegasus, 1969.

Grotius, Hugo. *De Jure Belli ac Pacis.* Translated by A. C. Campbell. Washington, D.C.: M. Walter Dunne, 1901.

———. *De Jure Belli ac Pacis.* Translated by Francis W. Kelsey. Indianapolis: Bobbs-Merrill, 1925.

———. *Prolegomena to the Law of War and Peace.* Translated by Francis W. Kelsey. New York: Liberal Arts Press, 1957.

———. *The Rights of War and Peace.* Edited by Richard Tuck. Indianapolis: Liberty Fund, 2005.

Hamilton, Alexander, James Madison, and John Jay. *The Federalist.* Edited by Clinton Rossiter. New York: Mentor Books, 1961.

Hegel, G. W. F. *Philosophy of Right.* Translated by T. M. Knox. New York: Oxford University Press, 1967.

Hobbes, Thomas. *Behemoth, or the Long Parliament.* Edited by Ferdinand Tönnies. Chicago: University of Chicago Press, 1990.

———. *A Dialogue Between a Philosopher and a Student of the Common Laws of England.* Edited by Joseph Cropsey. Chicago: University of Chicago Press, 1971.

———. *The Elements of Law Natural and Politic: Human Nature and De corpore politico with Three Lives.* Edited by J. C. A. Gaskin. New York: Oxford University Press, 1994.

———. *The English Works of Thomas Hobbes.* Edited by Sir William Molesworth. 12 vols. London: John Bohn, 1839–45.

———. *Leviathan.* Edited by Michael Oakeshott. New York: Collier Books, 1962.

———. *Leviathan.* With selected variants from the Latin edition of 1668. Edited by Edwin Curley. Indianapolis: Hackett Publishing, 1994.

———. *Man and Citizen: Thomas Hobbes's "De homine" and "De cive."* Edited by Bernard Gert. Garden City, N.Y.: Anchor Books, 1972.

Hooker, Richard. *Of the Laws of Ecclesiastical Polity.* Edited by Arthur Stephen McGrade. Cambridge: Cambridge University Press, 1989.

Hume, David. *Essays: Moral, Political, and Literary.* Edited by Eugene F. Miller. Indianapolis: Liberty Fund, 1985.

———. *A Treatise of Human Nature.* Edited by L. A. Selby-Bigge. 2d ed. Oxford: Clarendon Press, 1978.

Hunton, Philip. *A Treatise of Monarchy.* London, 1643.

James VI (James I). *The Trew Law of Free Monarchies.* In *Political Writings,* ed. Johann P. Sommerville, 62–84. New York: Cambridge University Press, 1994.

Jefferson, Thomas. *The Portable Thomas Jefferson*. Edited by Merrill D. Peterson. New York: Penguin Books, 1975.

Justinian. *The Institutes of Justinian*. Translated by J. B. Moyle. Oxford: Clarendon Press, 1913.

Kant, Immanuel. *Foundations of the Metaphysics of Morals*. Translated by Lewis White Beck. New York: Bobbs-Merrill, 1959.

———. *The Metaphysics of Morals*. Edited and translated by Mary Gregor. Cambridge: Cambridge University Press, 1996.

———. *Political Writings*. Edited by Hans Reiss, translated by H. B. Nisbet. New York: Cambridge University Press, 1991.

Kenyon, J. P. *The Stuart Constitution, 1603–1688*. Cambridge: Cambridge University Press, 1966.

Leibniz, Gottfried Wilhelm. *Political Writings*. Translated and edited by Patrick Riley. New York: Cambridge University Press, 1972.

Lewis, Ewart, ed. *Medieval Political Ideas*. 2 vols. London: Routledge and Kegan Paul, 1954.

Locke, John. *The Educational Writings of John Locke*. Edited by James L. Axtell. New York: Cambridge University Press, 1968.

———. *An Essay Concerning Human Understanding*. Edited by Alexander Campbell Fraser. New York: Dover Publications, 1959.

———. *Essays on the Law of Nature*. Edited by W. von Leyden. Oxford: Clarendon Press, 1954.

———. *A Letter Concerning Toleration*. Edited by James H. Tully. New York: Hackett, 1983.

———. *The Life of John Locke, with Extracts from His Correspondence, Journals and Common-place Books*. Edited by Peter King. 2 vols. Bristol: Thoemmes Press, 1830.

———. *Political Essays*. Edited by Mark Goldie. New York: Cambridge University Press, 1997.

———. *The Reasonableness of Christianity*. Edited by George Ewing. Washington, D.C.: Regnery Gateway, 1965.

———. *Some Thoughts Concerning Education and Of the Conduct of Understanding*. Edited by Ruth W. Grant and Nathan Tarcov. Indianapolis: Hackett Publishing, 1996.

———. *Two Tracts on Government*. Edited and translated by Philip Abrams. New York: Cambridge University Press, 1967.

———. *Two Treatises of Government*. Student ed. Edited by Peter Laslett. New York: Cambridge University Press, 1988.

———. *The Works of John Locke*. 10 vols. London, 1801.

Lutz, Donald S., ed. *Documents of Political Foundation Written by Colonial Americans: From Covenant to Constitution*. Philadelphia: Institute for the Study of Human Issues, 1986.

———. *The Origins of American Constitutionalism*. Baton Rouge: Louisiana State University Press, 1988.

Machiavelli, Niccolò. *The Prince*. Translated by George Bull. New York: Penguin Books, 1981.

Madison, James. *Writings*. Edited by Jack N. Rakove. New York: Library of America, 1999.

Mandeville, Bernard. *The Fable of the Bees: Or, Private Vices, Publick Benefits.* 1714. Edited by Phillip Harth. New York: Penguin Books, 1970.

Montesquieu. *The Spirit of the Laws.* Translated and edited by Anne Cohler, Basia Carolyn Miller, and Harold Samuel Stone. Cambridge: Cambridge University Press, 1989.

Morgan, Edmund S., ed. *Puritan Political Ideas: 1558–1794.* New York: Bobbs-Merrill, 1965.

[Mornay, Philippe du Plessis.] *Vindiciae contra tyrannos.* 1579. In *Constitutionalism and Resistance in the Sixteenth Century,* ed. and trans. Julian H. Franklin, 142–99. New York: Pegasus, 1969.

Nietzsche, Friedrich. *Beyond Good and Evil.* Translated by Walter Kaufmann. New York: Vintage Books, 1989.

———. *On the Genealogy of Morals.* Translated by Walter Kaufman and R. J. Hollingdale. New York: Vintage Books, 1969.

———. *The Will to Power.* Edited by Walter Kaufmann, translated by Walter Kaufmann and R. J. Hollingdale. New York: Vintage Books, 1968.

Otis, James. "The Rights of the British Colonies Asserted and Proved." In *Pamphlets of the American Revolution.* Vol. 1, *1750–1765.* Edited by Bernard Bailyn. Cambridge: Harvard University Press, 1965.

Paine, Thomas. *Rights of Man.* New York: Penguin Books, 1984.

Parker, Henry. *Observations upon some of his Majesties late Answers and Expresses.* London, 1642.

Pufendorf, Samuel. *De jure naturae et gentium libri octo.* Translated by C. H. Oldfather and W. A. Oldfather. Oxford: Clarendon Press, 1934.

———. *On the Duty of Man and Citizen According to Natural Law.* Edited by James Tully, translated by Michael Silverthorne. New York: Cambridge University Press, 1991.

Rawls, John. *John Rawls: Collected Papers.* Edited by Samuel Freeman. Cambridge: Harvard University Press, 1999.

———. *Justice as Fairness: A Restatement.* Edited by Erin Kelly. Cambridge: Belknap Press of Harvard University Press, 2001.

———. "Kantian Constructivism in Moral Theory." *Journal of Philosophy* 77, no. 9 (1980): 515–72.

———. *The Law of Peoples.* Cambridge: Harvard University Press, 1999.

———. *Political Liberalism.* New York: Columbia University Press, 1996.

———. *A Theory of Justice.* Cambridge: Harvard University Press, 1971.

———. "Two Concepts of Rules." *Philosophical Review* 64, no. 1 (1955): 3–32.

Rousseau, Jean-Jacques. *The Collected Writings of Rousseau.* Edited by Roger D. Masters and Christopher Kelly. 12 vols. Hanover: University Press of New England, 1994.

———. *The Confessions.* Translated by J. M. Cohen. New York: Penguin Books, 1953.

———. *The Discourses and Other Early Writings.* Edited and translated by Victor Gourevitch. Cambridge: Cambridge University Press, 1997.

———. *Émile, or on Education.* Translated by Allan Bloom. New York: Basic Books, 1979.

———. *The First and Second Discourses.* Edited by Roger D. Masters, translated by Roger D. Masters and Judith R. Masters. New York: St. Martin's Press, 1964.

———. *The First and Second Discourses and Essay on the Origin of Languages.* Translated by Victor Gourevitch. New York: Harper and Row, 1986.

———. *The Government of Poland.* Translated by Willmoore Kendall. Indianapolis: Hackett Publishing, 1985.

———. *La Nouvelle Héloïse.* Translated by Judith McDowell. University Park: Pennsylvania State University Press, 1968.

———. *The Political Writings of Jean-Jacques Rousseau.* Edited by C. E. Vaughan. Oxford: Basil Blackwell, 1962.

———. *Politics and the Arts: Letter to M. D'Alembert on the Theatre.* Translated by Allan Bloom. Ithaca: Cornell University Press, 1960.

———. *Reveries of the Solitary Walker.* Translated by Peter France. New York: Penguin Books, 1979.

———. *Rousseau—Political Writings.* Translated by Frederick Watkins. New York: Nelson, 1953.

———. *The Social Contract.* Edited by Roger D. Masters, translated by Judith R. Masters. New York: St. Martin's Press, 1978.

———. *The Social Contract and Other Later Political Writings.* Edited and translated by Victor Gourevitch. New York: Cambridge University Press, 1997.

Sanderson, Robert. *A Resolution of Conscience.* 1649. In *Divine Right and Democracy: An Anthology of Political Writing in Stuart England,* ed. David Wooten, 354–55. New York: Penguin Books, 1986.

Selden, John. *Table-Talk.* 1689. Edited by Edward Arber. London: Westminister A. Constable and Co., 1895.

Smith, Adam. *The Theory of Moral Sentiments.* Edited by D. D. Raphael and A. L. Macfie. Indianapolis: Liberty Fund, 1984.

Spinoza, Benedict. *A Theological-Political Treatise and A Political Treatise.* Translated by R. H. M. Elwes. New York: Dover Publications, 1951.

Suárez, Francisco. *A Treatise on Laws and God the Lawgiver* (1612) and *A Defense of the Catholic and Apostolic Faith against the Errors of the Anglican Sect* (1613). In *Selections from Three Works of Suárez.* Translated by Gwladys L. Williams, Ammi Brown, and John Waldron, 13–646, 667–725. Oxford: Clarendon Press, 1944.

Tyrell, James. *Patriarcha non monarchia.* 1681. Ann Arbor: University Microfilms, 1971.

Virgil. *The Aeneid.* Translated by Robert Fitzgerald. New York: Vintage Books, 1980.

Wise, John. *A Vindication of the Government of New England Churches.* In *Colonial American Writings,* ed. Roy Harvey Pearce, 318–45. New York: Rinehart and Co., 1950.

Woodhouse, A. S. P., ed. *Puritanism and Liberty: Being the Army Debates (1647–49) from the Clarke Manuscripts.* London: J. M. Dent and Sons, 1974.

Wooton, David, ed. *Divine Right and Democracy: An Anthology of Political Writing in Stuart England.* New York: Penguin Books, 1986.

SECONDARY SOURCES

Aarsleff, Hans. "The State of Nature and the Nature of Man in Locke." In *John Locke: Problems and Perspectives,* ed. John W. Yolton, 99–136. Cambridge: Cambridge University Press, 1969.

Ackerman, Bruce. *We the People: Foundations.* Cambridge: Belknap Press of Harvard University Press, 1991.

Allen, J. W. *English Political Thought: 1603–1660.* London: Methuen and Co., 1938.

———. *A History of Political Thought in the Sixteenth Century.* London: Methuen and Co., 1960.

Allison, Henry E. *Kant's Theory of Freedom.* Cambridge: Cambridge University Press, 1990.

Appiah, Kwame Anthony. *The Ethics of Identity.* Princeton: Princeton University Press, 2005.

Arendt, Hannah. *Between Past and Future.* New York: Penguin Books, 1968.

———. *Crises of the Republic.* New York: Harcourt Brace Jovanovich, 1972.

———. *The Human Condition.* Chicago: University of Chicago Press, 1958.

———. *Men in Dark Times.* New York: Harcourt Brace Jovanovich, 1968.

———. *On Revolution.* New York: Viking Press, 1965.

Ashcraft, Richard. *Locke's Two Treatises of Government.* London: Allen and Unwin, 1987.

———. *Revolutionary Politics and Locke's Two Treatises of Government.* Princeton: Princeton University Press, 1986.

Atiyah, P. S. *Essays on Contract.* Oxford: Clarendon Press, 1986.

Audi, Robert. *Religious Commitment and Secular Reason.* New York: Cambridge University Press, 2000.

Austin, J. L. *How to Do Things with Words.* 2d ed. Edited by J. O. Urmson and Marina Sbisa. Cambridge: Harvard University Press, 1962.

Aylmer, G. E., ed. *The Interregnum: The Quest for Settlement, 1646–1660.* London: Archon Books, 1972.

Bader, Veit. "Religious Pluralism: Secularism or Priority of Democracy?" *Political Theory* 27, no. 5 (1999): 597–633.

Barber, Benjamin. *The Conquest of Politics.* Princeton: Princeton University Press, 1988.

———. *Fear's Empire: War, Terrorism, and Democracy.* London: W. W. Norton, 2003.

———. "Foundationalism and Democracy." In Benjamin Barber, *A Passion for Democracy,* 19–30. Princeton: Princeton University Press, 1998.

———. "Liberal Democracy and the Costs of Consent." In *Liberalism and the Moral Life,* ed. Nancy L. Rosenblum, 54–67. Cambridge: Harvard University Press, 1989.

———. *Strong Democracy.* Berkeley and Los Angeles: University of California Press, 1984.

Barker, Ernest. *Greek Political Theory.* London: University Paperbacks, 1918.

———. "Introduction." In *Social Contract: Essays by Locke, Hume, and Rousseau,* ed. Ernest Barker, vii–xliv. New York: Oxford University Press, 1962.

———. *Principles of Social and Political Theory.* New York: Oxford University Press, 1952.

Barry, Brian. *Culture and Equality: An Egalitarian Critique of Multiculturalism.* Cambridge: Harvard University Press, 2001.

Baumgold, Deborah. "Hobbes's Political Sensibility: The Menace of Political Ambition." In *Thomas Hobbes and Political Theory,* ed. Mary G. Dietz, 74–90. Lawrence: University Press of Kansas, 1990.

———. *Hobbes's Political Theory.* Cambridge: Cambridge University Press, 1988.

Beiner, Ronald. *What's the Matter with Liberalism?* Berkeley and Los Angeles: University of California Press, 1992.

Beiner, Ronald, and William James Booth, eds. *Kant and Political Philosophy: The Contemporary Legacy.* New Haven: Yale University Press, 1993.

Benhabib, Seyla. "Liberal Dialogue Versus a Critical Theory of Discursive Legitimation." In *Liberalism and the Moral Life,* ed. Nancy Rosenblum, 143–56. Cambridge: Harvard University Press, 1989.

Beran, Harry. *The Consent Theory of Political Obligation.* London: Croom Helm,
1987.

Berkowitz, Peter. *Virtue and the Making of Modern Liberalism.* Princeton: Princeton University Press, 1999.

Berlin, Isaiah. "Two Concepts of Liberty." In Isaiah Berlin, *Four Essays on Liberty,*
118–72. Oxford: Oxford University Press, 1969.

Bickford, Susan. *The Dissonance of Democracy: Listening, Conflict, and Citizenship.*
Ithaca: Cornell University Press, 1996.

Black, Antony. "The Juristic Origins of Social Contract Theory." *History of Political
Thought* 14, no. 1 (1993): 57–76.

Bloom, Allan. "Rousseau's Critique of Liberal Constitutionalism." In *The Legacy of
Rousseau,* ed. Clifford Orwin and Nathan Tarcov, 143–67. Chicago: University of Chicago Press, 1997.

Bohman, James. "Public Reason and Cultural Pluralism: Political Liberalism and the
Problem of Moral Conflict." *Political Theory* 23, no. 2 (1995): 253–79.

Boonin-Vail, David. *Thomas Hobbes and the Science of Moral Virtue.* New York:
Cambridge University Press, 1994.

Boucher, David, and Paul Kelly, eds. *The Social Contract from Hobbes to Rawls.* New
York: Routledge, 1994.

Boyd, Richard. *Uncivil Society: The Perils of Pluralism and the Making of Modern
Liberalism.* Lanham, Md.: Lexington Books, 2004.

Brown, K. C., ed. *Hobbes Studies.* Oxford: Basil Blackwell, 1965.

Buchanan, Allen. "Political Liberalism and Social Epistemology." *Philosophy and Public Affairs* 32, no. 2 (2004): 95–130.

Butler, Melissa A. "Early Liberal Roots of Feminism: John Locke and the Attack on
Patriarchy." *American Political Science Review* 72, no. 1 (1978): 135–50.

Button, Mark E. "Arendt, Rawls, and Public Reason." *Social Theory and Practice* 31,
no. 2 (2005): 257–80.

———. "'A Monkish Kind of Virtue'? For and Against Humility." *Political Theory*
33, no. 6 (2005): 840–68.

Callan, Eamonn. *Creating Citizens: Political Education and Liberal Democracy.*
Oxford: Clarendon Press, 1997.

Carring, Joseph. "Liberal Impediments to Liberal Education: The Assent to Locke."
Review of Politics 63, no. 1 (2001): 41–76.

Carritt, E. F. *Ethical and Political Thinking.* Oxford: Clarendon Press, 1947.

Cassirer, Ernst. *The Philosophy of the Enlightenment.* Princeton: Princeton University Press, 1979.

———. *The Question of Jean-Jacques Rousseau.* Translated by Peter Gay. New York:
Columbia University Press, 1954.

Cavell, Stanley. *The Claim of Reason.* Oxford: Oxford University Press, 1979.

Christiano, Thomas. "Is There Any Basis for Rawls' Duty of Civility?" *Modern
Schoolmen* 78 (2001): 151–61.

Chwe, Michael Suk-Young. *Rational Ritual: Culture, Coordination, and Common
Knowledge.* Princeton: Princeton University Press, 2001.

Cohen, Joshua. "Reflections on Rousseau: Autonomy and Democracy." *Philosophy
and Public Affairs* 15 (1986): 275–97.

Colman, John. *John Locke's Moral Philosophy*. Edinburgh: Edinburgh University Press, 1983.

Coltman, Irene. *Private Men and Public Causes: Philosophy and Politics in the English Civil War*. London: Faber and Faber, 1962.

Connolly, William. *The Ethos of Pluralization*. Minneapolis: University of Minnesota Press, 1995.

———. *Identity/Difference: Democratic Negotiations of Political Paradox*. Ithaca: Cornell University Press, 1991.

———. *Neuropolitics: Thinking, Culture, Speed*. Minneapolis: University of Minnesota Press, 2002.

———. *Why I Am Not a Secularist*. Minneapolis: University of Minnesota Press, 1999.

Cooke, Paul D. *Hobbes and Christianity: Reassessing the Bible in Leviathan*. Lanham, Md.: Rowman and Littlefield, 1996.

Coole, Diana. "Women, Gender, and Contract: Feminist Interpretations." In *The Social Contract from Hobbes to Rawls*, ed. David Boucher and Paul Kelly, 191–210. New York: Routledge, 1994.

Cooper, Laurence D. *Rousseau and Nature: The Problem of the Good Life*. University Park: Pennsylvania State University Press, 1994.

Crocker, Lester. "Rousseau's *soi-disant* Liberty." In *Rousseau and Liberty*, ed. Robert Wokler, 244–66. Manchester: Manchester University Press, 1995.

Crowder, George. *Liberalism and Value Pluralism*. London: Continuum, 2002.

Dagger, Richard. *Civic Virtues*. New York: Oxford University Press, 1997.

Darwall, Stephen. *The British Moralists and the Internal 'Ought': 1640–1740*. New York: Cambridge University Press, 1995.

Deitz, Mary G. "Hobbes's Subject as Citizen." In *Thomas Hobbes and Political Theory*, ed. Mary G. Dietz, 91–119. Lawrence: University Press of Kansas, 1990.

De Jouvenel, Bertrand. *The Pure Theory of Politics*. New Haven: Yale University Press, 1963.

Deneen, Patrick J. *Democratic Faith*. Princeton: Princeton University Press, 2005.

Dent, N. J. H. *Rousseau: An Introduction to His Psychological, Social, and Political Theory*. New York: Basil Blackwell, 1988.

D'Entreves, Alexander Passerin. *Natural Law: An Introduction to Legal Philosophy*. New Brunswick, N.J.: Transaction Publishers, 1994.

Diamond, Larry, and Marc F. Plattner, eds. *The Global Divergence of Democracies*. Baltimore: Johns Hopkins University Press, 2001.

Digeser, P. E. *Political Forgiveness*. Ithaca: Cornell University Press, 2001.

Disch, Lisa Jane. *Hannah Arendt and the Limits of Philosophy*. Ithaca: Cornell University Press, 1994.

Dunn, John. *The History of Political Theory and Other Essays*. Cambridge: Cambridge University Press, 1996.

———. *Political Obligation in Its Historical Context*. Cambridge: Cambridge University Press, 1980.

———. *The Political Thought of John Locke*. Cambridge: Cambridge University Press, 1969.

———. "The Politics of Locke in England and America." In *John Locke: Problems and Perspectives*, ed. John W. Yolton, 45–80. Cambridge: Cambridge University Press, 1969.

———. "What Is Living and What Is Dead in the Political Theory of John Locke?"

In John Dunn, *Interpreting Political Responsibility: Essays, 1981–1989*, 9–25. Princeton: Princeton University Press, 1990.

Dworkin, Ronald. "Foundations of Liberal Equality." In *Equal Freedom: Selected Tanner Lectures in Human Values*, ed. Stephen Darwall, 190–306. Ann Arbor: University of Michigan Press, 1995.

———. *A Matter of Principle*. Cambridge: Harvard University Press, 1985.

Eisenach, Eldon J. *Narrative Power and Liberal Truth*. Lanham, Md.: Rowman and Littlefield, 2002.

———. *Two Worlds of Liberalism*. Chicago: University of Chicago Press, 1981.

Elazar, Daniel J. *The American Constitutional Tradition*. Lincoln: University of Nebraska Press, 1988.

———. *Covenant and Commonwealth: From Christian Separation Through the Protestant Reformation*. Vol. 2 of *The Covenant Tradition in Politics*. New Brunswick, N.J.: Transaction Publishers, 1996.

———. *Covenant and Polity in Biblical Israel: Biblical Foundations and Jewish Expressions*. Vol. 1 of *The Covenant Tradition in Politics*. New Brunswick, N.J.: Transaction Publishers, 1995.

Ellis, Elizabeth. *Kant's Politics: Provisional Theory for an Uncertain World*. New Haven: Yale University Press, 2005.

Elshtain, Jean Bethke. *Public Man, Private Woman: Women in Social and Political Thought*. Princeton: Princeton University Press, 1981.

Elster, Jon. *Ulysses Unbound: Studies in Rationality, Precommitment, and Constraints*. New York: Cambridge University Press, 2000.

Ewin, R. E. *Virtues and Rights: The Moral Philosophy of Thomas Hobbes*. Boulder: Westview Press, 1991.

Farr, James, and Clayton Roberts. "John Locke on the Glorious Revolution: A Rediscovered Document." *Historical Journal* 28, no. 2 (1995): 385–98.

Fermon, Nicole. *Domesticating Passions: Rousseau, Woman, and Nation*. Hanover: Wesleyan University Press, 1997.

Figgis, J. N. *Political Thought from Gerson to Grotius*. New York: Harper and Bros., 1960.

Flathman, Richard. *Pluralism and Liberal Democracy*. Baltimore: Johns Hopkins University Press, 2005.

———. *Political Obligation*. New York: Atheneum, 1972.

———. *Reflections of a Would Be Anarchist: Ideals and Institutions of Liberalism*. Minneapolis: University of Minnesota Press, 1998.

———. *Thomas Hobbes: Skepticism, Individuality, and Chastened Politics*. Newbury Park, Calif.: Sage, 1993.

———. *Willful Liberalism: Voluntarism and Individuality in Political Theory and Practice*. Ithaca: Cornell University Press, 1992.

Forde, Steven. "Natural Law, Theology, and Morality in Locke." *American Journal of Political Science* 45, no. 2 (2001): 396–409.

Forster, Greg. "Divine Law and Human Law in Hobbes's *Leviathan*." *History of Political Thought* 24, no. 2 (2003): 189–218.

Foucault, Michel. *The Essential Foucault*. Edited by Paul Rabinow and Nikolas Rose. New York: New Press, 2003.

———. *The Foucault Reader*. Edited by Paul Rabinow. New York: Pantheon, 1984.

———. *Power/Knowledge*. Edited by Colin Gordon, translated by Colon Gordon, Leo Marshall, John Mepham, and Kate Soper. New York: Pantheon, 1980.

Franklin, Julian H. *John Locke and the Theory of Sovereignty: Mixed Monarchy and the Right of Resistance in the Political Thought of the English Revolution.* New York: Cambridge University Press, 1978.

Freeman, Samuel. "Congruence and the Good of Justice." In *The Cambridge Companion to Rawls,* ed. Samuel Freeman, 277–315. Cambridge: Cambridge University Press, 2003.

———. "Political Liberalism and the Possibility of a Just Democratic Constitution." *Chicago-Kent Law Review* 69, no. 3 (1994): 619–68.

———. "Reason and Agreement in Social Contract Views." *Philosophy and Public Affairs* 19 (spring 1990): 122–57.

Fried, Charles. *Contract as Promise.* Cambridge: Harvard University Press, 1981.

Frohock, Fred. *Public Reason: Mediated Authority in the Liberal State.* Ithaca: Cornell University Press, 1999.

Gadamer, Hans-George. *Truth and Method.* Translated by Joel Weinsheimer and Donald G. Marshall. New York: Continuum, 1994.

Galston, William. *Kant and the Problem of History.* Chicago: University of Chicago Press, 1975.

———. *Liberal Purposes: Goods, Virtues, and Diversity in the Liberal State.* Cambridge: Cambridge University Press, 1991.

———. "Pluralism and Social Unity." *Ethics* 99, no. 4 (1989): 711–26.

Gaus, Gerald. *Contemporary Theories of Liberalism: Public Reason as a Post-Enlightenment Project.* Thousand Oaks, Calif.: Sage, 2003.

Gauthier, David. "Between Hobbes and Rawls." In *Rationality, Justice, and the Social Contract: Themes from Morals by Agreement,* ed. David Gauthier and Robert Sugden, 24–39. Ann Arbor: University of Michigan Press, 1993.

———. *Moral Dealing: Contract, Ethics, and Reason.* Ithaca: Cornell University Press, 1990.

———. *Morals by Agreement.* Oxford: Clarendon Press, 1986.

———. "Public Reason." *Social Philosophy and Policy* 12 (winter 1995): 19–42.

———. "Why Ought One Obey God?" In *The Social Contract Theorists: Critical Essays on Hobbes, Locke, and Rousseau,* ed. Christopher W. Morris, 73–95. Lanham, Md.: Rowman and Littlefield, 1999.

George, Robert P. *Making Men Moral: Civil Liberties and Public Morality.* Oxford: Clarendon Press, 1993.

Gert, Bernard. "Introduction." In Bernard Gert, *Man and Citizen.* Garden City, N.Y.: Anchor Books, 1972.

Gierke, Otto von. *The Development of Political Theory.* Translated by Bernard Freyd. New York: W. W. Norton, 1939.

———. *Natural Law and the Theory of Society, 1500 to 1800.* Translated by Ernest Barker. London: Cambridge University Press, 1958.

———. *Political Theories of the Middle Age.* 1900. Translated by F. W. Maitland. Bristol: Thoemmes Press, 1996.

Giesey, Ralph E. *If Not, Not: The Oath of the Aragonese and the Legendary Laws of Sobrarbe.* Princeton: Princeton University Press, 1968.

Gilden, Hilail. *Rousseau's Social Contract.* Chicago: University of Chicago Press, 1983.

Goldie, Mark. "The Reception of Hobbes." In *The Cambridge History of Political Thought: 1450–1700,* ed. J. H. Burns, 589–615. Cambridge: Cambridge University Press, 1991.

————. "The Revolution of 1689 and the Structure of Political Argument." *Bulletin of Research in the Humanities* 83 (1980): 473–564.

Goldsmith, M. M. *Hobbes's Science of Politics*. New York: Columbia University Press, 1966.

Gordly, James. *The Philosophical Origins of Modern Contract Doctrine*. Oxford: Clarendon Press, 1991.

Gough, J. W. *John Locke's Political Philosophy: Eight Studies*. Oxford: Clarendon Press, 1950.

————. *The Social Contract: A Critical Study of Its Development*. 2d ed. Oxford: Clarendon Press, 1957.

Grant, Ruth W. *Hypocrisy and Integrity: Machiavelli, Rousseau, and the Ethics of Politics*. Chicago: University of Chicago Press, 1997.

————. *John Locke's Liberalism*. Chicago: University of Chicago Press, 1987.

Gray, John. *Post-Liberalism: Studies in Political Thought*. New York: Routledge, 1993.

————. *Two Faces of Liberalism*. New York: New Press, 2000.

Green, T. H. *Lectures on the Principles of Political Obligation*. Edited by Paul Harris and John Morrow. Cambridge: Cambridge University Press, 1986.

Greenawalt, Kent. *Private Consciences and Public Reasons*. New York: Oxford University Press, 1995.

Grice, Geoffrey Russell. *The Ground of Moral Judgment*. Cambridge: Cambridge University Press, 1967.

Guthrie, W. K. C. *The Sophists*. Cambridge: Cambridge University Press, 1971.

Gutmann, Amy, and Dennis Thompson. *Democracy and Disagreement*. Cambridge: Belknap Press of Harvard University Press, 1996.

————. "Moral Conflict and Political Consensus." *Ethics* 101, no. 1 (1990): 64–88.

Haakonssen, Knud. *Natural Law and Moral Philosophy: From Grotius to the Scottish Enlightenment*. New York: Cambridge University Press, 1996.

Habermas, Jürgen. *Between Facts and Norms: Contributions to a Discourse Theory of Law and Democracy*. Translated by William Rehg. Cambridge: MIT Press, 1998.

————. "Constitutional Democracy: A Paradoxical Union of Contradictory Principles?" *Political Theory* 29, no. 6 (2001): 766–81.

————. *Justification and Application: Remarks on Discourse Ethics*. Translated by Ciaran Cronin. Cambridge: MIT Press, 1993.

————. *The Structural Transformation of the Public Sphere: An Inquiry into a Category of Bourgeois Society*. 1962. Translated by Thomas Burger. Cambridge: MIT Press, 1992.

Hampton, Jean. *Hobbes and the Social Contract Tradition*. Cambridge: Cambridge University Press, 1986.

Hanson, Donald W. *From Kingdom to Commonwealth: The Development of Civic Consciousness in English Political Thought*. Cambridge: Harvard University Press, 1970.

Hare, R. M. *Essays in Ethical Theory*. Oxford: University Press, 1989.

————. "The Promising Game." In *The Is-Ought Question: A Collection of Papers on the Central Problems in Moral Philosophy*, ed. W. D. Hudson, 144–56. New York: St. Martin's Press, 1969.

Harris, Ian. *The Mind of John Locke: A Study of Political Theory in Its Intellectual Setting*. New York: Cambridge University Press, 1994.

Harrison, J. R., and Peter Laslett. *The Library of John Locke*. 2d ed. Oxford: Clarendon Press, 1971.

Harsanyi, John C. "Morality and the Theory of Rational Behaviour." In *Utilitarianism and Beyond*, ed. Amartya Sen and Bernard Williams, 39–62. Cambridge: Cambridge University Press, 1982.

Hart, H. L. A. *The Concept of Law*. Oxford: Clarendon Press, 1961.

———. "Legal and Moral Obligation." In *Essays in Moral Philosophy*, ed. A. I. Melden. Seattle: University of Washington Press, 1958.

Herman, Barbara. "A Cosmopolitan Kingdom of Ends." In *Reclaiming the History of Ethics: Essays for John Rawls*, ed. Andrews Reath, Barbara Herman, and Christine M. Korsgaard, 187–213. Cambridge: Cambridge University Press, 1997.

———. "Training to Autonomy: Kant and the Question of Moral Education." In *Philosophers on Education: Historical Perspectives*, ed. Amélie Oksenberg Rorty, 255–72. London: Routledge, 1998.

Herzog, Don. *Happy Slaves: A Critique of Consent Theory*. Chicago: University of Chicago Press, 1989.

Hill, Christopher. *Society and Puritanism in Pre-Revolutionary England*. New York: St. Martin's Press, 1997.

Hill, Thomas E., Jr. *Dignity and Practical Reason in Kant's Moral Theory*. Ithaca: Cornell University Press, 1992.

Hirschman, Albert O. *The Passions and the Interests: Political Arguments for Capitalism Before Its Triumph*. Princeton: Princeton University Press, 1977.

Hirschmann, Nancy. *Rethinking Obligation: A Feminist Method for Political Obligation*. Ithaca: Cornell University Press, 1992.

Hollenbach, David. "Public Reason/Private Religion? A Response to Paul J. Weithman." *Journal of Religious Ethics* 22, no. 1 (1994): 39–46.

Holmes, Stephen. *Passions and Constraint: On the Theory of Liberal Democracy*. Chicago: University of Chicago Press, 1995.

Honig, Bonnie. "Dead Rights, Live Futures: A Reply to Habermas's 'Constitutional Democracy.'" *Political Theory* 29, no. 6 (2001): 792–805.

———. *Political Theory and the Displacement of Politics*. Ithaca: Cornell University Press, 1993.

Hood, F. C. *The Divine Politics of Thomas Hobbes*. Oxford: Clarendon Press, 1964.

Höpfl, Harro, and Martyn P. Thompson. "The History of Contract as a Motif in Political Thought." *American Historical Review* 84, no. 4 (1979): 919–44.

Horton, John. "Rawls, Public Reason, and the Limits of Liberal Justification." *Contemporary Political Theory* 2 (2003): 5–23.

Hulliung, Mark. *The Autocritique of the Enlightenment: Rousseau and the Philosophes*. Cambridge: Harvard University Press, 1994.

Hurka, Thomas. *Perfectionism*. New York: Oxford University Press, 1993.

Isaac, Jeffrey C., Matthew F. Filner, and Jason C. Bivins. "American Democracy and the New Christian Right: A Critique of Apolitical Liberalism." In *Democracy's Edges*, ed. Ian Shapiro and Casiano Hacker-Cordón, 222–64. Cambridge: Cambridge University Press, 1999.

Ivison, Duncan. "The Secret History of Public Reason: Hobbes to Rawls." *History of Political Thought* 18, no. 1 (1997): 125–47.

———. *The Self at Liberty: Political Argument and the Arts of Government*. Ithaca: Cornell University Press, 1997.

Johnston, David. *The Rhetoric of Leviathan: Thomas Hobbes and the Politics of Cultural Transformation*. Princeton: Princeton University Press, 1986.

Josephson, Peter. *The Great Art of Government: Locke's Use of Consent.* Lawrence: University Press of Kansas, 2002.

Judson, Margaret A. *From Tradition to Political Reality.* Hamden, Conn.: Archon Books, 1980.

Kahn, Victoria. *Wayward Contracts: The Crisis of Political Obligation in England, 1640–1674.* Princeton: Princeton University Press, 2004.

Kavka, Gregory S. *Hobbesian Moral and Political Theory.* Princeton: Princeton University Press, 1986.

Keenan, Alan. *Democracy in Question: Democratic Openness in a Time of Political Closure.* Stanford: Stanford University Press, 2003.

Kenyon, J. P. *Revolution Principles: The Politics of Party, 1689–1720.* Cambridge: Cambridge University Press, 1977.

Keohane, Nannerl O. *Philosophy and the State in France: The Renaissance to the Enlightenment.* Princeton: Princeton University Press, 1980.

Kingwell, Mark. *A Civil Tongue: Justice, Dialogue, and the Politics of Pluralism.* University Park: Pennsylvania State University Press, 1995.

Klosko, George. *Democratic Procedures and Liberal Consensus.* Oxford: Oxford University Press, 2000.

Korsgaard, Christine M. *The Souces of Normativity.* Cambridge: Cambridge University Press, 1996.

Kraus, Jody S. *The Limits of Hobbesian Contractarianism.* New York: Cambridge University Press, 1993.

Krieger, Leonard. *The Politics of Discretion: Pufendorf and the Acceptance of the Natural Law.* Chicago: University of Chicago Press, 1965.

Kukathas, Chandran. *The Liberal Archipelago: A Theory of Diversity and Freedom.* Oxford: Oxford University Press, 2003.

Kymlicka, Will. *Liberalism, Community, and Culture.* Oxford: Oxford University Press, 1989.

Langston, Douglas C. *Conscience and Other Virtues.* University Park: Pennsylvania State University Press, 2001.

Larmore, Charles. *The Morals of Modernity.* New York: Cambridge University Press, 1996.

———. "Public Reason." In *The Cambridge Companion to Rawls,* ed. Samuel Freeman, 368–93. New York: Cambridge University Press, 2003.

LaVaque-Manty, Mika. *Arguments and Fists: Political Agency and Justification in Liberal Theory.* New York: Routledge, 2002.

———. "Kant's Children." *Social Theory and Practice* 32, no. 3 (2006): 365–88.

Lessnoff, Michael. *Social Contract.* Atlantic Highlands, N.J.: Humanities Press International, 1986.

Levine, Andrew. *The Politics of Autonomy: A Kantian Reading of Rousseau's Social Contract.* Amherst: University of Massachusetts Press, 1976.

Lichterman, Paul. *Elusive Togetherness.* Princeton: Princeton University Press, 2005.

Lloyd, S. A. "Coercion, Ideology, and Education in *Leviathan.*" In *Reclaiming the History of Ethics: Essays for John Rawls,* ed. Andrews Reath, Barbara Herman, and Christine M. Korsgaard, 36–65. Cambridge: Cambridge University Press, 1997.

———. *Ideals as Interests in Hobbes's Leviathan: The Power of Mind over Matter.* Cambridge: Cambridge University Press, 1992.

Macedo, Stephen. *Diversity and Distrust: Civic Education in a Multicultural Democracy*. Cambridge: Harvard University Press, 2000.

———. "Liberal Civic Education and Religious Fundamentalism: The Case of God v. John Rawls?" *Ethics* 105 (April 1995): 468–96.

———. *Liberal Virtues: Citizenship, Virtue, and Community in Liberal Constitutionalism*. Oxford: Clarendon Press, 1990.

———. "Transformative Constitutionalism and the Case of Religion: Defending the Moderate Hegemony of Liberalism." *Political Theory* 26, no. 1 (1998): 56–80.

MacIntyre, Alasdair. *After Virtue*. Notre Dame: University of Notre Dame Press, 1981.

Macpherson, C. B. *The Political Theory of Possessive Individualism: Hobbes to Locke*. Oxford: Oxford University Press, 1988.

Maine, Henry Sumner. *Ancient Law*. Edited by Frederick Pollock. Gloucester, Mass.: Peter Smith, 1970.

Mansfield, Harvey C. "Liberty and Virtue in the American Founding." In *Never a Matter of Indifference: Sustaining Virtue in a Free Republic*, ed. Peter Berkowitz, 3–28. Stanford: Hoover Institution Press, 2003.

Marshall, John. *John Locke: Resistance, Religion, and Responsibility*. Cambridge: Cambridge University Press, 1994.

Martinich, A. P. *The Two Gods of Leviathan: Thomas Hobbes on Religion and Politics*. Cambridge: Cambridge University Press, 1992.

Masters, Roger D. *The Political Philosophy of Rousseau*. Princeton: Princeton University Press, 1968.

McClure, Kirstie M. *Judging Rights: Lockean Politics and the Limits of Consent*. Ithaca: Cornell University Press, 1996.

McCormick, Peter J. *Social Contract and Political Obligation: A Critique and Reappraisal*. New York: Garland, 1987.

Medina, Vincente. *Social Contract Theories: Political Obligation or Anarchy?* Savage, Md.: Rowman and Littlefield, 1990.

Mills, Charles W. *The Racial Contract*. Ithaca: Cornell University Press, 1997.

Mitchell, Joshua. *Not by Reason Alone: Religion, History, and Identity in Early Modern Political Thought*. Chicago: University of Chicago Press, 1993.

Moon, J. Donald. *Constructing Community: Moral Pluralism and Tragic Conflict*. Princeton: Princeton University Press, 1993.

———. "Engaging Plurality: Reflections on *The Ethos of Pluralization*." *Philosophy and Social Criticism* 24, no. 1 (1998): 63–71.

———. "Rawls and Habermas on Public Reason: Human Rights and Global Justice." *Annual Review of Political Science* 6 (2003): 257–74.

Mulhall, Stephen. "Promising, Consent, and Citizenship: Rawls and Cavell on Morality and Politics." *Political Theory* 25, no. 2 (1997): 171–92.

Murphy, Andrew R. *Conscience and Community*. University Park: Pennsylvania State University Press, 2001.

———. "Rawls and the Shrinking Liberty of Conscience." *Review of Politics* 60, no. 2 (1998): 247–76.

Myers, Peter C. *Our Only Star and Compass: Locke and the Struggle for Political Rationality*. Lanham, Md.: Rowman and Littlefield, 1998.

Nagel, Thomas. "Hobbes's Concept of Obligation." *Philosophical Review* 68, no. 1 (1959): 68–83.

———. "Moral Conflict and Political Legitimacy." *Philosophy and Public Affairs* 16, no. 3 (1987): 215–40.

Noble, Richard. *Language, Subjectivity, and Freedom in Rousseau's Moral Philosophy.* New York: Garland, 1991.

Nozick, Robert. *Anarchy, State, and Utopia.* Oxford: Basil Blackwell, 1974.

Oakeshott, Michael. "The Moral Life in the Writings of Thomas Hobbes." In Michael Oakeshott, *Rationalism in Politics and Other Essays,* 295–350. Indianapolis: Liberty Fund, 1991.

———. *On Human Conduct.* Oxford: Clarendon Press, 1975.

Oakley, Francis. "Locke, Natural Law, and God—Again." *History of Political Thought* 18, no. 4 (1997): 624–51.

———. *Omnipotence, Covenant, and Order: An Excursion in the History of Ideas from Abelard to Leibniz.* Ithaca: Cornell University Press, 1984.

Oakley, Francis, and Elliot Urdang. "Locke, Natural Law, and God." *Natural Law Forum* 11 (1966): 92–109.

Okin, Susan Moller. *Justice, Gender, and the Family.* New York: Basic Books, 1989.

———. *Women in Western Political Thought.* Princeton: Princeton University Press, 1979.

O'Neill, Onora. *Constructions of Reason.* Cambridge: Cambridge University Press, 1989.

———. "Constructivism in Rawls and Kant." In *The Cambridge Companion to Rawls,* ed. Samuel Freeman, 347–67. Cambridge: Cambridge University Press, 2003.

———. "Political Liberalism and Public Reason: A Critical Notice of John Rawls, *Political Liberalism.*" *Philosophical Review* 106, no. 3 (1997): 411–28.

Orlie, Melissa. "Forgiving Trespasses, Promising Futures." In *Feminist Interpretations of Hannah Arendt,* ed. Bonnie Honig, 337–56. University Park: Pennsylvania State University Press, 1995.

Orwin, Clifford, and Nathan Tarcov, eds. *The Legacy of Rousseau.* Chicago: University of Chicago Press, 1997.

Ostrom, Vincent. *The Meaning of American Federalism.* San Francisco: ICS Press, 1991.

Pangle, Thomas L. *The Spirit of Modern Republicanism: The Moral Vision of the American Founders and the Philosophy of Locke.* Chicago: University of Chicago Press, 1988.

Pateman, Carole. *The Problem of Political Obligation.* New York: John Wiley and Sons, 1979.

———. *The Sexual Contract.* Stanford: Stanford University Press, 1988.

Philips, Anne. "Dealing with Difference: A Politics of Ideas, or a Politics of Presence?" In *Democracy and Difference: Contesting the Boundaries of the Political,* ed. Seyla Benhabib, 139–52. Princeton: Princeton University Press, 1996.

Pitkin, Hanna. "Obligation and Consent—I." *American Political Science Review* 59, no. 4 (1965): 990–99.

———. "Obligation and Consent—II." *American Political Science Review* 60, no. 1 (1966): 39–52.

Plamenatz, J. P. *Consent, Freedom, and Political Obligation.* 2d ed. New York: Oxford University Press, 1968.

———. *Man and Society.* Vol. 1. New York: McGraw-Hill, 1963.

Pocock, J. G. A. *The Ancient Constitution and the Feudal Law: English Historical Thought in the Seventeenth Century.* Cambridge: Cambridge University Press, 1957.

————. "Cambridge Paradigms and Scotch Philosophers: A Study of the Relations Between the Civic Humanist and the Civil Jurisprudential Interpretation of Eighteenth-Century Social Thought." In *Wealth and Virtue: The Shaping of Political Economy in the Scottish Enlightenment,* ed. Istvan Hont and Michael Ignatieff, 235–52. Cambridge: Cambridge University Press, 1983.

————. "The Concept of a Language and the *métier d'historien:* Some Considerations on Practice." In *The Languages of Political Theory in Early-Modern Europe,* ed. Anthony Pagden, 19–38. New York: Cambridge University Press, 1987.

————. "A Discourse of Sovereignty: Observations on the Work in Progress." In *Political Discourse in Early Modern Britain,* ed. Nicholas Phillipson and Quentin Skinner, 377–428. Cambridge: Cambridge University Press, 1993.

————. *The Machiavellian Moment: Florentine Political Thought and the Atlantic Republican Tradition.* Princeton: Princeton University Press, 1975.

————. *Politics, Language, and Time: Essays on Political Thought and History.* Chicago: University of Chicago Press, 1971.

————. *Virtue, Commerce, and History.* Cambridge: Cambridge University Press, 1985.

Prichard, H. A. *Moral Obligation.* Oxford: Clarendon Press, 1949.

Putnam, Robert. *Making Democracy Work: Civic Traditions in Modern Italy.* Princeton: Princeton University Press, 1993.

Rapaczynski, Andrzej. *Nature and Politics: Liberalism in the Philosophies of Hobbes, Locke, and Rousseau.* Ithaca: Cornell University Press, 1987.

Rasmussen, Douglas B., and Douglas J. Den Uyl. *Norms of Liberty: A Perfectionist Basis for Non-Perfectionist Politics.* University Park: Pennsylvania State University Press, 2005.

Raz, Joseph. "Facing Diversity: The Case of Epistemic Abstinence." *Philosophy and Public Affairs* 19, no.1 (1990): 3–46.

————. *The Morality of Freedom.* Oxford: Clarendon Press, 1986.

Reath, Andrews. "Legislating for a Realm of Ends: The Social Dimension of Autonomy." In *Reclaiming the History of Ethics: Essays for John Rawls,* ed. Andrews Reath, Barbara Herman, and Christine M. Korsgaard, 214–39. Cambridge: Cambridge University Press, 1997.

Reisert, Joseph R. *Jean-Jacques Rousseau: A Friend of Virtue.* Ithaca: Cornell University Press, 2003.

Replogle, Ron. *Recovering the Social Contract.* Totowa, N.J.: Rowman and Littlefield, 1989.

Ridge, Michael. "Hobbesian Public Reason." *Ethics* 108 (April 1998): 538–68.

Riley, Patrick. *The General Will Before Rousseau.* Princeton: Princeton University Press, 1986.

————. "Rousseau's General Will: Freedom of a Particular Kind." In *Rousseau and Liberty,* ed. Robert Wokler, 1–28. Manchester: Manchester University Press, 1995.

————. *Will and Political Legitimacy.* Cambridge: Harvard University Press, 1982.

Ritchie, D. G. *Darwin and Hegel.* London: Swan Sonnenschein and Co., 1893.

Robins, Michael. *Promising, Intending, and Moral Autonomy.* Cambridge: Cambridge University Press, 1984.

Rosenblum, Nancy, ed. *Liberalism and the Moral Life.* Cambridge: Harvard University Press, 1989.

Ryan, Alan. "Hobbes and Individualism." In *Perspectives on Thomas Hobbes,* ed.

G. A. J. Rogers and Alan Ryan, 81–105. New York: Oxford University Press, 1988.

———. "Hobbes, Toleration, and the Inner Life." In *The Nature of Political Theory*, ed. David Miller and Larry Siedentop, 197–218. New York: Oxford University Press, 1983.

Salkaver, Stephen G. *Finding the Mean: Theory and Practice in Aristotelian Political Philosophy*. Princeton: Princeton University Press, 1990.

Sandel, Michael. *Democracy's Discontent: America in Search of a Public Philosophy*. Cambridge: Harvard University Press, 1996.

———. *Liberalism and the Limits of Justice*. Cambridge: Cambridge University Press, 1982.

———. "The Procedural Republic and the Unencumbered Self." *Political Theory* 12, no. 1 (1984): 81–96.

Scanlon, T. M. "Contractualism and Utilitarianism." In *Utilitarianism and Beyond*, ed. Amartya Sen and Bernard Williams, 103–28. Cambridge: Cambridge University Press, 1982.

———. "Promises and Practices." *Philosophy and Public Affairs* 19, no. 3 (1990): 199–226.

Schneewind, J. B. *The Invention of Autonomy*. New York: Cambridge University Press, 1998.

Schochet, Gordon J. *The Authoritarian Family and Political Attitudes in Seventeenth-Century England: Patriarchalism in Political Thought*. New Brunswick, N.J.: Transaction Publishers, 1988.

———. "Intending (Political) Obligation: Hobbes and the Voluntary Basis of Society." In *Thomas Hobbes and Political Theory*, ed. Mary G. Dietz, 55–73. Lawrence: University Press of Kansas, 1990.

———. "Radical Politics and Aschraft's Treatise on Locke." *Journal of the History of Ideas* 50, no. 3 (1989): 491–510.

Schouls, Peter A. *Reasoned Freedom: John Locke and Enlightenment*. Ithaca: Cornell University Press, 1992.

Schwoerer, Lois G. *The Declaration of Rights, 1689*. Baltimore: Johns Hopkins University Press, 1981.

———. "Locke, Lockean Ideas, and the Glorious Revolution." *Journal of the History of Ideas* 51, no. 4 (1990): 531–48.

Searle, John R. "How to Derive an 'Ought' from 'Is.'" In *Theories of Ethics*, ed. Philippa Foot, 101–14. New York: Oxford University Press, 1967.

———. *Speech Acts*. Cambridge: Cambridge University Press, 1969.

Seliger, Martin. "Locke's Natural Law and the Foundation of Politics." *Journal of the History of Ideas* 24, no. 3 (1963): 337–54.

Shanley, Mary Lyndon. "Marriage Contract and Social Contract in Seventeenth-Century English Political Thought." In *The Family in Political Thought*, ed. Jean Bethke Elshtain, 80–95. Amherst: University of Massachusetts Press, 1982.

Shapiro, Ian. *The Moral Foundations of Politics*. New Haven: Yale University Press, 2003.

Shelton, George. *Morality and Sovereignty in the Philosophy of Hobbes*. New York: St. Martin's Press, 1992.

Sherman, Nancy. *Making a Necessity of Virtue: Aristotle and Kant on Virtue*. Cambridge: Cambridge University Press, 1997.

Shklar, Judith. *Men and Citizens: A Study of Rousseau's Social Theory.* Cambridge: Cambridge University Press, 1969.

———. *Ordinary Vices.* Cambridge: Belknap Press of Harvard University Press, 1984.

Sidgwick, Henry. *The Methods of Ethics.* Indianapolis: Hackett Publishing, 1981.

Simmons, A. John. *Moral Principles and Political Obligations.* Princeton: Princeton University Press, 1979.

———. *On the Edge of Anarchy: Locke, Consent, and the Limits of Society.* Princeton: Princeton University Press, 1993.

Sinopoli, Richard. "Thick-Skinned Liberalism: Redefining Civility." *American Political Science Review* 89, no. 3 (1995): 612–20.

Skinner, Quentin. "Conquest and Consent: Thomas Hobbes and the Engagement Controversy." In *The Interregnum: The Quest for Settlement, 1646–1660,* ed. G. E. Aylmer, 79–98. London: Macmillan, 1974.

———. "The Context of Hobbes's Theory of Political Obligation." In *Hobbes and Rousseau: A Collection of Critical Essays,* ed. Maurice Cranston and Richard S. Peters, 109–42. New York: Anchor Books, 1972.

———. *The Foundations of Modern Political Thought.* 2 vols. Cambridge: Cambridge University Press, 1978.

———. "History and Ideology in the English Revolution." *Historical Journal* 8, no. 2 (1965): 151–78.

———. *Liberty Before Liberalism.* Cambridge: Cambridge University Press, 1998.

———. "The Limits of Historical Explanations." *Philosophy* 41 (1966): 199–215.

———. "Meaning and Understanding in the History of Ideas." *History and Theory* 8, no. 1 (1969): 3–53.

———. "The Paradoxes of Political Liberty." In *The Tanner Lectures on Human Values,* vol. 7, ed. Sterling M. McMurrin, 225–50. Salt Lake City: University of Utah Press, 1986.

———. *Reason and Rhetoric in the Philosophy of Hobbes.* Cambridge: Cambridge University Press, 1996.

———. "The Republican Ideal of Liberty." In *Machiavelli and Republicanism,* ed. Gisela Bock, Quentin Skinner, and Maurizio Viroli, 293–309. New York: Cambridge University Press, 1990.

———. *Visions of Politics.* Vol. 3, *Hobbes and Civil Science.* Cambridge: Cambridge University Press, 2002.

Slaughter, Thomas P. "'Abdicate' and 'Contract' in the Glorious Revolution." *Historical Journal* 24, no. 2 (1981): 323–37.

Sommerville, Johann P. *Thomas Hobbes: Political Ideas in Historical Context.* New York: St. Martin's Press, 1992.

Sorell, Tom. *Hobbes.* London: Routledge and Kegan Paul, 1986.

Spragens, Thomas A., Jr. *Civic Liberalism.* Lanham, Md.: Rowman and Littlefield, 1999.

———. *The Politics of Motion: The World of Thomas Hobbes.* London: Croom Helm, 1973.

Springborg, Patricia. "Leviathan and the Problem of Ecclesiastical Authority." *Political Theory* 3 (1975): 289–303.

Strauss, Leo. *Natural Right and History.* Chicago: University of Chicago Press, 1953.

———. *The Political Philosophy of Hobbes: Its Basis and Its Genesis.* Chicago: University of Chicago Press, 1963.

———. *What Is Political Philosophy? And Other Studies.* Westport, Conn.: Greenwood Press, 1959.

Tarcov, Nathan. *Locke's Education for Liberty.* Chicago: University of Chicago Press, 1984.

Taylor, A. E. "The Ethical Doctrine of Hobbes." *Philosophy* 13, no. 52 (1938): 406–24.

Taylor, Charles. *Sources of the Self: The Making of Modern Identity.* Cambridge: Harvard University Press, 1989.

Thompson, Martyn P. *Ideas of Contract in English Political Thought in the Age of John Locke.* New York: Garland, 1987.

———. "Locke's Contract in Context." In *The Social Contract from Hobbes to Rawls,* ed. David Boucher and Paul Kelly, 73–94. New York: Routledge, 1994.

Tierney, Brian. *The Idea of Natural Rights.* Atlanta: Scholars Press, 1997.

Tönnies, Ferdinand. *Community and Society.* Edited by Charles P. Loomis. New York: Harper and Row, 1957.

Trachtenberg, Zev M. *Making Citizens: Rousseau's Political Theory of Culture.* New York: Routledge, 1993.

Tuck, Richard. *Hobbes.* Oxford: Oxford University Press, 1989.

———. "Hobbes and Locke on Toleration." In *Thomas Hobbes and Political Theory,* ed. Mary G. Dietz, 153–71. Lawrence: University Press of Kansas, 1990.

———. "Hobbes's Moral Philosophy." In *The Cambridge Companion to Hobbes,* ed. Tom Sorell, 175–207. Cambridge: Cambridge University Press, 1996.

———. "The 'Modern' Theory of Natural Law." In *Languages of Political Theory in Early-Modern Europe,* ed. Anthony Pagden, 99–119. New York: Cambridge University Press, 1987.

———. *Natural Rights Theories: Their Origin and Development.* New York: Cambridge University Press, 1979.

———. *Philosophy and Government: 1572–1651.* Cambridge: Cambridge University Press, 1993.

Tuckness, Alex. "The Coherence of a Mind: John Locke and the Law of Nature." *Journal of the History of Philosophy* 37, no. 1 (1999): 73–90.

Tully, James. *An Approach to Political Philosophy: Locke in Contexts.* Cambridge: Cambridge University Press, 1993.

Tunick, Mark. *Practices and Principles: Approaches to Ethical and Legal Judgment.* Princeton: Princeton University Press, 1998.

Tussman, Joseph. *Obligation and the Body Politic.* New York: Oxford University Press, 1960.

Vaughan, Geoffrey M. *Behemoth Teaches Leviathan: Thomas Hobbes on Political Education.* Lanham, Md.: Lexington Books, 2002.

Viroli, Maurizio. *Jean-Jacques Rousseau and the "Well-Ordered Society."* Translated by Derek Hanson. Cambridge: Cambridge University Press, 1988.

Vitek, William. *Promising.* Philadelphia: Temple University Press, 1993.

Von Leyden, W. "John Locke and Natural Law." *Philosophy* 31, no. 116 (1956): 23–35.

———. "What Is a Nominal Essence the Essence Of?" In *John Locke: Problems and Perspectives,* ed. John W. Yolton, 224–33. Cambridge: Cambridge University Press, 1969.

Waldron, Jeremy. *God, Locke, and Equality: Christian Foundations in Locke's Political Thought.* Cambridge: Cambridge University Press, 2002.

———. "Hobbes and the Principle of Publicity." *Pacific Philosophical Quarterly* 82, nos. 3–4 (2001): 447–74.

———. *Liberal Rights: Collected Papers, 1981–1991.* Cambridge: Cambridge University Press, 1993.

————. "Religious Contributions in Public Deliberation." *San Diego Law Review* 30, no. 4 (1993): 817–48.

————. "A Right to Do Wrong." *Ethics* 92, no. 1 (1981): 21–39.

Wall, Steven. *Liberalism, Perfectionism, and Restraint*. New York: Cambridge University Press, 1998.

Walzer, Michael. *The Revolution of the Saints*. Cambridge: Harvard University Press, 1965.

Warner, Michael. *Publics and Counterpublics*. New York: Zone Books, 2002.

Warren, Mark E., ed. *Democracy and Trust*. Cambridge: Cambridge University Press, 1999.

Warrender, Howard. *The Political Philosophy of Hobbes*. Oxford: Clarendon Press, 1957.

Watkins, J. W. N. *Hobbes's System of Ideas*. London: Hutchinson Co., 1965.

Weithman, Paul J. "Rawlsian Liberalism and the Privatization of Religion: Three Theological Objections Considered." *Journal of Religious Ethics* 22, no. 1 (1994): 3–28.

————. *Religion and the Obligations of Citizenship*. Cambridge: Cambridge University Press, 2002.

White, Stephen K. *Sustaining Affirmation: The Strengths of Weak Ontology in Political Theory*. Princeton: Princeton University Press, 2000.

Williams, Melissa S. "Justice Toward Groups: Political Not Juridical." *Political Theory* 23, no. 1 (1995): 67–91.

Wittgenstein, Ludwig. *On Certainty*. Edited by G. E. M Anscombe and G. H. von Wright. New York: Harper and Row, 1969.

Wokler, Robert, ed. *Rousseau and Liberty*. Manchester: Manchester University Press, 1995.

Wolin, Sheldon. "Fugitive Democracy." In *Democracy and Difference*, ed. Seyla Benhabib, 31–45. Princeton: Princeton University Press, 1996.

————. "Norm and Form: The Constitutionalizing of Democracy." In *Athenian Political Thought and the Reconstruction of American Democracy*, ed. J. Peter Euben, John R. Wallach, and Josiah Ober, 29–58. Ithaca: Cornell University Press, 1994.

————. *Presence of the Past: Essays on the State and the Constitution*. Baltimore: Johns Hopkins University Press, 1989.

Wolterstorff, Nicholas, and Robert Audi. *Religion in the Public Square: The Place of Religious Convictions in Political Debate*. Lanham, Md.: Rowman and Littlefield, 1997.

Wood, Neal. *The Politics of Locke's Philosophy*. Berkeley and Los Angeles: University of California Press, 1983.

Wooten, David. "John Locke: Socinian or Natural Law Theorist?" In *Religion, Secularization, and Political Thought: Thomas Hobbes to J. S. Mill*, ed. James E. Crimmins, 39–67. London: Routledge, 1989.

Yolton, John W., ed. *John Locke: Problem and Perspectives*. Cambridge: Cambridge University Press, 1969.

————. "Locke on the Law of Nature." *Philosophical Review* 67, no. 4 (1958): 477–98.

Young, Iris Marion. "Communication and the Other: Beyond Deliberative Democracy." In *Democracy and Difference: Contesting the Boundaries of the Political*, ed. Seyla Benhabib, 120–35. Princeton: Princeton University Press, 1996.

————. "Polity and Group Difference: A Critique of the Ideal of Universal Citizenship." *Ethics* 99, no. 2 (1989): 250–74.

Zagorin, Perez. *A History of Political Thought in the English Revolution.* Bristol: Thoemmes Press, 1954.

Zerilli, Linda M. G. *Signifying Woman: Culture and Chaos in Rousseau, Burke, and Mill.* Ithaca: Cornell University Press, 1994.

Zuckert, Michael P. *Launching Liberalism: On Lockean Political Philosophy.* Lawrence: University Press of Kansas, 2002.

————. *Natural Rights and the New Republicanism.* Princeton: Princeton University Press, 1994.

INDEX

www.ingramcontent.com/pod-product-compliance
Lightning Source LLC
Chambersburg PA
CBHW021856020426
42334CB00013B/352